4/50

✓ **W9-DEU-396**

FLIGHT

STARS IN FLIGHT

STARS IN FLIGHT

A Study in Air Force
Character and Leadership

Edgar F. Puryear, Jr.

Introduction by Lt. Gen. Ira C. Eaker, USAF (Ret)

PRESIDIO PRESS

Copyright © 1981 by Presidio Press
Published by Presidio Press, 31 Pamaron Way, Novato, California 94947

Library of Congress Cataloging in Publication Data

Puryear, Edgar F   1930–
   Stars in flight.

   Includes bibliographical references and index.
    1. Generals—United States—Biography. 2. United
States. Air Force—Biography. 3. Leadership. I. Title.
UG626.P87   355'.0092'2 [B]   80-28631
ISBN 0-89141-128-3

Portraits of Generals Spaatz, Vandenberg, Twining, and White
courtesy of the U.S. Air Force Army Collection.

Cover design by Florence Stickney
Printed in the United States of America

CONTENTS

FOREWORD

Some eight years ago, a book, *Nineteen Stars,* appeared that marked a young writer, Edgar F. Puryear, Jr., as a promising biographer. *Nineteen Stars* consisted of brief biographies of Marshall, Eisenhower, Bradley, and Patton—three five-star generals and one four-star, all Army leaders. *Stars in Flight* fulfills the promise shown by this work. Only this time the topic is Air Force leadership, and the subjects are the first five Air Force Chiefs: Arnold, Spaatz, Vandenberg, Twining, and White.

Leadership, as exemplified by Army generals and Navy admirals, has inspired biographers for more than twenty centuries. Now, for the first time, a competent historian examines military leadership in a new environment—the air above contending armies and navies and above the enemy's bases.

The author employs two interesting techniques in all of the biographical sketches. First, he divides his effort into three distinct time periods: youth and the academic years; service through the grades of lieutenant to colonel; and the final productive years as Chief of Air Staff. Second, his data comes verbatim from reports, letters and interviews of each leader's contemporaries. These peer group evaluations are as entertaining and intimate as they are significant.

It would be difficult to name five military leaders more unlike and less stereotypical than Hap Arnold, Tooey Spaatz, Hoyt Vandenberg, Nate Twining, and Tommy White. Yet each was a successful leader of the U.S. Air Force.

True, they had some things in common. Each was a graduate of West Point, dedicated to its motto, "Duty, Honor, Country." Each was educated to lead ground forces. Each was tried and tested in the ultimate crucible, warfare, and in the greatest armed conflict of all time, World War II. Each was a flier, dedicated to military aviation, determined to demonstrate the influence airplanes could have on land and sea battles. And each believed ardently that air forces had an even more important and decisive role, far beyond the range of armies and navies.

But there the similarities end. Each of these preeminent air leaders was an individual with a unique personality, and distinctive methods of demonstrating command and control.

This book, as Gen. David C. Jones undoubtedly foresaw, is a comprehensive text on airpower leadership. General Jones was equally prescient in encouraging Dr. Puryear in this important task.

As an instructor at the Air Force Academy, Puryear had the necessary training. He also had the dedication, the tireless industry, and the writing ability to produce this valuable study. All the young military fliers of the future, preparing for eventual Air Force leadership will find this book an invaluable and inspirational guide.

I knew each of these five generals for many years. The author has recorded their service, their personalities, characters, and accomplishments with remarkable accuracy.

Stars in Flight permits the reader to compare Air leadership with that of Army generals and Navy admirals. He learns that the ten principles of war are generally as valid in air warfare as in land and sea campaigns. For example, air commanders have less time to make decisions, due to the greater speed and range of air weapons. These and other differences led to the early recognition that only fliers should command flying units. New tactics and strategies are needed for air forces. Only trained and skilled airmen can make correct decisions in the limited time available.

This book, *Stars in Flight,* considers most of the questions inherent in the air command problem and may well become the standard text for Air Force leadership. I commend it to all inquisitive students concerned about the future of air generalship.

Lt. Gen. Ira C. Eaker, USAF (Ret)

ACKNOWLEDGMENTS

The inspiration for this book comes from a continued desire to answer the questions of how one gets to the top of the military profession, how one leads on the way to the top, and what is the nature of the leadership role after achieving a high position of great responsibility.

The encouragement to follow that inspiration to publication comes from many sources, but especially from the Air Force Academy cadets and young Air Force officers who, after hearing my numerous lectures given on this work at the Academy and throughout the Air Force school system, made comments and offered ideas which helped define and mature the leadership concepts that unfold in this study.

In the process of researching this book, I have been aided by others too numerous to mention, particularly the hundreds of officers I interviewed and with whom I corresponded who gave of their time and wisdom gained through many years of experience as leaders. Their names appear repeatedly in the notes, and I am most grateful for their thoughtful responses.

During the course of my work on this book I have had the assistance of the office of the Deputy Chief of Staff of Personnel for handling the administrative responsibilities, correspondence, and other miscellaneous tasks. I want to express my appreciation to Gen. John W. Roberts, Deputy Chief of Staff of Personnel from October 1973 through September 1975; Lt. Gen. Kenneth L. Tallman, who held that position from September 1975 through June 1977, and for his assistance as Superintendent of the United States Air

Force Academy from 1977; and Gen. Bennie L. Davis, from August 1977 through March 1979. Also from the Deputy Chief of Staff of Personnel's office I had help from Maj. Gen. Robert E. Kelley; Brig. Gen. Robert C. Oaks; Col. Ralph E. Havens; Lt. Col. Charles A. Coble; and Col. Ronald M. Singer of the office of the Chief of Staff. CMS Dwight J. Collie and T/S Robert K. Staples were most helpful administratively.

I also want to thank Ann Fletcher, Donna DiToto, Debbie K. Simpson, Marie Dene, Carolyn L. Whittaker, and Kathleen M. Hurley for their secretarial and administrative assistance, and Katherine T. Beaver and Antonio Corto Cruz of Wainwright Hall, Fort Myer, Virginia, for billeting accomodations.

I have a very special appreciation for the positive, can-do input from Lt. Gen. Howard M. Fish, USAF (Ret.) and Air Force Counsel Gen. Stuart A. Richart. I also want to thank Brig. Gen. Pete Todd for his valuable insight, Wallace "Earl" Walker, USA, for his help, and Rebecca W. McCoy for her assistance.

This book has truly been a team effort and I am greatly indebted to many people for their assistance. Annette E. Hilgeman has been exceptional with her patience in transcribing the tapes of the numerous interviews, hundreds of letters, drafts, and many other administrative duties.

The extensive editorial assistance of Jinnie B. Mason has been invaluable. I will always be grateful for the editorial contribution of Edward A. Weeks, former editor of *Atlantic Monthly*. I also am most appreciative for the editorial advice of Adele Horwitz of Presidio Press. In addition, I have had helpful insight offered in the editing by Gen. Robert W. Porter, Jr., USA (Ret.); Brig. Gen. Phillip J. Erdle, USAF (Ret.); Brig. Gen. Thomas C. Pinkney; Lt. Col. John L. Sullivan; Lt. Col. Carol Habgood; and Dr. Wayne A. Knoll. I want to give credit to Col. Robert H. Baxter, USAF, for his role in getting this book started.

I was fortunate to have the opportunity to meet Maj. Gen. Chester V. Clifton, USA (Ret.), who was most helpful in putting me in contact with Presidio Press. General Clifton's experience and advice has been extremely valuable as has been that of the publisher of Presidio Press, Robert V. Kane.

I want to thank the members of my law firm who have been so patient during the process of research and writing: my partner L. B. Chandler, Jr., two of our associates, Daniel R. Bouton and John G. Berry, and Helen M. Slaven for secretarial assistance.

Most of all I want to thank my wife, Agnes, for her infinite patience during the extensive traveling and the many long hours of work on the manuscript, and a special thanks to my sons, Beverly Spotswood Parrish (Chug), Edgar F. (Chip), Scott Braxton (Colt), and Alfred Anderson (Cotton).

INTRODUCTION

This book gives the point of view of military leaders on leadership. The higher the leadership position, the more the leader is exposed to public view. The U.S. public, unfortunately, forms its opinions of leaders based on the values and the image of the leader as projected by the media. These public opinions of existing leaders are then impressed on the young men and women and junior leaders who are about to enter into, or who are in the process of embarking on, careers. As a consequence, today's military leaders not only must measure up to the values and abilities that the people they lead expect of them, but they must also overcome the prejudices that the media iconoclasts, as today's leading opinion formers of America, have instilled in the troops.

Enthusiasm, the "can do" attitude in approach to leadership and common tasks, is the sine qua non of leadership—positive attitudes toward the mission, commanders, and coordinating authorities. There is no place for iconoclasm. While our national television news broadcasters may make a significant contribution, would anyone want to go to war under the command of a Walter Cronkite, David Brinkley, or Howard K. Smith?

What is the value of studying the characteristics of leadership? There is an ancient proverb that says "The mill wheel is not turned by waters that have passed." Yet even when they no longer turn the wheel, our leaders' contributions provide a heritage that passes on life to the young officers now training for leadership. It serves as a stamp, a model, not necessarily to be copied, but certainly to be learned from.

During the course of the interviews and the research for this study, I became aware of many different definitions of leadership, of many words and phrases. Some authors and generals, referring to leadership, used terms such as "interpersonal relations," "dynamics of group action," "structures of personal interaction," "sensitive manipulation," "manpower dynamics," and "organization spirit." Some of the words were "generalship," "command," "management," and "charisma." One World War II general being interviewed on the leadership of General of the Army George C. Marshall, even commented, "He was not a leader, he was a staff officer."

To avoid any such problem of semantics, the objective of this work is simply to answer the question "How did the generals get to the top, how did they lead as officers on the way to the top, and how did they run the show when they were at the top?" The stories and anecdotes serve to teach, and the lessons are as fresh and valuable today as when they happened.

I am particularly interested in the junior officers as an audience. Lasting impressions of leadership and character are often derived when one is a junior officer. This book has as its goal the establishment of a model of the leadership of the early air generals.

All that one can say for certain with regard to war is that, however good the airmen may be, they will achieve little without good leadership. Yet trained and inspired leadership will strike a spark of response and will make the average and the above average perform better. The great wealth and reservoir of talent that in peacetime is channeled into what makes us the greatest industrial power in the world will in wartime make us, as in the past, the greatest, most awesome military power in the world.

Many thousands of young men and women serve in the Air Force for brief periods of two to four years. Part of the Air Force's responsibility is to help these young people to leave the Air Force better citizens than when they entered. Certainly nothing could be more inspiring for any young person seeking a worthwhile career than to know that if it is to be in the Air Force, he or she has a role in the most important task of our day—the security of our nation.

My research has been from primary sources and essentially from personal interviews. Over 1,000 officers of the rank of brigadier general or higher have been interviewed or have contributed their correspondence in answer to my questions about leadership. In addition, wherever relevant, I have sifted the testimony of some 5,000 men of all ranks, from private to five-star general, again, by letters or interviews. For more than a decade I have read everything in print by or about Generals Arnold, Spaatz, Vandenberg, Twining, and White. I am truly grateful for the insight given me by their wives, sons and daughters.

I have read over a thousand books on leadership. Although they showed varying ideas of what it is and how one leads successfully, they agreed that there are certain qualities that are indispensable for success in military leadership. Among these qualities are professional knowledge, decision, fairness, humanity, courage, humility, integrity, character, loyalty, energy, consideration, and selflessness. These qualities are given life and meaning in this study of the lives of Generals Arnold, Spaatz, Vandenberg, Twining, and White.

PART ONE
THE GENERALS

CHAPTER 1

GENERAL HENRY H. ARNOLD

General of the Air Force Henry H. "Hap" Arnold was the embodiment and personification of the U.S. Air Force. He was there for its birth, and he grew up with it. His career covered the entire gamut of Air Force history. He commanded it as the Air Service during World War I, devoted his life to its arduous and difficult development between the wars, and commanded it through the challenging years of World War II.

As a youngster, Henry Harley Arnold had no burning desire to make a career of the service. His early ambition was to go to Bucknell College and become a minister of the gospel. He was born June 25, 1886, in the town of Gladwyne, Pennsylvania; his paternal ancestry traced back to John Arnold, who had emigrated from England in 1740 and settled in Philadelphia. His mother was Louise Ann Harley; his father, Herbert A. Arnold, was a country doctor who practiced in the town of Ardmore, Montgomery County, Pennsylvania.

It was Henry's older brother Thomas who was slated to go to West Point, largely because their father had left his practice in 1898 to serve as surgeon to the Pennsylvania Cavalry in Puerto Rico in the Spanish-American War. "Thereafter," General Arnold commented, "my father wished to have one of his sons go to West Point, and he was able to bring a bit of influence there towards securing an appointment."[1] But Thomas refused to go to West Point, so Dr. Arnold decided that, as he had obtained this appointment, it was going to be used by one of his sons—Henry.

When Arnold entered West Point, he was the youngest member of the class of 1907 and one of the youngest ever to enter West Point. The minimum age for admission at that time was seventeen years, and Cadet Arnold was seventeen years and one month of age when he arrived on August 1, 1903. One of his classmates, Col. H. B. Hayden, who knew him for fifty years, commented, "At West Point he started in with papers from his last school indicating he was a fine student with high marks. In fact, he had so fine a mind that he memorized several pages of logarithm tables. Very soon after Arnold arrived at the Point, however, he greatly recovered from that reputation of being a student and abandoned any indication that he wanted to study at all" (personal communication, November 27, 1962).*

Academically, Cadet Arnold was in the lower half of his class throughout his career at West Point. Nor did he achieve cadet rank, serving as a private all four years at West Point. It appears that, rather than concentrating on academics or military achievements, he was devoting his energies to an organization of about twenty cadets known as the "Black Hand." The object of the Black Hand was "To raise all the hell it could without getting dismissed from the Academy." Col. Abbott Boone said that Arnold "was a leader of the Black Hand gang, the 'bandits' of the class, always up to mischief and bedevilment. These qualities made him exceedingly popular with most cadets, but not with the 'Sup,' the 'Com,' or the Academic Board, as one will see from his cadet record" (personal communication, December 7, 1962).

Arnold's activities as a member of the Black Hand showed great daring. Because of their class spirit, they decided to paint the class numerals, "1907," in a conspicuous place at the top of a chimney that was part of the heating plant at the Academy at the time. This chimney was over 100 feet high. When the Tactical Officers and cadets awoke the morning after the exploit was completed, there were the numerals "1907," painted vividly for all to see. It was a source of mystery to the "Tacs" as to how this feat was accomplished. No ladder was attached to the exterior of this chimney, nor was there any ladder at West Point tall enough to permit the scaling of the bastion. Cadet Arnold had climbed up the *inside* of the chimney. After reaching the top, he then, hanging on a rope thrown over the outside, went on to paint the numerals. Although the cadets knew that this deed had been executed by the Black Hand, only the members of the society knew that Arnold had done it.

Perhaps the most skillful achievement of this group was recalled by

*"Personal communication" refers to letter to the author.

Colonel Hayden as "their prize escapade." They succeeded in "disassembling the reveille gun, an ancient and honorable four-inch cannon." The Black Hand moved this reveille gun across the parade ground, took it apart, and put it back together in the cadet bathhouse, completely reassembled. The cadets accomplished this in only one night. "It took the entire Engineering Department," said Hayden, "an entire day to disassemble the gun and put it back together, and after it was put together, a team of six horses to pull it back to where it belonged" (personal communication, November 27, 1962). No one was ever apprehended for this particular prank.

Arnold thought that the greatest success of the Black Hand group occurred during his last year. It involved "smuggling fireworks and surpassed the most optimistic hopes the organization ever had. In the exploding glare that rose over the entire Academy, bugles blew, sirens sounded, officers and men tumbled from their beds—the whole reservation was alive. In the center of it all, on top of the barracks I touched off the piece de resistance. '1907' in pinwheels was spelled out and also the quotation, 'Never Again.' "[2]

The class of 1907 was convinced there would never be another one like theirs at West Point. The Superintendent, Commandant, and Tactical Department probably hoped not. It was no wonder that Arnold was assigned to another group—those who won the title of "A.B.," meaning "Area Bird"—"one who is awarded the privilege of walking the area on Wednesdays and Saturdays at the usually prescribed hours."

Arnold spent a considerable amount of time walking after the fireworks. The fireworks had gone off behind him, and he said, "Through bad luck I was left alone, silhouetted against the light of my own handiwork, in full view of the entire Corps."[3]

The change of pace provided by the Black Hand was certainly needed. Life at West Point in the early years of the century was austere and not unlike the training of Spartans. After arrival the first summer, a cadet was not permitted to return home until the end of the first two years, barring an emergency such as serious illness or a death in the immediate family. One reason for not permitting cadets to go home until the end of two years was fear by the staff, faculty, and Commandant that many cadets would not return. Comments from the yearbook of Arnold's class best described the cadets' own attitudes, an "institution that swallowed so remorsefully four years of their youth"; a "pitiless repression of the exuberant spirit of youth . . . which made training at West Point approach in harshness the religious military orders of the Middle Ages."

A review of the demerits he received further justifies his nickname of "Hap." The fourth recorded demerit he received was on September 5, 1903, for "smiling in ranks marching to dinner"; on February 5, 1904, he received a demerit for "smiling in ranks at gymnasium formation"; on May 31, 1904, for "talking and laughing in ranks at dinner formation"; on May 4, 1905, for "laughing in ranks at drill"; on March 9, 1906, for "smiling in ranks at inspection"; on March 20, 1906, for "talking and laughing in hall of Academic Building, 2:27 P.M."

"Hap" was not his first nickname. Arnold was very anxious to enter the Cavalry, in spite of the fact that he got seasick on horses. He was nicknamed "Pute" (also "Pewt") as a result of losing his lunch on more than one occasion while riding during the afternoon as part of his classes in horsemanship. Hayden tells us, "He disliked the nickname Pute so much that he asked us to call him something else, and since he was of such a happy disposition, we nicknamed him 'Happy,' which was abbreviated to 'Hap,' a nickname he carried all his life" (personal communication, November 27, 1962).

Cadet Thomas DeWitt Milling, class of 1909, two years behind Arnold at West Point but a classmate in later years in pilot training, described conditions at West Point as much like it was in the Civil War. There was no running water in the barracks and no baths, but a separate bathhouse. Running water was provided by a spigot in front of the barracks, and each room was provided with a bucket. One had to go downstairs, fill the bucket, and carry it up four floors.

Arnold's varsity sport was track and field. He participated in the indoor meet in his fourth, third, and first class years; in the outdoor meet, in his last three years. Competition was strictly one class against all the others, not against other schools. In the twelfth annual indoor meet on March 24, 1906, Cadet Arnold won third place in the sixteen-pound shot-put. The classmate in first place threw a distance of 35 feet, 11 inches, short of the Academy record of 39 feet, 6 inches. Cadet Arnold, however, tied for the best record during his four years as a cadet by putting the shot 36 feet, 1½ inches.

The Black Hand activities brought out the nature of Arnold's personality and character. He was described by classmates as independent, resourceful, daring, and determined. Arnold welcomed the undertaking of any project that offered a challenge—a quality demanded of anyone who wanted to go into flying during the pioneer years of aviation. At graduation, no cadet was permitted to go immediately into aviation. Indeed, in 1907 they gave very little thought to aviation—including Arnold. Arnold was set on being commissioned in the Cavalry; "Work or play," he wrote, "the thing that dominated the cadet lives of one little group of us was—the Cavalry! That was why we were here! It was what we lived for—our whole future. . . . It was the last romantic thing left on earth. The galloping charge! Indian fighting! . . . We dreamed night and day of being Cavalry officers, and the nearer graduation came, the more we dreamed."[4]

While waiting at home after graduating from West Point, young Arnold was so confident of being assigned to the Cavalry that he ordered his uniform with the extra width in the trouser stripe to stress the "glorious Cavalry yellow." There was never any doubt in his mind. When his commission came in the mail, he was sitting with his mother at breakfast, and he gaily tossed the correspondence to her without even looking at it. She read it slowly, then looked at her son saying, "You'd better read this, Harley." He did; it stated, "Henry H. Arnold . . . 2nd Lieutenant of . . . Infantry!"[5]

Arnold said, "My world collapsed." He was denied the branch of service he lived for. But he did not give up so easily. Arnold and his ex-Cavalry father decided to fight this assignment. They traveled to Washington to persuade their congressman and state senator to intervene with the War Department to change his assignment to the Cavalry. They were not successful; however, Arnold learned something from this experience: "to carry out the lawful orders of his superiors and accept whatever assignment he was given."[6]

His first assignment was to Fort McKinley, near Manila, in the Philippines. As often happens with a man who is carefree in his younger years, he now made an important decision. "I went to work," he said, "for the first time in earnest at my profession."[7]

In 1910, Arnold returned to the United States and was assigned to Governor's Island, New York. There he had his first airplane ride, as a passenger, in a bamboo-and-wire Curtiss biplane on a hop around the island. This flight gave him his first real interest in airplanes.

In 1911, after four years in the Infantry, Arnold, still a second lieutenant, took the exam to enter the Ordnance Department, primarily to get promoted to first lieutenant sooner than he would in the Infantry. He said:

> I . . . was awaiting word of whether I had passed it [the ordnance exam], when out of the blue an official letter arrived from the War Department. Would I be willing to volunteer for training with the Wright brothers at Dayton as an airplane pilot?
>
> Puzzled, I took the letter to my commanding officer. After reading it, he said, "Young man, I know of no better way for a

person to commit suicide!'' It was a challenge. Gone were all thoughts relating to the Ordnance Department.

Thus it was that on a night in the third week of April, 1911, I found myself on a train bound from New York to Dayton. In my pocket was a copy of War Department Special Order 95, paragraph 10. ''The following named officers are detailed for aeronautical duty with the Signal Corps, and will proceed to Dayton, Ohio, for the purpose of undergoing a course of instruction in operating the Wright airplane:

2nd Lt. Henry H. Arnold, 29th Infantry
2nd Lt. Thomas DeW. Milling, 15th Cavalry

The travel directed is necessary in the military service.''[8]

Actually, it was not really ''out of the blue.'' Someone had had him in mind. One of his key responsibilities at Fort McKinley was mapping duty, and while performing this job he had come to the attention of Captain Cowan of the Signal Corps in the Philippines. In 1911, Captain Cowan was assigned to Washington and was responsible for recruiting officers for aviation instruction. The relationship between Captain Cowan and Arnold that had begun in the Philippine Islands now resulted in this offer to Hap Arnold to become an aviation student.

One of Arnold's flying instructors was Orville Wright, co-inventor with his brother Wilbur of the world's first heavier-than-air aircraft to achieve sustained powered flight. But Arnold's main instructor was Al Welsh. Today it takes over a year and more than $100,000 to train a pilot, but training was shorter and less expensive in Arnold's days. His flying log read, ''Number of flights, 28. Total time in air 3 hours, 48 minutes.'' Thus, in ten days, Arnold became a rated military aviator, the fourth officer in the history of Army aviation. Of both military and civilian pilots, he received pilot's license number 29.

''Our airport was a miniature pasture,'' Arnold commented on his early flying, ''a rough small orchard with trees in it, outside Dayton. I first spent three hours in a balancing machine, an old airplane mounted on an edge so it would teeter. Operation of the warping lever, to warp the wings, enabled the student to learn its actions by keeping the machine laterally balanced. (There were no ailerons.) This was very necessary as there was nothing natural in the movements of the right controls—the handling of controls had to be instinctive, or disaster would result. The flying continued during my entire stay at Dayton.''[9]

One can capture the thrill that Lieutenant Arnold felt in a letter he wrote on May 13, 1911, to the Chief Signal Officer of the U.S. Army:

Dayton, Ohio
13 May, 1911

Sir:

I have the honor to report the following progress made by me in learning to operate a Wright airplane. During the week I have made twelve flights with an instructor and one flight by myself. My instruction under the personal supervision of the instructor in the machine is finished, and from now on all my flights will be made alone for experience.

Very respectfully yours

Henry H. Arnold
Second Lieutenant, 24th Infantry

At the time Lieutenant Arnold entered pilot training, courage was considered the main attribute necessary for an aviator. The Army policy then was that only young, unmarried, medium-weight junior officers would be allowed to enter pilot training, and then only after volunteering for this hazardous duty. "It was not uncommon," Arnold reflected years later, "for a pilot of 1916, 1917, and even as late as 1925 and 1926 to have a forced landing due to a faulty engine or a safe landing in a nettle or corn field, repair his damage, let down a few fences, and take off and return to his home airdrome. He took off with a prayer, as he had a 50 percent chance of engine failure on each flight. The annual toll taken by the grim reaper was about 33 1/3 percent of all those who stepped into a plane."[10] Arnold's primary instructor, Welsh, was killed in a flying accident less than a year after Arnold received his wings, and by 1925, when Arnold testified at Billy Mitchell's court-martial, 689 men had been killed in military aircraft accidents.

Thomas DeWitt Milling, Arnold's classmate in pilot training, reflected, "Everybody expected to be killed. . . . I still don't see how in the devil I wasn't, when I look back and see how close I came to being killed so many times."[11]

Many deaths occurred because the only aircraft available to the Air Service were obsolete, most of them of World War I vintage and of foreign make. The DeHaviland aircraft, for example, tended to burn when wrecked, and if the crash didn't kill the pilot, the fire would. Lack of up-to-date instruments caused fatal accidents in bad weather. And some of the aircraft had a bad propensity for spins.

On reflection, however, Arnold found humor in the situation despite the danger. "It was way back in 1912, in those days, an airplane was just a chain-and-sprocket box type, with three control sticks, and wooden paddles for props. While I was flying from Salem, Massachusetts, down to Bridgeport . . . I made a crash landing in the water. There I was, all tangled up in the wires and bleeding like a stuck pig, and just then I saw a couple of GAR [Grand Army of the Republic] veterans sailing past me. I yelled at them, and they hauled in close to the wreck, looked at me for a minute, and then squared away into the wind again. 'Anybody fool enough to get himself into one of these things,' I heard one of them mutter, 'he can get himself out again.' "[12]

The challenges of being in the Air Service (renamed the Air Corps in 1926) were not only the hazards of crash landings, injuries, and death. The Air Service competed with other branches in the Army budget for purchasing goods and materials, and the Air Service usually received the "short end of the stick." Naturally, the Air Service was interested in new aircraft and new weapons, just as the other Army branches were requesting new tanks, artillery, and other equipment. The result of this competition was often a great deal of bitterness.

An example of this was given by Ira C. Eaker, a very junior captain, who was the Air Service representative on a budget committee where everyone else was a brigadier general or higher. One key request by the Air Service at this hearing was for a decent ambulance. The ambulances used were horsedrawn or were old General Motors ambulances of World War I vintage. If an airplane crash-landed in a plowed field or in rougher country and the survivor was badly injured, it was not unusual for the jolting of such an ambulance to kill the injured flier being taken to the hospital. Ira Eaker recalled one ride in an archaic ambulance when jolting drove a broken bone through the flier's lung. Unfortunately, there was very little compassion on the part of the budget committee, which commented, "We have accidents in the Cavalry, too. Our people fall off polo ponies, and these ambulances are good enough for them, and they should be good enough for the Air Force" (personal interview, October 4, 1977). It was hardly a response to earn the respect of a flying officer.

There was an additional difficulty, because flying officers received extra hazards pay amounting to 25 percent of base pay. During the Depression, with limited appropriations, the Air Corps could not get aircraft engines or spare parts. Fliers were cut down to only four hours of flying a month, and the pay of all Army officers was reduced during the Depression, a combination that had a discouraging effect on morale.

After Lieutenants Arnold and Milling completed pilot training, they were assigned to College Park, Maryland, as instructors, where they taught the student officers essentially the way they had been taught by the Wright brothers in Dayton. On March 3, 1911, Congress made its first air appropriation—for $125,000—toward purchasing five airplanes. The only other airplane in the Army inventory at that time was one built by the Wright brothers in 1909, then being used for military missions in Texas.

As an aviator, Arnold established many firsts. He set an altitude record in a Burgess-Wright airplane on June 1, 1912, when he flew to a height of 6,540 feet at College Park, Maryland. The first Mackay Trophy was awarded to Arnold on October 9, 1912, for a reconnaissance flight over a triangular course from the Signal Corps Aviator School at College Park, to Washington Barracks in the District of Columbia, to Fort Myer, Virginia, and returning to College Park—a total distance of thirty miles.

When, as an observer, he took off from the College Park airport on that flight, it was a cold, gusty afternoon in November. During his flight, he observed a Cavalry detachment hidden in the woods across the Potomac River on the Virginia side. He made his observation sitting on the leading edge of the lower wing. On landing, he was so numbed from the cold and so exhausted from fighting gusty winds that he had to be taken to the hospital for treatment before he could make out his report. But he proved that reconnaissance observations could be made in bad weather conditions.[13]

Although he had been a second lieutenant for the six years prior to World War I, thereafter he was very quickly advanced from the rank of lieutenant to full colonel in his capacity of Assistant Director of Military Aeronautics. In May 1917, he was reassigned from the Panama Canal Zone, where he was organizing an aviation service, to Washington, D.C. When the office of the Director of Military Aeronautics was created in May 1917, he was appointed Executive Officer and, in April 1918, Assistant Director of Military Aeronautics. Thus, Arnold was responsible for supervising the extraordinary expansion of an air force that in April 1917 had only 35 pilots to a force of 10,000 pilots when the Armistice was signed on November 11, 1918! There were only two airfields in April 1917; there were thirty at the war's end.

The aircraft in which the American pilots trained and fought during World War II were not made in the United States. It was ironical that the Wright brothers had invented the airplane but that our own country did not have the vision to see its importance. Wilbur Wright wrote to Godfrey L. Cabot on May 10, 1906, and to Octave Chanute on June 21, 1906, "Previous to our entering into negotiations with foreign countries, we brought the subject before our own government. The answers of the department officials were so insulting in tone as to preclude any further advances on our part." There were only 131 officers in the Air Service, practically all of them pilots and student pilots, and only 1,087 enlisted men. There were 55 training planes, of which General John J. Pershing said "51 were obsolete and the other four obsolescent."[14] No American combat planes reached Europe before the Armistice, but 4,000 had come off the production line, with an additional 35,500 in production on November 11, 1918.

A classmate of Arnold's, Charles H. White, served with him during World War I and reflected on what Arnold was like as a leader of the Air Service (personal communication, November 12, 1962): "At that time we had only a handful of aviators, most of them young lieutenants with one to three years, or less, of flying. Still fewer were those who had been flying since about 1908. Among the older ones were Arnold, Foulois, and Mitchell. At Headquarters in Washington, the Chief of the Air Service was an aged colonel of the coast artillery. Apparently the War Department could not bring itself to having a young officer like Arnold at the head, so there was a titular head, who was the colonel in the coast artillery I have just referred to. Later in the spring of 1908, Major General Kenly, F. A., came back from France to be the Chief. . . .

"Arnold was constantly out in the airfields and manufacturing plants most of the time," he continued. "He was recognized, of course, as the best-qualified man (except for the age fetish of the time) to run the fledgling air arm. Understanding this, the Acting Chief had to more or less let Arnold have his own way. So Arnold would come back from the field, having seen the dire necessities, and would give orders, especially to the supply section, in a brusque, no-nonsense, and even violent manner in order to get things done. Many times he had no authority for what he ordered, and he would not use up time to seek it. If he thought something needed to be done, he would not let regulations stand in his way, nor did he hesitate to overlook any law that would delay getting things done. He got away with it because the War Department was in a terrible mess and he knew it. The times called for boldness and risk, and, as at West Point, he did not stand quietly under disciplinary restraint, formal channels, or methods. He was a maverick."

"From the start of World War I until the Armistice," Arnold reflected, "I was always asking for transfer overseas, but my requests were always turned down. I remained stuck in an assignment which left me, for most of the war, as the second-ranking officer in the War Department's Air Division, and for the greater part of those eighteen months, as the senior officer in Washington with wings. Promotion came rapidly in wartime— especially in an air force in which only a few relatively junior officers knew how to fly. By August 1917, I was a full (though temporary) colonel, the youngest one in the Army.

"My wife and I looked at those eagles on my shoulders," he said, "and though we were certainly pleased to see them there, they seemed unreal, even embarrassing. Youngsters, in those days, just didn't get to be colonels. At first, I used to take back streets when I walked to the War Department from my house, imagining that people would be looking at me incredulously. There had been thirty-year-old colonels in the Civil War, but that was before my time."[15]

An analysis of Arnold's leadership and the development of a separate air force would not be complete without the perspective offered by Billy Mitchell's contribution.

Perhaps Mitchell's first interest in aviation was reflected in an analysis of military ballooning. Long a member of the Signal Corps, which had the responsibility within the Army for aviation, he did not himself begin pilot training until the fall of 1916, doing so during his off-duty time at the Curtiss Aviation School in Newport News, Virginia. He received his pilot wings as Junior Military Aviator in September 1917, training at his own personal expense to the amount of almost $1,500 (then a large sum). But it was a sound investment, because in January 1917 the War Department decided to send an aeronautical observer to Europe, and as a result of his flying knowledge and interest Mitchell was selected. He arrived in France on March 19, 1917, and within two weeks, on April 2, 1917, the United States declared war on Germany.

This opportunity and experience developed Mitchell's knowledge of aviation and was the beginning of the real foundation as an expert. The British and French had long been involved in the combat aspect of the air. Unquestionably the people in Washington at first were not quick to accept the voluminous reports sent back by Mitchell because they were not by an expert. Before the war was over, this reluctance ended. By September 1917, Mitchell had been promoted to full colonel and selected by General John J. Pershing for a combat command in the Allied Expeditionary Force (AEF).

The chief of the Air Service in the AEF was Benjamin Foulois, one of the earliest Army pilots, who earned his wings in 1909. General Pershing and Foulois did not get along, so Foulois was replaced by a nonpilot, Maj. Gen. Mason Patrick, from the Corps of Engineers. Soon thereafter, Mitchell and Foulois did not get along, and ultimately Mitchell's star rose with Pershing as Foulois' went down.

The final result was the emergence of Mitchell as a man with great fighting ability and a definite flair for combat leadership. He was, in essence, the commander of the aviation combat forces. Pershing was extremely pleased with the results Mitchell achieved and recommended his promotion to brigadier general. In December 1918, Mitchell was returned to the United States as Director of Military Aeronautics. This had been the highest position in Army aviation, but after the war it was disbanded as the Army reorganized.

A fortunate result of Mitchell's World War I experience and growth was that he developed into an officer with a vision for an appreciation of air power. He could see the important role aviation would play in the next war, and he was now dedicated to a life of service in promoting aviation to prepare our country for that next conflict. To Mitchell, aerial warfare was as important as ground and naval warfare, and he believed there ought to be a separate air force. Until his death in 1936, he waged a battle to establish a separate air arm of equal status with the Army and the Navy.

The immediate post–World War I accomplishment that received the greatest publicity and for which Mitchell is perhaps most remembered was his insistence that airplanes were capable of sinking naval vessels, a feat that he proved, much to the irritation of the Navy, by sinking the ex-German battleship *Ostfriesland* on July 22, 1921, followed later by the sinking of the U.S. battleship *Alabama* (an overage target ship) in August.

Mitchell's advocacy of air power completely absorbed his life. After the end of World War I, he was often in the headlines. Both friends and enemies acknowledged his dedication to the cause and his stature as an expert in the field. But not all agreed with him on the importance of air power, and only a handful had his unique vision and enthusiasm. There were many ups and downs for Mitchell during the postwar period, which finally culminated in a showdown.

On September 5, 1925, an incident occurred that was a major turning point in the establishment of a separate air force. On this date, the prominent aviation hero of World War I, Col. William "Billy" Mitchell, held a press conference the impact of which will never be forgotten in Air Force history. Although I will not report in great detail the court-martial trial that resulted, I must cover the key issues because of their impact on the future of a separate air force and its air leaders.

On September 1 and 3, 1925, two air tragedies occurred. Strangely, the accidents involved the Navy. On September 1, 1925, Navy Commander John Rodgers and his crew of four were reported missing in the Pacific on an airplane flight from San Francisco to Honolulu. Considerable publicity was given to the allegation that the aircraft's fuel was insufficient for the headwinds encountered. Colonel Mitchell, assigned at that time in San Antonio, went on the radio on September 2, calling Rogers and his crew "martyrs."

On September 3, with Rodgers and his crew still missing, the *Shenandoah,* a lighter-than-air craft, ran into a squall; the Commander and fourteen of his crew fell to their death. The grief over losing so many was aggravated by a rumor that the Commander had made it clear to his superiors that he objected to the flight because of adverse weather but had been ordered to proceed. The situation was further agitated by the apparent lack of concern over the deaths implied by the Secretary of the Navy Curtis D. Wilbur, who said publicly, trying to minimize the two tragedies, that it was proof of our country's safety from invading air power.

These tragedies ended Billy Mitchell's public silence. On September 5, he called a press conference in San Antonio that exploded a controversy that had been building between Mitchell and his superiors for years. He charged that these "terrible accidents . . . are the direct results of incompetency, criminal negligence, and almost treasonable administration of the national defense by the War and Navy Departments."

There was no doubt that Colonel Mitchell had set the stage for either a court-martial or a reprimand. His charges were too grave to be ignored. Mitchell had deliberately forced a fight for air power and a separate air force, a cause dear to his heart. Those who knew him believed that he wanted the court-martial, to win support for his fight to replace the archaic air policy with a progressive and farsighted one. Mitchell was ready to sacrifice himself. He believed that if he were dismissed from the service the whole nation would pay attention to aviation and provide him with the opportunity to advance aviation more effectively as a civilian than as an Army officer.

A mere reprimand would not have accomplished one of Billy Mitchell's objectives—to force a congressional investigation. A reprimand attached to his record would not answer his public charge that military aviation was in the hands of "stupid" superiors who "knew nothing about flying" and who, as he put it, risked the lives of airmen as "pawns" in foolish and ill-timed ventures.

A court-martial would afford Mitchell an opportunity to prove his charges or be drummed out of the Army. At a court-martial, he would have the protection of due process of law, including representation of his own evidence and witnesses and the right to cross-examine the government's witnesses. It would thus bring to a head the controversy that had been raging for a long time between Mitchell and his superior officers in the War Department and the Army Air Service. President Calvin Coolidge decided to charge Colonel Mitchell with conduct prejudicial to good order and military discipline, insubordination, and utterances contemptuous of his superiors.

The court-martial record, when bound, composed seven very thick volumes. Although there had been more than twenty investigations of the Air Service since the end of World War I, the public had paid little attention.

This time the audience was the whole country; this time they paid attention.

The key issues debated were (1) whether there should be a unified air service—that is, a separate air force; (2) whether the development and progress of aviation had been retarded by the conservatism in the Army and Navy; (3) whether there was any discrimination in pay and promotion against officers of the Army Air Service; and finally (5) what importance and role should aviation have in fighting on land and sea.

In his defense, Mitchell pointed out, "In the Army, we have no air force, none whatever, either in materiel (that means airplanes and equipment), in personnel (pilots, observers, gunners, mechanics) or in operations (that is, method of using it) . . . and that the aircraft we have are worn out, they are dangerous, they are incapable of performing any functions of a modern air force."

The inadequacy of men and materiel was, as he put it, because "air matters are entrusted to the Army and Navy, which are handled and governed and dominated by nonflying officers. They not only know next to nothing about aviation, but regard it merely as an auxiliary of their present activities and not as a main force in the nation's military equipment. Their testimony regarding air matters is almost worthless—sometimes more serious than this." He added, "The voice of the air is smothered before it is heard," and, instead of having aviation needs explained by admirals and generals who knew what aviation was about, they were "selected on the principle of 'Tag, you're it; go and talk to Congress about aviation.'"

Colonel Mitchell was particularly bitter about the Army's system of recruiting and training mechanics, "which was so poorly done," he said, that "it amounts to training these men with the pilots' lives." He prophetically argued at his trial not only for a modernized separate air force but also for reorganization of the War and Navy Departments into a Department of Defense with the Army, Navy, and Air Force as subdivisions.

Countercharges were made by Mitchell supporters that the court-martial was the latest step taken by the General Staff in its efforts to get Mitchell; that years before the court-martial, Mitchell had been warned that if he did not stop his efforts for the air force he would be forced out of the service; and that there was a conspiracy among the General Staff to rid the Army of Mitchell.

Army Chief of Staff Major General Hines strongly opposed the separate air force that Mitchell advocated. To him, an air service was an essential element of an army or navy. It was tied to the ground or to a ship. The demands of neither the Army nor Navy would be met if the Air Service were an independent organization; that was efficiency in combat. He did not believe an independent air force would be as serviceable as one under the immediate control of an Army commander. General Hines was also concerned that a separate air force would increase the overhead cost of administration, concluding that the World War I experience illustrated that the cost of aviation was quite high.

The Navy's position was that a unified air service would remove from the naval commander the unified command needed in time of battle and the uniform training in time of peace that they thought essential to victory.

Mitchell's attack received mixed reactions within the military. Some of his fellow officers resented the accusation of incompetence, negligence, and treason. Certainly it was upsetting to those who believed the motives of Mitchell's superiors were beyond suspicion and had at heart the best possible provisions for our nation's security.

Some news commentators were more than unkind. A *New York Times* editorial published the day after his press conference stated scathingly that "Colonel Mitchell is plainly 'asking for it,' and he ought to get it, even if he is still under the delusion that it will add to his glory and induce sensible men to hold him in respect." The same editorial commented that his statement would break "the back of what reputation he had left."

"He has not altogether pleased some of his best friends by the tactics he is pursuing," said one news commentator, in the September 7, 1925, issue of the *New York Times*. "They feel he is hurting his own cause by making what they regard as reckless and inaccurate statements."

Mitchell's San Antonio manifesto startled the whole country, as well as civilian and military leaders. Mitchell dared the lightning to strike him. Mitchell defiantly challenged Army discipline; the Army could not let his challenge go unanswered because the effect on Army morale would be disastrous if he were not taken to task for the affront to his superiors.

Yet Mitchell had a strong following of officers who believed in his cause. Among them were two officers who testified on Mitchell's behalf and who were to become the most important air leaders of World War II—Hap Arnold and Carl "Tooey" Spaatz. Both were warned by a number of senior officers not to testify for Mitchell—to do so would hurt or perhaps end their careers.

At the court-martial, Arnold's testimony emphasized the fact that certain members of the Army and Navy had given false or misleading information to Congress. In other cases, Arnold maintained, his superiors had given misleading information on such matters as how current the aircraft of foreign powers were, such as Great Britain, France, and Sweden, and the organizational structure of the foreign services as separate and distinct air forces.

Arnold was asked about a statement by Gen. Hugh Drum in the earlier

U.S. Air Service unification hearings of the Military Affairs Committee that "It is evident from these figures, from a flying personnel viewpoint, the United States is well off and compares most favorably with all foreign powers." Major Arnold said that General Drum had not spoken accurately when he said our personnel compared favorably with that of foreign nations: "I mean that he [General Drum] gives the impression that our Air Service compares very favorably with other large powers' air services, and I mean to say that it does not compare favorably with those other powers' air services."[16]

Mitchell reflected on this episode in 1936: "Fighting from my side of the barricade was an officer whose convictions and courage may help to bring our Air Force to its required strength before the next war comes upon us. He was Major. H. H. Arnold, one of my boys, fearless before his bigoted superiors."[17]

After the court-martial which resulted in Mitchell's conviction, Arnold did not want to give up the fight. He wrote in his memoirs, "The first ones to try to keep the battle going were Maj. Herbert Dargue and myself. After such long service in Washington, we had many friends in Congress and in the press. We continued going out to Billy's house in Middleburg, and also over to Capitol Hill, and writing letters to keep up the fight.

"At once the boom was lowered with a bang. After all the trouble with Billy Mitchell—and the case unpopularly closed—there was no thought of allowing small fry to keep it going. It was understood now that President Coolidge himself had been the prime accuser. We were both called on the carpet to answer for our 'irregular' correspondence relative to changes in Air Service status. Dargue got off with a reprimand. I was, as the press announced, 'exiled.' "[18]

As noted earlier, Arnold had been warned that testifying for Mitchell might jeopardize his career. The issue that brought about his exile arose a year after the court-martial when a news release, highly complimentary of the Air Corps but critical of the Army General Staff, was circulated surreptitiously. "It was traced," said Ira Eaker, "to Arnold by the Army Inspector General. He had used a government typewriter and paper and was charged with misappropriating public property in a project inimical to the Army. The Inspector General recommended Arnold's court-martial, but instead, at General Patrick's intercession, he was relieved of duty on the Air Staff, banished from Washington, and assigned command of one air squadron at Fort Riley, Kansas, a Cavalry post" (personal interview, October 4, 1977).

Captain Eaker was then the assistant executive to Maj. Gen. Mason Patrick and was present during these difficult times. "Arnold carried out his functions and duties for Patrick," Eaker said of the exile incident. "Patrick thought he was a bright, able officer and was completely satisfied with the work he was doing for him. Then, aside from [Arnold's] official duties to Patrick, all of his extracurricular activities were devoted to helping Mitchell—which we all thought was right . . . and we were doing the same thing. . . . I think Arnold always felt that Patrick had been severe with him" (personal interview, October 4, 1977).

Eaker was standing outside the office when Patrick sternly rebuked Arnold for his activities in the Mitchell controversy and informed Arnold of his reassignment. "I remember when he came out," said Eaker. "He was tremendously emotionally upset. Patrick had been severe, but Patrick was an old soldier and he thought he was doing his duty. He said to someone else afterward that it was actually only through his intervention that Arnold was spared a court-martial. He was carrying out a disciplinary procedure, and if he had not done this to Arnold, Arnold would have had something more severe" (personal interview, October 4, 1977).

In a statement to the press, Patrick said that the issue was the distribution of circulars urging support for legislation and that the endeavors by these officers were "without his knowledge and through mistaken zeal." In response to allegations that a number of air officers were implicated, Patrick said, "The investigation disclosed the fact that only two officers in this office were concerned in an attempt to influence legislation in what I regard as an objectionable manner. Both of them will be reprimanded, and one of them [Arnold], no longer wanted in my office, will be sent to another station."[19]

Certainly the attitude of some of his fellow officers had much to do with Arnold's reaction. After reporting to Fort Riley, "When the children were in bed in our new quarters," Arnold recalled, "Bee and I started the uncomfortable walk to General Booth's house, the Post Commander, for our first official call. The house was all lit up. As we were admitted, we saw that the Commanding General was having a card party. The living room was full of people. We stood there, and General Booth looked across the room and apparently recognized me. He rose and came toward us. Then he held out his hand and put the other on my shoulder. . . . 'Arnold,' he said cordially, 'I'm glad to see you. I'm proud to have you in this command.' And then, so that everybody could hear, he added, 'I know why you're here, my boy. And as long as you're here you can write and say any damned thing you want. All I ask is that you let me see it first!' "[20]

General Summerall, who became Arnold's boss after the exile, sent a wire to the Commandant at Fort Leavenworth inquiring whether an additional officer could be accommodated in the next class at Command and

Staff School. The reply came back, "Yes, who is he?" Arnold's name was submitted. The answer came back—they didn't want him, but if he did come he would naturally be accepted.

"In a private letter to General Fechet, the Commandant at Leavenworth wrote," said Arnold, "that if I came to Leavenworth as a student I would be 'crucified.' However, I was determined to go. I remembered that the Commandant of the school had served on the court that had tried Billy Mitchell, which probably had something to do with his feelings. In spite of the lack of cordiality in his letter, I found the course there of great value. I didn't get into many difficulties, and I did not find the going very tough. Naturally, I did not agree with many of the school's concepts relative to the employment of aircraft and I thought the course, as far as the air arm was concerned, could and should be modernized."[21] He graduated twenty-sixth in a class of eighty-eight.

A few years later, Arnold said, "When Gen. E. L. King, who had been my Commanding Officer at Leavenworth, arrived for . . . maneuvers in 1931, he surprised me by saying he appreciated very much the paper I had submitted when I left Leavenworth, outlining my ideas of the proper instruction in air operations at the school. He also congratulated me on the way I had handled my job as G-4.* This, from the man who had said he would crucify me if I went there, made me feel good."[22]

The early pioneers in flying believed that the uses of aircraft in war, in order of their relative value, were (1) reconnaissance, (2) warding off hostile aircraft, (3) performing messenger service, (4) observing artillery fire, (5) carrying supplies, and (6) launching offensive operations. As early as 1913, Arnold began to speculate on the strategic role air power might play in the future. In an article published in the *Infantry Journal* that year, he wrote, "The actual damage that can be done to objects on the ground from an aeroplane is very limited. But if 200 or 300 bombs are dropped in or around a column of troops, there will be some confusion and demoralization even if the damage inflicted is slight." He went on to say, "It is certain, therefore, that some damage can be effected by dropping explosives from aeroplanes." He emphasized that if a power charge were "dropped into a city it would certainly cause considerable damage."[23] This was the first written analysis, however sketchy, of the role of strategic bombing.

Although his nickname was "Hap," there were those who sometimes wondered why. Robert S. Israel remembered, "During CCC** days back in the early 1930s, I was Adjutant to General (then Major) Arnold, for the

*Officer in charge of logistics.
**Civilian Conservation Corps.

March Field, California CCC area. One day he called me in and chewed me out for something (and he was a past master at it) that I had no knowledge of and was in no way responsible for. For some reason, I had sense enough to keep my yap shut and not try to alibi or say anything. The next day, having found out that he had taken the wrong man to task, he called me in, apologized and then with a twinkle in his eye he said, 'But, Israel, how many times have you done things and gotten away with them that you should have been bawled out for?' " (personal communication, June 28, 1963).

Arnold was a man with great drive and energy. A specific example was reflected in a story told by then Maj. Ira C. Eaker. On February 19, 1934, President Roosevelt issued an executive order that the Air Corps was going to carry the airmail, thus canceling the civilian airmail carriers' contracts.

This abrupt change was brought about because "the political system to which we subscribe in this country," said Benjamin B. Lipsner (the first Superintendent of the U.S. Aerial Mail Service), "adheres to the principle that to the victor belong the spoils. . . . As a method of keeping the spoils, the victor, immediately on taking over his new office, sets about to prove that the previous administration was wicked, corrupt, and grafting. . . . The Roosevelt Administration opened for business in March 1933 and began to operate as had all of the administrations before it. Anything of the Hoover Administration that appeared open for attack was given careful consideration, and plans for the attack were made."[24]

Allegedly there was the possibility of an airmail contract scandal. Charges were made by Postmaster General James A. Farley of favoritism for a few corporations in awarding appropriations, illegally extending airmail contracts, avoiding competitive bidding, allowing excess profits, awarding routes, and colluding. After investigation of these charges, almost all of which later proved false, President Roosevelt ordered all airmail contracts canceled.

The President relied on postal laws and regulations for the authority for the cancellation. Maj. Gen. Benjamin Foulois, the Chief of the Air Corps, was summoned to the White House and asked by the President if he thought the Air Corps could carry the airmail. The Air Corps was pitifully inadequate for the challenge because of years of neglect from the Army and Congress. The aircraft were too few and inadequate, the personnel not properly trained, the instruments archaic for weather flying. But the Air Corps considered this an opportunity to show that it merited more financial support; if it did not take up the challenge it would be even more ignored.

Ira Eaker said of this experience (personal interview, October 4, 1977), "I was on the golf course on a Sunday morning with General Arnold when

this happened. A messenger came and told us, 'General Arnold is directed
by the Chief of Air Corps to call him immediately.' When . . . he called, he
was told the Air Corps was to carry the mail and he, Arnold, was in charge
of the Western Region. He then called his squadron commanders in and
assigned their routes. . . . We were allowed but little time to prepare for this
new task.

"He was all up and down the route, inspecting every phase of it. He
had very bold concepts. I said, 'Where are we going to get the money for
this? We've got to rent those offices that Western Airlines has.' He said,
'Go ahead, take it over—I'll support you.'

'So we went in and hired people, hired office space, and hangars and
shop space, and took over as directed.'

"Within two weeks," reflected Arnold later, "we were forced to realize
that although the 'will to do' might get the job done, the price of our doing
it was to equal the sacrifice of a wartime combat operation. Courage alone
could not substitute for years of cross-country experience, for properly
equipped planes, and for suitable blind flying instruments such as the
regular airline mail pilots were using."[25]

The results were disastrous. Several days before the Air Corps was to
begin the airmail flights, three pilots were killed in crashes attempting to get
to their assignments. During the first week of the scheduled flight, five
pilots were killed, six others critically injured. Eight planes were destroyed.
These tragedies had some impact on the President, who ordered a sharp
reduction of the airmail service. Also, flights were only made during the day
and when weather conditions were appropriate for cross-country flying. But
death and injury continued. On March 9, 1934, four Air Corps pilots were
killed on the same day, and on March 10 the President announced that the
airmail service would be returned to the civilian airlines as soon as possible.
Before the transition was completed, however, the twelfth Army pilot was
killed, on March 31, 1934.

General Eaker commented on the airmail incident: "Partly because of
more favorable weather, but also to the foresight, leadership, and organization of Arnold, his was the most successful segment of the Army airmail
effort, sustaining fewer casualties, and with the highest rate of on-schedule
delivery" (personal interview, October 4, 1977).

Ironically, this unsuccessful try at flying the airmail provided further
momentum for a separate air force. "By the time we were relieved of carrying the airmail [on May 16]," commented Arnold, "public opinion was
clamoring for an investigation. . . . Out of this [investigation] . . . came the
formation of the General Headquarters or G.H.Q. Air Force, the first real
step ever taken toward an independent U.S. air force."[26]

Arnold was a dynamic man with tremendous energy and drive. J. L.

Atwood, a civilian aeronautical engineer with North American Corporation, had the key responsibility for the development of the "Mustang" P-51 fighter. Atwood commented that he first met Arnold in 1938. He said, "He was a pusher with the engineers—he was always urging and pushing technical improvements to get better performance out of the aircraft. He recognized the Germans were building ahead very fast, and we had to move very fast if we were going to get anywhere in competition with them. . . . I don't believe he considered himself a technical man. . . . He was more inspirational. In his position of leadership, I think he felt that it was incumbent upon him to do everything he could with the money he got and to push all of us as hard as he could. He was the kind of leader who could put pressure on without embittering people—rather, he attracted them to his point of view and objectives, and you wanted to do everything you could to comply. His subordinates in the Air Force, so it seemed to me, in spite of the pressure, were strongly addicted to him."[27]

"General Arnold was a 'goer,' " reflected Brig. Gen. LaVerne G. Saunders. "He had unlimited physical energy. . . . He 'ran' while everyone else walked. He had knowledge of his far-flung command. He would ask questions, knowing the answer, to obtain the personality and knowledge of the person whom he was interviewing. He would take quick action to relieve an incompetent person. He would get immediate reaction from an inspection—it would be short and to the point.

"I was one of the three deputies on the Air Staff," Saunders continued, "in the Pentagon from February 1942 to July 1942—and I could observe him daily. I accompanied him on some trips to large production centers of aircraft. He would walk through a group of civilian workers and get the same reaction as from the military. One group stopped working when he went into one place, and he said to them, 'Continue to work, don't stare at me, we have a war to win!" (personal communication, October 9, 1962).

Two journalists who accompanied Arnold on an inspection trip to various Air Force installations and manufacturing plants in January 1943 wrote, "He moves at almost a trot through the mile-long bomber plant, zigzags between the glistening rows of fuselage frames, threads his way past milling machines and lathes, dodges beneath the skeleton of a half-finished wing, cocks his head, and peers up at a radial motor dangling from a rack. He looks around and above and on either side, never missing a detail, and his lips curl at the corners in the famous grin."[28]

These writers continued, "He never seems to tire; he's turbo-supercharged, they swear; he'll go 18 or 20 hours a day like this without stopping, wearing out men half his age. He doesn't rely on second-hand reports or opinions but insists on finding things out for himself."[29]

He was further described during this trip as one who "has an insatiable curiosity about people as well; now and then, he'll halt abruptly in his inspection of a factory—to the considerable relief of the rest of the party, whose feet by this time are killing them—and engage in a conversation with a girl working a riveting machine, or crouch on his haunches beside the young mechanic with the grease gun. He would say to these people, 'Nice work. Keep it up. We're counting on you.' " These writers concluded that Arnold "likes people, is genuinely interested in what they think."[30]

These same reporters were with Arnold on a fishing trip. One of them commented, "He fishes as enthusiastically as he does everything else; you wonder whether if that's the secret of his energy. Maybe he finds his relaxation in the variety of his enthusiasms."[31]

General Kuter remarked, "To instill a better understanding in the Army and the Navy of the effectiveness of the strategic air offensive, General Arnold and the Air Staff found that their most convincing weapon was the old-fashioned stereoscope. In General Arnold's office, all top-level Army, Navy, and governmental authorities of the allied nations who visited him were forced more by his contagious enthusiasm than by respectful courtesy to look down through his stereoscope at the debris of gutted airplane factories, steel mills, submarine plants, ball-bearing factories, and industrial cities laid waste by the high explosives and the fire bombs of the Army Air Forces and the Royal Air Force. President Roosevelt was not only shown this stereoscopic evidence but was provided a specially built stereoscope and a set of the pictures, along with 'Hap' Arnold's dynamic, explosive, contagious, enthusiastic prompting to show them to the uninformed or doubtful visitors who reached his high office."[32] Arnold got this idea and his first stereoscope and slides from Air Marshal "Bomber" Harris.

There were other examples of his energy and enthusiasm. "During World War II," said Maj. Gen. Robert W. Douglass, "General H. H. Arnold gave orders and tasks which seemed almost impossible of attainment. His thorough knowledge of his people, their capabilities, their pride, and their desire enabled him to accomplish these seemingly impossible tasks. General Arnold's 'can do' spirit and attitude flowed down and made a 'can do' air force" (personal communication, April 17, 1963).

Gen. Laurence Kuter, one of Arnold's key staff officers during World War II, commented on how Arnold established a "can-do" air force. It was very rare, indeed, that any of the officers would go to Arnold and say, "Chief, this project you directed just can't be done." Kuter pointed out, "An officer who said that once was liable never to be given an opportunity to say it again. 'It can't be done' were fighting words to Arnold, and he held all the cards."[33]

"Once we got into the war," said Robert Gross of Lockheed Aircraft,

"I had some business contacts with General Arnold. He was a very stern and hard taskmaster; he was never satisfied with any performance—and always asked us to do more than we could, and in so doing I suppose got us to do more than we thought we could do." Gross gave a specific example: "The Lockheed Company's main projects for the U.S. Air Force were two: (1) the P-38 and (2) the Boeing bomber that we made over here, the B-17. (Lockheed and Douglass Aircraft shared in the production of the B-17 with Boeing.) But when the Air Force pounded on the desk and hammered the table with us, and they did, Arnold particularly—it was always the P-38: 'Why don't you give me more? Where are the ones you should have given me last month? When are you going to get more?'"[34]

"Hap Arnold was not an engineer, of course," continued Gross, "though he was scientifically oriented. Yes, you could discuss engineering problems with him. We didn't particularly, because when General Arnold visited us his time was always very, very limited. I don't suppose he ever spent a whole hour in this plant at one time, and I've seen him come in and spend less than half an hour, literally exhort us to do more and then leave. He'd tell us the cost of failure, urge us on to higher levels, and then go along. This was his real concern, his real contribution, I'd say—he was the driving force that got his suppliers to promise more and do more than they thought they could do."[35]

When asked why they responded to the exhortations of Arnold, Gross said, "In the first place, he personally was a very, very likeable, forceful person. . . . He sort of picked you up and carried you along. . . . The second point is, we were afraid of him. He'd curse us up one side and down the next, and we were afraid he'd order us out of the business or something, and take the place over—literally, we were apprehensive about our future. If we didn't produce, we didn't know what would happen. Finally, there was our own need to do our best. We had a conscientious feeling about wanting to make a record, and we were trying in our own way to do our best. The power General Arnold had to pressure us was his absolute dedication. . . . He was 100 percent in his work, no competitive diversions of any kind."[36]

At a congressional hearing on the selection of the B-36 aircraft, Arnold was asked whether or not he knew Gen. George C. Kenney and what his opinion was as to the soundness of Kenney's judgment. Arnold first responded that he would not have sent anyone to serve with Gen. Douglas MacArthur if he had not "been 100 percent tops." Then, when asked by Congressman Kennan whether or not Kenney's performance in the Pacific during World War II justified Arnold's confidence in him, Arnold responded that the record "speaks for itself. Kenney doesn't have to apologize to anybody for his air operations. Any officer who can take a look at a truck and say, after being told he has to haul it across from Australia to New Guinea by air and is told by the boys it can't be done . . . and say that 'The hell I can't, get an acetylene torch and cut it in half, and then put the two halves in the airplane and fly over,' and then when they got to New Guinea weld it together again and drive the truck away—you don't inquire to his ability.''[37]

Arnold's refusal to accept the impossible got results. Around 1943–44 when the B-36 was being designed, a group of aeronautical engineers came to Arnold and said, "We will have to have X million dollars."

Arnold asked, "What for?"

Their response was "Because we have to completely redesign our airdromes."

Arnold asked, "How?"

"Well, we have to put steel trusses with supports underneath the trusses, underneath all those airports."

"What for?"

They said, "So we can operate the B-36s."

Arnold's answer was "Take the B-36 out and cancel it. We will have no airplane for which we must rebuild all the airports in Germany before we get there. And that is what you're asking me to do. You're asking me to spend $2.5 million on every runway where we are going to use the B-36. If that is the kind of airplane it is, I don't want it, cancel the order."

"They looked at me," said Arnold later, "and saw that I meant what I said. I then said, 'Now, there's another solution, of course. Change your landing gear. So instead of having the impact on that many square inches, spread the impact and double and triple that many square inches, then you don't have to rebuild your airdromes.' This is what the manufacturers of the B-36 finally did."[38]

"I often have heard Hap Arnold referred to as an impatient man," said Adm. John H. Towers (a Navy officer who went through pilot training with Glen H. Curtiss at the same time Arnold was training with the Wright brothers and who was head of Naval aviation during World War II). "That is perfectly true, but his was the kind of impatience which bore fruit. He was impatient of unessential but required procedures, of delayed decisions upon matters which appeared obvious, of anything which impeded the buildup of the air power which he so rightly considered necessary to the winning of the war."[39]

Spaatz was asked if Arnold ever became impatient with him; Spaatz responded, "I know he got impatient with me when I was in England, because we hadn't started bombing for a couple of months; he asked what we were doing over there. Why didn't we go over and start bombing Germany? What were we waiting for? My reason was that when I thought our forces were seasoned and ready to bomb, we would start bombing and not before then. That was the end of that.

"I know he had confidence in me, because of the relationship we had before. With me, he might sound impatient, but when I responded and gave him the reason for what I was doing, that ended it. There was no more to it. He didn't hold that in the back of his mind as a grudge. . . . Hap just wanted results, and sometimes was impatient about it, but when something was explained to him, then his impatience died down."[40]

Spaatz said of Arnold, "He was very impatient with people who said something couldn't be done, but he was not an impatient person, in the way that he always expected someone to be doing something unexpected. He was very pleasant to be with . . . a man of his dominant characteristics would be impatient with inefficiency. . . . Hap was foremost in believing there were no limitations to the speed, altitude, and weight-carrying capabilities of the airplanes to do the military job."[41]

Arnold's energy got things done. Maj. Gen. Donald Wilson said, "General H. H. Arnold's outstanding quality of leadership was his refusal to think through to the difficulties which would have to be overcome to accomplish a desired project. This, in combination with his apparent faith and reliance on the staff, seemed to be a most comforting characteristic. Of course, one never knows how much gnawing at the heart goes on behind that built-in smile that he had" (personal communication, April 17, 1963).

There was, however, one occasion when his contagious enthusiasm and effort to inspire backfired. "General H. H. Arnold was quite a showman and quite dramatic in all his efforts. He was a great leader, but slightly unorthodox. In late 1942 and early 1943, during the time our war effort was quite strained, our morale was not the highest, we needed more equipment, more and better trained officers and airmen. The troops were overworked, etc., and with this in mind General Arnold made a trip to the Pacific area to check out the conditions and, more important, to bolster morale. In talking with the airmen, he commented that 'if you think things are bad here, you should see them in North Africa.' Two or three months later, he went to North Africa and made the same comment in reverse; namely, things are much worse in the Pacific. Unfortunately some men in North Africa had been in the Pacific and called his hand, so to speak. He passed it off by saying he had been traveling so much he had often forgotten where he was" (Maj. Gen. Milton W. Arnold, USAF Ret., personal communication, October 17, 1962).

After World War II started, Arnold continued to drive civilian industry to produce more, sooner, just as he drove his military people. Maj. Gen. Frederick W. Evans said of him, "I served under General Arnold initially as a staff officer and later as commanding general of the first troop carrier command. One thing that impressed me about him was his boldness and his readiness to accept and demand seemingly impossible tasks. Shortly after a visit to the conferences with the President, it was agreed that tonnage over the Hump would be increased substantially without delay. General Arnold accepted the commitment. It could not be met without substantial early delivery of C-46 transports, then getting into production. He called on the intercom and asked how many C-46s were ready to start for India 'tomorrow.' After investigation, I unhappily was required to inform him that the number was about five, as I recall. General Arnold knew of the many bugs that were being uncovered in the C-46s but he had made a commitment to the President, who would not accept that status quo. He assembled immediately the head of Curtiss Aircraft Company, all of the senior engineers in and out of the service, [and] all the supply people, and demanded an immediate speedup, and explained the reason why. . . . Things really started to hum. Here was a case where forceful pressure from the top produced results" (personal communication, October 29, 1962).

Arnold also appreciated energy and dynamism in others. One officer who knew him for years remembered a story that, he said, "should be preserved for posterity. Perhaps it illustrates potential leadership, or the ability of a leader to recognize leadership in spite of things.

"The story: One day during World War II, a group of staff officers, including several generals, was in Hap Arnold's office being thoroughly chewed out for something important that had not been done. At noon straight up, the wall clock in the office emitted a loud, deafening buzz, as did all clocks in the Pentagon. Irate at the interruption, General Arnold bellowed, 'Why doesn't somebody do something about that damn clock!' A young, obscure colonel in the group did something: He picked up a heavy, empty inkwell off General Arnold's desk, threw back his arm, took aim, fired, and shattered the clock into fragments, never to buzz again. The young colonel was 'Rosie' O'Donnell. He almost at once became a brigadier general. He rose to four-star general. He might readily have remained a colonel if not for the demonstration that particular day" (Gen. Jacob E. Smart, USAF Ret., personal interview, July 17, 1979).

But there were times when Arnold had to quell the enthusiasm of his key men. General Eaker, for example, wanted to lead the early raids of his Eighth Air Force. "I asked General Spaatz to let me do it," said Eaker, "but at first he demurred. Then he said OK. In our discussion, we thought it might be a good idea to have the commanders and the senior staff officers very familiar with the crew's full operation so that our planning would be practical. My feeling was that there was no better time to start than with the first. General Arnold stopped our enthusiasm for that sort of thing. He pointed out rather caustically that our job wasn't concerned with leading raids but with planning and directing the whole operation. 'Who takes your place if you get shot down?'—that sort of thing.

"Then, too, there was some danger the British side might think we were critical of their commanders. In addition, there was concern over the possible capture of the senior men, who knew too much about the invasion plans for Europe. Finally General Arnold issued an order that if a senior officer went on one of these raids he was to be sent home." Eaker wanted to go on the Schweinfurt raids over Germany and asked the senior Army Commander, Gen. Jacob Devers, permission. Devers responded, "No, General Arnold told me to send you home if you went on another raid" (personal interview, October 4, 1977).

Eaker remembered another incident that was indicative of Arnold's drive and energy. Then a brigadier general, Eaker received a telegram from Arnold to leave the West Coast and report to him immediately. On arriving in Washington, he walked into Arnold's office and said, "What's up, boss?" Arnold responded that he was sending Eaker to England to understudy British bomber operations preparatory to starting our own bombing effort. Eaker exclaimed, "Bombers? Why I've been in fighters all my Air Force life!" Arnold said, "Yes, I know. That is why I want you in bombers—to get the fighter pilot spirit in our bomber outfits" (personal interview, October 4, 1977).

It was fortunate that Arnold had such drive and determination, because even after the Air Force had received commitments on the number of aircraft needed he still had a fight on his hands. That fight was for what he considered to be the proper deployment of the aircraft being developed. With the invasion of North Africa, bombers were directed from the Eighth Air Force to the Northwest African Air Force for the strategic and tactical deployment to make the Tunisian campaign successful. Arnold could see that a crisis was developing: with the commitment of some of their aircraft to North Africa, the Eighth Air Force was only able to make token raids on selected targets in Germany. He was confident it was necessary to strategically bomb German targets to destroy their war-making machinery as well as the morale of their people. Arnold ultimately prevailed.

At the time Arnold was appointed Chief of the Air Corps in 1938 by President Franklin D. Roosevelt, the entire Air Corps consisted of 3,900 airplanes, most of them obsolete, and 22,000 officers and men in the combined services of Army, Navy, and Marine Corps. At the end of World War II, there were two and one-half million people and 80,000 aircraft in the Army Air Forces alone.

The impressive growth statistics of the Army Air Forces during World War II were due to the vision of the men leading the Air Corps during the 1920s and 1930s. All these incredible feats with thousands of airfields, airplanes, and pilots did not happen without a great deal of preparation. During the 1920s and 1930s, Arnold was planning an air force large enough and modern enough to do the job.

"Arnold's outstanding leadership marks," reflected Brig. Gen. Don E. Zimmerman, were his "foresight in prompt action towards farseen goals. One example of this foresight was the tremendously increased impact of science on war which was one of the great lessons of World War II. General H. H. Arnold recognized this change very early. As a result, he was instrumental in the establishment of Project RAND (Research and Development Corporation), which began shortly after World War II and which ensured the scientific study of air warfare" (personal communication, July 2, 1963).

One of these scientists and engineers, J. L. Atwood, commented on Arnold's friendship with the Cal Tech people, "It was pretty far-fetched kind of activity for a military man in the early '30's. I always thought of Arnold as very forward-looking and thinking, and he supported science . . . strongly in the Air Force and the country as a whole. It was a pretty unusual quality in an Air Force officer."[42]

"Arnold had an inquiring mind," Carl Spaatz said in relation to Arnold's contact with Cal Tech. "He was interested in everything. . . . He was one of the first to be interested in aviation, and that was a new science in a way. . . . Milliken was a very brilliant man, the type that Hap liked to talk to. He suggested this idea to Hap (that is, about making flights to check cosmic rays), and Hap said, 'Well, we've got the planes out here at March Field, let's take the thing up and see what happens.' "[43]

Spaatz continued, "I can think of other people in the same position who would have checked up on Army regulations and found that there was nothing in Army regulations that covered that particular procedure, and he would have then said, 'Well, I don't think I can do it, because it's not covered.' General Arnold would have said, 'My duties are my regulations on the way to operate.' "[44]

It is fortunate that Arnold was a man of vision, because lead time was critical in developing our air power. The B-25 was originally designed in 1938, but the first aircraft was not delivered until 1941. The P-38 was designed in 1939 but was not used until 1941. And the P-47, which was designed in 1937, was not operational until 1941. Certainly the most outstanding aircraft of World War II was the early B-17, which was designed in 1934, but it was 1936 before the first B-17 was delivered.

Part of this lag was due to the requirement of securing support from

Congress, the War Department, and the public in developing aircraft. It was hard for the public to realize that it took almost five years to develop an aircraft. Funds for aircraft had to cover this period, because without continuity of funds development and procurement were difficult, if not impossible.

Eaker remembered that "one of the things that always impressed me about General Arnold was his tremendous vision about the future. And then the executive steps he took to get the information, and to do the things that had to be done. I don't think there was anybody in the War Department at that time who had the broad vision, coupled with the energizing executive capacity to come through" (personal interview, October 4, 1977).

Arnold realized the importance of recruiting the best people for the Air Corps. Maj. Gen. Charles F. Born said, "General H. H. Arnold was well known for being forceful, aggressive, dynamic, positive and a hard-driving leader with great foresight. In 1937 I was assigned to the U.S. Military Academy as an instructor. Being ambitious and an air officer, I felt I was losing three years of my tactical career by being assigned to the Military Academy. I approached General Arnold, who was then Chief of Staff of the Air Corps, about my being relieved from this assignment. His answer to me was, 'What the hell do you think I sent you there for, to be an instructor? I want you there to recruit the best graduates of each class for the Air Corps; we are going to need them badly in the future. Do I make myself clear?' " (personal communication, November 21, 1962).

One reason for Arnold's concern was illustrated by Theodore R. Milton, who entered the Air Force after graduation from West Point. Milton commented, regarding his experience with Arnold, "I knew him as a boy. He was a friend of my family; in fact, he gave me my first airplane ride when I was about 12 years old. But I didn't know him; after all, I was a second lieutenant and a first lieutenant when he was Chief of the Air Corps. After my graduation from West Point, he did make me report to him one Sunday, right after graduation, demanding to know why more of my class had not chosen the Air Corps. I graduated in the class of 1940. Our class was slightly below the norm that year, and he wanted to know why and decided that his best source would be the newly graduated cadets. . . . it was easy to answer that question. We had a very bad time with the Air Corps during our first class year. They had not treated us like grown-ups. They had been overly rigid on discipline. For example: we were taken to different Army posts throughout the United States, such as Fort Monmouth to see what the Signal Corps was like, to Fort Benning to observe the Cavalry and to Mitchell Field to observe the Air Corps. Mitchell Field was absolute disaster as far as their program of indoctrination was concerned. It was dull, and they lectured us all day long with the most stupid ground school subjects, and they flew us around in B-18s. . . . We wanted to get into pursuit planes and transports where the instructors would give you a hand in flying.''

Milton, who went on to become a full general in the Air Force, concluded that the next year the Air Corps did a good job, and there was a decided increase and interest on the part of West Point cadets for going into the Air Corps. Milton remarked that when the cadets stayed at Mitchell Field, the Air Corps officers that summer were "peeking around all night seeing if they could catch anyone out after taps, and if so, they proceeded to punish them. The Cavalry at night, where you slept on the ground and were camping, had such a hard, grueling day every day in the week that the senior Cavalry officer simply said to us that if we wanted to try to slip out after taps, go ahead. 'I don't care,' said the senior Cavalry officer, 'because you are going to be sorry tomorrow with the grueling schedule that we have in mind.' Indeed some of them did go down the road and drink beer. He had them up at 3 A.M., all day long on a horse, and by the time he put them through the rigors of the day it was quite obvious there was no need for punishment of the individuals who went out after taps. We all thought that this was funny and concluded that this was certainly the way to handle us as far as what we would do after taps. I told him [Arnold] all this, and he made notes. . . . He then made the comment, 'This was the last time that would ever happen' '' (personal interview, April 9, 1976).

While Arnold was a man of great drive and energy, he stressed that a commander should not try to do everything. "Until his staff is thoroughly trained," he said, "he will supervise all the duties himself, but it is more than one man can undertake and he will be wise, indeed, if he early ensures the adequate training of these assistants and then delegates to them the responsibility, retaining supervisory power."[45]

When an officer is a squadron or group commander, there are many other details he can take care of personally, and there is certainly a tendency and desire to attempt to run these things with a minimum of delegation. But a commander must learn to control his organization from a detached point of view. As he goes up in rank, he can no longer concern himself with petty details or even work with his hands. "He must get away," said Arnold, "from the shovel handle and out of the ditch so that he can oversee all the workmen on the project."[46]

One reason for Arnold's successful leadership was his ability to pick good people and to then delegate full authority to them, with only general directives. Brig. Gen. Clarence P. Cain remembered Arnold's early years of leadership: "I served under General Arnold as supply officer during the air mail. General Arnold picked specialists for key jobs and then left them alone. He would back his subordinates to the hilt. He never forgot a favor. But if he took a dislike to an individual he could be mighty tough" (personal communication, June 12, 1962). A specific example that another officer remembered was that of Maj. Gen. Rush P. Lincoln: "When I was ordered to Australia, General Arnold showed his confidence in me by giving me only one order, 'Rush, go out there and take action to stop the Japs. Something is wrong out there and you correct it' " (personal communication, October 9, 1962).

Spaatz commented, "All the money that was spent for national defense between World War I and World War II was spent on the Navy, which was sunk at Pearl Harbor. We were just a small smattering of people in the Air Force—400, 500 officers . . . and some of them were not too good. That's what we had to expand to two or three million people for the war."

Did Hap choose his staff well? "I would say he picked his staff very well," said Spaatz, "from what he had to pick from. . . . He took the resources he had and put them to the best advantage that they could be put to."[47]

It was surprising, however, that with all his vision Arnold was reluctant to advance quickly some of the brilliant younger officers early in World War II. Gen. George C. Marshall suggested, to assist Hap Arnold with this dilemma presented by the large increase in the size of the Air Force, that Arnold select a few relatively junior Air Corps officers to be jumped in rank, to prepare younger talent for effective leadership in the rapidly growing Army Air Forces. Arnold replied that if he promoted these officers he did not believe he could sustain the morale of the World War I flyers among the senior colonels. Many of these colonels had been reduced from war-time rank in 1919 and had served as long as seventeen years as lieutenants. Jump-promoting "youngsters" in their thirties, he thought, would shatter the morale of the older, more experienced group. Marshall therefore proceeded on his own and, for example, promoted Lt. Col. Laurence S. Kuter immediately to the rank of brigadier general. Kuter had only been a lieutenant colonel for some three weeks when this promotion was made. Arnold was then instructed to place the thirty-six-year-old Kuter in a high position on his staff and to be less concerned about the morale of the older officers and more concerned with providing incentives for the younger ones.[48]

One of Arnold's West Point classmates, who was also with him in both world wars, commented on Arnold's leadership. "He was able to turn over to other men, his subordinates, their definite jobs and leave them alone. . . . if they did not do their jobs on time, they were replaced by other men. He learned to keep good discipline and looked after his men" (H. B. Hayden, personal communication, November 27, 1962).

His key plans officer during World War II, Gen. Orville A. Anderson, said of Arnold that he gave "almost total leeway. I never went to Hap's office. Now, there were times when I wanted to brief him and say, 'Here's a big issue coming up,' and I wanted to let him know what the issue is. But as his planner, until he says, 'Now you've gone berserk,' I'm supposed to do what I think Hap would do if he had the same opportunity to read as deeply into the problem as I had. In other words, as long as I think I have logic and reason to support the stand that I take . . . I'm not afraid of Hap or anybody else."[49]

Immediately after Pearl Harbor, in January 1942, Army Chief of Staff George C. Marshall selected then Maj. Gen. Joseph T. McNarney and three other officers to form a committee to reorganize the War Department to meet the needs of the rapidly building fighting force required to win World War II. One officer selected for this reorganization—which as matters developed was another step toward an independent and separate air force —was Laurence S. Kuter. "I was Assistant Secretary of the War Department General Staff and was selected as one of General McNarney's three assistants, responsible for a radically new Army Air Forces organization," Kuter said. "In my job, I relied heavily on the assistance and collaboration of Gen. Byron E. 'Hungry' Gates. Hungry in turn assembled a group of newly inducted Army Air Forces officers with credentials in management and organization. Among them was a twenty-six-year-old M.B.A. from Harvard, Lt. Col. Robert S. McNamara . . . also Col. Charles B. 'Tex' Thornton—who, not long after the war, organized and managed Litton Industries. Also in the group were Guido Perera, subsequently a leading corporation lawyer and corporate director in Boston, and Joseph S. Clark, future mayor of Philadelphia and later U.S. Senator from Pennsylvania."[50]

Guido R. Perera reflected on this historic move toward a separate air force: "On February 5, 1942, I was a junior officer at a meeting in General Marshall's office called to discuss the proposed reorganization of the Army. The others present were the Chiefs of the several divisions of the War Department General Staff and Generals McNarney, McNair, Somervell, Kuter, Smith, and Harmon, and Colonels Harrison and Gates. . . . General Marshall led the discussion and did so with both tact and authority. Two of his passing comments intrigued me: (1) 'The War Department becomes a madhouse by 9:15 A.M. and it is difficult to find time after that to do any constructive planning; and (2) in reply to a comment that the proposed plan was 'abnormal,' 'Yes, the plan may seem abnormal but all wars are abnormal and this one is particularly abnormal.' "[51]

The reorganization eliminated the Office Chief of Air Corps and the General Headquarters Air Force. Arnold became Commanding General of the Army Air Force. Although he was not given any combat functions, in essence he did have these responsibilities through his position as Deputy Chief of Staff, then later as a member of the Joint Chiefs of Staff, and because of his personal relationship with the air commanders in the field. As a result of this reorganization, as Perera succinctly put it, Arnold now had an influence "on the strategic command of the war beyond all authority. This was particularly true of matters involving the strategic use of air power."[52]

In early March of 1942, the Army Air Corps officially became the Army Air Forces. An autonomous air staff was created, separate from the War Department's General Staff. One of the brilliant young staff officers with that group was Kuter. He thought that the resulting increase in staff size "seemed to generate a diffidence of uncertainty in commanding General 'Hap' Arnold toward his own staff." With the reorganization of March 1942, General Arnold no longer had the small, tightly knit staff to which he was accustomed; instead, he had an immense organization with branches, sections, and offices with hundreds of officers and civil servants —far too many for Arnold to know personally. Kuter said that "Arnold sometimes seemed to regard the Air Staff not as his own personal staff, not as an extension of his own mind and will, but as an obstacle to be hurdled, to be dodged or evaded."[53]

This created real problems for Arnold, who as a man of dynamic energy was used to making fast decisions. He expressed concern to one member of his staff after this change: "I toss a new idea to you staff fellows and what happens? A long time later I get a list of the staff's projects that will have to be deferred if mine is to be implemented and sometimes the implication that my idea isn't as good as yours anyway. All I get back are reasons why it can't be done! I got all of that kind of support I needed from the great War Department General Staff when I was in the aviation section of the Signal Corps of the Army."[54]

There were obvious frustrations for Arnold with this tremendous increase in the Air Staff, as Kuter recognized: "Even as Chief of the Air Corps in Washington, he [Arnold] had been a highly personal leader in face to face contact with his subordinates. He was not nearly as well attuned to the task of guiding the leaders of this new, large Air Staff as to struggle to create airpower. The General just had to get things done himself. He found it difficult to sit quietly as he projected his thoughts into the future. He had to be talking to people. He wanted to advance new ideas, have them picked up with enthusiasm, bounced around a bit, augmented here and there, and put into operation immediately."[55]

During Arnold's tenure as Commander of the Army Air Forces in

World War II, the Assistant Secretary of War was Robert Lovett. General Anderson said, "Lovett was an appraiser, an advisor, and his council was always sound. Lovett was a very able, thinking man. . . . [When] Hap . . . at times [got] too enthusiastic and [went] off the deep end . . . Lovett would come in and sit and talk for a while and get him toned down, and roll him off to a safer area."[56]

To cope with the huge size of the Air Staff, Arnold created a group called on the organization chart "Council." This group of officers reported directly to the Commanding General of the Army Air Forces. In this office, there were normally two to four very carefully selected brilliant prospects as career officers in the Army Air Forces and very talented civilians serving in the military during the war. They had far above average potential and considerable reach and experience, and Arnold could and did talk freely and easily with them. They were not subject to Air Staff assignments. If they had been, Arnold believed, they would be too busy with day-to-day business to be imaginative and to evaluate new ideas that he might throw to them. Membership of this council rotated, but some of them—such as Rosie O'Donnell, Jacob E. Smart, "Pre" Cabell, and Fred Dean later earned three and four stars—an obvious indication of Arnold's wisdom in selecting junior officers who had potential for key positions in the future.

When Marshall learned of this small group of advisors, he became very distressed, as indicated in the following conversation between himself and Kuter:

Marshall:	What is the Council I saw on the latest version of the organizational chart of the Air Staff?
Kuter:	A very small office, which General Arnold uses on matters of special concern to him.
Marshall:	Who supervises it?
Kuter:	General Arnold.
Marshall:	Now see here! Your Air Staff has been operating reasonably well, and I'm not going to have a superstaff by any name imposed on top of it!
Kuter:	General Marshall, the members of the Council have become very important aides to our staff operation and are by no means superimposed on top of the staff.
Marshall:	Tell me how it works.

Kuter: Well, General, basically that office serves as a valuable
point of contact between General Arnold and the Air Staff.
Those officers on the Council have no other duties than to
keep their attention in line with General Arnold's thinking
and be alert and available to him all the time. They are
officers whose imaginations, experiences, and judgment
General Arnold respects. They respond to his thinking, and
they are the type with whom he bats new ideas around. And
what is more important, they understand and respect the
work of the staff in Washington as well as the commands in
the field. They are painstaking in passing on to the staff up-
to-the-minute information on our Chief's changing interest
and actions. Through them we are kept current on General
Arnold's rapidly developing ideas. Through them the staff
knows what our Chief wants and what he doesn't want.[57]

Kuter's evaluation was that this staff "served as a smooth and incon-
spicuous transmission or gear box between the mercurial interests of the
Chief and the minor inertias inevitable in this huge organization. The rare
personalities in that council buffered the Chief's changes of pace in direction and added stability to the Air Staff's contact with its commander."
The evaluation eased Marshall's concern.[58]

To some individuals, Arnold's type of drive and energy was not leadership. Some believed that he was driving, not leading. "Not all the
casualties," related Kuter, "in the Army Air Force were in the battle areas.
During a high-pressure conference at about 11 A.M. on Sunday morning in
early 1942, a key officer in the Air Staff dropped dead on the carpet in front
of General Arnold's desk. He had apparently been killed by the intensity of
his responsibility as a staff officer.

"As the news reached the hallways of the Munitions Building, there
followed a brief flurry of comment that the Chief was 'a slave driver who
was working his officers to death.' Such remarks came more frequently
from outside the staff than from officers on it, and even then it was sparse
and short-lived. At the top of the staff, all knew that General Arnold was
'driving' no one. However, he was leading at a very fast pace. It was essential if the Army Air Forces were to be built in time to forestall disaster in
Europe and the Pacific. As the leader, none worked under the pressure he
did. As far as their matters were concerned, he took the brunt of the
demands of the President, Harry Hopkins, and the White House staff, as
well as other high outside agencies."[59]

Another solution Arnold used to overcome the large staff—which seemed to him to stand in the way of getting his projects accomplished—was to select Air Corps officers in whom he had confidence, give them projects, and send them off "right away." Arnold would then conceal this assignment from the rest of his staff. The staff had to intercept each project officer to learn what the chief had instructed him to do. It was not unusual that such a project would be beyond the officer's knowledge or control. Then the staff stepped in to help expedite the project.[60]

Although Arnold left his people alone to do their work, he still "had a custom of checking on different operations that he might have assigned to you," said Brig. Gen. Lawrence J. Carr. "It was normal, perhaps, that for various reasons some projects fell behind schedule, in which case he would review your actions in the matter and of course question you on why you didn't get certain things done. He would always carefully listen to your reasons and then remark pleasantly, but firmly with his well-known smile, 'Well, Lawrence . . . do you want to do this project or do you want me to do it for you? Invariably I went on and got the job done.

"General Arnold issued a directive at the beginning of the war that if any problems arose that could not be solved in the command or if his assistance was needed, to pick up the phone and call him. It appears now perhaps as being an unnecessary directive, but at the time in the middle of all our problems we had the feeling General Arnold was right at our elbow ready to assist us if we required it. His 'presence' there unquestionably forced a solution without a call" (personal communication, October 3, 1962).

Another officer, Maj. Gen. K. B. Wolfe, was less kind. "Hap Arnold," he said, "was a very impatient man. He was never satisfied with what we were doing. One of his favorite sayings to me was, 'Well, K. B., how long is it going to take you to do this?'

"I'd say, 'It's going to take six months, or sixteen months.'

"He'd say, 'Well, that's fine. Take all the time you want, but do it in three months.' He's that kind of guy, impatient, and I'd say unreasonable."[61]

But Arnold's drive and energy did not mean that he ran roughshod over people. He cared about others, and consideration for others goes far in making a successful leader. At one military installation where Arnold inspected an enlisted mess, something immediately caught his attention. He called for the mess sergeant, asking, "Where's the menu?"

The sergeant responded, "It's on the bulletin board, sir."

General Arnold said, "No. I mean a big menu over the counter so the men can see it before they get to the hot plate. They like to look up and see what they're going to have to eat. I know I do." Then over his shoulder as he started back for the flying line, he added, "Better get one made."[62]

During World War II, Arnold often visited the enlisted men's mess as part of any visit to an installation, even if only to land for refueling. One reporter traveling with him recounted such an incident. He went up to the chow line and said to the man behind the steam table, "Let's taste that." He sampled it and remarked to the man behind the steam table, "I wondered why in the hell the men weren't eating." Then he turned to the base commander, obviously intending that the latter correct the poor-quality meal being served.[63]

He was concerned for feelings as well as for physical comfort. Once Arnold called in a colonel on his staff and instructed him, "Pack your bags. We're going somewhere."

The colonel responded, "May I ask where we're going?"

"You may not," was the response.

As it turns out, their destination was an advanced flying school of the Army Air Forces. They arrived in time for graduation exercises, which were in progress. Each young man who had earned his wings stepped forward to get his wings and be commissioned. One young man in the crowd was obviously excited, constantly looking up at the visiting colonel who was with Arnold. As the anxious young man came forward, Arnold turned to the colonel and said, "All right, Thomas, step forward and pin the Air Force wings on your kid."[64]

Arnold's concern for his men included personal and professional satisfaction. Any professional officer is anxious, if his country is at war, to go where the action is, to get involved in the fighting. This opportunity passed by Arnold in World War I. "My ambition to take an air outfit to France," he said, "was never realized. In a sense, it remains a disappointment to this day. During World War II, in Washington, I deliberately deprived myself of the aid of a whole series of fine chiefs of staff and valuable topflight advisers so that these men would not miss out on wartime experience that I never had."[65]

Arnold went on, "Early in 1941, trying to get better information about the war in Europe, we sent officers abroad from all parts of the Air Force organization—combat units, staff, training center, and materiel command. Whether they could be spared or not made no difference. I followed the same procedures during the war because I thought it far more important to give these men a crack at combat operations than to keep them on duty in Washington. I always remembered my own frustrated attempts to get overseas in World War I.

"Chiefs of Staff of the Air Force, like Spaatz, Eaker, M. F. Harmon, Stratemeyer, Delos Emmons, and such advisers as George C. Kenney and the late Frank M. Andrews were sent overseas to big commands of their own. Acting Chiefs of the Air Corps and Deputy Chiefs were changed as often, no matter how good they were, but, unfortunately, many good men never had a chance to demonstrate their ability in combat'' (personal interview, October 4, 1977).

Once, a long-time friend, stationed at Wright Field, needed a good young officer to understudy one of his department heads. Arnold told this friend, ''I'll recommend one who'll be an answer to your prayer. Your gain will be my loss. . . . But this young man is too good to be held to the confines of one squadron. He can benefit the whole Air Corps if you take him with you, but first you must promise me you'll give him a chance. He is not prepossessing in appearance.''[66] The man was given his chance and performed brilliantly.

His concern for people encompassed civilians as well as military. Eaker was with him in California in the 1930s, and told this story: ''Well, this particular night in 1930, they had this big earthquake in Long Beach. He was sitting home at night and somebody phoned him about it. He marshalled the whole post, called everybody in—emergency, war footing—and rushed trucks down to Long Beach, and took over the police duty, issued blankets, and turned out little camp kitchens—just took over. The Corps Area Commander threatened to charge him with the price of the government property that he had distributed and used! You would think he'd have gotten a commendation for this action that he had taken, but he almost got a court-martial rather than a commendation for it!'' (personal interview, October 4, 1977).

Arnold gave a particularly appropriate example in an appearance before the House Committee on Armed Services on August 19, 1949, of a World War II experience with the press. The newspapers were making comments to the effect in 1943 that the Air Force under General MacArthur was not defeating the Japanese and General Spaatz was not licking the German air force because of the quality of our airplanes. These commentators, in their newspaper columns and over the radio, made such comments as, ''Why don't you get airplanes as good as the Jap Zeros?'' ''Why don't you get airplanes as good as the Messerschmidts and the Focke-Wulfs?'' These same writers panned the P-38s and the P-47s and all the rest of the U.S. aircraft. ''It got so bad,'' said Arnold, ''that I finally decided that something had to be done. I knew I didn't dare tell them the relative characteristics of these airplanes, for general broadcast. . . . I called in the worst of my critics from New York. . . . And when he came down, I said, 'Now, you're an expert and I am not. . . . You have 5 million readers, and they all look to you for advice and you are [telling] them . . . that the German airplanes are better than anything else we have in the United States.'' Arnold then said, ''I have here on this chart, unidentified, every airplane built by Germany,

Japan, and the United States. I wish you would look at that chart and decide, if you were in my place, which one of these airplanes you would supply for our combat units."

The newspaper reporter responded, "Obviously I couldn't do a thing like that; it doesn't mean anything to me."

Arnold said, "You must be an expert because you've told the people of the United States—by God, you know all about it. Now, which one of these would you pick out? You will notice that this one is a single supercharger, so it is at best performance up to probably 7,000 feet. Now this one is a Douglas supercharger, so it is not so good at 7,000 feet but between 7,000 and 14,000 feet it is a little bit better, and beyond 18,000 it is tops. There they are." The newspaper reporter then said, "Well, I can't do it, but I'll try. OK, I pick that one." Arnold informed him that the one he had picked was the P-38.

He said, "Try again," and the newspaper reporter picked the P-51.

The reporter finally said, "Listen, you've got me. Why don't you tell us this?" the reporter continued. "Why don't you give it to us so that we can put it in our papers?"

Arnold answered, "You supposed that I would be foolish enough to tell Hitler and Hirohito everything that I know about our planes?"[67] Arnold never had any trouble with that newspaper reporter again.

On March 19, 1943, Henry H. Arnold became the first four-star general —and later the first five-star air general—as an air officer. When the nomination went to the Senate of the United States, it broke all records for speedy confirmation, the nomination having been unanimous and by acclamation on the day it came up for approval. He had begun by commanding a squadron of only five planes at Fort Riley after he was exiled, and ended commanding 80,000 planes and 2.5 million men in all parts of the world.

"He always had been doing something," Spaatz commented on Arnold's career. "He was never satisfied with conditions that existed. He always had to be doing something else. That was the dominant characteristic he had. That's what some people call impatience. He was not satisfied to sit back and view a scene that looked perfectly smooth and operated smoothly, and say, 'All right now, sit down and rest.' That was not Hap. He always had to be some other place. That was the impatience I think that some people attributed to Hap."[68]

Frederick Lewis Allen wrote, of his first press conference with General Arnold, "At the head of the table sat General Arnold, a merry, rosy, white-haired man, with a smile on his lips so much of the time that it was obvious his nickname 'Hap' must stand for 'Happy.' A solid man, friendly, energetic, conveying force when he turned serious—as he did later when addressing us; but it was the smooth-shaven pinkness of him, and the merry smile, which lingered in my memory: I thought of a beardless Santa Claus."[69]

And, finally, his smile was described as "a fighting grin, you realize, as you study him across the aisle. There are sparks in it; his aides will tell you, 'You haven't lived until you've been bawled out by the old man.' It's more than a term of affection; it's a tribute. They know his achievements, know the spectacular string of firsts that he has hung up in the course of a record-breaking flying career."[70]

The comment was once made of Arnold, "He's a very even-tempered man—always angry." Secretary Lovett said it wasn't true. Ambassador Averell Harriman said, "Arnold could get angry, you know. He controlled his temper, but he used his temper to get results" (personal interview, August 16, 1978).

Another perspective was offered by Gen. Leroy T. Lutes, who said, "Arnold was a very determined man. . . . He was very persistent when he wanted something. He had a very calm manner up to a point, but Hap could get mad. It wasn't the type of madness or anger that you would resent at all; you knew why he was mad. He had good judgment, and he had a damn good disposition. When you won your point, he was always ready to slap you on the back, make some facetious remark and let it go at that. But he'd fight for his point."[71]

One might think that in time of war the rivalry between the Navy and the Air Corps would cease, but it did not. The Navy was extremely jealous and felt threatened by the prospect of a separate air force. "It was obvious to other members of the Joint Chiefs of Staff, that despite the present edict, Arnold did not get recognition from Leahy and King," commented Gen. Orville A. Anderson, Arnold's plans officer during World War II. "Unless they were just cracking jokes or something, they didn't talk directly to Arnold. It wasn't their habit to talk to Arnold."

One of Arnold's major strengths was his capacity to grow and develop. After becoming Chief of Air Corps in 1938, he found himself in less than two years involved actively in international relations. From a somewhat isolated life of thirty years of military service, he was suddenly in regular contact with President Franklin D. Roosevelt and Prime Minister Winston Churchill, and to a lesser degree, with Stalin and DeGaulle. He had not had such contacts before, but, as Ambassador Harriman remarked, Arnold was "not unduly awed and certainly wasn't affected by it. He was tremendously interested by it. He always had an inherent dignity. He took them in a mature manner; although not sophisticated, although they were a new experience for him, he had a natural dignity so that he never did or said anything gauche, nor did he ever put his foot in the wrong place'' (personal interview, August 16, 1978).

It was, perhaps, best summed up by Kuter, who wrote, "In the beginning God created the Heaven and the earth. Considerably later, General H. H. 'Hap' Arnold created the Army Air Forces. The axioms of sound business management were not adhered to very closely in either case."[72]

Several reporters who traveled extensively with Arnold during World War II commented that, after inspecting an air base or aircraft factory, they would return to their plane, where Arnold often relieved the pilot by taking over the controls to fly to the next destination. "He guides the ship with a veteran hand, and you realize as you watch him what it is that makes it possible for him to be a cloak to every last member of his outfit."[73]

Hap Arnold personified the U.S. Air Force. He was there for the early pioneer years of aviation and was part of its growth. He commanded it through the challenging years of World War II. He never doubted that he would build an air force that would win the war. "I was tired," he wrote, "quite ready to turn over the reins of air power to others—for I'd spent most of my adult life in airplanes."[74]

He had certainly earned a rest. Eight years as Chief of Air Corps, from 1938 to 1946, was an incredible demand on any man's endurance and health. He fought a war in peacetime as well in his efforts to enhance air power against strong opposition. No one could have accomplished what General Arnold did in the development of air power before and during World War II.

Arnold died on January 15, 1950, of a heart attack. On the day of his death when he arose, he told his wife that he felt well. A few minutes later, however, he sat down on the bed and collapsed. By the time the local doctor arrived, Hap Arnold was dead at the age of sixty-three. The doctor, Russell V. Lee, said, "He should have quit during the war when he had his first heart attack in 1944. But things were hot then and he decided to take his chances with the rest of the soldiers and went back to duty."[75]

General Hayden recalled, "When I learned that Arnold's heart was not in good shape, I urged him to retire. He refused to do so, and made the comment to me on more than one occasion that so long as young men were flying and getting killed, he would stay on active duty and if that meant that he had to die while serving as Chief of the Army Air Corps, he did not see that that was any different from somebody who had to die in combat."

Perhaps the most intimate tribute paid to Arnold was in the obituary published in the West Point alumni magazine, *Assembly,* written by Benjamin F. Castle, who knew Arnold as well as, or better, than any other man. He said, at Hap Arnold's services at Arlington Cemetery, where he was joined by many of the "long gray line," that a "great and valiant spirit was reporting for duty." Castle further said, "As we sat quietly together that January day, we remembered all the big and little things that go to make up many years of close association. We were glad that in his lifetime appreciation and recognition had been his—Arnold's reward for the great service he had given his country—that as 'General of the Air Force' he ranked with other great Army leaders like Washington, Grant, MacArthur, Marshall, Eisenhower and Bradley; that high honors had been awarded him. We remembered too, his great simplicities, how he would come to the class meetings whenever possible and recall with the rest of us those cadet days we all liked to talk over. We were glad, too, that he had those quiet hours in the Valley of the Moon (his retirement home) and the deep satisfaction it must have been to him to know that after all the tumultuous years it was he who was the Chief of the Air Force when final hard-fought victory was ours. There is so much more that should be said—so much more that will live in our memories and in the memories of many men in the ranks of life. The phrase which comes to mind which best expresses Hap is one from Kipling: he could 'walk with kings—nor lose the common touch.' "[77]

NOTES, Chapter 1

1. Gen. Henry H. Arnold, *Global Mission* (New York: Harper, 1949), p. 6.
2. Arnold, *Global Mission,* p. 7.
3. Ibid.
4. Arnold, *Global Mission,* pp. 7–8.
5. Ibid., p. 8.
6. Ibid., pp. 8–9.
7. Ibid., p. 11.
8. Ibid., p. 15.
9. *Colliers,* February 23, 1946, p. 8.
10. Maj. Gen. Henry H. Arnold and Col. Ira C. Eaker, *Science Digest,* 9 (May 1941):23–24.
11. Interview by Donald Shaunessey with Brig. Gen. Thomas DeWitt Milling, February 1959.
12. Cory Ford and Allister McBain, "The Sky's the Limit," *Colliers,* January 9, 1943, pp. 18–19.
13. Ben H. Pearse, *His Job Is Giving Us World Air.*
14. Frank Wesley Craven and James Lea Cate, eds., *The Army Air Forces in World War II.,* Vol. 1, *Plans and Early Operations, January 1939 to August 1942* (Chicago: University of Chicago Press, 1948), p. 7.
15. Arnold, *Global Mission,* p. 22.
16. Testimony of Maj. H. H. Arnold at Court-Martial Trial of William D. Mitchell, pp. 482–84.

17. William D. Mitchell correspondence.
18. Arnold, *Global Mission,* p. 122.
19. *Journal,* February 20, 1926.
20. Arnold, *Global Mission,* p. 123.
21. Ibid., p. 131.
22. Ibid.
23. First Lt. Henry H. Arnold, U.S. Infantry, "Air Corps and War," *Infantry Journal,* 10 (July 1931–June 1941): 229.
24. Capt. Benjamin B. Lipsner, *The Airmail* (Chicago: Wilcox & Follett, 1951), pp. 238–40.
25. Arnold, *Global Mission,* p. 143.
26. Ibid., p. 145.
27. Interview by Donald Shaunessey with J. L. Atwood, May 15, 1959.
28. *Colliers,* 113 (January 9, 1943): 18.
29. Ibid.
30. Ibid.
31. Ibid., p. 20.
32. Laurence S. Kuter, *Airman at Yalta* (New York: Duell, Sloan, & Pearce, 1955), pp. 31–32.
33. *Aerospace Historian,* December 1974, p. 186.
34. Interview by Donald Shaunessey with Robert Gross, May 15, 1959.
35. Ibid.
36. Ibid.
37. *Investigation of the B-36 Bomber Program Hearings on H.R. 234,* 81st Congress, 1949, p. 378.
38. Ibid., p. 376.
39. Adm. John H. Towers, USN (Ret.). "My Friend 'Hap' Arnold," *United Aircraft Corporation,* 25 (Spring, No. 2): 9.
40. Spaatz comment.
41. Ibid.
42. Shaunessey-Atwood interview.
43. Interview by Donald Shaunessey with Carl A. Spaatz, January 29, 1959.
44. Ibid.
45. Lt. Gen. H[enry] H. Arnold and Brig. Gen. Ira C. Eaker, *Army Flyer* (New York: Harper, 1942), p. 168.
46. Ibid., p. 169.
47. Shaunessey-Spaatz interview.
48. *Aerospace Historian,* December 1974, p. 186.
49. Interview by Donald Shaunessey with Gen. Orville A. Anderson, October 1959.
50. Gen. Laurence S. Kuter, "How Hap Arnold Built the AAF," *Air Force,* September 1973, p. 89.
51. Guido R. Perera, *Leaves from My Book of Life* (Boston: privately printed, 1975), pp. 55–56.
52. Ibid., p. 58.
53. Kuter, op. cit.
54. *Aerospace Historian,* p. 185.
55. Ibid.
56. Shaunessey-Anderson interview.

57. Ibid.
58. Ibid, p. 188.
59. Ibid.
60. Ibid., p. 186.
61. Interview by Donald Shaunessey with Gen. K. B. Wolfe, March 14, 1959.
62. *Colliers,* 113 (January 9, 1943): 19.
63. *Colliers,* 112 (December 25, 1943): 26.
64. Ibid.
65. Arnold, *Global Mission,* p. 48.
66. Ibid.
67. B-36 Bomber Program Hearings, pp. 372–73.
68. Shaunessey-Spaatz interview.
69. Frederick Lewis Allen, "Marshall, Arnold, King: Three Snapshots," *Harper's,* February 1945, pp. 287–88.
70. *Colliers,* January 9, 1943, p. 18.
71. Interview by Donald Shaunessey with Gen. Leroy T. Lutes, April 15, 1959.
72. Kuter, "How Hap Arnold," p. 88.
73. *Colliers,* p. 63.
74. General of the Army H[enry] H. Arnold, "My Life in the Valley of the Moon," *The National Geographic,* December 1948, p. 689.
75. *Time* Magazine, June 23, 1950.
76. Hayden correspondence, op. cit.
77. Benjamin F. Castle, *Assembly,* April 1951, p. 52.

CHAPTER 2

GENERAL CARL A. SPAATZ

Carl A. Spaatz was born on June 28, 1891, in Boyertown, a small town in Berks County, Pennsylvania. The Spaatz family was of German background, his grandfather being the first to come to the United States. His father, Charles B. Spaatz, was born in Boyertown; his mother, Anna, whose maiden name was Muntz, in Reading. Spaatz's father was the publisher of the *Berks County Democrat,* which his own grandfather had founded and which originally was printed in German, then in German and English, and, finally, only in English.

As a boy, Carl worked around his father's printing shop, setting the old lead type and running the printing press. "I graduated from Boyertown High School," he recalled, "at fourteen and went to Perkiomen Academy. I was part way through the second year when they had a very bad fire in Boyertown, in which my father was very seriously injured. I had to leave school and go back and run the paper until my father was well enough to take over again. I stayed in Boyertown about a year and then went to Army-Navy prep school in Washington to prepare to enter West Point. I wanted to go. I was nine at the time of the Spanish-American War, and that may have influenced me. I think my father hoped that I would take over the newspaper, but he didn't object to my going to West Point."[1]

Spaatz received his appointment from Congressman John H. Rothermel. "He was a political friend of my father's," remembered Spaatz. "Periodically, ever since I can remember, my father ran for Congress on the

Democratic ticket, but he was never elected. Berks County at that time was the only Democratic county in Pennsylvania. As I recall, Rothermel was a Democrat. I always felt that the only time my old man had a real chance to win a seat to Congress, he gave it up by agreeing not to run and in return I was to get an appointment to West Point."[2]

His beginning at West Point was auspicious. On his first day, in March 1910, Carl Spaatz was involved in an altercation that showed much about his character. Classmate John H. Jouett related, "If you are a Military Academy graduate, you will know what Beast Barracks is like. There is utter mental confusion. We had to go to the cadet store window to draw all of our equipment—mattress, chair, blanket, sheets, pillow cases, etc., etc. —and we stood in a queue to reach the window. Tooey was one removed from reaching the window when another cadet, obviously experienced, stepped into line ahead of him. This cadet happened to be a turnback (one who flunked the previous year and returned to repeat that year), but Tooey didn't know who he was, and Tooey challenged his right to step into line ahead of him. The interloper told Tooey off, and Tooey, undaunted, persisted in his claim. A challenge was passed, and the two met behind closed doors in the gymnasium that afternoon. It so happened that the interloper was the best lightweight boxer at the Academy; I am afraid that Tooey did not know too much about the fine art of self-defense, and he took the drubbing that you can imagine, and he took it like a man" (personal communication, March 28, 1963).*

It was at West Point that young Spaatz was pinned with a nickname that stayed with him the remainder of his life, that of "Toohey," later "Tooey." When Spaatz was in his first year at West Point," reflected classmate Harrison Brand, Jr., "there was an upperclassman in the class of 1913 named Francis Joseph Toohey, from Michigan. Spaatz looked very much like Toohey, slight, wiry build, red-thatched, and freckled. So because of this resemblance, his classmates jocularly began calling Spaatz 'Toohey,' which with time was slurred to 'Tooey,' the name which stuck. He was sometimes called 'Red' and 'Toughie,' the latter a holdover from his prep school, Perkiomen Academy, that illustrated his conduct on the football field, where at 120 pounds he was the lightest, but gamest halfback in the school's history" (personal communication, March 21, 1963).

On entrance to West Point, Spaatz's name was spelled with only one a, Spatz. Later, his wife Ruth and three daughers—Katherine, Rebecca, and Carla—did not like their name pronounced "Spats." The correct pronunciation was as if it were spelled with an o; that is, "Spots." So an extra a

---

*"Personal communication" refers to letter to the author.

was added. When the family asked him to make the change, in 1937, he told them amiably to do what they wanted and he would go along (Mrs. Carl A. Spaatz, personal interview, February 11, 1976).

Spaatz participated in a few extracurricular activities as a cadet—basketball during his fourth year, for instance. He also qualified as an expert rifleman. Spaatz, like Arnold, was a "cleansleeve," remaining a private all four years at West Point. He was also an "area bird," a perennial walker of punishment tours assessed for excessive demerits.

"My first year at the Point was very difficult," Spaatz reminisced. "The first year always has been, probably always will be. It's not hazing, but a disciplinary period, a different kind of discipline from what you're used to when you're pretty much on your own around a small country town. When you are subjected to this kind of discipline, it's pretty tough."[3] He received 122 demerits that first year, 142 the next, made a marked improvement with 86 in his junior year, but regressed completely in his final year, accumulating a whopping 166 demerits. These resulted in the main from his lack of attention to housekeeping duties, such as sweeping the floor, dusting his shoes, piling his bedclothes, and otherwise keeping his "gear" and room in order. But he also showed up from time to time wearing improper uniform, was late to drill, did not always remain silent in ranks, and failed to keep his rifle in A-1 condition. Once he was even cited for "repeatedly counting off wrong at guard mounting," suggesting either recalcitrance or a spirit of fun, neither of which was looked on favorably by the tactical officers or upperclassmen.

The most serious disciplinary challenge for Cadet Spaatz occurred in 1912, at the beginning of his junior year. On September 28, Spaatz was charged with "conduct to the prejudice of good order and military discipline," and more specifically that on August 12, 1912, he "did drink intoxicating liquor."

To the surprise of the Tactical Department at West Point, Cadet Spaatz, who had been very average academically, had shown a sudden interest in the library. When he and several of his friends started going to the library on Saturday night, the Tacs became suspicious. Spaatz and his group purportedly had made arrangements with the janitor to buy them beer, which was delivered to the cadets and consumed in the basement of the library. At that time, such an offense was regarded as a severe breach of military discipline; hence the court-martial. The decision of the court to the charges and specification was, fortunately, "not guilty." It would have been a great loss for the future Air Force had the court-martial been successful, and the history of the Air Force might have been considerably different.

With such a collection of demerits, one can see why a classmate,

William H. Holcombe, said, "Carl Spaatz was one of our number who was known to take things easy, play bridge and poker and enjoy life as much as possible for a cadet, and still maintain a creditable class standing without much apparent effort. He was always himself and seemed never to be troubled by the stresses and strains that plagued engineers who were striving for tenths and goats who were struggling to remain cadets" (personal communication, March 21, 1963).

Spaatz stood 102 out of 107 in conduct in his senior year. His roommate, C. E. Fosnes, was 105 out of 107 that year—they must have been quite a pair. In fact, Cadet Spaatz was walking the area on graduation day. "He walked the area," remembered Mrs. Spaatz, "until twenty minutes before graduation. He had to go back and change into dress uniform. It was that close with him" (personal interview, February 11, 1976).

Academically, Spaatz stood 57 out of 107. "I rather liked mathematics," he said, "but I wouldn't say I was most efficient in math. Drawing I had no yen for at all. I couldn't even draw a brick. I was interested in reading and courses in literature. We had courses in English composition, but I didn't care much for those."[4]

But the side that most endeared him to his classmates was his musical skill. "Aside from being outstanding as a carefree good fellow, Spaatz attracted attention as the leader of an outlaw orchestra," wrote classmate James C. Waddell. "His group of string instrument players, recruited mostly from classes behind ours, could be heard most any hour during release from quarters" (personal communication, April 8, 1963). Classmate Brand's memory of Spaatz's music was that "he was a great guitarist and I have enjoyed his strumming many a time. I think he still does some now and then. I used to accompany with the ukulele" (personal communication, March 21, 1963). Holcombe recalled, "Spaatz would entertain us with his fund of delightfully risqué songs, accompanying himself on the guitar" (personal communication, March 21, 1963). The guitar was Carl Spaatz's salvation. "I really and truly think that the thing that saw him through West Point," said his wife, "was his guitar. He got together with a group to play. During academics, there was little time for it, but at summer camp they used to have lots of summer concerts. Oddly enough, when you think of the way the guitar has swept the country today, it is hard to realize that in his day there were very, very few guitar players. Many played the mandolin, or banjo, but at West Point I think Tooey was the only guitarist. He was very good—had a marvelous ear and was a good accompanist. I have heard him leap from key to key accompanying a drunk at a party who fancied himself a singer" (personal interview, February 11, 1976).

In the early years of this century, West Point had only two officially sanctioned activities other than athletics and studies: YMCA and the Dialectic Society. Spaatz seems to have ignored the YMCA, but he was deeply involved in the Dialectic Society. These two organizations took the place of the clubs and fraternities in colleges. The best description of the Dialectic Society was provided by the cadets in their yearbook:

> The Dialectic Society claims a most ancient and honorable title among the now existing Corps organizations. More than a century ago, when life here was not so crammed with studies and drills, we find the Cadets taking advantage of every opportunity to gather and discuss all the interesting, pertinent questions of life in general. These decisions became so important a factor in the life of the Academy that in 1824 a definite organization was created and the present name adopted. Here it was that Grant, Lee, Longstreet and others thrashed out many momentous questions which influenced so strongly the future history of our country. In the time-marked archives of this old society we find recorded the names of many of our most illustrious graduates who were in truth the builders of our Alma Mater.

> For a period, the society seems to have suffered a marked decline, probably due to the [civil] war, until it became merely a name. Interest was revived, however, and the society again played an important role in the life of the Academy. Questions arising in the Corps on subjects of honor and ethics were referred to its offices for settlement and in this way it exerted a potent sway. But the original purpose had been lost sight of and the society continued to change until today its scope of endeavor embraces an entirely different field. It encourages literature to the extent of furnishing a good reading room with all the important papers and periodicals; and, more important still, is the encouragement it has given to music.

> At present the Dialectic makes itself chiefly felt through the annual play on 100th night. In this play, the idea has always been to give our visitors a comical picture of Cadet life through the medium of light opera, and in addition, to enlarge the field of Cadet enjoyment.[5]

The president of the Dialectic Society for the academic year of 1913–1914 was Tooey Spaatz, and his election is clear evidence of his popularity and leadership. One classmate said, "He is a splendid example of the fact that you cannot use a man's history as a cadet to predict what he will do as an officer. Our class had 107 graduates. Toohey was No. 57 just ahead of Bull, who was a three-star. Another good example was Milburn, who was 99th and also became a three-star. And look what became of the first 15 of the class: one four-star (the four-star was General Brehon B. Somervell), two major generals, two brigadier generals, four colonels" (Harrison Brand, personal interview, March 21, 1963).

Class standing and cadet rank are not necessarily the criteria for studying these men. Rather, one should study their personality and character as cadets. There are some common denominators among these future leaders. Both Arnold and Spaatz were well liked by their fellow cadets, and there was no condescension in their popularity.

Classmate John P. Markoe put the fist fight described earlier into perspective: "Tooey Spaatz was among my closest and most intimate friends. At that time I never would have predicted for him the brilliant military career that followed. . . . There was a certain modesty and reserve about him which concealed the seeds of leadership that lay, at that time, more or less dormant within him. He never aspired to be a cadet officer. He seemed always to feel sure of himself and to know just what to do in any situation. Coupled with this self-assurance was a great courage. This was instinctively sensed by others, so that no one risked trying to push him around, especially after one cadet tried this and failed. The weapons, bare fists. Tooey was beaten, but gave a good account of himself against this ex-professional pug. The fight was finally stopped by upperclassmen. No one tangled with Tooey after that—not that they feared him but that they deeply respected and admired him" (personal communication, March 20, 1963). Brigadier General Woodberry said, "His classmates loved him. He had a casual way of ingratiating himself with everyone, and was a favorite, though scarcely a leader in our class. My biggest surprise was when he was out of the Academy several years to find him a leader in thought and action in promoting the Air Corps as an independent service" (personal communication, March 24, 1963). This quality of independence had a clear bearing on his entry into the Air Service, as it was first called.

One of the finest compliments to Spaatz as a cadet was made by classmate John H. Carruth, who suspected even then that Spaatz would play a larger role. "To sum up my impression of him, he was the sort of man you would like to have on your side in a fight or any other serious situation. His outstanding career in the service was no surprise to me" (personal communication, March 23, 1963).

Carl Spaatz was commissioned a second lieutenant in the Infantry on June 12, 1914. As was then the tradition, on graduation he was granted a three-month leave, after which he traveled to his first post, the Twenty-fifth Infantry at Schofield Barracks, Hawaiian Territory, reporting on October 4, 1914.

Something of Lieutenant Spaatz's record at West Point followed him to his first station. As was then routine, his personnel file started with the assessment of the Commandant of Cadets of the U.S. Military Academy, Lt. Col. Morton S. Smith: "Attention to duty and habits very good. General bearing and military appearance good. Attitude towards discipline, fair. Cadet rank: third class, second class, first class—private."

It was rather remarkable that the reporting officer was as kind as he was in commenting on "attitude towards discipline" as "fair," when one stops to consider that in his final year at the Academy he stood 102 out of 107 in conduct. It is also clear that note was taken of the fact that he received no cadet rank. It was not exactly a clean start for Lieutenant Spaatz after graduation from West Point. Moreover, the tactical officer reported that Spaatz was "not athletic," but at the same time evaluated him as being very good in horsemanship, reported his qualification as an expert rifleman, and rated him good in swordsmanship.

Yet Captain Sinclair, who was Lieutenant Spaatz's company commander of Company B in the Twenty-fifth Infantry, was impressed with Spaatz's performance during his first year of service: "Attention to duty, professional zeal, general bearing and military appearance, intelligence and judgment shown in instructing, drilling and handling enlisted men, excellent. Should be trusted with important duties. I would desire to have him under my immediate command, in peace or war."

"I hadn't decided anything at first about my future branch of the service," Spaatz reflected. "I don't know whether it was the first year I was there [at West Point] or the second year when Glen Curtiss flew up the Hudson River and we all watched him. I decided then that I wanted to get into the flying game. I entered the Academy in March 1910. I think the flight was in the summer or fall of 1910, a flight from Albany to Governor's Island in New York, making about three stops en route to refuel. I just watched him fly by West Point. I think witnessing this flight is what influenced me toward a flying career" (personal interview, September 19, 1962).

At the end of his mandatory year in the infantry, Lieutenant Spaatz fulfilled his desire to fly. When later asked why, he said, "Well, the airplane was just beginning to become a practical thing, I mean take it up in the air and land it without breaking it up. When I first went to West Point there was an air section—the Signal Corps—to which young officers could go and learn to fly. When I graduated from the Point, there was no doubt in my mind that I wanted aviation. But the requirement then was to serve a year with another service—in my case, the Infantry. As soon as that year was up, I was allowed to transfer to the aviation section, Signal Corps, and remained in that from then on until it became the Air Service, then the Air Corps and later on the separate Air Force" (personal interview, September 19, 1962).

"Usually," remembered Mrs. Spaatz on the occasion of his applying for pilot training, "there was a fatherly colonel who would call in the young officer interested in flying to his office and say, 'My boy, I want to talk seriously to you about this flying aberration of yours' and then go into the fact that he was not only throwing his military career out the window, but he might be throwing his life away. So Tooey and Sam Wheeler, a classmate who went over with Tooey to the Twenty-Fifth Infantry, and also yearned to fly, made application. When they put in their applications, it went through the general, company commander, and others. There was a magnificent old colonel in command of the Twenty-fifth Infantry, Colonel Cannon. I can see him now. He was about six feet two inches and had mutton-chop whiskers and the bluest eyes I've ever seen. He was quite a figure of a man. So Tooey and Sam went in, they had been sent for, prepared for the fifty-cent lecture. They went in and smartly saluted. Colonel Cannon rose from behind his desk and put his hands out and took one of Sam's and one of Tooey's and said, 'My boys, if I were your age, I would be doing the same thing!' " (personal interview, February 11, 1976).

"I went to San Diego in October 1915, to the Signal Corps Aviation School," Spaatz said. "There was no difficulty. All you had to do was put in your application and pass the physical examination. There weren't too many applicants then. Besides the flying instructions, which consisted of between two and five hours with an instructor, and the rest of the time alone, there was the question of being able to take care of your own motor. We disassembled and assembled motors and balanced propellers—we had the old wooden propellers then. We learned how they made the airplanes, and how to inspect them and see whether it was safe to fly.

"This was my first time up in the air, at the school. The planes we were flying were built by Martin. They'd just changed from the pusher type to the tractor type. The only instructor I had was a man named Oscar Brindley —that is, in the airplane. The mechanic on the airplane was a corporal named Albert Smith. I think he became a major or a lieutenant colonel in the last war. And there was a civilian by the name of George Hallett, an instructor on the motors.

"We didn't get too much instruction. The day's work consisted of getting over there in the morning, to North Highland, at 7:30 or 8:00, and finishing up by noon, during which time we might have had fifteen or twenty minutes of flying. To do that twenty minutes of flying, you did a lot of waiting around for your turn. Then, classwork. There was no class in the theory of flight, or anything like that. Theory then was all practice" (personal interview, September 19, 1962).

Later in his career, when General Spaatz was asked what particular flying experience stood out most in his mind, he replied, "I think probably the first thrill was flying alone for the first time. On that particular occasion, I believe I had had one hour [of] dual instruction. The motor quit after I got a hundred feet in the air. We were told to land straight ahead when the motor quit, and not to try to turn, which I did, and landed without any damage" (personal interview, September 19, 1962).

The evaluations of Lieutenant Spaatz by Capt. Arthur S. Cowan, Signal Corps, the Commander of the Pilot Training School, were a distinct change in Spaatz's career. On the report covering from January 1, 1916, to April 2, 1916, Cowan wrote, "He has shown peculiar fitness for details in the Signal Corps aviation duties." This reporting officer went on to say, "I would desire to have him under my immediate command in peace and in war. In the event of war is best suited for aviation duty." Captain Cowan's final comment was "He cooperates energetically and loyally with others."

After completing pilot training in May 1916, Lieutenant Spaatz joined the First Aero Squadron at Fort Sam Houston, Texas. It had fifteen pilots and a total of nine aircraft—six JN3s and three Burgess planes. Shortly before he was assigned to the First, an event occurred that presented a real challenge to his future outfit.

On the evening of March 9, 1916, Francisco "Pancho" Villa crossed the border between the United States and Mexico with a guerrilla force of almost 1,000 men and raided Columbus, New Mexico. Seventeen Americans were killed, and much property was destroyed before the U.S. Cavalry drove the Mexicans off. The next day President Woodrow Wilson ordered Brig. Gen. John J. Pershing into Mexico to "assist" the Mexican government in catching Pancho Villa. Secretary of War Newton Baker was ordered by the President to have the U.S. Army pursue Villa and his men into Mexico until Villa's group was broken up. The Secretary specifically instructed Pershing to make all practical use of the airplanes for observation. The Commander of the First Aero Squadron (the only air squadron in Texas), Maj. Benjamin D. Foulois, in anticipation of being called into action, reflected on the challenge:

> I mentally planned what I would do if the First Aero Squadron were ordered to help Pershing. During the three days after Villa's raid, I made it a point to talk to all of my men individ-

ually to find out what problems they were having, both on and off the job. I checked over the eight planes, ten trucks, and one automobile assigned. I looked at maps of Mexico. . . . reviewed the airplane maintenance problems we had, inventoried the stocks of spare parts, gasoline, and personal equipment of the men. The answers to my . . . questions were disturbing. We might be able to last thirty days. . . . The sand and heat in the daytime and the cold Mexican nights would probably take enough toll of parts, planes, and men. To add a requirement to fly many missions in support of ground troops would be a severe strain on the squadron.[6]

On March 12, 1916, Major Foulois was directed to proceed by rail to Columbus, New Mexico, where the raid had occurred. The men flew their planes to the Fort Sam Houston drill grounds where they were disassembled and loaded on rail cars. Some thirty hours later, the eleven pilots, eighty-two enlisted men, and one civilian mechanic arrived in Columbus by railroad. The next day they began flying reconnaissance missions.

One of the pilots, Lt. R. H. Willis, while on a reconnaissance flight, made a forced landing in Mexico. Because he was in hostile territory, he left his airplane and hid in the mountains that night. When a repair crew arrived the next day, the Mexicans had chopped it to pieces and destroyed everything but the engine.[7]

A day later, Lieutenant Bowen's aircraft got caught in a vicious whirlwind; he landed "end up" with a broken nose, cuts, and bruises, and the plane was a total wreck. Thus, in the first two days, they lost two of their nine airplanes, a loss of one-fourth of the squadron.[8]

Spaatz said of the experience, "It was mostly a question of trying to keep your plane operating. We spent a lot of time on that, although we had a mechanic and he was responsible for your plane. Still, you spent a lot of time tinkering it into shape. There was no such thing as radio in the plane. Any communication we had would be by dropped messages or signals. There were attempts made to signal by firing guns, but they were just experimental. A man named Culver made some experiments with radio in the planes, but it was not anything you could use in the service.

"You'd fly over, and see a column, and you'd fly over the column and signal as to whether you saw anything that you thought should be investigated, which as a rule was not very successful, because as soon as Villa's troops (if there were any around) would see a plane, they'd know damn well that it could only be an American reconnaissance plane, and all the troops would get into the patios and when our troops arrived in town, there'd be nothing there" (personal interview, September 9, 1962).

Several days after their arrival, Lt. Herbert A. Dargue was attempting to escape from some hostile Mexican citizens after landing on a mission in Chihuahua, Mexico. The entire top section of the fuselage behind the cockpit blew off in flight and struck the vertical stabilizer on his plane. Thus another aircraft was demolished. A fourth was damaged landing on rough terrain near Ojito, and a fifth during a forced landing on a photographic mission between San Antonio, Mexico, and Chihuahua. Thus within just a few days, six of the nine airplanes were destroyed or damaged, leaving only two serviceable aircraft in the squadron. It was so bad that General Pershing wrote to Washington about his disapproval of "the old wrecks" the pilots in the First Aero Squadron had to fly. In his words, they "have already too often risked their lives in the old and useless machines which they have patched up and worked over in an effort to do their share of the duty in this expedition."[9]

In addition to having to cope with the antique planes, the pilots had trouble with the severe rain, hail, and, in the mountains, snowstorms. The engine did not have enough power for the mountain flying, and the dry weather warped the laminations on the propellers, causing them to come apart. Everything considered, it was quite an introduction for Lieutenant Spaatz but it did not discourage him. As his wife recalled, he "constantly asked General Pershing about taking a flight. Tooey would go to Pershing, 'General, sir, I certainly would like to take you up for a flight today.' He said it once too often and General Pershing fixed him with a steely eye and said, 'Young man, when I wish to fly, I will order you to take me up.' But Pershing never did" (personal interview, February 11, 1976).

Major Foulois, Commander of the Squadron, went on to become a major general and Chief of the Army Air Corps in the 1930s, and Spaatz was one of his favorites. "Spaatz literally grew up under me," said his former superior. "He was with me back in 1916, he was with me as one of my officers when I was Chief of the Air Services in World War I in the theater of operations. Spaatz came over with me and was with me throughout World War I and practically throughout the rest of my service career. . . . He grew up with me and he has long been one of my closest and dearest friends." When Foulois was asked what qualities took Spaatz to the top, he replied, "Spaatz, like Arnold, was someone that moved out. I never had any question that he was going to be successful as a leader, because he always stood out and reached out. That was true of these other men, such as Ira Eaker. Eaker and these other young men, particularly Spaatz, were individuals who had initiative. Spaatz never waited until he was told that he had a job to do. He accepted responsibility, he was given authority. . . . You have to let them have responsibility and when you are senior, to give them the chance to carry out the job and to do what they are supposed to do. . . . There have been radical changes in the last fifteen years or more in separating authority from responsibility. As a result, an officer who isn't willing to get reprimanded once in a while doesn't want to take responsibility. He tries to pass it off to someone else" (personal interview, September 18, 1962).

After completing his duty with the First Aero Squadron, Lieutenant Spaatz was assigned to the Third Aero Squadron, holding this position until July 14, 1917. On August 11, 1917, he left San Antonio, Texas, for war duty in France, and on September 21, was assigned to Aviation Headquarters, Paris, France. "This was my first meeting with Billy Mitchell," Spaatz said. "He was quite a dynamic person. He was always on the go. He lived in the same chateau as I did—we all lived together, Mitchell and his staff. He was very energetic, had a very alert mind, a man with a lot of ideas. I got along with him pretty well" (personal interview, September 19, 1962).

Spaatz's first real challenge began when he was assigned as Commanding Officer of the American Aviation School in Issoudun, France, which he took over on November 15, 1917. He wrote of this experience in a letter dated December 12, 1919: "At this time very few buildings had been erected at this school. No course of instruction outline and no very definite plan of organization thought of. I served either as Commanding Officer or the Officer in Charge of Training from this time until August 30, 1918, with the exception of one month, which time was spent at the British front. This school grew to be probably the largest aviation school in the world. The greater percentage of all the American aviators and mechanics sent to the front were trained at this school. As Officer in Charge of Training, it was my duty to outline the different courses of flying and technical instructions and see that they were carried out. Practically every plan for the location of the field and buildings, for the methods of maintenance and supplying of airplanes and accessories, and for the arrangement and method of instruction was either drawn up by myself or submitted to me for approval."

Spaatz said later, "When I was given my first command at the training school in France in World War I, which was a big training school, I had only been out of West Point for three years (and flying school less than two years). I happened to be the one available that could be given the job and that was because I knew training" (personal interview, September 19, 1962).

One of the students at Issoudun, then Capt. Edward P. Curtis, commented on Spaatz's first command. "He was not highly regarded by the cadets at Issoudon, nor did they have any personal affection for him. The Adjutant of the outfit was named Wedenbach, and Spaatz and Wedenbach were affectionately known to us as the 'German spies.' Our estimate of our commanding officer, the then Maj. Carl Spaatz, was somewhat less than enthusiastic. In fact, we hated his guts. Wedenbach changed his name after the war to his mother's maiden name, Willoughby. His father had been an officer in the German army. As Willoughby he went on to become a major general in the U.S. Army and served as General of the Army Douglas MacArthur's G-2" (personal interview, April 20, 1978).

When asked why the cadets and officers "hated Major Spaatz," Curtis responded, "Issoudun was the hell hole of France. It was terrible. The mud was thick on the ground. The weather was awful, and there was an acute shortage of airplanes with which to keep us flying. Although we were supposed to be getting our final training before going into battle, much of our time was spent picking up rocks on the runways and other mundane pursuits. The reason they gave for picking up the rocks was because they were getting into the propellers, but the chief reason was the fact that morale was low—we had time on our hands. I was already trained to fly when I arrived and I thought I was pretty good, but the first weeks I was there, I never had any opportunity to fly. But eventually things were straightened out" (personal interview, April 20, 1978).

Captain Curtis went on to become Spaatz's Chief of Staff during World War II. He said, about Issoudun, "It was an assignment Tooey didn't like very much. He did everything he possibly could to get out of it and get into combat, which he finally did toward the end of the war. It would have been incredible to imagine at that time that in the years to come he would become the outstanding air commander of World War II, and one of my closest friends" (personal interview, April 20, 1978).

Major Spaatz was certainly a contrast to Cadet Spaatz. Now he was the disciplinarian and not the disciplined. His reporting officer wrote in evaluating him during performance, "Did very well as C.O. at Issoudun. Is forceful, courageous, and a good man in a tight place." The reporting officer was Brig. Gen. Mason M. Patrick, the officer who was later assigned by Gen. John J. Pershing as Commanding General of the Air Service, specifically directed to instill discipline in the Army pilots, and Spaatz worked for him again in that position.

On September 2, 1918, "I joined the Second Pursuit Group," said Major Spaatz, "for a little experience at the front before returning to the United States for the purpose of outlining the methods we used at Issoudun for flying instruction at the schools in the United States. I remained there until September 21, 1918. Most of the time I served as a pursuit pilot for the

Thirteenth Squadron and was promoted to flight leader just before leaving for the United States. As a result of that experience at the front, I was one of a number of men who were made military aviators, like Billy Mitchell, Rickenbacker, Hall, Reed Chambers, and several others. When you were made a military aviator, that gave you an automatic increase in rank, that was the law. Although I reverted to the grade of captain after the war, being a military aviator, I retained the rank of major" (personal interview, September 19, 1962).

Captain Spaatz was too modest. Because of his leadership, he was awarded the Distinguished Service Cross for extraordinary heroism during the St. Mihiel offensive in 1918. The citation read:

> Although he had received orders to go to the United States, he begged for and received permission to serve with the pursuit squadron at the front. Subordinating himself to men of lower rank, he was attached to the squadron as a pilot and saw conditions and arduous service through the offensive. As a result of his efficient work, he was promoted to the position of Flight Commander. Knowing that another attack was to take place in vicinity of Verdun, he remained on duty in order to take part. On the day of the attack west of Meuse while with his patrol over enemy lines, a number of enemy aircraft were encountered. In the combat that followed, he succeeded in bringing down two enemy planes. In his ardor and enthusiasm he became separated from his patrol while following another enemy far beyond the line. His gasoline giving out, he was forced to land and managed to land within friendly territory. Through these acts he became an inspiration and example to all men with whom he was associated.

There was peculiar irony in the fact that the next officer who wrote an evaluation on Major Spaatz was Brig. Gen. Billy Mitchell. Anyone familiar with Mitchell's personality and the events surrounding his court-martial would find it particularly interesting that he said of Major Spaatz, "This officer has handled all of his jobs with energy and courage, an excellent officer of the highest quality." Mitchell then added, "But lacking to some extent in tact."

Major Spaatz's activities in World War I sent him on his way. He had received a battlefield promotion to major, which could not be taken away. Immediately on his return, he took part in a "circus." He wrote, "Since returning to the United States, I've been oscillating between California and

Texas. On April 10, 1919, I left San Diego, California, in charge of a flying circus which covered the western states, to assist in the Victory Loan drive. This flying circus traveled by train, the planes being set up on arrival at each city. We made approximately 27 flights in 27 cities, traveled to California, Nevada, Utah, Idaho, Texas, New Mexico and Arizona. An average of about nine planes were flown in each city. This circus was on the road 30 days.''

In December 1919, Major Spaatz was assigned to Rockwell Field, California. "This was my first post with Hap Arnold," he said. "I think it was called the Western Department at that time, under Liggett's command. Arnold was the Air Officer, and I was his assistant. His duties were quite varied. He supervised all the air installations in the area for the commanding general. His report as to whether they were operating well or not was accepted by the commanding general, usually as a matter of form. The principal thing he was interested in then was starting a forest fire patrol, which was established shortly after World War I. There wasn't much else for us to do. Training, forest fire patrol, and there wasn't much training going on'' (personal interview, September 19, 1962).

That contact began a twenty-five-year relationship in the course of which Spaatz was eventually to succeed General Arnold in running the largest air force in the post–World War II period. At this time, Colonel Arnold wrote of Spaatz, "Always did more than expected—work very seldom criticized, and always praised. Always on the job. Energetic and reliable. Does his work right up to the handle."

An incident that occurred gives insight into the affectionate relationship between Spaatz and Arnold at this time. In his memoirs, Arnold wrote, "It was while I was at General Liggett's headquarters, in 1920, that we lost our temporary war rank and reverted to our permanent status. Major 'Tooey' Spaatz, my assistant, had won his temporary rank in combat and so retained it by law. I went from the rank of colonel to captain. On the morning the orders came through, I arrived at the office first and moved all of Tooey's stuff into my desk in my office, and vice versa.

"When he arrived, he was aghast. 'What the hell is this all about?' he exclaimed. I explained that he was in command now, and I was his assistant and ready to carry out any orders he cared to give me.

"I said, 'Look, Tooey. Law is law. You are in command now, and you can't change it.' Tooey looked at me for a moment and then left the office. A few minutes later he returned and said, 'Well, everything is fixed up.' It developed that he had gone straight to General Liggett himself, had submitted the case for a Solomon's judgment, and had gotten orders out, having himself transferred to Mather Field rather than take my job away from me.

So, because of Tooey Spaatz's Pennsylvania Dutch stubbornness, I was left in charge as West Coast Air Officer, as a captain. A few months later I was made a major."[10]

In 1922, Spaatz became Commanding Officer of the First Pursuit Group at Ellington Field, Texas, and in June he was ordered to move the group to Selfridge Field, near Detroit. Spaatz took advantage of this transfer. Instead of crating up the aircraft and sending them by train as was done when his outfit went on the Pancho Villa expedition, he decided to fly the aircraft from Houston to Selfridge. It was an adventure. Spaatz described it in a letter to a friend on July 6, 1922. "We flew from Ellington Field," he wrote, "with 14 Spads, 2 SE5's, and 5 DH4's. All the planes arrived here safely. Camblin, in maneuvering takeoff at Belleville, taxied his machine into a gas house on the line, wrecking the two left wings. This damage was repaired, and he continued the flight. Tinsley knocked down a few high tension wires upon gliding in to land at California, Mo. He landed without doing any further damage. Stace had a number of forced landings due to an overheated motor; the last one was at Bryan, Ohio, 100 miles from Selfridge, upon which occasion he cracked his landing gear. This was repaired and the plane came in the next day."[11]

Maj. Gen. Mason M. Patrick, Chief of the Air Service, was ecstatic over the maneuver and sent his congratulations to Spaatz: "It is a source of gratification to me and to the Air Service at large that the First Pursuit Group has accomplished with such marked efficiency the movement of twenty airplanes from Ellington Field, Texas, to Selfridge Field, Mt. Clemens, Michigan, by air. Considering the obstacles encountered, this flight, covering a distance of approximately 1,500 miles, was accomplished in a remarkably short space of time. The mission of the pathfinder airplane was well performed. . . . A flight of so great a distance over a country of such a nature, without the loss of any airplanes would be considered an excellent performance with any type of airplane, but when performed by pursuit airplanes, its accomplishment, without mishap, is a fine illustration of efficiency and skill.

"It is a pleasure to me to commend you as Commanding Officer and the officers and enlisted men of your group for your zeal and efficiency in the accomplishment of this flight."[12] Spaatz had made his point, and immediately passed on Patrick's letter to his men, who undoubtedly appreciated it, although the general's comment "without mishap" here may have left Camblin, Tinsley, and Stace wondering about how he defined the word.

Selfridge Field had been abandoned for some two years, and the condition of the field was a challenge. On arrival, Spaatz found a single officer and two enlisted men in charge of the whole base. The officer, Maj. W. C.

McChord, had written to Spaatz in June 1922 what was probably the under-statement of the year: "Much work will have to be done before the field can be gotten into shape for occupancy." The heating plant of the Commanding Officer's quarters had been allowed to freeze the previous winter and was entirely useless; more important, the central heating plant, which served the barracks, headquarters, and all the buildings around, did not have enough pressure, and a new heating system would be required before winter. The underpinnings of all buildings were rotting, and the roofs leaked so badly it was difficult to keep anything dry. There was practically no furniture, no commissary on the post, and insufficient cooking utensils in the mess. There were no gasoline trucks, so servicing of airplanes had to be done with hand carts. There was absolutely no oil for the aircraft on their arrival, and no bombing and machine ammunition.[13]

Spaatz, however, approached it all with great cheerfulness. "A month or two of work," he said, "will make a very neat post."[14] And he wrote to General Patrick that "the morale of the officers and enlisted men has gone up tremendously since arriving at this station. Whereas at Ellington Field it was necessary to be constantly on the alert for slackers, at this place everyone has pitched in to the best of their ability."[15]

In early June, just before leaving Ellington Field, one of the pilots, Lt. John K. Cannon, was injured in a mid-air collision. His aircraft had fallen 3,000 feet, fracturing his skull, along with many other bones, and causing severe shock. This might have been averted had he been able to bail out, but he had no parachute—there were none available in the whole squadron. Spaatz took corrective measures. He learned on arriving at Selfridge that McCook Field in Dayton, Ohio, had parachutes and wrote at once to Maj. Thurman H. Bane, "I am instructing all pilots who take cross-country flights which take them near Dayton to stopover for the purpose of being fitted with a parachute. I understand that you have a number on hand. . . . I am very desirous of having every pilot report there as soon as possible to procure this equipment."[16] On July 19, 1922, he received a response from Major Bane, Chief of the Engineering Division, that "your request is a bit irregular, as you know we are not a supply depot. However, we are very anxious to help you out in this situation and will fix up your pilots as fast as they fly in here until we are ordered to stop by higher authority."[17] Spaatz had once commented about his World War I flying, "We had no parachutes until after the war, and we weren't bothered with insurance salesmen at all!" He joked about it when it concerned himself, but when it involved his men, he had a different outlook.

Cannon's accident also emphasized the need for better medical sup-port. As mentioned in Chapter 1, Captain Eaker once requested an ambulance to take injured flyers to a hospital, to which the Army general had responded that horse-drawn carts were sufficient for their injured polo players and should fulfill the needs of the Air Service! But when he saw Cannon's injuries, Spaatz ordered a civilian ambulance to carry Cannon to the hospital. The horse-drawn ambulance ride would have killed him. Spaatz had considerable difficulty in getting the Army to pay for his initiative in making this unauthorized expenditure. His justification, written to the Commanding Officer of the Eighth Corps Area, Fort Sam Houston was that "the nature of the skull and superior maxilla fractures were such as to require the most careful handling in transportation. The distance from Ellington Field to Camp Logan (to a hospital) is twenty-five miles, and it was feared that to transport Lt. Cannon in any of the ambulances on this post would result in jarring which might prove fatal."

Preparing for future accidents could not be delayed. Spaatz wrote to a friend on June 30, 1922, "I am calling on you for help. The nature of the work carried on by a pursuit group requires the services of a highly efficient surgeon, and some well-trained nurses." This overture began dealings to establish flight surgeons to fulfill the specialized needs for flying personnel.

Spaatz's personal leadership was well tested during his tour at Selfridge. He had some real problems there as a postwar leader. "In the Twentieth Pursuit Group," said Ira Eaker, "he had as wild a bunch of Air Force fliers as we had ever had. He had, for example, Hunter, who had been an ace in World War I; Elmendorf; and, indeed, all of the First Pursuit Group was composed of pilots who were easy livers and who wanted to do only one thing, and that was fly. I noted that Spaatz could control these fellows without any difficulty. He flew with them. He led them in formation flying, and he was also a great believer in physical exercise. He organized these pilots into athletic teams, played with them, particularly squash. He controlled this wild bunch of pilots and kept them from being court-martialed and, possibly, eliminated from the Air Corps. Part of Spaatz's hold over this gang was the fact that he would not tolerate inferiority. He demanded of all of these men their best, and a pilot did not stay very long in the First Pursuit Group if he lacked courage; if he lacked or had an inability to be disciplined or discipline himself, or lacked flying ability" (personal interview, October 4, 1977).

But he also gave his men the opportunity to learn from their mistakes. There was one officer, Lieutenant Meredith, whose lack of discipline was so marked that Spaatz wrote to General Patrick concerning his possible dismissal from the service. "Some time ago I wrote to your office," Spaatz said, "about Lt. Russell L. Meredith, in which letter I stated that he needed some knowledge of military discipline. At the time of writing that letter, I spoke rather sharply to Lieutenant Meredith and cautioned him.

"Since that time his performance of duty has been such as to warrant, I believe, a special report to you. He has been working exceptionally hard. In addition to performing his duties in an excellent manner, he volunteered for a very difficult flight, going to the rescue of an injured man on Beaver Island. The flight was made in a bad snowstorm, a distance of 275 miles, and involved landing on uncertain landing fields due to snow. He accomplished this mission successfully.

"Today he left in the worst snowstorm of the year for Camp Borden, Canada, to carry supplies to General Mitchell . . . knowing that the airdrome has three feet of snow on it and that the skis he is using are experimental.

"These two flights elevate Lieutenant Meredith, in my opinion, to the position of the highest type of pursuit pilot."[18]

Some idea of the challenges Spaatz faced was revealed in the correspondence he received. On May 2, 1923, Milton G. Goff wrote to him, "One of the planes, presumably from Selfridge, passing over the club grounds at a plane's fair rate of speed (about 60 miles per hour), appeared to make a descent, and skimmed about five or six feet above the ground directly at me, ascending, however, again while still some feet away. This may be quite a joke to the aviator, but to the civilian, it has the same effect as having an automatic fired at you point blank."[19]

About a month later, a representative of a construction company, Greiling Brothers, requested that the planes fly at a higher level when passing over the new Belle Isle Bridge they were building. "The reason for this request," the letter related, "is that when Plane Number 10 passed over between the hours of eight and nine o'clock today, he flew so low that several of our employees were frightened to the extent of jumping into the river, and if it had not been for the foreman restraining them, it might have ended in a very serious accident.[20] Spaatz grounded the pilot responsible for this complaint for two weeks.

Nor did he give up quickly on his men. "I have been thinking," Spaatz wrote to his friend Maj. Frank D. Lackland at Fort Sam Houston on August 22, 1922, "of submitting a report, thru channels, about Asp. As far as ordinary routine work is concerned, he is incompetent as an officer, it is difficult to keep him on the job. On the other hand, he has a natural bent for engineering and technical matters; he will work all day and night trying to learn something about a new motor or a new airplane. If he could be placed in some position where he could exercise this natural inclination, I believe he would become a fairly valuable officer. The difficulty has been in deciding whether an officer with these inclinations was valuable enough to the service to keep . . . I would like a little advice from you in this connection . . . there is no use in giving up hope until the end (i.e., submitting his official report)."[21]

These were the days of Prohibition—and of widespread disregard for it. "General Patrick had had reports that there was a liquor problem at Selfridge Field," related Ira Eaker. "He called Spaatz in and asked him if that were the case, and Spaatz responded, 'No, sir. We do not have a liquor problem at Selfridge Field. All of my officers are on duty when they are supposed to be on duty and they abide by rules and regulations meticulously.' He went on to say that we did serve liquor in the evenings. 'When we have it, and it's scarce as you know. I don't prohibit liquor on the field because it would be unrealistic. They would simply just go off the base and get into trouble. I keep them on the base. I make it pleasant for them to be at the officers club and remain on the base.' Patrick told me later that Spaatz's response appealed to him." Patrick also remarked, "Spaatz had the courage to disagree with me." Spaatz himself was not aware the conference had gone so well. "I remember too," said Eaker, "that when Spaatz came out he said, 'Well, I guess I'll have a new assignment. I'd appreciate it if you'd let me know where it is—I'll be going as soon as you know' " (personal interview, October 4, 1977).

He was not moved. What's more, he soon had the opportunity to distinguish himself and his command. One of the responsibilities that fell to Spaatz was arranging for the 1922 Pulitzer Races, which were held at Selfridge Field on October 12, 13, and 14. The amount of work required to prepare for these races was prodigious. There were hundreds of aircraft, thousands of spectators. The world's most prominent leaders of aviation attended. Competing in these races were pilots from the Air Service, Navy, Marine Corps, and foreign air forces, as well as civilian pilots from the United States and abroad. The Pulitzer trophy was won by Lt. R. L. Maughan of the Air Service, flying the 154-mile course at an average speed of 206 miles per hour—a new record.

The Army's overall success at these races and what it meant were best expressed by Rear Adm. W. A. Moffett of the Navy, Commander of the Navy Air Force, who wrote graciously to Patrick, "I wish to congratulate you and the Army Air Service on your victory in Detroit. The achievement of breaking all existing world's records by such a substantial margin is conclusive evidence of the superiority of American aviation over that of any nation.

"And through you, I desire to express to the Commanding Officer at Selfridge Field, and to the officers who are associated with him, the deep appreciation that is felt by the Navy for the generous cooperation and unfailing courtesy which they extended us."[22]

Secretary of War John W. Weeks wrote to Spaatz, "I know that you are greatly responsible for the splendid organization exhibited during these contests and for the efficient handling of the unusual number of visiting airplanes. Great credit has been brought to the Air Service and to the Army at large by the creditable manner in which the Air Service officers and men connected with this event conducted themselves. The successful culmination of this meet, with no casualties or serious accidents, speaks well for the efficient ground organization of the contests and is indicative of the high morale and esprit de corps of your command."[23]

From October 1, 1922, to April 16, 1923, Major Spaatz was Post Commander at Selfridge Field, Michigan. But this tour was to take its toll on Spaatz. Earlier in 1923, he had a near-fatal mid-air collision in the landing pattern. "The same thing which happened to me on the last review during your visit took place again today," Spaatz wrote to Brig. Gen. William Mitchell of another near miss during a landing approach. "This time the escape was a little narrower. The incident convinces me that I have gone stale, and consequently I have put in for a sick leave. The combination of the Joy case [an earlier complaint], Ruth [his wife], and post work has been too much." But he was incorrigible. In spite of his condition, he wrote to General Mitchell, "If sick leave is granted, I shall go to San Antonio and since it will be impossible to keep away from work all together, I shall spend part of the day at Kelly Field going over the pursuit course with Hickam." He felt guilty about his request, saying in the close of the letter, "I trust my request for this leave will not be considered with disapproval on your part."[24] He took the sick leave, spending time with his family and resting, and returned to Selfridge with new energy.

As Spaatz was preparing to leave Selfridge for his next assignment—as a student at the Air Corps Tactical School at Langley Field, Virginia, he was shocked to learn that one of his finance officers, Lt. Howard Farmer, was probably guilty of embezzlement. Farmer was relieved from duty as Finance Officer on April 29, 1924, and the trial was held in June. Farmer was found guilty, dismissed from the service and sentenced to five years' confinement in the penitentiary. The amount embezzled was large, over $16,000. Just as Spaatz had been accorded credit for his command's handling of the Pulitzer races, now he was blamed for the conduct of one of his officers. The Army Corps Commander responsible for Selfridge Field was Maj. Gen. Harry C.

Hale. He received the court-martial transcript and wrote to the Adjutant General of the Army, Washington, D.C. of "considerable evidence to the effect that the accused had for months previous to his trial been drinking to excess, gambling, and playing the stock market. I was unable to understand how such a condition of affairs could have existed for the length of time without the knowledge of the Post Commander [Spaatz] . . . it seems impossible to escape the conclusion [based upon his reading of the court-martial testimony] . . . that the Post Commander was either lax in his dealing with the accused officer or that, if ignorant of the accused weaknesses, was negligent in the execution of his office as Post Commander."[25]

Hale concluded in his letter to the Adjutant General that, because Major Spaatz was serving at another station, "it might be considered proper to drop the entire matter, but . . . the conduct of the Post Commander, Maj. Carl Spatz, A.S., does not appear creditable to him, and it is believed that he should have an opportunity of clearing up the matter if possible."[26] The Adjutant General Hale's comments passed on to the Inspector General, who in turn asked Spaatz to make such remarks as he desired to make.

Spaatz's reply was contained in a letter to the Commanding Officer of Langley Field on December 10, 1924. He related that as soon as he heard of Lieutenant Farmer's gambling he had taken disciplinary action: the rules for conduct of government agents entrusted with government funds had been read to Farmer, and that any gambling in the future would result in charges being preferred. All this occurred six or seven months before the shortage of funds was discovered.

"I believe," Spaatz wrote, "that any impression of negligence on my part has arisen from a misunderstanding of my testimony as to the time when I became aware of Lieutenant Farmer's inability to control his appetite for liquor. This became known to me between the time I placed him under arrest and the time he was tried. . . . The drunken spree to which the testimony relates took place after—and not before—he was placed under arrest by me; and finally that I did not neglect the work of Lieutenant Farmer but gave to it a measure of supervision which I deemed appropriate and which consisted principally of observation of his ability to perform what I considered the main test of his efficiency—by his ability to pay troops efficiently."[27]

The investigation was long and tedious. Spaatz wrote in his diary of May 10, 1925, "Am now a student at the A.S. Tactical School, almost a graduate. Am suffering a slight degree of mental anguish pending the outcome of Farmer's embezzlement of $16,000 at Selfridge Field while I was commanding officer."[28]

On August 6, 1925, the axe fell. Spaatz received a reprimand from the Adjutant General. The letter criticized him for failing to report immediately Lieutenant Farmer's gambling to the Corps Commander and to the Chief of Finance, and "you elected to take his pledge that he would not gamble while under your command and entrusted with government funds." There was more. "Your duties [were] . . . clear, definite and mandatory. The action you were to take was not left to your judgment or discretion. Your disregard of . . . regulations was so flagrant as to indicate either dense ignorance of your duties in this regard or a presumptuous setting of your opinion against those of your superiors. Even did regulations permit you to handle this case according to your own ideas, your judgment was bad and your action futile." The letter closed, "Your administration of your duties as Commanding Officer at Selfridge Field in this regard does you no credit and calls for severe censure."[29]

On June 30, 1925, before Spaatz received his letter of censure, he had come to much the same conclusion. His diary entry for that date included the following: "Tendency to assume everyone acts with right motives, hence no effort to differentiate between men to separate those whose mental makeup prevent their acting with right motives as in case of Farmer."[30]

Soon after the censure, Major Spaatz considered leaving the Air Service. On September 9, 1925, he wrote to Col. Bert M. Atkinson, in the office of the Adjutant General for the State Arsenal, St. Augustine, Florida. "Dear 'Atch'—I was overjoyed to hear from you. I am seriously considering going into commercial aviation, but have made no definite move as yet. What is your general idea of the chance of success of a company operating in Florida?" closing with "Let me hear from you as soon as possible."[31]

But he bounced back quickly from this heavy blow. On October 19, he wrote to Wilson, one of his former students from Kelly Field, who had appeared to interview for a job with Spaatz's proposed airline. "I have no intention of leaving the Air Service and establishing myself in commercial aviation at the present time."[32] And on November 6, Spaatz wrote to Colonel Atkinson, "I have given up any idea of going into commercial aviation and I shall stick along in the Army for the present at least."[33]

Spaatz was missed after he was reassigned from Selfridge. "Naturally, Major Lamphere's personality," wrote one of his pilots from Selfridge, "is being reflected in the group, which has somewhat changed its character since you left, and I am sorry to say the change has been for the worse. Several of the officers have confessed a desire to transfer. The general morale of the enlisted men is beginning to wane, and a considerable number of the old men are also attempting to transfer. I think probably the reason for this may be that Maj. Lamphere is more interested in creating an impression in Detroit and elsewhere than on the post. Lately, he has spent very little time here.

"There has been absolutely no social life on the post since you left, with one exception—the New Year's calls."[34]

From October 8, 1924, to June 18, 1925, Spaatz was a student officer at the Air Service Tactical School, Langley Field, Virginia. One objective of the Army schooling system was to remove the officers from the burden of their normal duties and give them the opportunity to study, think, and reflect. A diary kept by Spaatz while at Langley reflected that he read widely and did not limit his study to strictly professional matters: "May 10, 1925: Am reading Huneker's *Steeplejack;* May 18, 1925: Finished Don Marquis' *The Dark Hour;* May 25, 1925: Literature by Arthur Schnitzler. . . . *Monsieur Lamblin* by George Ancey presents a character which is difficult to visualize as an actuality."[35] Most meaningful was the comment, "Read *Steeplejack* until noon—quotation: 'But to pass our interval between two eternities raking in gold is simply absurd to me.' . . . henceforth I am to acquire sufficient gold to cease any worry about old age. It may be ridiculous for an aviator to worry about old age but I do coupled with apprehension that some day I may quit my Army career, either thru my own volition or otherwise."[36] He was an ardent poker player, and on June 6, 1925, he wrote, "Book on Poker by Geo. Ade and others received. Seems to have put on paper much of psychology of poker and poker players."[37]

The Assistant Commandant of the Air Service Tactical School at that time was then Maj. T. D. Milling, Hap Arnold's classmate in pilot training in 1911. Major Milling was one of the early pioneers in aviation and one who made very great contributions to the development of the Air Force. He evaluated his friend Spaatz thus: "An excellent officer in every respect. Would prefer to have him as a pursuit pilot commander to anyone else that I know."

Spaatz had been worried that he might be reassigned because he had stood up to General Patrick, but he underestimated the latter's regard for him. For on June 18, 1925, he was ordered to report for duty to the Office of the Chief of the Air Staff in Washington, D.C. It was to be an important assignment both for his personal development and his career.

Six months later, he was involved in Billy Mitchell's fight for air power, which ultimately resulted in a court-martial. Spaatz decided to testify, although he was warned by his superiors it might jeopardize his standing. The attorney for the defense asked Spaatz, "Would you tell the court the condition of the equipment at the present time that the Air Service is supplied with?"

Spaatz responded, "The equipment in the Air Service has reached a condition where it is very difficult to figure out how we're going to continue to fly. . . . The bulk of equipment in the Air Service is very obsolescent or obsolete."

As the testimony continued, Spaatz was asked, "What percent of the aircraft on hand were available for the pursuit mission with fighter aircraft?"

He replied, "None of those that we have on hand—I would not care to go to war with any of them on hand. They are a very hard maintenance job to start with and have no performance that would meet pursuit conditions; they have been in use for approximately three years. I think the greater portion of them have been to the depot at least once for repairs and reissued to the units."[38] As for the shortage of aircraft, Spaatz estimated that it amounted to 355 airplanes.[39]

Next came an inquiry into the availability of personnel. Spaatz stated that they were short 660 officers in tactical units: 85 officers short in Hawaii, 55 for the Philippines, and 54 for Panama.

Mitchell's council was aggressive and tenacious. He went for the Army's jugular: "Are the officers of the General Staff qualified by training or experience to lay down principles for military aviation?"[40] Spaatz at first was not permitted to answer because of the challenge to authority. After strenuous objection and a lengthy discussion, Spaatz was permitted to continue: "With the exception of Maj. M. F. Harmon and Maj. C. G. Brant, no officers of the General Staff have had Air Service training [but were still placed] in command of tactical units of the Air Service—as the result of having been in command of tactical units of the Air Service."[41]

Spaatz thus directly challenged the qualifications of his superiors. He was asked the question, and he gave an honest answer. Spaatz displayed no tact that day, and if Billy Mitchell had not appreciated this quality before, he did then.

As the trial proceeded, Spaatz received encouragement from his friends in the Air Service. Capt. Frank O. D. Hunter wired to him on November 10, 1925, "That a boy," and from a man named Pickering, "Congratulations on your testimony and nerve. Best to Mitchell. Can I help?"

Later Spaatz put the whole Mitchell controversy in perspective. "I think the basic factor was the old one that goes down to history: resistance to change. When you're well drilled and trained in your profession, you don't like something to come along that makes you have to learn all over again, and the older you are in your profession, the more you resist change. . . . If the old order has to give way to a new order, then the appropriations to the old order become decreased, their advantages lessened, and the career and rank go to the new order. Essentially it's a psychological mass prejudice against change on the part of the military, and I think that's been true enough through history."[42]

"I testified for Billy Mitchell," Spaatz said later in life, "against the General Staff position, and they never did anything to me. They can't do anything to you. When you're under oath, you have to tell them the truth when you answer their questions."[43]

Some months after the trial, Mitchell wrote a letter that Spaatz kept the rest of his life.

Washington, D.C.
February 5, 1926

Dear Major Spatz:

The aid you gave me and my counsel, the Honorable Frank R. Reid, in connection with the recent court-martial is deeply appreciated.

I feel you have assisted in bringing to the people a presentation of facts relating to the national defense of our country which will undoubtedly lead to its improvement.

With grateful thanks for your help and support, I am,

Cordially yours,
[signed]
Wm. Mitchell[44]

Spaatz was keenly interested in the recruitment of West Point cadets for the Air Service. A close friend, Maj. George Stratemeyer of the Air Service, was teaching at West Point. They had been classmates and had been together in pilot training. On March 30, 1927, Stratemeyer wrote from West Point, "The Supt. and the authorities here have approved the idea of cadets going to Langley Field. . . .

"There were 131 cadets in the present first class who took the 609 exam [for aviation]. About 66 passed and I think about 25 will apply for detail in the Air Corps. . . . I really believe about 45 percent of each class would elect Air Corps if they felt they could do as they desired. These cadets graduate between the ages of twenty-one and twenty-five, after having been caged up here for four years."[45]

As Training and Operations Officer for the Chief of the Air Service, Spaatz had considerable authority on the assignment of aircraft to the few existing Air Force installations. In this role, he did not forget his friend Major Hap Arnold, as revealed in the following letter from Arnold.

> Ft. Riley, Kansas
> August 20, 1926

My Dear Tuey,

Please accept my thanks for your help in relieving the plane shortage at this place. Everyone from the Commanding General, Seventh Area; Chief of Cavalry; Commanding General here; various inspectors take a perfect delight in asking me how many planes that I have and will have to carry out this year's schedule. Thanks to you, within a few weeks I will be able to satisfy them as to my ability to meet their demands.

Personally I do not believe that you will get a better place to test out the 0-1 with the Liberty engine for we have such a variety of work to carry out. Cavalry liasion (it looks wrong to me but you get my idea), artillery fire control, reconnaissance, machine gunnery, bombing, and carrying student officers for instruction in observation. We have to do these things all day and almost every day after we get started in the fall. Hence I believe that this is an ideal place to give that plane a service test. Please use your influence to have it sent out here.

Remember me to all my friends and give Ruth the kindest regards of the entire family.

Yours till the Air Corps is more than a mere name,

[signed]
H. H. Arnold[46]

Spaatz also helped Arnold in other ways. He wrote, "The gasoline shortage in the Air Corps as well as the airplane shortage is going to restrict considerably our activities during the next year. Based on the total number of observation planes available, a new distribution has been worked out in which an attempt was made to distribute airplanes as equitably as possible based on the personnel at the stations and the work being done. The gasoline distribution has been reworked, and your allotment increased 17,000 gallons over the original allotment made earlier in the year of 28,000 gallons, making a total for this year's allotment of 45,000 gallons. Even this is short of your requirements, but the same shortage exists throughout the service and cannot be helped.''[47]

During this tour in training and operations, Spaatz had brought to his attention for the first time a young officer with whom he was to later have a very close association, Hoyt. S. Vandenberg. Capt. J. H. Davidson wrote to Spaatz on May 19, 1926, an evaluation of all of his instructor pilots at Headquarters, Third Attack Group of the Air Service Advanced Flying School (ASAFS), Kelly Field, Texas. The list included over thirty officers assigned to Kelly Field at that time. Captain Davidson wrote of Lieutenant Vandenberg, "Assigned to group, September, 1924. Excellent officer. Good attack pilot with enough attack training to be of some value. I was informed by the Commandant of the ASAFS today that he would be transferred to the School Group within two weeks. This transfer will cripple our group considerably, as, with the exception of myself, he is the only other officer present for duty with the group who has had enough attack experience to train other officers."

A random example of Spaatz's travel orders during his tour gives considerable insight into his exposure to the entire Air Service: March 1, 1927, he traveled from "Washington, D.C. to Ft. Bragg, North Carolina; thence to Ft. Benning, Georgia, thence to Ft. Crockett, Texas; thence to Brooks Field, San Antonio, Texas; thence to Kelly Field, Texas; thence to Ft. Sill, Oklahoma; thence to Ft. Riley, Kansas; thence to Ft. Leavenworth, Kansas; thence to Scott Field, Illinois; thence to Chanute Field, Rantoul, Illinois; thence to McCook Field, Dayton, Ohio, for conferences with the commanding officers of these places with reference to Air Corps activities and training, and upon completion, proceed, by air or rail, to your proper station, Washington, D.C."

Spaatz was adjusting to the responsibilities he had on the staff, although he had not yet sought staff duty. Spaatz much preferred flying airplanes to being involved in a staff job in Washington, D.C., at the Air Corps Headquarters and in December 1928 he had a welcome relief.

On December 12, 1928, he received orders to "proceed, by air or rail, from Washington, D.C., to Rockwell Field, Coronado, California, on or about December 18, 1928, for the purpose of carrying out instructions received from the Chief of the Air Corps in connection with the refueling endurance flight at that place." This was to be the *Question Mark* flight. The objective was to inform the people and members of Congress that air power was not a vision but a reality, no longer a barnstorming carnival sideshow. On New Year's Day in 1929, Spaatz prepared for an endurance flight that involved air-to-air refueling, hoping to establish a record for time in the air. The crew was composed of Maj. Tooey Spaatz, Flight Commander; Capt. Ira C. Eaker, Chief Pilot; Lt. Elwood R. Quesada, Lt. Harry A. Halverson, pilots; and the mechanic, Staff Sgt. Roy W. Hooe.

Spaatz later commented, "At the time . . . the possibility of war [was remote]. But we saw it as a means of testing the endurance of a crew of men, a means for testing the engines—to know how long they would run without any checkup on the ground. And also, to . . . add to the knowledge of refueling in the air. It had been done before but just as sort of a stunt, but by having this operation as a real military operation, it would establish the fact that refueling was possible as means of extending the range of an airplane."[48]

The aircraft was named *Question Mark,* and the takeoff was at Metropolitan Airport, Van Nuys, California, on January 1, 1929. They had obtained a fire hose for transferring gasoline from the refueling tanker aircraft. A sling arrangement was improvised to lower the cans of oil, water, food, and other necessities from the refueling plane. The *Question Mark* was a Fokker C-2, a high-wing, three-engine monoplane with a speed of 100 miles per hour. The refueling aircraft was a C-1, single-engine biplane with a speed of 95 miles per hour, which during refueling would reduce speed and hook the hose onto the *Question Mark.* Then both would descend in a shallow dive. This procedure precluded the danger of either aircraft stalling out while refueling.

The tanker aircraft was fitted out at Middletown Airport in Pennsylvania. There were some real challenges in modifying the tanker for the mission. Quesada remembered that the tanker was so heavily loaded with gasoline that it was difficult to get it rolling from a standstill. But there was no question that the aircraft would be able to fly, once they obtained the momentum that was needed. Eaker, Quesada, and Capt. Ross Hoyt were responsible for modifying the tanker. They did not lack imagination. To resolve the problem of moving the aircraft forward, the crew members dropped their feet on the ground through a hole that they cut in the fuselage and physically pushed the aircraft forward. Once they were started, the rest was quite easy.

The takeoff of the *Question Mark* occurred at 7:24 A.M. The skies were clear, with not a cloud in sight. There was a strong wind, but the big aircraft lifted off with almost the ease of a small pursuit aircraft. The flying conditions were ideal. There were less than 100 gallons of gasoline in the wing tanks—about a three-hour supply.

On the first day of refueling, tanker pilot Lt. Otis Moon reported, "We held contact for eight minutes. We started at 2,800-feet altitude and Major

Spaatz, the flight commander, found that 2,000 feet was the best after he dropped 800 feet in experimenting for ideal conditions.''

There was considerable danger involved in the mission, as they discovered during the first morning of the flight. Spaatz entered in the official log the comment, ''Contact Number 2 established at 10:25 A.M. over Point Loma and maintained until 10:31, northeast Rockwell Field. Air rough, hose jerked out of hands three times; tanks registered 270 gallons received. Captain Eaker at controls, Halverson along side, Hooe at pumps, Spaatz at hose, Quesada along side.'' Actually this log entry was quite an understatement. Spaatz, for protection, wore goggles, a rubber face mask, rubber gloves, and a raincoat, to protect him from the wind during the course of the refueling and also from spraying gas. And, in fact, a sudden gust of wind separated the two aircraft, and the gas line from the tanker sprayed Spaatz with 72-octane gasoline.

Eaker said, ''When I saw what happened, we tore off all of Major Spaatz's clothes and covered his body with lubricating oil. He then said to me, 'If this doesn't work and I need emergency medical aid, I'll get out in a parachute. You take command. Under no condition abandon this flight. That's an order! Do you understand?' I returned to the cockpit, flew out over the ocean where the air was smoother, and we completed the refueling. Our first-aid proved effective; Major Spaatz suffered no serious discomfort, although he was rather greasy for the rest of the flight'' (personal interview, October 4, 1977).

Spaatz had directed at the beginning of the mission that all crew members would wear parachutes during refueling because of the fire danger. Each man was to be ready to jump immediately. Spaatz now insisted they continue the refueling even though he had been sprayed. Eaker remembers looking back after returning to the controls: ''Spaatz was the only nude I ever saw in a parachute'' (personal interview, October 4, 1977).

There was great concern on the ground that the gasoline might have affected Spaatz's eyes, but the log showed that ''Major Spaatz took control of the aircraft at 3:30 A.M.''

The flight was a great success, and did not end until they had flown over six days—a total of 150 hours, 40 minutes, and 15 seconds. After the first 37 hours, 15 minutes, and 40 seconds in the air, the flight surpassed the previous American refueling endurance record. As the flight continued, it gained national and international attention. Even though the crew was spending New Year's Day in the air, they were not forgotten. A turkey dinner provided by a church in Van Nuys was lowered to their plane.

It had been anticipated that perhaps the greatest challenge would be refueling at night. The schedule established for refueling was for 4 P.M., midnight, and 8 A.M. Tests at San Diego prior to the flight proved that the night refueling presented no difficulty, after electric bulbs were fitted to the wheels of the refueling aircraft. Night refueling was carried out nine times during the mission without incident.

Although one objective of the *Question Mark* flight was to keep air power before the American public, it also demonstrated that refueling in mid-air was safe and practical. The aircraft was refueled forty-three times, and the two planes were linked together 5½ hours, all told.

The country and the world were watching the exploit, and while they might have been impressed there were some who were not. Mrs. Spaatz and their three daughters were staying with her parents during the flight. The children were playing outside as the *Question Mark* passed overhead, and Mrs. Spaatz called to one of her daughters, "Look, Your father is in that plane. He has been in the air a whole week, a new world record. What do you think of that?" The ten-year-old girl responded curtly, "I think it's silly" (Mrs. Carl A. Spaatz, personal interview, February 11, 1976).

Although Spaatz, as the commander, received most of the fame for this mission, it was clearly a team effort. On March 6, 1929, the *Question Mark* crew was awarded the Distinguished Flying Cross. And Spaatz sent a memorandum on January 19, 1929 to the "commanding officer, Rockwell Field, California. In order to reimburse personnel of Rockwell Field for expenses incurred during the flight of the *Question Mark*, the following sums are to be paid out of a total of $1,106.80 turned over to Capt. H. M. Elmendorf, Air Corps." The amounts varied among the forty-one contributors (officers, enlisted men, and civilians) from a low of $6 to a high of $55.

The *Question Mark* flight was the forerunner of the air-to-air refueling that was to become commonplace for the Air Force in years to come. It was the beginning, too, of ties between what were to become the Strategic Air Command (SAC) and Tactical Air Command (TAC). On September 16, 1975, Gen. Robert J. Dixon, TAC Commander, presented Gen. Russell E. Dougherty, SAC Commander in Chief, the newly created Carl "Tooey" Spaatz Trophy, an award "in appreciation of superb air refueling support for worldwide tactical fighter forces—past, present, and future." The objective was to bind these two commands together, with this symbolic trophy to be awarded to the best refueling tanker crew in SAC each year.

After completing his tour in Washington, Major Spaatz was again assigned to Rockwell Field, Coronado, California. Shortly after his demonstration of air-to-air refueling, on June 13, 1931, he published a prophetic article in the San Francisco *Call:*

Only thirteen years have elapsed since the great war closed, yet pioneers of aerial warfare who braved and found death overseas would hardly recognize their squadrons, decked out with new equipment and employing modern tactical theories.

In these few years the picture of great swarms of airplanes wandering blindly towards the fighting front has changed to one of well-organized units, flying precise, highly maneuverable formations, which are strictly controlled. However many planes may be in the flight, all are responsive to the order of the commander in a moment's notice while within a radius of 200 miles.

Radio, of course, is the answer.

In the next war, instead of each pilot fighting his own battle in his own way, large formations will move as units resembling well-drilled infantry regiments. The commander, officers, and all, will actually be in the sky.

The walls of his aerial office will be prepared with maps upon which colored pinheads will mark the locations of his units. The radio operator will hand him a message; a pin will be moved. A weather report will come in and he will tell a squadron a hundred miles away to change its route. An order will come in from a division commander, and a squadron 20 miles away will be moved to the aid of the friendly bombers operating in its vicinity.

This may all sound theatrical, but it has already been worked out, and training activities now are directed to those lines.

Radio, I say without trepidation, is the most important single factor in the development of aerial tactics since the war.[49]

Spaatz tested this advance at every opportunity. For example, after attending maneuvers in Hawaii in 1932 he sent his observations to the Chief of the Air Corps, Maj. Gen. Benjamin D. Foulois: "The lack of suitable radio sets in their pursuit airplanes prevented the Black forces from committing their forces into action following the attack by the Blue forces."[50] He again wrote to Foulois on April 21, 1932: "The First Bombardment Wing has progressed to the point where I think you might be interested in a report of its activities to this time. . . . Great emphasis has been laid on the rapid clearing of airdromes, both on takeoff and landing, and on the use of radio. In my opinion, radio is rapidly reaching the point where it is no longer a tinkering affair but something that can be counted on, and definite procedure in its use must be developed."[51] Spaatz's insistence on the value of radio may have influenced Arnold, who recommended him for promotion to brigadier general and said that he was, "One of the most efficient and best all-around officers in the Air Corps. One of the few who can efficiently command a wing."

After an additional year of staff work in Washington, Spaatz was assigned to duty as a student at Command and General Staff School, Fort Leavenworth, Kansas, an assignment to which he did not look forward. As Mrs. Spaatz recalls, her mother was a very old friend of Gen. Malin Craig, then Chief of Staff of the Army. He asked Mrs. Spaatz's mother, " 'Edith, what about that Air Service son-in-law of yours. What do you think of him?'

"Mother said, 'I adore him, I love him.'

"Craig responded, 'I'm disappointed in him. He has not put in for Leavenworth. You know officers are asking to be assigned—even beg to go.'

"My mother said, 'I doubt if he ever would ask for it. It really isn't his dish of tea.'

"Craig said, 'He's never going to get anywhere in the Army if he is not a graduate. I will not wait for an application from him. I will order him to go.' That's how Tooey got to Leavenworth" (personal interview, February 11, 1976).

When Arnold, a strong believer in the value of the Leavenworth training, congratulated Spaatz on being selected, Spaatz replied, "Glad to get your letter of Jan. 31st, however, I cannot agree. . . . I am going to Leavenworth not because I expect it will do me any good, but primarily because I am ordered there and secondarily to get away from here [Washington]."[52]

"I got the idea," wrote Brig. Gen. William T. Fitts, Jr., a classmate of Spaatz at Leavenworth (personal communication, April 5, 1978), "that Spaatz thought he was wasting his time being there. He was not interested in infantry division, our main concern, but in air power. We were taking an exam one day. I looked up and saw Spaatz slam his paper down on his desk a few minutes after we started. He got up and walked out, and I heard him say, 'Nobody but a damn fool could answer questions like that.' Most officers would probably have been relieved from the course for such action." Obviously, Spaatz was not.

In his class was Capt. Hoyt S. Vandenberg, and Brig. Gen. E. W. Timberlake commented on the two of them, "These two men's outstanding leadership potentialities were evident . . . they both took a dim view of some of the precepts of the school, particularly on mobility . . . their ability to move troops rapidly by air was a new concept in our ground training. Ground training by the Army only conceived of moving troops by truck or by foot! So Tooey and Hoyt were always able to get there the 'fustest and the mostest' in our tactical problems and astonished the training classes" (personal communication, April 9, 1978).

It was clear, however, that when something intrigued Spaatz he performed exceptionally well. "At Leavenworth during the years 1935–1936," remembered Maj. Gen. John K. Rice, "Tooey's desk in the classroom was immediately behind mine. One of many 'problems of decision' that year required actual area reconnaissance. As it was announced, Tooey tapped me on the shoulder and said—'Ricky, you fly with me. I'll drive the plane; you watch the ground, and we'll turn in a report!' So, he did, and I did and we managed to get a pair of good grades." General Rice observed that "in our four-hour map problems, Tooey habitually arose and turned in his paper in approximately one and one-half hours. This was conspicuous to the class, and many wondered somewhat facetiously whether Tooey might have been assured of graduation and was being carefree about it. He was carefree by nature, but not, in any sense, for any such reason. He was rapid in reading and with comprehension; he was quick and discerning in weighing the factors involved and direct in bringing himself to clear-cut, firm decision. He was a man of action and, although a delightful 'hail-fellow-well-met,' he detested waste of time in either work or play" (personal communication, April 7, 1978).

"There was never a time," reflected Brig. Gen. Andrew C. Tychsen, "that Tooey bothered himself with the study requirements handed out to all students. A number of times I witnessed Tooey taking out the sometimes bulky material from his slot and slide it all into the nearest wastebasket. At the same time I never heard Tooey give an unsatisfactory answer when called upon in class. We all wondered how he got away with it. In every class that required written solutions to be submitted, often with a required time, Tooey would invariably finish ahead of all of us, smiling broadly, while the rest of us had barely gotten down to the requirements of the problem. We gradually determined that Tooey was possessed of a lightning mind, and was able to get at the root of the test and, to my way of thinking, [was] the top man of the class in that regard. Tooey took a lot of bantering from his classmates, but never lost his jolly good nature.

"He would remark to me when we were pulling out the ever-growing books and papers from our slots for home study and preparation, usually for the weekend, that surely I was not going to actually read that tripe! And looking back on those grinding days, I think Tooey was right. It was just impossible for anyone to cover that much material, and I am sure the faculty knew that it was" (personal communication, April 5, 1978).

Spaatz stood 94th in a graduating class of 121, and the official report on him was not favorable. He was not recommended for further training in high command or general staff duty. Nevertheless, his reporting officer termed him "diligent, dependable, and self-reliant."

Once he was back with the Air Corps, a more favorable view was taken of Lt. Col. Carl Spaatz (he had at last been promoted in 1936, after spending nineteen years as a major). From July 1, 1937 to February 28, 1938, as the war clouds gathered, he served as executive officer for the 2nd Wing, General Headquarters of the Air Force, and his effectiveness was noted by Brig. Gen. Arnold N. Krogstad, who called Spaatz, "An officer of exceptional ability. Very quick to grasp essential or critical points, and stick to his objective. An experienced Air Corps officer."

After Germany's invasion of Poland in September 1939, Hap Arnold later remembered, "I at once sent two of the best officers in the Air Corps, Lt. Col. 'Tooey' Spaatz and Maj. George C. Kenney, to Europe as combat observers. I didn't know how close they could get in touch with the actual war theater, but I knew those officers, and their flow of accurate reports presently affected our preparations and plans through the fall of France and the Battle of Britain."[53]

It was characteristic of Spaatz that he could maintain an optimistic outlook during the most serious adversity. After Dunkirk, he became an observer with the RAF. During these critical days, U.S. Ambassador Joseph F. Kennedy, Sr., was sending back fatalistic reports to Washington, indicating that Britain was doomed and that Germany would launch an early and successful invasion. Spaatz learned of these reports and urgently cabled Arnold his own estimates in defiance of the Ambassador. He believed the RAF would stop the Luftwaffe bombers, and he wrote Arnold a personal letter on July 31, 1940, that was remarkable for its foresight: "We are now trying to visit the southeast part of England to get a little closer view of the action of the German AF. Unless their attempt to take England is launched during August, I am inclined to believe it will have been indefinitely postponed. Unless the Germans have more up their sleeve than they have shown so far their chance of success in destroying the RAF is not particularly good. In air combat, German losses in daylight raids will be huge. In night attacks, the accuracy of their bombing is of a very low order. A tremendous effort using all planes regardless of loss and with prodigious use of gas might be successful, but if not it would be the beginning of the end for the German air supremacy. I am more inclined to believe that the German effort will be more of the nature of an air and submarine blockade of the British Isles rather than a risk of defeat in an attempted invasion of the islands."

"The Spaatz prophecy," concluded General Eaker, "accurate by a very narrow margin, impressed President Roosevelt favorably and endeared Spaatz to British leaders. He was thus a logical and certain choice to head our own air effort in Europe in World War II."[54]

Back in Washington, in August 1940, Spaatz, now a colonel, was assigned to the Office of the Chief of the Air Corps, and two months later was promoted again, to brigadier general, and appointed assistant to General Arnold. He served in that position until he became Chief of the Plans Division of the Air Corps in November 1940, and in July was named Chief of the Air Staff at Army Air Force (AAF) Headquarters.

In January 1942, after the bombing of Pearl Harbor, Spaatz was assigned as Chief of the AAF Combat Command at Washington and promoted to major general. He was selected as commander of the Eighth Air Force in May and was transferred to Europe in July to prepare for the American bombing of Germany. On July 7, 1942, he was appointed commanding general of all U.S. Army Air Forces in the European theater in addition to his responsibilities as commander of Eighth Air Force.

World War II built a close relationship between Gen. Dwight D. Eisenhower and Spaatz. On December 5, 1942, it was announced that Major General Spaatz had been sent to Africa "to organize allied air strength in Tunisia as Chief Air Adviser to General Eisenhower." Spaatz commented, "I knew him at West Point. He was in the class after mine. I did not know him very well, didn't see anything of him at all until after the war after I left West Point. Of course, I had very close connections with him during World War II. I think his ideas of leadership were pretty much the same as mine" (personal interview, September 19, 1962).

At that time the British forces were commanded by British, and the Americans by Americans. The decision was made to combine the forces. This required a meeting between the British and the Americans to divide up the two forces into the combined commands. They set up a bomber command, the tactical command, and the coastal air force command. Then the problem came as to who was going to command them. "The British," said General Quesada, who was present at this meeting, "as you can well understand were arguing that each of these commands should be commanded by an Englishman. An RAF type. The Americans, obviously, wanted the Americans in command. The Englishmen presented the argument over and over that they had experience. Well I was just a kid at the time, about thirty-nine years old, but I was more brash than the rest. I spoke up for the first time, as a new brigadier general. I commented to the British during the course of the discussion that, 'Well, what is your experience? Is it Dunkirk, Crete, Greece, Singapore?' " Obviously, these were all failures on the part of the British. After the point had been raised, there was silence. "General

Spaatz had let me go on, but after I had made that comment, he reached over to me and said, 'Take it easy, Pete,' and he stopped me. Henceforth, do you know who was on my side of the argument? The RAF. Because they saw it had merit'' (personal interview, June 22, 1977).

Publicly, Spaatz's new assignment was not supposed to affect the job of Maj. Gen. James H. Doolittle as Commander of the Twelfth Air Force in Africa, but in reality it did. "I was taken from command of the whole operation in North Africa," remarked Doolittle, "and given one of the lesser commands. I realized that General Spaatz knew more about the job than I did. He was more experienced than I. I was disappointed, but I was in no way despairing and I was very anxious to take a lesser command and prove myself in that" (personal interview, February 7, 1977).

"I'll give you an example of General Spaatz's leadership," Quesada said. "During the campaign in North Africa during World War II, things were not going very well. There was a great deal of friction among the various commands, particularly between British and Americans. . . . Some of this friction was between General Doolittle and the senior British airmen. . . . and Eisenhower . . . did not like friction. He liked tranquility. So he sent for General Spaatz. Actually, General Eisenhower wanted to send General Doolittle home. . . . But General Spaatz was successful in persuading General Eisenhower to leave General Doolittle there; Spaatz felt that General Doolittle had good qualities, and he called Doolittle in and talked to him like a Dutch uncle. Doolittle had that wonderful capacity that some men have where they're able to examine themselves and correct their own faults. That is what Doolittle did" (personal interview, June 22, 1977).

Doolittle's attitude explained why Spaatz wanted to keep him. Doolittle commented, "Maybe I should just say a word about a philosophy I have. I feel that you should do everything possible to make those things over which you exercise any control come out the way you want them to come out. I believe that when things are completely beyond your ability to affect in one way or another you should accept them and do the best you can under those conditions" (personal interview, February 7, 1977).

Later, on September 16, 1943, Doolittle justified Spaatz's confidence in him when, at Allied Headquarters in North Africa, Eisenhower pinned the Distinguished Service Medal on Doolittle. The citation read in part, "His energy, good judgment, exceptional qualities of leadership and his wholehearted cooperation contributed to the ultimate success of the operations during the Tunisian campaign."

On taking over his position in North Africa, Spaatz announced to the officers in his new command, "We have just begun, much remains to be done. Teamwork is the answer to successful aerial warfare. The entire Army

Air Force must operate as a team smoothly and efficiently, with minds, hearts, and hands." His first objective was to establish better teamwork between the British and American air forces and better cooperation between ground and air forces than had prevailed when the Allies had made their move for Tunisia.

"Early in that campaign Eisenhower called Spaatz to a fateful conference," General Eaker recalled. "Eisenhower said, 'Tooey, my morning reports shows you have 400 planes, while the British have 200, and the French show 100. Rommel has only 500 planes by today's intelligence estimate, yet every day he clobbers us. How come?'

"Spaatz responded, 'Ike, your figures are about right; when Rommel's planes hit me they outnumber me 5 to 4; when they hit the British they have the advantage 5 to 3. The Germans have overwhelming superiority over the French, 5 to 1. Our tactics have been all wrong. The airplane is a poor defensive weapon. Air power must always be used on the offensive. The first mission of the tactical air force is to win air superiority over the battlefield. Only then can it be diverted to the secondary roles like observation, directing artillery fire, shooting up tanks, or defending headquarters.'

" 'I get the point,' said Eisenhower. 'Tooey, hereafter as long as I am in command, you have the operational control of all the airplanes made available to me by our government or any allied nation' " (personal interview, October 4, 1977).

Spaatz's new, joint command, Allied Air Forces in North Africa, included the Eastern Air Command under Air Marshal Sir William Welsh, the Twelfth U.S. Army Air Force under Major General Doolittle, and units of the French air force. It was the first time British fighters and bombers had been brought under the direct command of an American general.

It did not take long for Spaatz to get the desired results. On April 9, 1943, it was announced that his Northwest African Air Force had secured "supremacy of the air." Since the beginning of the Mareth Line battle on March 20, the Allies had shot down 519 Axis planes while losing only 175 of their own. The highlight was the shooting down on April 17 and 18, 1943 of 96 enemy aircraft with the loss of only 11 Allied planes. Over 1,000 enemy planes were destroyed on the ground. The Luftwaffe was so weak that it was reduced to sneak raids. Allied planes denied the resupply of the Afrika Korps; without gas, Rommel's tanks were halted. In a statement printed in the *New York Times,* April 19, 1943, Spaatz commented:

> Our fighters have constantly beaten the enemy in the air, as the
> record shows. The planes we have can cope with anything the

Germans have. Naturally, the lessons we learned we sent home for incorporation in future designs. I want to emphasize that American planes here are good. Our pilots are as good as the pilots of any nation and the RAF admits that freely. The operations of the Northwest African Air Forces have thrown us together in intimate contact, and there is the highest admiration between the Americans and the RAF for each other.

It may or may not have been absolutely accurate then, but saying it publicly helped make it come true all the sooner.

Part of the success was Spaatz's planes and his knowledge of how to best use them. In the same issue of the *New York Times,* he said, "I would not have a Stuka type [the German dive bomber] in any air force I would ever run. The best dive bomber we have is the fighter. All of our fighters have good points, but use them the wrong way at the wrong levels and you get into trouble. The combination of planes we have here meets our requirements very adequately."

The evaluation of Spaatz's performance in the North African campaign is best summed up in a letter dated May 12, 1943, from Eisenhower to Spaatz: "With the campaign in North Africa now drawing rapidly to a completely successful conclusion, I take this means of letting you know how deeply I am personally and officially obligated to you for your contribution to the common victory.

"From the day when you entered this theater, your effectiveness in securing cooperation among British and American air forces, in organizing the whole air force to assure accomplishment of its mission, in sustaining and building morale and cooperating effectively with other arms and services, has been most noticeable. As the Commander of the Northwest African Air Force in the later stages of the campaign, you and your staff have done a remarkable piece of work. The physical results you have achieved are largely a matter of record. But beyond all this, you have been of great assistance in proving that Allied forces can work as a unified and effective team; a lesson that will grow more and more important as we enter future phases of the war."[55]

After defeating Germany in North Africa, the Allies turned their attention to the war in Europe. There were a number of issues to be resolved. Of particular concern to the Army Air Corps were these: Who would command the D-Day invasion? Who would command the Air Forces? What would be the nationality of the leaders selected? How would the air staffing be determined?

On December 24, 1943, some of these questions were answered. After extensive consultation with Prime Minister Churchill, President Roosevelt made the formal announcement that General Dwight D. Eisenhower was to command the invasion of Europe. At the same time it was announced that Lt. Gen. Carl A. Spaatz would command the entire American strategic bombing force operating against Europe. With these leadership matters settled, a new set of questions emerged for Spaatz. How would strategic bombing be accomplished? What targets would be bombed? Where would the bombing be done?

The RAF wanted the Army Air Corps to join their efforts in night bombing, believing that this would defeat Germany. The AAF believed strongly in high-altitude precision daylight bombing. The turning point for the opposing views was the Casablanca Conference in January 1943.

Arnold called his key air commanders to the conference to uphold the U.S. position; Lt. Gen. Tooey Spaatz as Commander of the Allied Air Force in North Africa; Lt. Gen. Ira C. Eaker as Commander of the Eighth Air Force; Lt. Gen. Frank Andrews, Commander of U.S. Forces in the Middle East. Arnold went round and round with Prime Minister Churchill over the issue, but the day was really won by Eaker, who persuaded Churchill to give the United States a chance with daylight precision bombing.

Also at issue was the selection of targets. Spaatz wanted to hit the German weapons plants (particularly the ball-bearing plants) and oil refineries. His reasoning was that the Germans would defend these targets, whose destruction would have brought Germany's industry and transportation system to a standstill, and that the American fighter aircraft would then have an opportunity to flush out the German Luftwaffe and destroy it. In Spaatz's opinion, the Germans would fight to defend their oil supply and would risk losing fighter aircraft and crews.

On the other hand, Field Marshal Tedder of the RAF wanted to hit the railway centers, bridges, viaducts, and rolling stock. Tedder convinced General Eisenhower these air strikes were necessary for the success of the D-Day invasion, to ensure that the Germans would not be able to mass sufficient forces to throw our invasion troops off the beachheads.

Spaatz was not successful at that time in overcoming the positions of Eisenhower and Tedder. As a soldier, he accepted the decision that the bombers would first be sent against transportation targets, but he did obtain from Eisenhower permission to hit oil targets in Germany when the weather was right. But the tug-of-war continued. It even reached a point where Spaatz threatened to ask to be relieved of his command if he was not given the opportunity to give priority to these oil and ball-bearing targets that he considered to be so terribly important in crippling the Wehrmacht.

Air Marshal Sir John Slessor commented on Spaatz's strategic planning:

> On the President's instructions, Spaatz and Eaker had produced a detailed and comprehensive plan for the destruction of the German War economy, based on the assumption that the RAF would continue bombing by night, aimed at devastation, dislocation of normal life, and the undermining of the morale of the industrial population, while the Americans singled out the vital war industrial targets one by one and destroyed them by high-altitude precision bombing by daylight. Spaatz showed me this plan, and I thought well of it; in some ways it was unduly optimistic. . . . But it was an impressive bit of work and contained all the essentials of the program that ultimately tore the heart out of Germany.[56]

Robert A. Lovett, Assistant Secretary of War for Air, a close friend and confidant and an unusually keen and accurate observer, felt that Spaatz had an instinct for strategy and that his instinct generally proved correct. Spaatz, himself, was not a systematic planner, allowing his intuition to guide him to the right decisions.[57] As one of his staff officers, Brig. Gen. Laurence S. Kuter, said, "A staff study was an anathema to General Spaatz. The staff studies were made, but Tooey would want to be told immediately what the conclusions were, what the options were, what were the recommendations, and who should do it. . . . He did not read the whole staff study. He wanted the conclusions, the results, the options and little more" (personal interview, July8, 1978).

In selecting the German targets, Spaatz was opposed to bombing urban areas, primarily because he did not think it would win the war. "There were various target systems proposed," he said. "There was the industrial complex, transportation, the aircraft industry, and oil. Our plan was daylight bombing; precision bombing of whatever system was given top priority. The British didn't believe at the time that daylight bombing could be successful. We felt it would be. At the back of our minds, including mine, was the idea that there would be a need for fighter cover. Some of our people were opposed to taking fighters over when we went in 1942. They said the British had enough fighters to take care of us. There was some argument about it, but Arnold and Stimson supported me, and Marshall decided the fighters would go over with the bombers.

"We always attacked only legitimate military targets with one exception —the capital of the hostile nation. Berlin was the administrative and communications center of Germany and therefore became a military target.

Other than that, our targets were always military targets. One stand was that we'd bomb only strategic targets—not areas. I believed that we could win the war more quickly that way. It wasn't for religious or moral reasons that I didn't go along with urban area bombing."[58]

No fighters, either U.S. or British, had enough range to accompany bombers into Germany. This problem, at Spaatz's insistence, was solved by developing a long-range fighter, the Mustang, and extending its range with wing tanks that could be jettisoned.

Alfred Goldberg wrote:

> It is to Spaatz's credit that he personally directed the aggressive strategy and tactics in the onslaught of the fighters against the Luftwaffe. He insisted that the fighters not be tied to the bombers as escorts and that they surge ahead of the bomber formations, seek out the German fighters in the air and on the ground, and destroy them. This brilliant stroke derived from Spaatz's boldness and his confidence in the strength and quality of his forces. The Luftwaffe never recovered from the crippling effects of these great air battles.[59]

After the war, Spaatz was asked, "Do you feel that the faith of the Army Air Force in daylight strategic bombing was justified by the results?" He responded, "Why, certainly. We might have won the war in Europe without it, but I doubt it very much. I think it was the combination of the two bombings, the night bombing of the RAF and daylight bombing, that was largely responsible for successful conclusion of the war there. Everyone thought a year or two before the invasion that to invade the continent of Europe was an impossible undertaking, that the German air forces would smother it as they did at that first operation at Dieppe by Mountbatten. But actually, the result of the, and I say primarily, of the daylight bombing, which forced the German air force back to defend Germany, prevented any large German air force [from appearing] at the invasion. I think that there were only two or three German planes that appeared during the whole landing in Normandy."[60]

Indeed, little was seen of the Luftwaffe during the landing at Normandy. There is no question that before the D-Day invasion was launched on June 6, 1944, the German air force had been defeated. One of the primary reasons was the leadership of Tooey Spaatz in formulating and executing plans for the tactical and strategic use of airpower, particularly the emphasis on hitting the German oil refineries, electrical producing and distributing systems, transportation systems, and ball-bearing factories. "The damage we did to German targets," said Spaatz, "was less than half the battle; the real purpose was to flush the Luftwaffe, to force it to battle. We knew we could beat them."[61]

The wisdom of Spaatz's judgment was later corroborated by Albert Spear, Minister of Armaments and War Production for Germany during World War II. He wrote in his memoirs that the bombing campaign against German oil was decisive and suggested the Allies would have done better to have pursued the oil target bombing as well as select key industrial targets. "The idea was correct, the executive defective," said Albert Spear, "for not having pursued it with vigor."[62]

Spaatz had keen ability in picking good people for command and for staff assignments. He once said facetiously to Maj. Gen. Robert E. L. Eaton, "I owe my success to two things: I drink good whiskey and get other people to do my work. I give a man a job. I never tell him how to do it. He's supposed to know how to do it" (Eaton, personal communication, April 18, 1963).

"General Carl 'Tooey' Spaatz had, in my opinion," remarked Brig. Gen. Harold A. Bartron, "more ability to inspire confidence in his commanders than anyone with whom I ever came in contact. He did this by reposing confidence in them.

"The general officer in command of service troops in the Mediterranean theater in World War II had a nervous breakdown and had to be replaced overnight. General Spaatz selected me for the job. . . . He took me to one side, and said, 'Bartron, Duncan is sick and is going to be sent home. You will replace him. This is the toughest job in the theater, he has just broken down, I hope that you, too, do not break down. You run the job the way you think it should be run; go any place any time you want to go. Take time off and often whenever you like. If you're going to be away from your office for more than three or four days, let me know.'

"In more than a year, during the war, General Spaatz visited me only once, and in that time it was more of a social visit than otherwise. As he left he said to me, 'Bartron, I know you think it funny I didn't ask you a lot of questions as to how things are going. I get that from reports before I made a visit. When I inspect a commander, I look for only one thing, 'his frame of mind.' I guess he wanted to check and see if I was going to crack up" (personal communication, October 17, 1962).

But in crucial moments Spaatz stayed in touch, as Maj. Gen. Robert B. Williams remembered: "On the night of October 13, 1944, the First Air Division, which I commanded, had been briefed for a full-scale attack on the fighter factories around Anklam in northern Germany. About 3 A.M. in the morning of October 14, I was in my operations office checking the weather at our bases. They were all 0–0 with dense fog. An operations officer came over and said General Spaatz wanted me on the scrambler phone. I picked up the telephone, and General Spaatz said to me, 'Bob, how are things in your area?' I responded to him that we were socked in and couldn't see to even taxi. He then said to me, 'We have the first perfect bombing weather in Northern Germany that we have had in many months, and there is no telling when we would get another day of good weather as this.' I was, of course, aware of the fact. But General Spaatz went on to say to me, 'However, if you're fogged in and can't take off, there is nothing we can do about it. I'll leave it entirely up to you.'

"I told General Spaatz," continued Williams, "that I would get my division airborne and that we would bomb Anklam with the ones that did not crack up on take off. Our pilots did an unbelievable job of getting several hundred B-17s off the fog-bound fields without a single fatal accident. The operation against Anklam was an outstanding success.

"I mentioned this because I consider the manner in which General Spaatz handled this situation is an excellent example of fine leadership. If he had ordered us on that mission I would have tried to convince him that it was impossible. However, when he left it squarely up to me, what else could I do?" (personal communication, October 31, 1962).

This leadership style probably detracts from a leader's getting credit, and Spaatz was very unassuming about his role. Gen. Curtis E. LeMay commented, "To me, Spaatz was lazy. I think Ira Eaker was twice the leader that Spaatz was. I have a suspicion that a lot of Spaatz's success was due to the people he had around him. That very fact, however, makes him a good leader. To get the people around you to do your work. General Spaatz used to brag about the fact that he was lazy and would have everybody else do the work. Spaatz was able to set the goal and say, 'This is what we have to do to get it done without my having to do it myself' " (personal interview, August 28, 1975).

Spaatz did not alter his leadership style when he became Chief of Staff. "I'll tell you a significant story about General Spaatz," commented Gen. William F. "Bozo" McKee, "and then you can see why he was so successful. When General Spaatz was Chief of Staff, Hoyt S. Vandenberg was Vice Chief and I was Assistant Vice Chief. By that time I had gotten to know General Spaatz quite well. It was on a Saturday morning, and Vandenberg was gone. I had three papers that had to be signed by the Chief of Staff, or at least I thought they had to be signed by the Chief of Staff. So I took these three papers in to General Spaatz shortly after 11 o'clock that Saturday morning. I said to him, 'Sir, I've got three papers here that require your signature as Chief.'

"I was a major general at the time, and General Spaatz looked up to me and he said, 'Bozo, didn't you just get promoted?'

"I said, Yes, sir.'

" 'Who promoted you?'

"I said, 'You did, sir.'

"He said, 'Why in the hell do you think I promoted you?'

"I said, 'Sir, I don't know.'

"He said, 'Well, I'll tell you. I promoted you to sign papers like these. Do any of these papers have to do with war starting tomorrow?'

"I said, 'No sir.'

"He said, 'Then you sign them.' He then said, 'If you make a mistake, I'll forgive you once. If you make a mistake two times, you're fired. Furthermore,' he continued, 'I'm in a hurry because I'm due to meet some friends at 11:45 and I've got to go. So you sign these papers.'

"I went back to the desk, and I read these papers three more times with great care before I signed them and that was the last I heard of it. The reason I tell this story is that General Spaatz, when he had confidence in somebody, believed in the world's simplest fundamental of leadership; that is, to give your subordinates responsibility. Spell out the responsibility and then give them the authority to discharge it" (personal interview, July 6, 1977).

"I was at once impressed," said then Lt. Gen. Ira C. Eaker, "with General Spaatz's command ability. I noticed that he was very taciturn, and did not make friends easily. He was not as literate as General Arnold was, and did not attempt to be. But he did have a very warm personality once you knew him." General Spaatz was aware of his "taciturn" manner. He wrote in his diary on June 9, 1925, "Read article by Arnold Bennett on conversation. He deplores silent or taciturn people, and advises one to talk even if what they say is trivial or seems silly. That by talk, life becomes more enjoyable. Dead hours at meals, etc. can be made into pleasant moments. Believe he is right and that I am a serious offender."[63]

Spaatz and Eaker enjoyed a long and close friendship. Eaker recalled, "Perhaps it wasn't so much that General Spaatz was taciturn as he was short of speech. He was never loquacious at any time, and I can remember so well that we spent [vacations on] nineteen successive years in a fishing cabin that I had on Rogue River. We would sit in the evening over cocktails or over a game of cards and exchange very few words. He was not a talkative individual. When you asked him a question, he would reply in monosyllables or in the briefest possible way. When Spaatz was in command of the fighter selection board between the wars, about the years 1930, 1931, and 1932, I was the recorder of the fighter board for the year that he was chairman of it. General Spaatz decided that the B-12 was the best of the fighters that we had examined. So I wrote a report about three-quarters of a page in length. He read it and said to me, 'This is much too verbose.' I said to General Spaatz, 'Okay, you write it.' So he said, 'Here's what I think your report should state: We've examined all of the airplanes entered in the competition as we were directed. The B-12 is the best. We recommend its early procurement.' Thus, we had about three sentences, a very brief paragraph, which is quite a contrast to the McNamara whiz kids who spent two years studying the F-111 report'' (personal interview, October 4, 1955).

Eaker and Spaatz worked their way up the promotion ladder together between World War I and World War II. "I remember that we served,'' said Eaker, "on several fighter selection boards together and also together during spring and autumn maneuvers, which are held almost every year. For many years, he was Commander of the First Pursuit Group, and I noticed General Spaatz was not only given command, but that he also was frequently given the senior staff roles on the Air Staff. I served with him on the Air Staff twice, for two or three years. I think that his briefness was very much to his advantage. He was unique in that regard. He always had definite ideas and never failed to express them, and expressed them in much briefer terms than most staff officers. That probably added to the conviction that the seniors had that he was a capable staff officer, rather than to detract from it. I also served with him on many boards, tactical boards, and what we now term 'strategic' boards. . . . We would propose something in the current budget coming up for that year and would present a paper defending it. General Spaatz and I worked together more often than most people, and this getting to the heart of the matter was part of General Spaatz's success.

"A careless historian once said in my presence that he thought that I, Ira C. Eaker, was the voice of Spaatz, intimating that I wrote many of the things that we signed together. That gives a false impression. We arrived at the same conclusions that I wrote, but they were the result of a mutual discussion. So although General Spaatz was not verbose by any means, I always knew what his view was and respected it. Most times I agreed with it because he would generally listen before he would express a view. In other words, I generally outlined my view and the reasons for it and then he commented on his position. General Arnold, for example, would usually state a case in General Spaatz's presence and in the presence of his other key staff members. Usually General Spaatz was the last one to comment, and he generally buttoned it up and summarized it in a very few sentences'' (personal interview with Lt. Gen. Ira C. Eaker, October 4, 1977).

RAF Marshall Sir John Slessor, during World War II, made a similar comment. "I saw a lot of him in those summer months (that is, the summer when then Lt. Col. Spaatz was sent to Great Britain as an observer) and thus began another treasured friendship—I remember him turning up one day when I was enjoying 48 hours' leave, cutting corn in Oxfordshire, and we lay on our backs in the stubble chewing straws and looking up at the summer sky where the Battle of Britain was then being fought away to the Southeast. Spaatz is Pennsylvania Dutch, a man of few words but with a dry sense of humor. . . . He was one of their earliest airmen, with a fine record in the Kaiser's war, and has other characteristics in common with our Lord Trenchard—a man of action rather than of speech, rather inarticulate, with an uncommon flair for the really important issue and a passionate faith in the mission of air power."[64]

An example of Spaatz's briefness was also provided by Brigadier General Bartron, whose Mediterranean command of the service troops was mentioned earlier. There was a worldwide shortage of B-17 engines. "I informed General Spaatz of this dilemma, and he replied, 'Don't you run out of engines—I'm not running out of war'" (personal communication, October 17, 1962).

Shortly after the United States entered World War II, a directive was handed down instructing senior air commanders not to fly on missions (as noted in Chapter 1). One commander who was nonetheless anxious to get into action was General Cannon, who preferred flying single-seaters. After he went down in the water and narrowly escaped death, Spaatz issued the following order to Cannon: "You will hereafter confine your overwater flights to multiengine aircraft. We have plenty of airplanes, but we have only one Cannon" (Bartron, personal communication, October 17, 1962).

"General Spaatz had an incredible capacity," said Quesada, "to put a very profound thought in a few words. He was that way all of his life. He could pick a broad spectrum of thoughts and express it in a few words because he was not verbose. He was rather quiet, really. He was extremely thoughtful—I don't mean thoughtful in the sense of being kind to other people. I mean thoughtful about what air power is. Arnold was not adverse to exaggerating the potential of air power. Indeed, usually Arnold did exaggerate. Whereas Spaatz was not inclined towards exaggerating anything. If anything, he played things low-key, but was very persuasive. General Eisenhower's confidence in Spaatz was boundless during the war" (personal interview, June 22, 1977).

Tooey Spaatz was unpretentious and unassuming. Robert Lovett, Assistant Secretary of War for Air, was visiting Spaatz at his headquarters in North Africa in 1943. "It was a Sunday, an off day," recalled Secretary Lovett. "There weren't any staff people around, but there was a guard outside the villa. Spaatz was up on the roof of the villa sunning himself, wearing just a pair of khaki shorts and nothing else except sandals. I was in the villa, and a guard came to me and said there was a French officer outside who wanted to see General Spaatz. I think it was either a French colonel or a brigadier but he was all dressed up, full uniform, full regalia and he was going to present his compliments to the Commanding General. I spoke with the French officer and said, 'All right, I'll go get General Spaatz.' So I went up on the roof and told Spaatz that the French officer was waiting below to present his compliments. Spaatz demurred and didn't particularly want to be bothered at that time, but I succeeded in persuading him that he ought to see the French officer. He said, 'All right,' and started down in just his shorts. I said, 'Aren't you going to change?' Spaatz said, 'Hell no,' and he went downstairs to receive this French officer dressed in khaki shorts and nothing else, much to the amazement of the French officer, who nevertheless went through all of the proper punctilio of the occasion and departed. The Frenchman was obviously very much surprised and astonished at the uniform of the Commanding General of the American Air Forces in North Africa" (personal interview, September 12, 1978). According to Lovett, this was not uncommon—Spaatz did not stand on ceremony. He was not a spit and polish type.

This casual approach to things also made an impression on one of the key Army field commanders of World War II, Gen. George S. Patton, Jr., who noted in his diary on April 16, 1943, "Had a long talk with Spaatz on air support. I think he will do, but he lacks any idea of discipline." Several months later, Patton noted in his diary on August 5, 1943, "General Spaatz came to see me. As usual he was dirty and unshaved."[65]

This casual approach was humorously portrayed by Laurence Kuter. "In January 1943, I reported to Algiers under orders to be General Spaatz's Chief of Staff. I finally found his headquarters building and looked for somebody to show me where Tooey's offices were. No one met me, and after looking around I finally found an office with a sign that said 'Chief of Staff.' I went in, and I found an Air Vice Marshal sitting there named Robb. I introduced myself and said I had a set of orders designating me to be Tooey Spaatz's Chief of Staff and I was looking for him. 'That's odd. I've been looking for him too, and I'm his Chief of Staff.' We talked about it for awhile and sorted things out between us. I decided his assignment probably preceded mine. But Robb was delighted to see me, asking 'What was Tooey's Chief of Staff supposed to do?' Nobody could tell him. I couldn't either." Kuter also served under Spaatz in the Pacific and there, he said, "I don't think he ever went to an office. I don't think he had an office. He wouldn't admit he did." Kuter commented, "Tooey's operating methods in the field just defied any standards of anybody" (personal interview, July 8, 1978).

New York Times correspondent Hanson Baldwin described Spaatz after a visit to North Africa in June 1943. "Like Eisenhower, Spaatz has restless energy; at a desk he is like an eagle chained to its nest."[66]

But this casualness, so far as it was reflected in Spaatz's command, concerned Eisenhower, who looked on it as a lack of attention to discipline. Indeed, Eisenhower even held up promotions of several key members of Spaatz's staff. Eisenhower wrote to Spaatz on May 12, 1943, "I have sent forward to the Chief of Staff the recommendations for promotion in the four cases, concerning which you feel so deeply. In this connection, I wish you would read again the letter I wrote on promotions to senior commanders a month or so ago. I particularly want to emphasize the need for discipline among our troops. If you could drop into the headquarters for Fifth Army at Oujda, you would see what I mean. Soldiers there are smart, clean, and salute punctiliously and correctly. The effect created is most pleasing and, more than this, it inspires a feeling of confidence. Frankly, I think our air forces have been behind in this matter. I am struck by the number of times I walk across flying fields to be classicly ignored by officers, to say nothing of enlisted men. If we are to continue to promote your officers, they must deliver the goods in this respect as well as in others.

"I know that you do not consider me harsh in this matter. No one loves a good soldier more than I do, but we must demand results, and I honestly hope that you will make this matter, during the ensuing weeks, one of particular concern."[67]

What Eisenhower did not understand was that Spaatz tolerated no relaxation of discipline in the air. There was a marked contrast between his relaxed approach on the ground and his absolute and strict discipline in air procedures.

"General Spaatz is and has been for many years a close personal friend," commented Maj. Gen. Frank O. D. Hunter. "There is one fact that stands out in his career; he never commanded any outfit that didn't turn out tops. I think his most outstanding characteristic as a number one leader was that he kept the objective always in front of him and nothing would cause him to divert an inch" (personal communication, October 3, 1962).

Spaatz's professional qualifications as a leader were derived in part from his long and unusually broad and deep experience as an airman. Certainly his leadership had the chance for more rapid growth in very responsible positions with pressures, challenge, and exposure to decision making and outstanding decision makers at the highest level. In a discussion, Spaatz made this point, "The one thing that is necessary is that you know the tools of your trade. In my case, it was knowing the airplane—knowing what the airplane could do at all times" (personal interview, September 19, 1962).

The final achievement of General Spaatz was the establishment of an air force separate from the Army and Navy. One of his reasons for remaining in the Air Corps after Arnold's retirement, and for accepting the position of Commander of the Army Air Corps, was to assist in bringing this to fruition. In a letter he wrote to a young debater on January 29, 1926, he explained why a separate air force was needed:

> Mr. Gerald Garard
> 1208 Main St.
> Mendota, Ill.
>
> My dear Mr. Garard:
>
> Reference yours of January 26, I shall try to define "air service" and "air force."
>
> "Air Service" is that part of aviation which works directly with and in conjunction with ground troops, such as observation aviation which regulates artillery fire, conducts Infantry liaison missions, and such other work as is directly connected with ground troops—in other words "service," i.e., "air service."
>
> "Air force" is that part of aviation capable of independent action without regard to ground operation, such as bombardment, pursuit, and attack. These branches of aviation strike independently at enemy centers such as cities, factories, railroad yards, docks, etc., without regard to location or operation of ground troops. In other words it is a "force" within itself; i.e., "air force."
>
> I am glad to hear you have won a debate for an air force, and hope you can win many more.[68]

Throughout his life, Spaatz was a leading architect of air power. In particular, he originated and developed the bombing techniques that were so important in bringing Germany and Japan to surrender. He played the decisive part in the way the air war was conducted. Spaatz was responsible for shortening the war, which saved many lives. He was a quiet, effective evangelist for air power. Although he was often described as a "prosaic" person, it was quite clear to those who knew him that he felt intensely about our country's need for air power to ensure security and survival, to win war and to keep peace. It was fortunate for the United States that we had such a leader. We can always remain grateful for the contribution he made.

NOTES, Chapter 2

1. Personal interview between Gen. Carl A. Spaatz and Donald Shaunessey, January 29, 1959. (The permanent records at West Point list the spelling as *Spatz,* but throughout this work the name will be spelled *Spaatz.*)
2. Ibid.
3. Ibid.
4. Ibid.
5. *Howitzer* (West Point Yearbook), 1914, p. 184.
6. Benjamin D. Foulois, "From the Wright Brothers to the Astronauts." *The Memoirs of Major General Benjamin D. Foulois,* with Col. C. V. Glines, USAF (New York: McGraw-Hill, 1968), p. 122.
7. Ibid.
8. Ibid.
9. Ibid, p. 134.
10. Gen. Henry H. Arnold, *Global Mission* (New York: Harper, 1949), p. 98.
11. Letter from Maj. Gen. Carl Spaatz to Maj. E. H. Branard, July 6, 1922.
12. Letter from Maj. Gen. Mason M. Patrick, chief of Air Service, to Maj. Carl Spaatz, July 11, 1922.
13. Letter from 1st Lt. C. G. Brenneman, A.S., to Maj. Carl Spaatz, June 17, 1922.
14. Spaatz letter to Branard.
15. Letter from Maj. Carl Spaatz, A.S., to Maj. Gen. Mason M. Patrick, July 20, 1922.
16. Letter from Maj. Carl Spaatz to Maj. Thurman H. Bane, A.S., July 13, 1922.
17. Letter from Maj. Thurman Bane, Chief, Engineering Division, to Maj. Carl Spaatz, July 19, 1922.
18. Letter from Maj. Carl Spaatz to Maj. Gen. Mason M. Patrick, February 21, 1923.
19. Letter from Milton G. Goff to Maj. Carl A. Spaatz, May 2, 1923.
20. Letter from E. A. Pasha to Maj. Carl A. Spaatz, June 12, 1923.
21. Letter from Maj. Carl Spaatz to Maj. Frank D. Lackland, Air Officer, 8th Corps Area, August 22, 1922.
22. Letter from Rear Admiral W. A. Moffett to Maj. Gen. Mason M. Patrick, October 20, 1922.
23. Letter from John W. Weeks, Secretary of War, to Maj. Carl A. Spaatz, October 21, 1922.
24. Letter from Maj. Carl Spaatz to Brig. Gen. William Mitchell, April 24, 1923.
25. Letter from Maj. Gen. Harry C. Hale to the Adjutant General of the Army.
26. Ibid.
27. Letter from Maj. Gen. Carl A. Spaatz to the Commanding Officer, Langley Field, Virginia, December 10, 1924.
28. Personal diary of Maj. Carl Spaatz, May 10, 1925.
29. Letter from Adj. Gen. A. B. Braxton to Maj. Carl Spaatz, through chief of Air Service, August 6, 1925.
30. Spaatz diary, June 30, 1925.
31. Letter from Maj. Carl Spaatz to Col. Bert M. Atkinson, September 9, 1925.
32. Letter from Maj. Carl A. Spaatz to Lew C. Wilson, October 19, 1925.

33.   Letter from Maj. Carl A. Spaatz to Col. Bert M. Atkinson, November 6, 1925.
34.   Letter from Blackburn to Maj. Carl Spaatz, January 10, 1925.
35.   Spaatz diary, May 10, 18, and 25, 1925.
36.   Ibid., May 12, 1925.
37.   Ibid., June 6, 1925.
38.   Testimony of Maj. Carl Spatz, Air Service, U.S. Army, as witness for the defense, p. 382.
39.   Ibid., pp. 421–22.
40.   Ibid., p. 411.
41.   Ibid., p. 413.
42.   Shaunessey-Spaatz interview.
43.   Ibid.
44.   Letter from William Mitchell to Maj. Carl A. Spaatz, February 5, 1926.
45.   Letter from Maj. Stratemeyer to Maj. Carl Spaatz, March 30, 1927.
46.   Letter from Maj. Henry H. Arnold to Maj. Carl Spaatz, August 20, 1926.
47.   Letter from Maj. Carl Spaatz to Maj. Henry H. Arnold, November 9, 1926.
48.   Interview by Alfred Goldberg with Gen. Carl A. Spaatz, May 19, 1965, USAF Oral History Program. K239.0512-755.
49.   Maj. Carl Spaatz, U.S. Air Corps, San Francisco *Call*, June 13, 1931.
50.   Letter from Maj. Carl Spaatz to Maj. Gen. B[enjamin] D. Foulois, Chief of the Air Corps, February 29, 1932.
51.   Letter from Maj. Carl Spaatz to Maj. Gen. B[enjamin] D. Foulois, Chief of the Air Corps, April 21, 1932.
52.   Letter from Maj. Carl Spaatz to Lt. Col. H[enry] H. Arnold, March Field, February 5, 1935.
53.   Arnold, *Global Mission,* p. 192.
54.   Ibid.
55.   Alfred D. Chandler, Jr., ed., *The Papers of Dwight David Eisenhower of the War Years,* Vol. 2 (Baltimore: John Hopkins University Press, 1970), p. 1126.
56.   Sir J. Slessor, *The Central Blue: The Autobiography of Sir John Slessor, Marshal of the RAF* (New York: Praeger, 1957), p. 430.
57.   Field Marshal Sir Michael Carver, ed., *The War Lords* (Little, Brown, 1976), p. 580.
58.   Goldberg-Spaatz interview.
59.   Carver, pp. 570–71.
60.   Goldberg-Spaatz interview.
61.   Lt. Gen. Eaker, "Gen. Carl A. Spaatz, USAF," *Air Force Magazine,* September 1974.
62.   Albert Spear, *Memoirs: Inside the Third Reich* (New York: Macmillan Company, 1970).
63.   Spaatz diary, June 9, 1925.
64.   Slessor, pp. 315–16.
65.   Martin Blumenson, ed., *The Patton Papers—1940-1945* (Boston: Houghton Mifflin, 1944), p. 222.
66.   *New York Times,* June 20, 1943, Section VI, p. 6.
67.   Chandler, p. 1125.
68.   Letter from Maj. Carl Spaatz, A.S., to Gerald Garard, January 29, 1926.

CHAPTER 3
GENERAL HOYT S. VANDENBERG

Hoyt Sanford Vandenberg was born in Milwaukee, January 24, 1899. His family had settled in Lowell, Massachusetts, and young Hoyt attended Lowell High School, where for four years he was very active in athletics. He was a regular in the backfield of the football team, a sprinter in track, and first base on the baseball team. His favorite sport was ice hockey, and he played on defense for four years. From this record one pictures a tall youth, fast on his feet, quick and with long arms to cover the throws to first base, and one who enjoyed bodily contact, especially in hockey.

At school he had some exposure to military training: four years of high school ROTC, reaching the rank of cadet captain, and two months at Plattsburg Training Camp. After graduation from high school, he spent a year at Columbia Prep School in Washington, D.C. Upon receiving an appointment to West Point from Senator William A. Smith of Michigan, he was sworn in on June 13, 1919, as a member of the class of 1923.

Vandenberg's demerits at West Point present a graphic record of his performance as a cadet. He was repeatedly cited for inattention to commands, being consistently late, and for carelessness with his clothes. His first class year was his best performance, with only fifty-four demerits, a number that placed him 176 out of 263 cadets. During his second year, he received demerits—for the twenty-eighth time—for being absent at dinner formation, for improper uniform, for a dirty gun, and for being late at formation for athletics (fifteenth incident).

During his third year, his demerits increased to 118, placing Vandenberg 276 out of 293 in "military efficiency and conduct." Again, the offenses were repeated—eleven more counts of being late, sixteen instances of improper uniform, for falling asleep in chapel, for leaving lights on in his room, and for failing to take the seat assigned to him after having been repeatedly directed to do so—and now the punishment was severe, five demerits, with ten hours to walk.

The compound interest on his casual, sometimes defiant, attitude toward regulations naturally detracted from his record in military efficiency. And his classmates held rather different views of him. When asked to describe what leadership Vandenberg exhibited during his cadet years, one commented, "How can you tell a cadet the best way to success is to be a poor student, make influential friends, never worry, drink beer with the right people—yet success as a leader seems to point to this in many cases" (Col. Robert M. Smith, personal communication, December 27, 1963).*

Yet there was another side to Hoyt's behavior. He was a member of "A" Company, many of whom became cadet leaders. This company instituted reform in the summer camp in 1922, which, as one cadet put it, "in no small measure was successful in advocating the fundamental rights of men and cadets. A spirit of reform swept like wildfire through the Corps," and essentially it meant that they treated new cadets like human beings.

In their senior year, out of the forty men in the Corps who had earned their letter, seven were in "A" Company. One of the seven was Vandenberg, who earned his letter in hockey, having played on the team all four years. The hockey team played fourteen games, against some of the best teams in the East and against the Royal Military College of Canada. Van must have been a valuable asset—the *Howitzer* of 1923 commented, "By graduation of '23, Army will lose O'Shea, Lord, and Vandenberg." The hockey team was handicapped by the conditions under which they were forced to practice and play. They played their home games outside because West Point had no indoor rink. The snowfall on some occasions was so heavy that practice was often impossible and many scheduled home games were delayed or canceled. They went to Princeton, New Jersey, to practice on Princeton's indoor rink on weekends and during Christmas leave.

Like cadets "Hap" Arnold and "Tooey" Spaatz, Vandenberg was a "cleansleeve," with no stripes to show cadet rank. Perhaps the fairest estimate of him at West Point comes from his classmate, Col. D. H. Galloway, who lived for three years directly across the hall from him: "Van was a youthful-looking cadet *with a most attractive personality,* gay spirit, and

*"Personal communication" refers to letter to the author.

was completely without sham or pretense. As I look back on it, there was a tendency in the Corps during that period to predict great things for the articulate cadet who paraded his disciplinary record, his moral conduct, and seriousness of purpose. Van did none of these things but was extremely well liked by his friends and close associates for his personal charm and loyalty. He had one quality to which I attached no significance at the time and that was his ability to listen while others were talking and then come forth with a pertinent and wise remark. He retained this faculty during his entire lifetime" (personal communication, December 23, 1963).

A fellow "goat" remarked of their four years, "The system tended to make nonconformists of a certain percentage of cadets. We resented what happened to us as plebes. We were skeptical of what seemed to be the superficial judgment of those in authority of who was superior and who was not. We scorned the apple-polishing efforts of some cadets who were bent on obtaining high efficiency ratings and were often successful in getting them. Such nonconformists as Van and I were labeled as being 'indifferent.' I believe the failure of people such as Van and I to attain high rankings as cadets was as likely to be a matter of attitude as a matter of lack of potential" (Paul P. Hanson, personal communication, January 13, 1964).

"Van was unassuming. He was a respected and well-liked member of the class," said classmate Col. Henry L. Shafer, "and made a fine impression as a hop manager. I am confident that his popularity stemmed more from his general personality and natural latent leadership ability than from any conscious effort on his part" (personal communication, December 26, 1964).

As Alfred L. Johnson remembered him, "Van had a sense of humor and enjoyed a good story, well told. He, himself, was an able raconteur, and was always 'one of the gang' in any gathering" (personal communication, January 10, 1954).

Cadet Vandenberg never marched in close step with the Academic Department. His final standing for the four years was 240 out of 261. He had the most trouble with mathematics, standing 290 out of 298 in his plebe year. "Jerry Rusk, my roommate in 'A' Company during our first class year," writes Alfred Johnson, "on many occasions tutored Van in difficult math assignments. Van never forgot this. We were all flying cadets at Brooks Field, Texas, when Jerry Rusk was killed in an airplane crash. Van was deeply upset. Often he later said, 'If it were not for Jerry Rusk's assistance, I would not have graduated with the class of '23' " (personal communication, January 10, 1954).

Hanson suggested about Van's scholastic performance, "Intelligence tests were comparatively unknown at that time, so I don't know what

Vandenberg's IQ was. But in the light of subsequent events I would guess it was high. This need be no surprise; the academic standards were high for those days. Many high school teachers of that time would have been unable to pass the entrance examinations. Our casualty rate was high; of 520 who entered in my class, only 261 graduated. Again, attitude may have had much to do with Vandenberg's academic standing'' (personal communication, January 13, 1964).

The class of 1923 was the first permitted to enter pilot training immediately. But there was little interest among his classmates in flying, and service preference was based on class standing. "I recall," reflected his son, Sandy Vandenberg, "that my father told me when I was going to West Point that he was interested in getting into the Cavalry. He once made the comment to me there was no way he could compete for the Cavalry because he was down so far in his class. One day an Army guy flew an old jenny up and landed on the Plain. He was there to sell the Air Service. Dad went and looked at this guy in his boots, goggles, and scarf and said, 'That's not too bad.' He told me that convinced him that's what he wanted to do and he applied for the Air Service" (personal interview, August 12, 1977).

Despite this apparent casualness, Vandenberg was eager to be successful in pilot training. Laurence C. Craigie, a classmate, said, "I don't know of anybody who really wanted to complete pilot training as badly as Van did, or who would have been more upset in getting washed out than Van" (personal interview, February 8, 1977).

Craigie and Vandenberg roomed together in pilot training. "There were eight of us," Craigie continued, "who were given a little house that had been built for two married families, so they put eight bachelors in the house. This was just fine with us. We ate our meals up at the club. Vandenberg, Rosey Wolfe, and I and one other lieutenant lived in one side of the house, and there were four others who lived on the other side. Van and I had the same flight instructor, Jimmy Taylor, one of the World War I pilots in the Air Service. He lived with his wife next door to the little bungalow we eight bachelors were sharing. Things were much less formal in those days than they are now. I'll give you an example. Jimmy Taylor went off on a cross-country flight and cracked up. He was delayed somewhere in the Midwest, and it was winter. He was away for over three weeks, but no effort was made by those in charge to assign us to another instructor. Van and I just soloed day after day after day, sort of comparing notes on what we were doing. Gradually we both developed some very unsafe methods of flying. Particularly, I can remember him doing the so-called one-eighty, where you come over the spot, turn 180 degrees, and land directly under the spot that had been picked. Finally we had a check pilot, John McCorkle, who stopped us, and said we could not fly again until we had more instruction. He assigned us to another instructor temporarily. Van and I were probably lucky we got through flying school because Jim was a very different type of instructor than most—he was very excitable. I recall one day, for example, I was doing this same maneuver of the one-eighty, and I did something wrong early in the maneuver. Jimmy Taylor started to cuss me out, and before I got down to the ground, which probably took all of 30 to 45 seconds, he told me what time I'd gotten in the night before, which was late, and he confined me to the post for a week. During all of this chewing, I was trying to maneuver the airplane. So he was not the best applied psychologist in the world, because there is no worse way to instruct somebody than to get him so damned upset in the middle of a maneuver and then hold him for it. Van and I had our troubles with Jim, but we both got through. Van got married at Christmas time, to Gladys Rose. I had gone with Gladys Rose, indeed, dated her at West Point before Van did" (personal interview, February 8, 1977).

After completing their training at Brooks Field, the two then went to Kelly Field for more advanced training. They had been at Brooks Field for six months and now were scheduled at Kelly for three. There they were divided into four sections; pursuit, bombardment, attack, and observation. "Van," said Craigie, "was assigned to the attack section and I was assigned to pursuit, so we were in different sections in the last three months of advanced pilot training. I can recall vividly the interest that Van had in attack aviation, and as soon as we graduated and he got his wings he was sent down to Fort Crockett with an attack group" (personal interview, February 8, 1977).

Asked how he would evaluate Vandenberg's aptitude for flying, Craigie, who became a lieutenant general, responded, "He was a good pilot, but he had one weakness which showed up, which was more psychological than a flying weakness. He just hated a physical exam. He had this same attitude toward check rides. He'd get himself all psyched up and just scared to death he was going to wash out. As a result he wouldn't do anywhere nearly as well as he could have or should have. This is why I think he was lucky to get through Jim Taylor without getting washed out, because Jim was so excitable. I think I was a bit lucky too" (personal interview, February 8, 1977).

Joseph H. Davidson saw Hoyt Vandenberg on completion of pilot training and made the comment, "Lieutenant Vandenberg was assigned to my flight and flew on my left in the leading echelon—I found out that he had learned his formation flying very well indeed. His airplane was always exactly where it was supposed to be. It was evident that he was sincere and thorough in learning his duties, and he quickly became one of the best-qualified low-altitude bombers and machine gunners in the group. I soon noted that Lieutenant Vandenberg's bombs always fell within the target area and close to or on the target itself. To maintain our proficiency with machine gun fire . . . we loaded the ammunition belts with a dummy round between each live round, and in this way we were able to fire with one round in each dive. It became apparent that some of our pilots were able to put a bullet in the bull's-eye in each dive. As the keeper of the records, I noticed that Lieutenant Vandenberg was one of those excellent marksmen.''[1]

Vandenberg served two tours as a flying instructor. He instructed at the Air Corps Primary Flying School at March Field, California, from 1927 until May 1929. After the tour at Schofield Barracks, Hawaii, with the Sixth Pursuit Squadron, he returned to the United States in September 1931, as an instructor at Randolph Field, Texas, serving as flight commander and deputy stage commander until March 1933.

One of then Lieutenant Vandenberg's students was John P. McConnell, who graduated from West Point in 1932 and went on to become Chief of Staff of the Air Force, succeeding Gen. Curtis E. LeMay. "I would always forget to fasten my safety belt," remembered McConnell. "The PT-3s we were training in had mirrors in front of them. Van was always in the front seat, and I was in the back seat. He would look at me in the mirror and say, 'fasten your safety belt!'—so I would. Why I always forgot to fasten it, I'll be damned if I know. One morning we went up and he took us right on up to 8,000 feet, which was just about as high as that thing would go. So he had me doing lazy eights, then he shook the stick and said he'd take it. All we had to talk back and forth with in the air was the gosport. We could hear each other that way. I had again forgotten to fasten my safety belt, so to make a point, he took the airplane and turned it over on its back, and pushed forward on the stick to throw me out. Boy, I grabbed everything in that cockpit to stay in. He turned the plane over and then signaled me to take the stick. Vandenberg never said a word. I'll guarantee you that I always remembered to fasten my seat belt after that" (personal interview, summer 1975).

General Spaatz later wrote that Vandenberg had remarked that "his work as a flying instructor was the most satisfying of all because he had the chance to work closely with the finest and most capable young Americans. He could, in a few months time, transform a bewildered and awkward young man into a self-confident and capable pilot. It was this opportunity to work with men of unusual ability and promise, and to contribute directly to their progress that he enjoyed the most."[2]

From May 1929 until September 1931, Lieutenant Vandenberg was assigned to Schofield Barracks in Hawaii with the Sixth Pursuit Squadron, which gave him his first real experience in command. One of his pilots at that time has this to say about Van's consideration and audacity: "After pilot training," said Maj. Gen. Richard A. Grussendorf, "I arrived in Hawaii on March 21, 1930, and stayed there for two years, assigned to the Sixth Pursuit Squadron commanded by Lieutenant Vandenberg. That was then considered overseas duty, believe it or not. I was a bachelor, and I was having the time of my life. I went to Lieutenant Vandenberg after a year, and said, 'Sir, I would like to extend,' and he said, 'No way. You're in the Army, and this can spoil you for the rest of your time. You better just call it quits here in Hawaii after your two years and do something else.' At that time he knew he was going to Randolph, and he asked if I was interested in being an instructor in the training setup, and I said, 'No sir,' I was not interested. He did not force it, and I went to Langley Field'' (personal interview, July 8, 1978).

"I was a brand new second lieutenant in the air reserve and knew practically zilch about the Army and its procedures. Lieutenant Vandenberg called me in right after I arrived and said, 'I'm assigning you as Assistant Adjutant of the squadron, Supply Officer, and Mess Officer of the squadron.' Well, you could have pulled me through the eye of a needle. We had an outstanding Sergeant Major, so that took care of the Adjutant's job. The mess was a different matter. I went into it blindly, but I must have a certain affinity for food, I guess; I always liked it. The then Mess Sergeant was someone I didn't like from our first meeting. (Part of the trouble with the mess was that the man was not qualified.) Under then existing Army regulations, the maximum rank of a mess sergeant was three-striper, a buck sergeant. Well, I found out that on the line, there was a three-striper ready to be promoted to staff, but he was a crew chief and a very good crew chief. He also had the reputation of being an outstanding Mess Sergeant. So I went to Van and said, 'Sir, to get this mess straightened out, we need this sergeant on the line who is about to be promoted to staff. He can't be promoted to staff as a Mess Sergeant but,' I said, 'he would help me.'

"Van said, 'What do you mean he can't be promoted to staff?''

"I said, 'Army regulations.'

"He said, 'To hell with Army regulations. If he's the man, get him in there now.'

"That was all I needed. Well, that mess in a very, very short time turned out to be outstanding. We actually had to put senior noncoms on the mess door to keep the men from the other squadrons from coming in.

"After one of these jobs was finished, Van would call you in and say it was a good job. When that happened, I would say to myself, 'My God, if he ever asks me to do anything again, I'm going to do it better.' At that time, I didn't know anything about efficiency reports. Lieutenant Vandenberg called me in one day and told me, 'Grussey, I have your ER here.' I wasn't sure what the hell he meant. 'Well,' he said, 'this is an efficiency report of how you're doing; this is going to go in your record. In time, this might make you general.' A general! I was thinking that maybe, with luck, after thirty years service, I'd end as a lieutenant colonel. [In fact, Grussendorf was promoted to major general.] He was just all in all nice, considerate, thoughtful, and helpful—he had all those qualities. This was my feeling as a brand new officer and also for all the rest of us that came into Van's outfit."

If one got into trouble or needed assistance on a job, Van would "just casually, so to speak, drop around and say, 'Well, how are things?' or 'You're doing all right, but have you tried this? I don't know if it'll work, but have you tried it or have you thought about it?' He didn't say, 'Do it this way, do it that way'—well, that to me was thoughtfulness on his part" (personal interview, July 8, 1978).

But Lieutenant Vandenberg made mistakes too. "When we first got the P-12s, which was then a real fine airplane," reflected Grussendorf, "Van took the squadron—I think at that time we just had nine airplanes—up in our khaki slacks and leather jackets. He didn't tell us what he had in mind. He kept boring up and up and he got up to well over 20,000 feet. We had no oxygen, and it was colder than be damned. Anyway, we all hung in there, and we were getting wobbly as hell because we were lacking oxygen. Then he tipped on over and came practically straight down, all of us yelling like Banshees to keep our ears cleared out. When we landed, my legs were wobbly. A couple of the pilots actually fell down when they got out of the airplane. We met in the ops [operation] office afterwards and he apologized to us for doing it. He said it was very foolish on his part, and he hoped that there would be no aftereffects, but he just wanted to see what the outfit would do under his leadership if he'd kept going. We all hung in there, and I think he was pleased with that but a little bit ashamed that he had extended his test that high" (personal interview, July 8, 1978).

The period beginning 1934 was a formative time in Vandenberg's career. In August 1934, he entered the Air Corps Tactical School at Maxwell Field, Alabama, the first of five years of professional education for Vandenberg, largely as a student and partly as an instructor. The course at the Air Corps Tactical School lasted until June 1935. A classmate of Vandenberg's at the school, Laurence S. Kuter, was asked what sort of student Vandenberg was, how he got along with his classmates, and whether he showed any leadership. He responded, "Well, I'd say he was an all-around poor student, but got along with the class fine. He never missed a party; he was with the lively set. He was much more interested in partying than in school work. He liked to fly, he liked people. As for leadership, I couldn't say that he exerted any among the class of students, but you wouldn't expect that among a class of students. I can't name any student who did" (personal interview, July 8, 1978).

Another classmate at the Air Corps Tactical School at Maxwell Field remembered most of all that "Van loved to fly and was probably one of the best fliers in the class, and he and two or three others loved to engage in various maneuvers which were not wholly part of the exercise" (Col. Sheffield Edwards, personal communication, January 10, 1964).

On completion of Command and General Staff School, he was reassigned to the Air Corps Tactical School, this time as an academic instructor. "Van and I were together at Maxwell quite a while," reflected Kuter. "I had stayed there on the faculty in bombardment while Van had gone to Command and General Staff School. Then he came back to Maxwell as an instructor in pursuit. We had offices across the hall from each other and were somewhat competitive, as one really had to be at that time. We were competitive for budgetary retention, really, in our specialties. I was for bombers, and he was for fighters. He and Clair Chennault for a while, then he and Pat Partridge, then Jimmy Parker. There were usually two, sometimes three, in the pursuit section. In the bombardment section, I happened to be alone for a while. I was there for four years. When Van and I were instructors, yes, there was some leadership there, instructors were supposed to. He did it not by being a boss, not by being a dictator. He wasn't a gang leader; his leadership was on the subtle side, not overpowering by any means. He and Pat Partridge were much alike, both outstanding people. As a leader, Van was better than average at anything he did. There were members of the faculty who, I think, showed more intellectual leadership, such as Fairchild or George—particularly George, Possum Hansell, Gordon Saville. Van didn't take things too seriously *ever,* as instructor or student. He didn't miss any parties on the faculty ever. He was good at that. I don't want to disparage him, but I'm trying to be honest in recalling it to the best of my ability. We liked him and Gladys, no doubt about that; they were good people. We had children the same age, we saw lots of them" (personal interview, July 8, 1978).

From September 1938 to June 1939, Vandenberg attended the Army War College; he was then assigned to the Plans Division in the Office of the Chief of the Air Corps, and served in that capacity until immediately after Pearl Harbor, when he became Operations and Training Officer of the Air Staff. Promotion came fast and was eagerly accepted. In June 1942,

Brigadier General Vandenberg was assigned to the United Kingdom, where he was involved in the planning of the Air Force operations in North Africa. He wanted action, and as Chief of the Staff of the Twelfth Air Force, Van participated in the invasion of North Africa in the Tunisian and Sicilian campaigns.

Recognition of Vandenberg's admirable conduct of the Air Force campaign in North Africa is spelled out in the citation for the Silver Star, which he was awarded on April 14, 1943, for gallantry in action.

Since February 18, 1943, when he assumed the duties of Chief of Staff of the Northwest African Strategic Air Force, this officer by his untiring efforts, keen professional knowledge, and personal example has been an inspiration to the personnel of this command. During the recent operations, many exceptional victories have been credited to the Strategic Air Force. In no small measure these victories are attributable to the expert service rendered by General Vandenberg in the planning of these missions. The intrepidity he displayed in participating in many of the missions he assisted in planning inspired the units of his command to renewed successful efforts against the enemy. By his display of gallantry and courageous leadership, General Vandenberg has upheld the highest tradition of the Air Forces of the United States Army.

The example he set for his junior officers is emphasized in his citation for the Distinguished Flying Cross, reading:

For extraordinary achievement while participating in numerous aerial flights over Tunisia, Italy, Sardinia, Sicily, and Pantelleria during the North African campaign. These missions were flown in all types of bombardment airplanes of the strategic air force. Types of missions included attacks against shipping at minimum, intermediate, and high altitudes and attacks against lines of communications, airports, and landing grounds. General Vandenberg has flown in various capacities, such as gunner, co-pilot, and observer. By means of these flights, he has attained firsthand knowledge of operating conditions, which has permitted him to recommend approved methods of operation. General Vandenberg's recommendations added immeasurably to the improvement in tactics and technique in radio and air discipline of the strategic air force. General Vandenberg volunteered for these missions knowing full well the hazards involved. This achievement, far above and beyond the requirements of his position, reflects high credit on General Vandenberg in a military service of the United States.

Like every airman, he wore the Air Medal for five sorties against the enemy and Oak Leaf Clusters for each additional five, and these were followed by the Legion of Merit, attesting the "personal courage and coolness of his leadership."

Vandenberg's record in North Africa made a deep impression on General Arnold. Brig. Gen. Laurence Kuter was General Arnold's primary staff officer on combat operations, and also appreciated Vandenberg's leadership: "Van was flying lots of missions. He was out with the troops. He was a good commander. He may have been a staff officer at that time, but he was acting like a commander and doing well. All of Van's papers came through my office, across my desk, and it was all good. I could see vigorous employment of fighters; using aircraft we once thought of only as dog-fighting World War I pursuit aircraft as very effective offensive weapons and close work with the ground force commanders, good relations with RAF, never anything unfavorable" (personal interview, July 8, 1978).

In the summer of 1943, Averell Harriman was appointed U.S. Ambassador to the Soviet Union, which immediately affected Vandenberg's career. "When it was finally agreed that I should become Ambassador" said Harriman, "sometime in early September 1943, I went to President Roosevelt and said I wanted to establish a military mission to work according to the Joint Chiefs of Staff, but also to be under my direction because if we wanted to get cooperation with Russia, it was necessary to have a high-level group. . . . I talked with Hap Arnold, and also to Bob Lovett, and they were both anxious to have a high-level officer there. Hap Arnold got the idea we wanted to establish bases in the Soviet Union for shuttle-bombing, but there'd never been any foreign command on Russian soil. It was an ambitious plan from the standpoint of getting Russian approval. It was also ambitious to get all the material necessary to establish air bases" (personal interview, August 16, 1978).

Actually, the air mission had three objectives: (1) to establish shuttle-bombing of industrial Germany by providing available bases on which U.S. aircraft could refuel, receive repairs, and rearm; (2) to set up a more effective exchange of weather information, and to ensure that U.S. and USSR signal communications be improved; and (3) to expedite air transport between the United States and the USSR.[3]

Arnold selected Vandenberg to head the air mission. "I had great respect for Vandenberg," Harriman commented. "I knew him before and I was thrilled that he was appointed because I knew he was one of the really top officers of the Air Force. I had asked Arnold to give me one of his good men. Robert Lovett, whom I knew well as a businessman, was Assistant Secretary of War for Air. Lovett and Arnold said Vandenberg couldn't stay long. Vandenberg was a senior officer—he had force—he had ability both as a staff officer and a commanding officer. The Russians would pay attention to an officer with his prestige."

Harriman continued, "Vandenberg did a very good job. He stayed four months instead of the six weeks as initially scheduled. In my talks with Stalin, I got his agreement in principle to establish our air bases. Accordingly, Vandenberg was eagerly involved, along with Deane, in this program for the shuttle bombing. But it was all very difficult and trying. We soon found out that agreement in principle was no agreement at all. Vandenberg got fairly restless . . . there was frustration because of the length of negotiations for the bases; it would be days between meetings. We expected in wartime that they'd make a decision. I don't blame Vandenberg for getting restless. Vandenberg wanted to fight the war. He left as soon as he thought it was right for him to do so. Then we sent in an Air Corps team later that handled the details of the shuttle bases and ran the operation" (personal interview, August 16, 1978).

It was strange to the Americans that they should have to suffer through time-consuming and unnecessary delays when they were simply trying to end the war. The first planes did not land until June 2, 1944. But the perspective of this mission must not be forgotten. We had to be patient. There was always the threat hanging over the United States and Britain that the Soviets would make a separate peace with Germany, just as they had during World War I under a Communist regime.

Vandenberg learned some lessons in this period negotiating with the Soviets; first that "approval in principle" meant nothing. He learned that no subordinate official in the Communist government could make a decision—each had to consult a higher authority, which in the end meant Stalin. And he was forced to be patient with seemingly endless, unnecessary delays in making decisions that could and should have been made in minutes.

He met Soviet officials up through V. M. Molotov, Minister of Foreign Affairs—the equivalent of our Secretary of State. He learned what a Communist dictatorship was like and, in particular, learned of their goal for world conquest.

The Soviets might be slow in the negotiations, but Vandenberg realized that they were not slow in the development of air power. "General Vandenberg's visit to Russia was one of the most enlightening experiences of his career," General Spaatz wrote. "He was impressed by the restless energy of Red technicians and the importance attached to the buildup of Red air power. He gained an understanding of Soviet progress which caused him to call attention repeatedly, both in high councils and in public statements, to the generally unrecognized threat of growing Russian power in the air."[4]

The Soviets gave as their reason for hesitating on the shuttle bases the possibility that foreign aircraft might mistakenly be fired on by their anti-aircraft defenses. "I believe," said Maj. Gen. John R. Deane, "the real reason was that the Russians wished to avoid any precedents which would encourage foreign governments to believe that transit rights over the Soviet Union would be forthcoming in the postwar civil aviation scramble. Regardless of the reason for the Russian attitude, it certainly was not that of a friendly ally."

This was an educational assignment for Vandenberg as one can see from this conclusion of General Deane's, "As far as our future relations with Russia are concerned, I feel that the shuttle-bombing venture will be of value in pointing to the vast difference in the attitude towards Americans that exists between the rank and file of the Russian people and their leaders. Starting with Novikov and Nikitin, the entire staff, and extending down to the women who laid the steel mat for our runways, we encountered nothing but a spirit of friendliness and cooperation. . . . Starting in the other direction and working up through the General Staff, the NKVD, the Foreign Office, and the Party leaders who lurk behind the scenes as Stalin's closest advisers, we found nothing but the desire to sabotage the venture which they had reluctantly approved. Everything was made difficult, including approval of visas, control of communications, selection of targets, and clearances for landings and departures, and in the end we were literally forced out of Russia by restrictions which had become unbearable."[5]

Vandenberg was restless in Moscow, and he was no happier on his return to Washington as Deputy Chief of the Air Staff. The thing he was most anxious for was a combat command. So Arnold sent him to Europe, this time as Commander of the Ninth Air Force.

The Ninth was primarily a tactical air force. Vandenberg had more than 3,000 aircraft under him, and his principal responsibilities were to give close support to Gen. Omar Bradley's ground troops, to provide armed reconnaissance, and to isolate the battlefields by fighter-bomber interdiction. This command rounded out Van's experience in all phases of air power.

The teamwork finally achieved between the Ninth Air Force and Bradley's Twelfth Army Group was described by Bradley in a statement printed in the *New York Times,* on December 16, 1944: "The confidence of our ground men in air support has been firmly established, and now you cannot find a ground commander who will think of an operation without thinking in terms of air as well." But that confidence had not always been there. "Before D-Day, we had little opportunity to train with the Ninth Air Force, and we came in on the beach without as full confidence in air support as we might have wished. But after the breakthrough in Normandy it really began to function, and four or more planes were over every column to take out resistance all the way across France." Bradley went on to say that the "German Army and Air Force in their heyday never had the degree of cooperation that we have. Only through that kind of cooperation were we able to continue the advance."

At the same conference, Vandenberg explained to the newspapermen how a tactical air force does its work. "We are operating a flexible, balanced air force that includes many types of airplanes and the most modern equipment we are able to assemble." He then went on to point out that the ground action was planned with the full understanding of the air officers in staff meetings; the ground people told them what they wanted done; and the Ninth, "after studying the plans, do it wherever feasible and possible. Our techniques and equipment are constantly improving, and we are able to get the job done if we get the flying weather. Although a self-contained functioning military arm with many branches, we fit into the picture as an integral part of the war machine."

Vandenberg won high marks from the Army. One officer said, "While I was on the staff of an Army Corps I ran into several staff officers who served with General Patton, and they were most enthusiastic about General Van and the Ninth Air Force for the support given General Patton's ground forces. They were most impressed by Vandenberg's ability to understand and appreciate the problems and tactics of the ground forces and by the way the two services cooperated and accomplished their missions" (Galloway, personal communication, December 23, 1963).

Usually the only pilots to receive public recognition were those who shot down enemy planes and became aces. To right the balance, Vandenberg established an award known as "Busters"—specialists who had harassed the Nazis by destroying bridges, locomotives, buildings, tunnels, and trains. In announcing the honors, he commented, "By the nature of tactical air power, which attacks dozens of targets simultaneously . . . our daily operations are reported in an impersonal and statistical fashion. However, tactical air power's total effect rests squarely on the personal skill and achievements of individual pilots in destroying enemy material and snarling communication systems.

"That effort is just as real and worthy of special recognition as the skill involved in shooting down enemy planes. The personal achievements of these nine pilots [receiving the award that day] reflect the initiative and the battle wisdom of all of our tactical airmen, who have learned how to knock out ground force material which is of the utmost value to the enemy." Vandenberg noted that while the fighter-bomber pilots, who concentrated on ground targets, were exposed to ground fire, they would seldom meet German planes, but he emphasized that "their job is just as exciting as that of the high-scoring pilots." This statement appeared in the March 25, 1945, issue of the *New York Times*.

At the end of World War II, Vandenberg's career took a new turn when he was made Chief of Army Intelligence. The importance of this appointment was stressed by President Harry Truman who, exasperated by the undigested mass of intelligence reports from the Army, Navy, and State Departments that were flooding across his desk, established by executive directive a Central Intelligence Group (CIG) on January 22, 1946. One of the first duties of the CIG was, of course, to coordinate a daily Intelligence bulletin for the President, and Vandenberg was the ideal choice to enforce the reports from the Army. He had been outspoken in his belief that our sources of Intelligence must be greatly strengthened. "In my opinion," he said, "the vital importance of effective military intelligence is not generally understood. Our first line of defense is neither the Navy nor the Air Force, but Intelligence. If another war comes, it will be almost without warning. A 'sneak attack' might end the show. Without a military intelligence organization that is alert, tireless, and directed with purpose and strength, another 'Pearl Harbor' might be our last." Vandenberg set up the framework for training Intelligence officers in Washington, and he planned to expand the schooling of Intelligence at the reorganized Command and Staff College at Fort Leavenworth, Kansas, which was done in September 1946. He was determined to develop an Intelligence system, equal to, if not superior, to those famous and highly active systems of the British and the Soviets.

As Chief of Army Intelligence, he realized that two factors were necessary: money and trust. "We will need a large operating sum," said Vandenberg, "and I don't think the amount should be revealed. And we will need almost a blank check in trust. I mean that if the authorities responsible for the expenditure of public funds are convinced of this nation's need to know what is going on in the world, they should give us the funds we need and trust us to do the job without a public accounting of what we are doing.

"Obviously, if military intelligence is to be effective we cannot publish our actions for the world to read. The British, whose intelligence work has been superb and a model for us, do not do it. Neither do the Russians.

"It is a popular misconception, that a military intelligence system should be based on the Army's numerical strength. In time of war we are certain who are our allies and who are our enemies, and we can amplify our intelligence with that of our allies. In peacetime, deprived of the assistance of allied intelligence, it is necessary for us to provide complete global coverage in order that we may be certain to determine the war-making potentiality of any possible enemy."

He also made it quite clear that he favored what was later named the Central Intelligence Agency (CIA), which in time would replace the CIG, linking together the combined intelligence activities of the Army, Navy, and State Department.

The individual Truman selected to head CIG was Adm. Sidney Souers, a very successful businessman in St. Louis before World War II, described as "the only man around President Truman who didn't want anything for himself—except to go home." One of the early members of the CIG said of Souers, "He was the only person who really everybody could agree on. He wanted to get home as soon as possible, to start to recover his business. He picked Van or recommended Van as his successor, which commended itself to President Truman because of the man General Van called 'Unc,' who was, of course, Senator Arthur Vandenberg. I think President Truman thought it might be useful for him to have a director who had something to do with Capitol Hill and who at least couldn't hurt him there" (Walter L. Pforzheimer, personal communication, July 25, 1978).

"Having agreed to serve as the Director of the Central Intelligence Group only until the Agency learned to walk," suggested a news commentator for *Newsweek,* "Souers at once began casting about for a successor against the time he would return to his St. Louis business affairs. Within four months, he found his man. Vandenberg, home from the wars, had been named to Souers' advisory staff. Checking into his record, Souers found three traits required by the job. Vandenberg had proved his fearlessness in numerous combat flights; he had inspired an almost legendary loyalty among his men; his talent for intelligence had been demonstrated. Although not a brilliant military student, Vandenberg, throughout his Army career, had one high mark in leadership. He had a reputation for discussion."[6]

There was a humorous note in the choice of Vandenberg, this journalist remarked: "When the movies get around to making atomic-age espionage thrillers, they will have trouble finding an actor to play the part of Lt. Gen. Hoyt S. Vandenberg, Director of Central Intelligence, U.S. Government top cloak-and-dagger agency. Actors don't come handsome enough. The real Vandenberg has bat wing shoulders, a 30-inch waist, and just the right touch of gray at the temples for his forty-seven years."[7]

Vandenberg's leadership changed the current attitude toward intelligence activities. He made it very clear to a congressional committee that we must get over the feeling that there is something "un-American about espionage and even about intelligence generally." He pointed out that in the last war we were handicapped by our unpreparedness and that as a result "for months we had to rely blindly and trustingly upon the superior intelligence system of the British." Although our trust in the British was certainly well placed, it must be understood that in the future, "the interest of others may not be our interest" and that we have a great need to become "self-sufficient." This statement appeared in the May 2, 1946, issue of the *New York Times.*

When Vandenberg took over, there were real problems: difficulties with funding, wrangling with the State Department, and inevitable differences with the Army and Navy. The CIG did not really have the authority to hire and fire; they could not even make firm promises on longevity to those hired. This simply was not the organization to serve the needs of U.S. Intelligence. "Vandenberg had, right from the start, the definite concept of a central agency which would produce intelligence and not just coordinate other people's. Soon after Vandenberg came, he called me," said Lawrence Houston, a CIG member, "and said, 'I think we need legislation [without legislation, the CIG would end one year after President Truman's executive order] and I'd like it by next Monday.' After he looked at my first draft," reflected Larry Houston, "he was bothered by its length and by all sorts of little things that were in it. The draft was revised and shortened to meet his approval. General Vandenberg then said, 'You go down with Jimmy Lane and clear this legislation with Clark Clifford.' So we took it down, Clifford read through it and then he gave a long whistle. He said, 'I thought you boys were supposed to be sort of just a coordinating unit. This is a real operating entity.' I said, 'That's exactly the change we're trying to make in Admiral Souer's concept. General Vandenberg has given his okay on it.' So in effect that was our clearance with the White House on the legislation" (personal interview, July 25, 1978).

Vandenberg made a lasting impact on the U.S. Intelligence organization during his ten months with the CIA. He both gave and learned a great deal. It was an opportunity to gain a deeper understanding of the political realities, and of our need to develop a sensitive, vigilant agency, which the old Army had neglected. Added to his experience in Moscow, this was all extremely helpful to him when he became Chief of Staff of the Air Force. As Chief of Staff, his responsibilities required that he have an alert understanding of what other nations were doing with air power. He also had to edit a daily bulletin that contained the significant intelligence gathered over the previous twenty-four hours, with his detailed analysis of its significance,

quite often presenting this in person to President Truman. It was a significant part of his education in the CIA.

In the latter part of July 1947, President Truman signed legislation that
established a separate air force. For forty years, it had been attached to the
Army as part of the Signal Corps. At the anniversary banquet, Vandenberg
spelled out his philosophy as one of the Air Force leaders: "We are a young
organization. It behooves us to buckle down and develop a compact, highly
efficient, well-organized and fully trained arm of the service. We intend to
concentrate on an air force immediately ready for action. . . . To all of us
who know that air power is peace power, the fifth decade upon which the
Air Force now embarks holds the opportunity to justify the faith we have all
had through the years."

When the separate Air Force was formed, W. Stuart Symington was
selected as the first Secretary for Air. General Carl Spaatz became the first
Chief of Staff and his Vice Chief of Staff was General Vandenberg,
appointed on October 1, 1947, and promoted to the rank of four-star
general. He was only forty-eight, the youngest four-star general then on
active duty.

When Spaatz retired, Vandenberg moved up to Chief of Staff. Not only
did Spaatz help select his successor, but it was quite clear that he had begun
grooming Vandenberg for the position as soon as he himself became Chief
of Staff. General Norstad was asked to comment on Spaatz's desire to have
Vandenberg succeed him. "Spaatz," said Norstad, "had such stature that
whatever he recommended at that time would certainly have been accepted,
but General Spaatz would have told you of the many discussions that Secretary Symington had with him and with me, and sometimes with others
about this. There were some very strong contenders, particularly the late
George Kenney and McNarney, who were great people who had to be considered. You couldn't really pick somebody, you had specifically to
eliminate some people before you could pick someone else. . . . But it is true
that Spaatz favored Vandenberg and one reason is [that] Van had worked
with Spaatz on the Air Staff when Tooey was the Chief of Staff to Arnold,
at the beginning of the war. I've forgotten the name of the job then, but
Van was really in operations and training. . . .

"While the discussion was going on of Van as a possible successor to
General Spaatz, I remember a conversation among Stuart Symington,
myself and General Spaatz when Symington made the comment, 'I'll start
talking to the President about Van.' I think that I was the one who suggested that one of the first things to be done would be to get him out as head
of the CIA. If something were to slip and go wrong, which is so easy over
there, then General Vandenberg would be ruined, he'd be through. So we

had to get him out. . . . Symington said he would arrange the replacement of General Vandenberg with the White House. Shortly after that, Van came back as Vice Chief of Staff for Tooey. General Vandenberg took over from Ira Eaker. You can't let a man make mistakes, nor get caught with somebody else's mistakes because he might be destroyed" (personal communication, August 22, 1977).

Spaatz had made it clear after accepting the position that he didn't intend to hold the job as Chief of Staff very long. "There was some general conversation on the subject among all of us," said one of the senior Air Force generals, Laurence S. Kuter. "Van had not been the obvious choice. On the other hand, there was no consensus of objection of any sort either. It seemed reasonable, it seemed natural" (personal interview, July 8, 1978).

An insight into General Vandenberg's selection was provided by one of his closest associates, Lieutenant General Craigie: "Van, as he grew older, had had good success in the various assignments that he had, and this success impressed him enough so that he realized he had ability. I believe he had some misgivings about himself earlier, which, I think is one of the reasons why he was always afraid of check rides. He did not have the confidence early that he later developed in himself, but he did very well at the tactical school because Van was able to talk easily and he made a good impression. I think he impressed his associates and that he gradually built up confidence in himself, and at the same time, he was impressing the people who were above him. They would say, now here's somebody with a real future, so Van was given an opportunity, and when he was given these assignments, he came through" (personal interview, February 8, 1977).

Some, less kind and less objective about the reason for Vandenberg's selection, at each promotion of Vandenberg's, referred to him as the nephew of U.S. Senator Arthur H. Vandenberg. After Vandenberg's selection as Air Force Chief of Staff, an article in *Newsweek* made the fairest statement, "Washington is a city of cynics, skeptics, and plain old-fashioned wiseacres; and in Washington there are a good many people who have acidulous doubts about Hoyt S. Vandenberg's ability. He's the nephew of Republican Senator from Michigan Arthur H. Vandenberg, for one thing; and he's too good-looking.

"These may not seem very cogent criticisms on Main Street, U.S.A., but no one will ever convince the Washington know-it-all's first, that Vandenberg doesn't owe his job to his uncle's influence, and second, that anyone as handsome as Vandenberg could have brains.

"The facts, however, belie the critics; Vandenberg was made Air Force Chief of Staff in spite of his uncle, not because of him. The Senator never made any attempt to push his nephew along because he was convinced the

Pentagon brass would bend over backward to avoid the appearance of yielding to pressure, particularly from a Republican."[8]

It is clear that Hoyt was his uncle's favorite nephew and equally clear Vandenberg wanted to go his way without any assistance from his influential uncle. On one occasion, the Senator visited Lieutenant Vandenberg when he was stationed at Fort Crockett prior to World War II. Vandenberg introduced him to his commanding officer, simply as "My uncle, Mr. Vandenberg." "I immediately recognized the Senator," recalled Joseph H. Davidson. "We chatted a few minutes and then they left. Shortly thereafter Lieutenant Vandenberg was back in my office and asked me not to tell anyone that his uncle was a Senator."[9]

After the war, when Vandenberg was concentrating on Intelligence, he did call on his uncle for advice. "Let me give you another sidelight," reflected his legislative officer, Walter Pforzheimer of the CIG. "General Vandenberg had left Washington a lieutenant colonel in effect, and in effect he came back a lieutenant general. Somewhere up there was something called Capitol Hill and the Congress. He did not have much experience with them, except with the mysterious man called 'Uncle.' Once in a while, General Vandenberg would come up against a problem, he'd say, 'I think we ought to go up and talk to "Unc" about that.' We would drive up to Capitol Hill. Why I went along I don't know, because I sat in the outer room. I never got into a meeting with 'Unc' when he went to talk to Senator Vandenberg. He'd come out and say, 'Come on, let's go home.' That's all that ever happened. Once in a while, he might say, well, the Senator suggested maybe we do this or that, particularly with the fighting over the National Security Act of 1947" (personal communication, July 25, 1978).

The challenge for the new Chief of Staff was almost overwhelming as Vandenberg disclosed in an article he wrote in 1951. "After the surrender of Japan, the AAF shrank rapidly from its wartime peak of 2,400,000 men and officers and 80,000 planes to a low point (in May 1947) of 303,614 military personnel. Hasty demobilization weakened the training facilities of the Air Force and reduced it to such a low state of operational efficiency that there was a deep concern for its capability."[10] Equally important, the aircraft crew personnel decreased from a high of 413,890 at the end of World War II to only 24,079 when Vandenberg succeeded Spaatz. Even more disturbing, the Air Force supposedly had 52 wings in 1948, but some believed that only two wings out of the 52 were combat-ready.

In a speech before the annual convention of the American Legion in Miami, Florida, printed in the *New York Times* on October 22, 1948, Vandenberg acknowledged that the superb fighting force of 1944–45 "is no more." But he affirmed that "we now are on the way back to recapture our position as a truly great air force. This time we are growing for peace and not for war, and it is practically the unanimous opinion of those who know war that the seventy-group Air Force equipped with modern planes at top strength will be our best investment for peace and our strongest insurance against war.''

Vandenberg had to fight hard for the needs of the Air Force in the early years of the cold war. But he was also realistic. In a speech after the House had approved the seventy-group Air Force, printed in the *New York Times* on April 16, 1948, he made it very clear that such a program could not be carried out speedily and that a new buildup would require six or seven years. "Once the wheels stopped turning in World War II," said Vandenberg, "the reduction of the Air Force and stagnation of the aviation industry began. And now the empty factories cannot be refilled overnight."

Our inadequacy became very apparent in the Korean conflict. At a congressional hearing, Vandenberg made the alarming statement that our Air Force was so weak that we could not undertake operations against the Manchurian bases and still be ready to fight a major war with the Soviet Union. "We cannot do both," he said, "because we have a shoestring air force."[11]

The lesson learned in Korea developed a sense of urgency, even of desperation, in Vandenberg. As was so often the case in the history of this country, as soon as there was peace, anxiety diminished and there was an effort to reduce the Air Force budget by $5.1 billion. Vandenberg vigorously opposed such a drastic reduction; he said it would endanger this country. He emphasized that if the free world was to survive, or the United States was to fight a major war, it must have an air force that is second to none";[12] "air power is no longer a faith—it is a fact. The problem is not whether air power is real, but whether we shall be its masters or its victims." He stated, "The potential power of the U.S. Air Force is not only our first line of defense, it is the greatest single factor in keeping the peace."[13]

General Norstad was frank in his opinion: "Even though Tooey was the first Chief of Staff of the separate Air Force, Van was the one who really had to establish the Air Force as a new service. I can remember we had long discussions on how to approach this, and I think that this is an important point. It was decided that in the Chiefs of Staff, for instance, we had to establish ourselves within the Joint Chiefs of Staff. We had to take positions on behalf of the Air Force, strong positions, based upon principle, and we would always have to fight for and stick to these principles. We would never quibble. So we worked like hell, and we mastered the papers that we presented and developed the positions to the Joint Chiefs. I had to write many of these papers, and I went down with General Vandenberg to the meeting of the Joint Chiefs, and we did quite well in those days. We obtained some good positions through old man [Admiral] Leahy, who had no love for our shade of blue uniform and God knows he had no great love for younger people. One time we put in something and General Bradley, who did support us generally, criticized us, and old man Leahy turned and he said, 'Brad, I see the basis of your comment, but I must tell you that I've learned to think twice before I criticize the younger people in the Air Force. They do their work, they've got a good record of being right!' That from an old turtle is quite important" (personal interview, August 22, 1977).

One of the most important decisions Vandenberg made was to give primary emphasis to strategic air power as the essential force for the defense of the United States and the free world. Vital to this decision was his selection of Curtis E. LeMay in 1948 as the Commander of the Strategic Air Command (SAC) to succeed General George Kenney. History has proven that a wise choice. Vandenberg stated publicly, "In my opinion General LeMay has had more experience than any other man in the world today in strategic bombing. I think he probably has more competence in that particular phase than any man alive."[14]

This emphasis on strategic bombing was not an easy decision to stand on. There was disagreement within the Air Force on such a heavy emphasis on SAC. After the Korean War began, some complained about the performance of the Air Force in supporting ground troops. Vandenberg's critics accused him of neglecting tactical aviation. SAC supporters dismissed these charges by pointing to Vandenberg's record before and during World War II as a member of the tactical air team. Actually, however, as Vandenberg explained, his concern was the defense of the United States, but he did not believe that air defense alone, in the narrow sense, could accomplish this. He cited the Battle of Britain and the experience of the Luftwaffe in World War II as proof that defending fighters can stop only a relatively small percentage of attacking bombers. When the enemy is carrying atomic bombs, every air attack can result in holocaust.[15] Vandenberg felt that the way to counter the enemy's strategic air power was not only with interceptors but with our own strategic air power—by destroying the enemy's ability to strike at U.S. industry.

Although Vandenberg believed strongly in strategic air power, in a speech made before the American Legion's thirteenth National Aerial Round-Up banquet, published in the *New York Times* on May 2, 1949, he emphasized the fact that strategic bombing was not the only way to defend world freedom, nor was the Air Force the only service. He did not believe that a large fleet of the long-range B-36 strategic bombers, the largest and most up-to-date bombers at that time, carrying atomic bombs, could win a war without the assistance of the other services. He stressed that American strategic air power was "Primarily a deterrent to war and a means of quick retaliation against aggressors," and, he continued, "If conflict were forced upon us, our strategic [bomber] force would pass from the role of deterrent to that of heavy retaliation. Our insurance against defeat and our hope of future victory would depend in large measure upon the effectiveness of this attack." He then said that the B-36 was "by no means the solution to all our security problems. The Air Force has never held that this airplane is a suitable basket for all our eggs." He closed his talk with the statement: "References to strategic bombers as evidence of 'Maginot-Line psychology' are difficult to understand. All military planners recognize that there are certain purposes bombers can accomplish and certain purposes they cannot accomplish."

"Destroying the enemy's homeland from the air might not be enough," he said in another speech, published in the *New York Times* on April 6, 1946. "We need ground troops in Europe sufficient to force the enemy to use their stockpile of war material . . . we are the only nation equipped and able to furnish the strategic air efforts to destroy the enemy's war-making potential. And, today, we also have to supply the tactical aviation. It is my hope that eventually the nations now building new armies will eventually be able to furnish a great portion of their own tactical air."

Before Vandenberg became Chief of Staff, the defense money was apportioned among the services, and the idea of a "balanced force" was one in which equal sums of money were spent by the Army, the Navy, and the Air Force. Military leaders felt that if the respective services could not receive the necessary funds in order to accomplish the mission as they saw it, then the only thing to do was to divide what money was available equally among the three services.

In an unprecedented speech for the Air Force Association in Los Angeles in the fall of 1950, Vandenberg urged that the defense dollar should be distributed in accordance with the expected value to national security. Under his leadership there was a departure from the standard policy that each of the three military services received one-third of the budget for defense. The turning point came in 1951 with the approval for the forthcoming budget of 1953 allocating $22 billion to the Air Force, $14 billion to the Army, and $13 billion to the Navy. Vandenberg defended this new policy. "The Air Force recognizes that air superiority over enemy nations cannot alone win a war, though loss of air superiority could lose it. Total victory in modern war is a product of ground, air, and sea power. Nothing can be gained, everything will be lost, if one component is sacrificed to such a point that it is unable to contribute to the big objective. We are building the Air Force as rapidly as possible without sacrificing the integrity of our already existing forces. Because we refuse to weaken these hard-core combat-ready units, our ability to effect an immediate increase in total strength is limited: ninety-five wings is about all we can achieve in fiscal 1951 and 1952. Obviously, however, if the world situation continues to worsen, ninety-five wings isn't enough.''[16]

But there had been grumblings of discontent from the senior services. In April 1949, an anonymous letter was circulated to congressmen, senators, industrial leaders, and the press, accusing Floyd B. Odlum, president of the Atlas Corporation, a holding company that included as a subsidiary the company that manufactured the B-36, of being "unscrupulous." It charged that Odlum had made substantial contributions to the Democratic campaign amounting to "very large sums, ranging up to the extraordinary figure of $6.5 million" for the alleged purpose of influencing aircraft contracts for the benefit of his corporation. It further stated that Air Force Secretary Stuart Symington and Odlum "have been much in each other's company. The log of Mr. Symington's plane . . . shows frequent trips between Washington and Palm Springs, allegedly to visit with Mr. Odlum. . . . that on one occasion this year Symington and General Vandenberg spent a week at Odlum's ranch in California."

The letter further suggested that the Air Force and its leaders had lied about the capabilities of the B-36 and that even some members of the Air Force were not convinced that it could perform its stated mission. There were many other allegations, implying corruption, incompetence, and payoffs.

In May 1949, Congressman James E. Van Zandt, Republican from Pennsylvania, in a speech to the House, cited this anonymous letter with further insinuations about Secretary Symington, Air Force high command, and its civilian counterparts. These allegations led to a prompt investigation by the House Armed Services Committee, which was chaired by Congressman Carl Vinson, Democrat from Georgia.

Much more was involved than the utility of the B-36. At the heart of the investigation that began in early August was the vexing question of the balance in our military establishment. At issue was the gravity of strategic bombing and the high priority it received. Was there too much attention to the long-range heavy bomber, which carried the atomic bomb great distances, but not enough attention to medium-range attack bombers, fighter bombers, and fighters? Equally controversial was the Navy's tactical air power and its fleet carriers of the size of *Midway* and *Essex,* which had been reduced from eleven ships to eight. Were more cuts contemplated?

The Army was unhappy about the tactical support given to their ground forces. Gen. Jacob Devers, who commanded the Army Field Forces, and other Army officers, believed there might be a greater need for tactical air power in the event that atomic weapons were outlawed, just as poisonous gas was outlawed in World War I.

Secretary Symington took complete responsibility for the entire B-36 bomber program. In very vigorous language, he answered the attacks made on him, the Air Force leadership, and the B-36. In his testimony before Congress, he stated positively that the B-36 had lived up to its predicted capabilities; it had flown more than 10,000 miles, carrying a 10,000-pound bomb load, and that, midway through its 10,000-mile trip, had dropped its bomb load and returned to its destination.

He also emphasized that, with only so much money to go around, the B-36 required an Air Force sacrifice, as it did of other services, because there would be less money for other bombers and for tactical, cargo, and reconnaissance aircraft.

Symington's 32-page statement categorically denied the fifteen allusions to his personal character made in Van Zandt's speech and denied the smirching of Vandenberg and other Air Force leaders. And he demanded that whoever was responsible for the anonymous charges be revealed.

The anonymous letter had actually been written by Cedric R. Worth, formerly special assistant to the Assistant Secretary of Navy for Air and later to the Under Secretary of the Navy. When the investigation determined that he was the author of the letter, he was suspended from his employment by the Navy Department. The essence of the congressional finding was the committee's conclusion that the anonymous letter contained not "one iota, not one scintilla of evidence . . . that would support charges that collusion, fraud, corruption, influence or favoritism played any part whatsoever in the procurement of the B-36 bomber. There has been very substantial and compelling evidence that the Air Force procured this bomber solely on the ground that this is the best aircraft for its purpose available to the nation."

The guilty Worth stated that the Navy admirals had no part in his anonymous letter, but the controversy did not end with that denial, because the fight was continued by the Navy admirals. On October 19, 1949, General of the Army Omar N. Bradley, Chairman of the Joint Chiefs of Staff, openly rebuked the Navy's complaining admirals and accused them of being in "open rebellion against civil authority" and of doing "infinite harm to the United States and its world position." He referred to them, some of whom were sitting there during his statement in silent anger, as "Fancy Dans," who owed a public retraction of the allegations that they had made against high military policy and Secretary of Defense Louis Johnson. The admirals had complained of low morale in the Navy. Bradley commented that if morale was low in the Navy it was because the Navy leaders did not "realize that the esprit of men is but the mirror of their confidence in their leadership."

Bradley pointed out that Pearl Harbor might well have been averted by complete understanding, cooperation, and trust among the armed services. He emphasized that that "fatal day" and the lessons since "should have taught all military men that our forces are one team—and the game to win regardless of who carries the ball. This is not [the] time for 'Fancy Dans' who won't hit the line with all they have in every play unless they can call the signals. Each player on this team—whether he shines in the spotlight of the backfield or eats dirt in the line—must be an all-American team." Bradley went on to say "that there must have been something seriously wrong in our military establishment, and that this wrong lay in the attitude of the Navy, which had opposed unification of the services from the beginning and has not yet accepted it 'in spirit.' "

Then Vandenberg had his opportunity to comment on the Navy's position. He made it quite clear that the Navy had caused dangerous disclosures to be "spread before those who would destroy us," and he suggested that Congress decide how much freedom with "classified information should be given to military officers." Vandenberg said that the disclosures by the Navy and the fact of the hearing itself were an "extraordinary episode" that "had shaken the military establishment." To answer once and for all the Navy's argument about the $1 billion allocated to the B-36 as being of no value as a national weapon, Vandenberg said:

"You have heard recommendations that we place less emphasis on strategic bombing and devote more resources to tactical aviation—fighters, fighter bombers, and light bombers. If we should decide to make this change, here are the things we give up. First we would give up the deterrent value of this country's atomic weapons, and we would place ourselves in disagreement with all those people on both sides of the ocean who believe that Soviet aggression is in fact now being deterred.

Second, we would inform the Russians that they need now take no defensive measures against a possible atomic attack on their heartland. . . .

Third, if war is forced upon us, the proposal deprives us of the opportunity of checking off enemy war-making power at its source (in Congressional Testimony at Investigation of B-36 Bomber Program, 81st Congress, 1949: Washington, D.C., GPO).

In summing up, Bradley protested against the "insinuations" that the Army and Air Force representatives stood together against the Navy in "an old school tie" arrangement and "outvoted" the Navy. "This suggestion

. . . is hard to answer patiently. It indicates that we would prefer to build up the other two services at the expense of our entire security." He said that the Navy had so often been outvoted in the Joint Chiefs of Staff because Navy officers were still preoccupied with past "island-hopping" campaigns and sometimes showed "no conception" of big continental operations such as war with Russia would involve. Bradley added, "There has been a continuing undercurrent and an occasional specific outburst of the insinuation that those responsible for war planning—the Joint Chiefs of Staff—are ignorant as to how war should be carried on.

"Even if I were not personally involved, I would harbor a distaste for such lack of loyalty and for the unfounded insinuation about men who have earned their way on record in accomplishment to positions of great national responsibility.

"In my opinion, the Armed Forces have a very big and very important job to do and should get on with it."

The essence of Vandenberg's military philosophy was his response to those who argued that strategic bombing could be stopped by locating the bombers with radar and by then proceeding to shoot them down with jet fighters and guided missiles:

> The people who have said these things seem not to realize that the B-36s, B-47s, and B-50s by merely existing can and do force the Soviet Union to channel the industrial power, technological skill, manpower, and money into purely defensive measures and thus cut down resources which could otherwise be devoted to offensive purposes.
>
> And what is the alternative?
>
> It is this: Tactical aviation supports ground troops and ground divisions. It is proposed that we build and maintain a standing army capable of meeting the masses of any enemy army on the ground in equal man to man, body to body, gun to gun combat.
>
> This alternative offers us the prospect of a wholly defensive war. We wait until we are attacked. Then we undertake to hold the masses of enemy troops on the ground. Finally, if we seek victory, we undertake to provide the ground force power to press the enemy back into his homeland until he gives up—and in this we might be following the fairly unattractive example of Napoleon and Hitler.
>
> Mr. Chairman, this alternative is militarily unsound. A prime objective of this country must be to find a counterbalance

to the potential enemy's masses of ground troops other than equal masses of Americans and, allied ground troops. No such balancing factor exists other than strategic bombing, including the atomic bomb.

Vandenberg squarely addressed the issue of Navy aircraft carriers: "First, I'm not only willing but insistent that the types of carriers which can help meet the threat of the enemy submarine fleet shall be developed fully and kept in instant readiness. The sea lanes must be kept open. . . .

"I do not believe that there is justification for maintaining large carrier task forces during peace time unless they are required by the strategic plans of the Joint Chiefs of Staff. In my judgment, they are not required by those plans."

The B-36 investigation was the climax of years of built-up frustrations within the Navy brass, who were not pleased with the mission assigned to the Air Force and, more particularly, the larger allocation of scarce dollars to the Air Force. Then, on April 23, 1949, Secretary of Defense Louis Johnson canceled the Navy's new aircraft carrier. The Navy believed in the role of the aircraft carrier and challenged the very basis of strategic bombing. The Air Force believed that the new $188-million carrier the Navy wanted was unnecessary. The Air Force won the day and the Navy, dedicated as it was to its mission, was a bad loser.

The false allegations by Congressman Van Zandt, based primarily on newspaper clippings and rumors, were insulting. Actually, the Air Force showed remarkable restraint over the whole issue when one considers how ugly and vicious the charges were. The Air Force not only won the role it thought appropriate for the best defense of our country, but the incident actually served as a forum for the discussion of the mission of air power that reached out into the thinking of people all over the country. They were made more aware of air power in the defense of our country and the free world.

An officer who was extremely close to Vandenberg, Brig. Gen. Noel F. Parrish, commented, "Strictly realistic, Van abhorred exaggeration and fanaticism. When tactical Air Force planners demanded he speak out on how 'Operation Strangle' in Korea would starve out Chinese armies in weeks, he replied, 'From Italy we closed the Brenner Pass every day. The Germans opened it every night.' Once I wrote in a position paper for him that a tactical air base could launch more planes than an aircraft carrier.

" 'How many planes in a tactical wing?'

" 'Seventy-five.'

" 'How many on a super-carrier?'

" 'One hundred twenty-five—but etc.'

" 'Never mind the explanations. My statement may be challenged when I am not there to explain. Never leave me on a limb. The case for air power is good enough without compromising it by stretching. Stick to the cold facts.' Needless to say, he got no more warmed-over facts from me, and few from anybody."

One of the first decisions Vandenberg made as Air Force Chief of Staff, and an example of his tendency to delegate authority, was the necessity of retiring some thirty officers of the rank of brigadier general or higher. He called in his Deputy Chief of Staff of Personnel, Lt. Gen. Nathan F. Twining, and instructed him to proceed with the retirement of these thirty generals. Gen. Lauris Norstad was also involved in the incident: "I was in the midst of that because I was Vice Chief of Staff for Van at that time. I remember very well our discussions and our decision that some of the older colonels, particularly people who were holding temporary general rank, should retire because there was no proper place for them to go. I remember going over with Van the list of these people and there was the case of one man, who was a very good friend of mine, an old-timer, who had done great things in the Air Force. General Vandenberg decided that he would either have to retire or be reduced in rank because he would never get another assignment which called for the rank that he held. I can remember saying, 'Van, he's a friend of yours and you've known him longer than anybody. You're the Chief so you owe it to him to call him in and talk to him, and he'll understand it from you and take it.' And I can remember Van looking at me with those big eyes and saying, 'Yes, I'm the Chief, but you help the Chief, you work with the Chief, so help me out, and you talk to him' " (personal interview, August 22, 1977).

Norstad was asked whether each of these men was given the courtesy of being called in for a private talk. "Oh yes," he replied, "that was the case. I had to do it with many of them, Van called many of them in and discussed it with them, and General Twining did some of them as well" (personal communication, August 22, 1977).

Vandenberg was very effective in backing up his people. "I had normal contact with him as Chief with regard to the Berlin airlift," related Gen. Laurence S. Kuter, then Commander of Military Air Transport (MATS). "MATS was responsible for all the maintenance, for all the training crews, replacement of all personnel. Van's instructions to me were to 'go to it. If there are any Air Force resources you have trouble getting, call me.'

"We had a newly published policy," remembered Kuter, "that related to new legislation which specified the conditions under which senior officers would retire. It's still unchanged, I believe. There was a point at issue on this policy where a brigadier general who was not promoted to major general would be retired after thirty years' service if he had been a brigadier general for five years. Once the policy was established, you couldn't draw a line, it had to be firm. You couldn't make it case by case. Nobody but God could do that, and I'm not so sure that he always got it right.

"In Massachusetts we had an electronics laboratory," he continued, "an important one, with a brigadier general commanding it. He was good, and he didn't want to be retired when his thirty years were up, and he had not been promoted to major general.

"This brigadier general's age," said Kuter, "was fifty-two at that time, I think. He went to elaborate political channels to upset our policy. He took his case to that famous Senator from Massachusetts named Kennedy and to a former Mayor of Boston, named Curley; they may have even had the President in, I don't know. They certainly had Secretary Johnson, who was a political politician. Secretary Johnson had working for him Anna Rosenberg, who we won't go into much detail about. She was the Deputy Secretary of Defense for Personnel. She called me in and told me that I just couldn't retire this man, he's only fifty-two and he looked good to her. They liked him in Boston, anyway. I said, yes, he was only fifty-two. He was able, he was competent, or he wouldn't have been a brigadier general. We had a policy, however, and we had a tier of colonels and under them a bigger tier of lieutenant colonels who all had promise of being electronic experts. If we kept this fellow on in violation of the policy, that meant there would be no promotion at that point, and we were already losing some of these brilliant youngsters, and we could not afford to lose them. So logic said we had to adhere to the policy. She said, 'Yes, I heard that. Now you write him a letter that he will not be retired.' 'Not while I'm Assistant Chief of Staff [for] Personnel,' I replied. She said, 'Well, I'll fix that too,' and called in General Vandenberg, who took my position. She was going to fix Van by calling in Tom Finletter, who was then Secretary of the Air Force. Tom weaseled on it a bit, said he'd talk to me and have to do some investigating. He talked to me and, bless his heart, he backed me up. The policy stood. This able fellow was retired, and for the rest of my duty, as a matter of fact, I'm sure for many years there was never a deviation from that policy" (personal interview, July 8, 1978).

General McKee served as Deputy Vice Chief of Staff under General Spaatz and continued in that position after Vandenberg succeeded Spaatz in 1948. McKee was asked why, in his opinion, Vandenberg was outstanding as a leader. "General Vandenberg," he said, "was very much like Spaatz and very much like Arnold. They both had a tremendous personality. Secondly, Vandenberg was a real professional in the flying business, and a real leader in terms of knowing how to handle people and also in evaluating people. His whole background in the Air Force was a flying career, although he was certainly a professional as a commander and a staff officer as well. When Vandenberg was announced as Chief of Staff before General Spaatz left, there was a great deal of thought and searching as to who would be the Vice Chief of Staff. General Vandenberg came over to me at a party at Bolling Air Force Base the evening the announcement was made. He sat down beside me and said, 'Bozo, what would you think of Sandy Fairchild down at Air University being Vice Chief?'

"I said, 'I don't think you could do better,' because I felt General Fairchild was one of the brightest men the Air Force had. A couple of days later, Vandenberg came to my office, and said he put Sandy Fairchild in for his third star to make him Vice Chief.

" 'Well,' Van said, 'he's a major general, and he can't be jumping from a major general to a four-star general.'

"I said, 'Why in the hell not? He's going to have the responsibility, let's give him the tools to do the job. If you don't trust him, then hell don't make him Vice Chief of Staff.'

"General Vandenberg replied, 'I agree with you, but General Spaatz would never go for that.'

"I said, 'I'll bet you he will.'

"He said, 'OK, you call him and see if you can get him to do it.'

"General Spaatz was on leave. I got him wherever he was and he said, 'Bozo, I couldn't agree with you more. Put him in for four stars right now.'

"But Vandenberg was that kind of guy. He just didn't think General Spaatz would go along with it, and I thought he would so he said OK, 'Bozo, you go ahead and do it' " (personal interview, July 6, 1977).

Gen. Robert E. Lee worked closely with Vandenberg when he was Chief of Staff, serving in the capacity of Plans officer. He had also been very closely associated with Vandenberg when the latter commanded the Ninth Air Force during World War II. "I wasn't a yes man," said Lee. "I probably knew more about air support than General Vandenberg did because I had been in the business of air support all of my life. General Vandenberg told me on a couple of occasions that he appreciated the fact that I would say what I thought on things." He then went on to give an example of how he continued this when he served on the Air Staff after Vandenberg had become Chief of Staff. "General Vandenberg was looking for an officer to fill a three-star position on the Joint Chiefs of Staff, and to serve as a liaison officer to the National Security Council. General Vandenberg told me during one of our conversations that I'd better start looking for an Air Force general to take this position, since it was presently filled by a Navy admiral, but it soon was going to be the Air Force's turn for this job. The job rotated among the Army, Navy, and Air Force. So I went down to General Laurence S. Kuter, who was Deputy Chief of Staff for Personnel. He had a list of all of the general officers who were assigned throughout the world on a wall in an office adjoining his office. He and I discussed this matter, and we had several candidates, most of them men who had the rank of major general, since it was the normal policy to pick out a man who would be promoted into the job. So we decided upon an individual. I went down to see General Vandenberg and I suggested the individual who I had decided upon in conjunction with General Kuter. He said, 'No, he's no good. Go back and try again.' So I had a couple of more sessions with General Kuter and we really scanned the group of officers, looking for a man who had a retentive memory and who mixed well with both the civilian and the military side of the National Security Council. We also needed someone who could talk with the President when he was present at National Security meetings. Well, we thought that the man we had just suggested was the best. So I went back again, and again General Vandenberg rejected the one we had come up with, saying to me, 'You mean to tell me you haven't got anybody better than this in the Air Force? If that's the case, we're in one hell of a shape. Go back again and find somebody else.' So again, General Kuter and I reviewed all the candidates, and I decided that the man I had suggested to him on the second go around was clearly the best man for the job. I went back again and told General Vandenberg that I was again recommending the individual I had last suggested. It is the only time I ever saw Van get upset, but he damn near threw me out of the office. He said, 'You mean you have come back here with the same name?'

"I said, 'Listen, General Vandenberg, your Deputy Chief of Staff of Personnel and I have really searched this thing and have reviewed this thing and have reviewed all of the qualities necessary for the job. I don't know what your objective is but this is the man for the job.'

"Well, suddenly General Vandenberg said, 'All right.' But he added, 'If he doesn't work out, you'd better not come back' " (personal interview, April 1976).

When Vandenberg thought he had a weakness, he delegated authority and relied on the help of others. His chief research and development officer was Lt. Gen. Laurence C. Craigie. Craigie commented that "I think Van had a weakness in math and science as a student at West Point, and I don't think he ever got over that. When he was Chief of Staff, he did not get directly involved in research and development matters. He really didn't feel comfortable getting involved in a technical discussion or a technical conference. He wanted to stay clear of that if he could, and I'm sure that this is one of the reasons why he leaned so heavily on Jimmy Doolittle, who, of course, was the first individual to get a Ph.D. in aeronautical engineering in the United States. Jimmy Doolittle was very sound in that line, and he and Van were very close friends. Van relied heavily on Jimmy Doolittle and his advice during all the time he was Chief" (personal communication, February 8, 1977).

Vandenberg considered it essential to visit the troops in the field, to gain firsthand information. During the Berlin Airlift, Vandenberg, along with Symington, visited Europe to inspect the progress. They made a point to congratulate Lt. Gen. Curtis LeMay and his people for the job they had done.

As Chief of Staff of the Air Force during the Korean conflict, Vandenberg got into combat any way he could, as he had in World War II. He often visited the battlefield and sized up the situation. He would climb in an airplane and fly around the front on his own. He was very much concerned that the military effort was relying too much on air support to do everything. He decided he was going to find out for himself, firsthand, what the appropriate support should be. While he was there in January 1951, inspecting things from a helicopter, he ordered the helicopter to land near the front lines so he could join some of the Army patrols to get an idea of what was really happening on the ground.[17]

His executive officer, Major General Grussendorf, accompanied Vandenberg on one of these Korean trips and commented, "You couldn't see a hell of a lot but he could from the chopper. He could see some ground action or where there had been, and he visited with the combat air people over there, not just the officers or the commander. He would go right on down to the mess, the squadron, ops, out on the line. He could speak their language. He knew these airplanes almost as well as they did and he knew, because of the European business, what the hell aerial combat was, and the men loved him. He would stand up and get in a jeep and pass down the review line, he'd get out on his two feet and nobody was called to attention, all of a sudden there he was" (personal interview, July 8, 1978).

He made a point to talk with the enlisted personnel as he toured and inspected. "He was popular with his airmen and enlisted men, talking air slang with the best of them," commented one observer. "He played volleyball and ping pong with them and usually beat them. A dashing figure in impeccable uniform, cap at a rakish angle, he always seemed to be in action."[18]

"General Vandenberg wanted to get closer to his people," said Grussendorf. "The staff and I made the suggestion that you had to get closer to the peons, the captains and the majors that are around here. They are working like hell, and all they see are four walls in their inside office or their basement operation. I said, 'Will you meet with this group sometime if I get them together?' He said, 'Yeah.' So in one of the big staff meeting rooms there on the fifth floor—not as big as a theater but it holds 150 people. So I got word out to the various staff agencies that the Chief would like to speak to X number [of men]—and I practically had it allocated by numbers—not above the rank of major, maybe it was lieutenant colonel.

"We had a full house," Grussendorf continued. "Van came in and everybody [stood] at attention and he says, 'As you were, as you were.' He gets up on the podium and you could see this, you know, stiff neck looking out and then suddenly he said, 'To hell with this, let's get closer!' So he comes down off the stage, sits cross-legged on this big table and said, 'Now, let's talk,' and that opened up the thing. They all joined in.

"He started off saying what he was trying to do as Chief, that he had been in roughly a similar position and that he knew that they were aware of everything that was going on. He wanted to make them feel completely aware of their importance on the Air Staff, even though their names did not appear on the letterhead or the signature, they were important to the running of the Air Force" (personal communication, July 8, 1978).

Vandenberg took a personal interest in his men. He made a point to congratulate in public Air Force Staff Sgt. Melvin G. Whitfield, who was the only track and field winner from the armed services in the 1948 Olympics. Vandenberg asked Sergeant Whitfield to come to Vandenberg's office at the Pentagon on his return from England and asked him, "When did you learn to run?" The young sergeant, embarrassed, smiled and said, "When I was quite young, sir." Whitfield had won two Olympic gold medals: the 800-meter and as anchorman of the American 1,000-meter relay team. In addition, he took third place in the 400-meter run. This exchange was noted in the August 28, 1948, issue of the *New York Times*.

Vandenberg was just as considerate in dealing with his contemporaries. "I remember one time," reflected Lt. Gen. William E. Kepner, "when George Kenney was supposed to move the Strategic Air Command headquarters. Van was Chief of Staff, and Kenney Commander of Strategic Air Command. The decision was made to move the headquarters to Omaha, Nebraska. Kenney was stationed down somewhere around Washington.

Old George was a very fine character. I loved him, and so did Van and everybody else. But Van had decided that he was going to move that outfit to Omaha, Nebraska, and George was taking plenty of time—to say the kindest thing—to get ready to go to Omaha. He wasn't getting ready to go fast enough, so finally Van called him in and made it very clear that the Chief of the Air Force was ordering him to do something and just when can the Chief of the Air Force expect to have this job done. Whereupon George said, 'Right away, sir,' and out he went. Van had given him lots of time. I personally would probably have been on the warpath, and I think anybody else would too, but Van wasn't. Van knew a way to get in there and still have everything smooth. In other words, his smile was a smile of steel, and like we used to say about Arnold, God, you had to be careful if Arnold started to smile because he was getting ready to just saw somebody's neck in two and don't ever then talk back to him" (personal interview July 7, 1978).

Gen. Laurence S. Kuter was appointed to succeed Gen. Richard E. Nugent as Deputy Chief of Staff for Personnel during Vandenberg's tenure as Air Force Chief. When Kuter was asked about his appointment, he replied, "Van moved me in there over my objection. . . . Dick Nugent was sick with a heart attack. Van needed somebody he could count on. To tell the truth, he wanted a berth for his classmate, Joe Smith, too. Van was fond of Joe. Joe had been for years in the plans work, which he didn't like very much, and Van wanted to give him a chance—a command" (personal interview, July 8, 1978). When Kuter went to personnel, Smith succeeded him at MATS.

Probably the finest compliment came from General Spaatz, who wrote of Vandenberg, "He studiously avoids claims or statements that could not be justified by cold facts. His steady, objective attitude, his self-control in public appearances, and particularly in congressional hearings, are already a tradition in the Air Force."[19]

Lieutenant General Kepner elaborated on this theme: "There was this four-star general who was in charge of all the supplies; he was a crusty fellow, and he roamed around the European theater—we always said this fellow stuck his chest out too far. So he came to some Air Force station in France one day, and Van said, 'You know, I was in the midst of running an operation in a battle and this fellow called up and said I want you out here right now at this base.'

"Van said, 'I'm in the midst of a battle and I don't think it's in the interest of the command that I leave until I take care of this situation. I will see you when the battle is over.'

"Van laughingly told me, 'You know, I waited until I was ready to go out there, which was not until all my reports were in.' Then, he said, 'I went out. This fellow said to me, "It's been a long time; you were told to be out here immediately!" ' He was a four-star general, Van was three.

"So Van said, 'Well, yes sir. You told me that.'

" 'Why didn't you come?'

" 'Well,' Van replied, 'you know, I thought this thing over, and I gave it serious study and decided that I had to win that battle. Now that I've won the battle, what can I do for you?" The general, of course, just snorted and walked off" (personal interview, July 7, 1978).

In addition to being handsome, Vandenberg's looks belied his years. "This is something he can't change," wrote Sidney Shalett, "despite his twenty-five years service in the Air Force, his sensational war record as a fighting and planning commander, his seven rows of decorations, and a large dose of poise acquired through years of functioning as a trouble-shooter for the Air Force, the Army and even the White House. Though forty-nine is not exactly a tender age, and Vandenberg, in fact, is a grand-father, he has kept himself in such fine trim that he looks better and younger than most men of forty.

"As an example of how people are fooled by the flying grandfather's appearance, Vandenberg recently was the object of some misguided sym-pathy on the part of one of Washington's impressive dowagers. It was just before that fourth star was pinned on his shoulders. Vandenberg, a mere lieutenant general at the time, was attending a diplomatic function. He was wearing civilian clothes, which he prefers to his uniform, and the dowager didn't quite catch the introduction when the host presented 'Lieutenant General Vandenberg.' She was quite impressed with him, however, and spent the rest of the evening buttonholing some of her influential colonel and brigadier general friends, demanding, 'Why can't something be done with this fine young Lieutenant Vandenberg?' "[20]

Vandenberg selected Colonel Grussendorf as executive officer. Grus-sendorf soon found that he was being by-passed as the executive officer. "There were things that belonged to the exec and not down in the staff sec-tion, so I directed that the papers start coming to me. Everything seemed to be going all right. Van would say good morning to me when he came in and at night he'd leave with a smile, so I was happy as a bee. But after about ten days, I got a call on the intercom from General McKee, the assistant Vice Chief of Staff, who asked if I had some time. He'd like to speak to me. So I got down to General McKee's office as soon as I could and he proceeded to tell me, 'This is lesson number 12. Now these papers come in to me. I decide who they go to or what's to be done with them' I listened very attentively and I said, 'Thank you, sir,' and I left. I never changed a damn thing of what I was doing and after—very shortly thereafter—I got a buzz from General Van, so I dashed into his office with my note pad. Van was standing behind his desk looking out over the River Entrance of the Pentagon and turned around and with a big grin said, 'Grussey, I just want to let you know I've never had it so good.' That did it. General McKee or the whole rest of the damn Air Force was not going to change my procedures'' (personal communication, July 8, 1978). This approach inspired loyalty and was an important part of General Vandenberg's leadership.

"General Vandenberg made a trip to Korea during the Korean conflict, and I traveled with him," recalled Grussendorf. "In General MacArthur's headquarters, the aide asked Collins and Vandenberg to come on in and I found a seat outside General MacArthur's office. I was about to sit in it when Van said, 'You come with me,' and so, I followed him in. I met General MacArthur, and he was very cordial and accepted the fact that there was a colonel in the room, but Van said, 'I want you to listen to this.' It was very considerate of Van but I think it was also part of my training—I would better understand messages and JCS papers and so on. Also, thoughtfulness, it wasn't just a 'come on in with me and meet the big man thing so you can tell your grandchildren' '' (personal communication, July 8, 1978).

Vandenberg's four-year tour of duty as Chief of Staff was scheduled to end on April 30, 1952, but at the time that his four years ended he still had fourteen months to serve to complete thirty years for retirement. It was an awkward situation. If he was not reappointed as Chief of Staff, he would have had to step down and hold a lesser job; he might also have been reduced in rank from four-star general to three-star general. There had been a strong tradition, in peacetime, against keeping anyone in the position of Chief of Staff for more than four years. But there were compelling reasons for permitting Vandenberg to finish out his thirty years, even if it broke tradition. He had led the Air Force through the internal struggle between the proponents of a greater role for strategic air power and the proponents of tactical air. In spite of the B-36 controversy, he had been diplomatic enough to avoid an irrevocable breach with the Army and the Navy.

The matter was ultimately resolved by President Truman's announcement that Vandenberg was reappointed for the remaining fourteen months, thus finishing out a full thirty years. The reason given by the White House was that "The president does not wish General Vandenberg to be put in a subordinate command before he reaches retirement."[21]

Secretary of the Air Force Finletter denied any desire to retire Vandenberg. "I always liked Vandenberg very much," he said. "I admired his capacity as a public servant. Until this day, he stands out to me as a very important officer. He knew what the problems were, taking them up with great vigor and not trying to show off, but trying to do what was best for the United States. He was really a great public servant."

Secretary Finletter then spoke quite candidly of their relationship. "I had a great respect for his opinion, otherwise he wouldn't have continued in office. I would have gotten somebody else. He was, in my judgment, and I was not a great expert by any means when I went into the job, but my judgment was that this was a man of great quality. I thought that he was a very good man for the Air Force and I must say, in retrospect, I'm sure he was" (personal interview, October 11, 1977).

Few leaders have had as difficult a challenge as Vandenberg did as Chief of Staff. When he took command, the Air Force had just gone through rapid, total demobilization of aircraft, materiel, and personnel. His job was to build it up again. At the height of World War II, there were 80,000 aircraft and 2.5 million officers and men. When Vandenberg took over from Spaatz, there were only 375,000 officers and men—on paper, 55 wings, most of them with obsolete planes. At his retirement, Air Force personnel had grown to 960,000 officers and men, 137 wings, all of them combat ready. It was a remarkable achievement, the result of brilliant leadership.

In the cold war, he had to lead in reforging the Air Force. Vandenberg grasped the essentials of our national security: Training was as vital as technology. "Air power doesn't guarantee America's security," he said, "but it exploits the nation's greatest asset—our technological skill. We cannot hope to match enemy nations in manpower but we can, as in the last war, produce more and better airplanes than any other country. And we have young men with the mechanical facility for flying all the airplanes we build. Training can quickly give them efficiency."[22]

As Chief of Staff, he continued to fly, a crucial way for an Air Force leader to stay in touch. He flew the new model fighters and checked out in the early jet planes, something few generals had done in the early years of jets. When he flew on official trips, his pilot would automatically move to the co-pilot's seat, and the co-pilot moved back into the cabin to play gin rummy with the General's aide so that Vandenberg could fly the aircraft. His preoccupation with flying may seem an affectation. But, as one of the Air Force's smart thinkers observed, "Most of the strategic mistakes of the German Air Force were made by generals who no longer knew the air."[23]

Vandenberg was the Air Force leader who ushered in a period of revolution in weapons, with jet aircraft, atomic weapons, and electronic technology. Vandenberg was not a scientist, but had the good judgment to surround himself with people such as Doolittle and civilian scientists in a program for internal development of Air Force personnel.

One of the most important technical developments was breaking the invisible barrier and flying faster than the speed of sound. This was pioneered by Capt. Charles E. Yeager in the experimental X-1, opening a new threshold in air power weaponry and potential. Vandenberg called it "the greatest aeronautical achievement since the flight of the Wright brothers at Kitty Hawk."[24]

During his career, General Vandenberg was confronted by a number of significant challenges. First, the Berlin Blockade confrontation was brilliantly neutralized by the Berlin Airlift. Next came the ugly and irresponsible attack on the Air Force by the anonymous letter—the B-36 controversy—which educated the American public on the role of strategic bombing. Then came the Korean war, imposing such immediate demands on our "shoe-string" Air Force that Vandenberg was alarmed, wondering if we were so overextended that we could not keep up our guard elsewhere in the world.

In the line of duty, it was occasionally necessary for Vandenberg to dispute presidential decisions. He disagreed with President Truman's $5 billion budget cut; on more than one occasion, he differed with Truman and then later with President Eisenhower, his Commander in Chief, yet there is little question that Truman and Eisenhower both had great appreciation for the job Vandenberg did. As noted, Truman extended his tour to an unprecedented additional fourteen months, although Vandenberg did not live to complete that final mission.

At Vandenberg's death on April 2, 1954, Eisenhower summed up his appreciation: "The nation mourns the passing of a devoted and able military leader and will hold him in grateful remembrance. Gallant commander, a decade ago, of our tactical Air Force in Northwest Europe; unswerving advocate of the precepts and cause of the U.S. Air Force, a forceful fighter for a strong national offense—General Vandenberg was a courageous and tireless leader. He has left a lasting imprint on the service he loved so well and on the nation he served with all his strength and skill."

NOTES, Chapter 3

1. Letter from Brig. Gen. Joseph H. Davidson, USAF (Ret), to William H. Davidson, February 21, 1966, cited in an unpublished manuscript entitled *Air Command and Staff College Thesis* by Maj. William H. Davidson, entitled "General Hoyt Sanford Vandenberg, the Man, the Advocate, the Architect," p. 7.
2. Gen. Carl A. Spaatz, "Hoyt Sanford Vandenberg," *Assembly,* 1954, *8*(3): 53.

3. John R. Deane, *The Strange Alliance* (New York: Viking Press, 1947), pp. 19–20.
4. Spaatz, p. 54.
5. Deane, p. 124.
6. *Newsweek,* July 22, 1946, p. 34.
7. Ibid.
8. "U.S. Air Force and Its Boss Are Ready," *Newsweek,* February 19, 1951, p. 22.
9. Davidson manuscript.
10. Gen. Hoyt S. Vandenberg, "This Is Your New Air Force," *Flying,* May 1951, *48:* 32–41.
11. *Life,* June 11, 1951, *30:* 28.
12. "Do Air Force Cuts Endanger the United States?" *U.S. News and World Report,* June 12, 1953, p. 40.
13. "Message from the Chief of Staff, U.S. Air Force," *Flying,* March 1953, p. 27.
14. U.S. Congress, House, Committee on Armed Services, *Investigation of the B-36 Bomber Program,* Hearings on House Resolution 234, 81st Congress, 1949 (Washington, D.C.: Government Printing Office, 1949), p. 186.
15. "Vandenberg Speaking: Our Air Might," *Newsweek,* February 19, 1951, pp. 22–24.
16. Vandenberg.
17. Robert F. Futrell, "Korea—A Shoestring Air Force Goes to War," p. 262.
18. John A. Giles, "General 'Van,' " *Flying,* July 1948, *43:* 271.
19. Spaatz, p. 53.
20. Sidney Shalett, "Man on a Hot Spot," *Saturday Evening Post,* May 29, 1948, p. 23.
21. "Vandenberg, LeMay, Twining Team," *U.S. News & World Report,* March 14, 1952, pp. 62–64.
22. Vandenberg, op. cit.
23. Shalett.
24. Alfred Goldberg, *A History of the United States Air Force, 1907–1957* Princeton, N.J.: Van Nostrand, 1957), pp. 202–203.

CHAPTER 4

GENERAL NATHAN

FARRAGUT TWINING

Nathan Farragut Twining was born on October 11, 1897, and, as his name shows, of a family proud of its military record. His earliest ancestors landed at Plymouth, Massachusetts, in 1635; two of his forebears fought in the Revolutionary War, one in the War of 1812, four in the Civil War. His uncle, Nathan C. Twining, for whom he was named, graduated from Anna-polis in the class of 1889, rose to the rank of captain during World War I, and was ultimately retired as a rear admiral.

Nate Twining was one of eight children, six boys and two girls. His father, Clarence Walter Twining, was a moderately prosperous banker who encouraged his sons to serve their country. Robert, the eldest, entered the Naval Academy, graduating in the class of 1916 and retiring at the rank of captain. Nate saw service in Mexico before he entered West Point. His younger brother, Merrill, in turn graduated from the Naval Academy, rising to the rank of lieutenant general in the Marine Crops at the time that his brother Nathan was Chairman of the Joint Chiefs of Staff.

Although he was born in Wisconsin, Twining's family moved to Oregon when he was a child. At the turn of the century, Oregon was pioneer territory, and as a youngster Nate devoted many hours to fishing, tracking animals, and hunting. He came to be a superb rifle shot and joined H Com-pany of the Oregon National Guard because, he said, "they had a good rifle range and I liked to shoot" (personal interview, September 18, 1962). His guard unit was mobilized for duty with General Pershing's expedition in

Mexico in 1916, and Nate was promoted first to corporal, then to sergeant, quite an accomplishment for a young man of only eighteen.

When asked why he decided to go to West Point, he responded, "Since I was a kid I was always interested in the military, and my folks were military all the way back. My grandfather was a Quaker and took part in the Civil War, and because of this was fired from the Quaker organization. I had an uncle who was in the Navy, and I always wanted to get into the service. I was in the National Guard and was under General Pershing when he stopped Pancho Villa, who was raiding the United States from Mexico. I was just a kid then, and after it was over I came back and finished high school and took my examination for West Point and that was it" (personal interview, September 18, 1962).

Twining actually received his appointment to West Point from the Oregon National Guard, and was admitted as a cadet on June 14, 1917, at the age of nineteen years, eight months. He graduated on November 1, 1918, with an overall standing of 138 in a class of 284 members, leaving only seventeen months after he entered because of the accelerated program in World War I. He and his classmates returned to West Point a month after the Armistice to resume their courses; he graduated June 11, 1919, and was then commissioned as a second lieutenant in the Infantry.

Twining's class spent the initial summer in "beast barracks," as the foreword of their yearbook described facetiously:

June 14th we all came up on the seven o'clock train. There must have been a couple hundred of us get off at West Point. The first thing we did was to climb a great long hill and line up in front of a door where we had to turn in all our money. I hated to turn in the $10 that Aunt Rowena gave me and I didn't spend in New York. After that, things began to happen in a hurry. A big, handsome man in a gray uniform came up to four or five of us and said just like he was mad about something, "You men stand up around here. Turn down the cuffs on those trousers. You man, put your hat on the front of your head. Now form a column of twos and come with me." I didn't see why he acted so angry. We hadn't done anything. I soon learned how they all treat you here, though. Then we had to report to a lot of men, and they all got mad because we didn't say 'Sir' to them. How were we to know? After that I stood around for a moment, until some one came up to me and said "Mr. Ducrot, what are you doing standing here? You pick up a D.T. and get your equipment! Speed up about it, you understand?"

I never had a clear idea of what happened those next few days. I ran around with a mattress and laundry bags, I double timed up and down stairs, I drilled and drilled and drilled some more. I went over to the gymnasium and raised my chest for an officer over there, until I thought it would split, and all the time I never got a chance to eat in peace. They're always bothering you in the Mess Hall. You have to sit up so straight, and they keep yelling at you all the time to do this or that. It's the noisiest place I was ever in. I'd think they'd have better manners. And we do nothing but shine our shoes and polish our breast plates and take baths and go around to the company officer and get crawled. Some of those upperclassmen that drill us are awfully mean. They get mad if you have a speck of lint on your coat, or even if you look at them sometimes. We can only write one letter a week, and that has to go home. I fooled them last week though, 'cause I put a letter to Sue inside my letter to mother. There are some good fellows in this division. The upperclassmen are always calling out orders that none of us can understand, and there's one fellow, named Joe Cranston, who always pipes up afterwards, "May I ask a question? What was that last order, Sir?" and some one always comes up and crawls him.

It's Fourth of July today. They sent me over to the cadet store to get a laundry bag of firecrackers this morning, but they must have made a mistake, because it wasn't open. We didn't have any drills this afternoon and can visit each other in different divisions of barracks and here I've wasted most of the afternoon writing this.[1]

Twining was not bothered by this harassment of cadet life. He just took it all in stride. "I recall seeing Twining one evening during our beast barracks," reflected Col. Donald H. Nelson (personal communication, August 29, 1963).* " 'How are you doing?' he asked me.

" 'They've about got me,' I said, nodding my head at the three pair of perfectly polished shoes I was taking to reshine and clean the soles. I asked of him, 'How are you making out?'

"Twining responded, 'I don't think they know I'm here, we got this stuff, this basic stuff in the National Guard and I brought along my old cleaning kit.' "

During his fourth-class year, he played football with the scrubs, those

*"Personal communication" refers to letter to the author.

of insufficient experience or too small for varsity. Classmate Henry Baldwin Nichols said, "It has been a long time since Twining and I were at West Point, but I recall him very vividly. He was not physically big enough to play varsity football, but he did play on the Cullum Hall squad, which corresponded to the junior varsity, and in spite of the physical beatings he took, he stuck with it, and he showed the characteristics with his determination which later made him one of the first general officers from the class" (personal communication, September 18, 1963).

"Hockey was probably the sport he most enjoyed," reflected classmate John V. Dominey. "Its demand for sustained endurance and toughness in contact as well as the consistent change in tactics that requires split-second thinking and quick decision seemed natural to his temperament. Although he was usually of a quiet disposition, when on the ice he played with great intensity. He had the faculty of concentrating and applying all his powers at the moment they were needed" (personal communication, September 20, 1963).

In addition to football and hockey, "Nate was shortstop on the baseball team and a pretty good one too. I remember," said classmate Col. Roy Green, "that in one game he made two errors. Then he made a brilliant stop and throw, and our class comedian, Ralph (later General) Stanley, Air Force, yelled above the noise, 'Like the Ancient Mariner, he stoppeth one of three' " (personal communication, June 9, 1963).

Twining's intensity and determination were not limited to competitive sports—they were in everything he did. "The thing I remember about Nate Twining that made a lasting impression upon me," said classmate Richard Rick, "occurred forty-six years ago when we were in the West Point gym. Twining's behavior during calisthenics class impressed me conclusively; his attitude seemed more like that of a contestant aiming for a goal, rather than that of people performing simple gymnastics. Months later, my roommate, Panzarella, who chose a West Point class ring in lieu of the world's lightweight boxing crown, he was that good, made the similar comment to me after observing Twining's intensity in doing calisthenics" (personal communication, August 30, 1963).

Academically, the best perspective was offered by classmate Col. Edward M. Scar. "Nate was in that part of our class about the middle, where he found no need to worry about his studies nor was he concerned that he was not number one, thereby leaving his mind free to derive the maximum benefits of the Military Academy. His leadership qualities in early life were exemplified by his constant alertness and desire to participate in all activities" (personal communication, August 28, 1963).

Twining was popular and, because of his experience in the National Guard, more mature than his classmates. As has been stated, Twining's classwork was accelerated because of World War I, and the highest cadet rank for anyone at the outset was corporal. Twining was the second-ranking corporal out of eight for "G" Company. Col. William H. Dunham remembered that "at the end of Plebe year, Twining and I were selected as the two senior corporals in 'G' Company. We were assigned to tents in summer camp across from each other and were charged with the discipline of the new cadets who joined our compnay. Twining had had some military experience before entering West Point, and he exercised his authority with firmness and fairness. I was particularly impressed with his capacity in the case of a new cadet who didn't really want to be in West Point, but who was there because his father's being a VIP had put him there. This young man was indifferent and surly and finally made a false statement officially to then Corporal Twining. It was a very sticky situation, because of the fact that the cadet's father was influential, but Corporal Twining stuck to his guns, and the cadet left the Academy" (personal communication, September 7, 1963).

At graduation, Twining was one of the 33 percent of his class who chose Infantry because, he said, "I thought I would get overseas faster in World War I and into the action" (personal communication, September 18, 1962).

"Our class has an outstanding number of generals. There were five four-star generals on duty at the same time, something no other class had ever had, not even the class of 1915, Ike's class. As I look over my service, I am sure that the long period we had as company officers after West Point paid dividends and also gave us opportunities for professional schooling. Then when World War II came along, we were prepared and willing to accept the responsibilities" (Maj. Gen. J. H. Phillips, personal communication, September 14, 1963).

Assigned to the Infantry on July 21, 1919, Twining joined the American forces in Germany. In September, he returned to the United States and was ordered to Camp Benning, Georgia, as a student officer at the Infantry School, where he remained until he completed the course in June 1920.

At Fort Benning, Twining continued to participate in athletics. "It was at Fort Benning," said CWO Charles R. Jackson, "that I first got to know Nate, and this was as a football player. The Infantry School fielded a team, which was composed mostly of lads in the class of 1919, and on this team Twining played end. He was a real star. I was on the squad, and I had to try to tackle him several times at practice. I still recall the impact; his body was as hard as a rock, and tackling Twining hurt. He had now developed from a boy into a young man.

"We played Auburn that fall at Auburn and they really had a great team. I can remember that it took all of their best men to defeat us by a score of 14 to 7. Nate scored our first touchdown on a short pass and a long, broken field run, and the first half ended with Benning ahead, 7–0. During the fourth period, however, Auburn scored two touchdowns, but it took everything they had to do it" (personal communication, August 27, 1963).

Another member of the team remembered an incident that was particularly revealing. "We had a football team made up from officers on the post," related John Dominey. "Our most famous player was Van de Graaf, a former All-Southern tackle at Alabama, who coached our team and also played fullback. After several days practice, Vandy announced we needed a scrimmage on a hot September afternoon. Twining, who weighed about 165 pounds soaking wet, was the left end when Vandy, with his 210 pounds of muscle, decided to run right through him. That was a sad mistake; he should have run the other end. There was no deception on the play, and as he shot towards the line Nate hit him hard and low. Vandy's ankle was badly sprained, and he was out for half the season. We all felt badly, including Nate. As in everything that he did, he gave it his best" (personal communication, September 20, 1963).

While all of this was going on, Twining had thoughts elsewhere. According to Stuart Little, who was with Nate as a cadet and later at Fort Benning, "At the Infantry School it was the policy to toss decision-making problems at the students at unexpected moments. Twining stood up well in those tactical problems, although, even then, he kept looking up at the sky and saying his future was in the air" (personal communication, September 18, 1963).

Bernard A. Byrne recalled some problems in leadership that occurred at Fort Benning: "Nate and I were among a small group in the class who were kept at Fort Benning to serve jointly as the commanders of demonstration troops and as faculty members. Nate and I commanded platoons—and sometimes companies—in the same battalion. Our troops were predominantly men sent back from the European theater as, 'unfit to represent the United States in a foreign country,' and the undesirables shipped out of the Second Division when its strength was reduced. Our job often felt more like running a disciplinary barracks than commanding a tactical outfit. Nate was a driver and fit well in the requirements of that task, where the element of persuasive leadership was of little use a good deal of the time." (personal communication, September 1, 1963).

Another officer wrote, "I remember when Second Lieutenant Twining got the unpleasant detail of sand-ratting. This, for your information, is the target detail on the rifle range. As his assistants, he had several World War I officers who had been reduced from lieutenant colonel to captain, with the resultant indifference toward any duty that they might be assigned. I remember so well that one of these officers was Capt. C. R. Heubner, who went on to become a lieutenant general and corps commander in World War II. Then Captain Heubner had made a comment to me about the target detail: he told me how much he admired young Lieutenant Twining's performance. Twining was all business and there was absolutely no loafing permitted of any of the officers by Twining, although Twining was far junior to most of them. Neither their former jobs as battalion commanders or their decorations in any way affected Twining's carrying out of the mission that was assigned to him" (Maj. Gen. John B. Murphy, personal communication, September 5, 1963). Twining remained there at Fort Benning as an instructor until he became Aide to Brig. Gen. Benjamin A. Poore, serving that capacity at Camp Travis, Texas; at Fort Logan, Colorado; and at Fort Sam Houston, Texas, until June 30, 1923, when he left to enter pilot training.

It was during an athletic event when Fort Benning was playing a football team at a flying school that Nate finally decided to get into aviation. As a special treat, members of the flying school football squad offered rides to the members of the Fort Benning team in a Jenny aircraft the morning of the game. For some of the football team, it was not so much a treat as a treatment, because some of them became sick in the air—as a result Fort Benning lost the game 13 to 7. But for Nate Twining the flight was a joy, and he decided on the spot to get into flying on a full-time basis.

"Twining and I went through flying school together," reflected Lt. Gen. Laurence C. Craigie. "He was a wonderful guy. Warm, fun-loving, he had a great sense of humor and a light side to him. We all just loved him. He was a bachelor, but yet he was just one of us." Craigie also noted that Twining had to apply several times before he finally made it into the Air Service. "I decry the unfortunate situation, but it was a fact that a group who formed the Army Air Force, a group of World War I pilots, were jealous. They had put the outfit together, meaning the Army Air Service, and they just didn't want outsiders to come in. That clique had very little rank. Most of the Air Service officers were junior to hundreds of other Army officers. It was a very difficult time to go through pilot training because of this attitude on the part of the instructor pilots. What I remember so well about Twining is that he wanted to get through just as badly as the rest of us did. That was uppermost in our minds" (personal communication, February 8, 1977).

Twining entered pilot training and had his first flight, lasting sixty minutes, on August 23, 1923. He then had approximately one flight a day for the next month when, with a total of fifteen hours and five minutes, he soloed. "Hap" Arnold, back in the very, very early days of aviation, had soloed and earned his wings in approximately ten days. Obviously, training and technology had greatly altered the requirements to become a pilot since then—Twining continued in the flight program for almost a year before earning his wings.

Twining's logbook shows his meticulous ground schooling and his better-than-average grades.

SUBJECT	HOURS	GRADES
Military sketching and map reading	35	97%
Motors	45	71%
Aerodynamics	25	93%
Parachute rigging	15	87%
Instruments	10	95%
Aerial radio communications	35	91%
Codes and signals	50	82%
Meteorology	25	79%
Photography	12	87%
Browning automatic machine gun	10	74%
Lewis machine gun	10	88%
Synchronizing gears	9	94%
Aerial sites	8	71%
Camera gun	5	89%
Marlin machine gun		93%
Parachute	6	92%
Machine gun range work	48	No grade

There was one subject, aerial navigation, of twenty-five hours, for which his logbook showed the grade in red: 57 percent. Twining had failed that subject and had to take a second examination, in which he received the grade of 90 percent.

Twining began his pilot training August 22, 1923, at Brooks Field, Texas, and after seven months he went on to Kelly Field, Texas, to complete the advanced part. Then he received his wings and was retained as a flying instructor.

As Craigie has indicated, there was a sour attitude on the part of many pilot instructors, which was partially responsible for a washout rate in excess of 50 percent. But Nathan Twining was different. Student after student who had been exposed to him as an instructor made comments such as that of Maj. Gen. Robert O. Cork, who remarked, "As a flying cadet, I was about to wash out. Nathan Twining was my final check pilot. He quietly put me completely at ease, and patiently put me through the flying basics. His understanding of my difficulties and his forbearance became stimulants that guided my entire future career. I went on to the rank of major general, but had it not been for Nathan F. Twining and his understanding and his example, I don't believe I would have achieved the success that I did" (personal communication, April 17, 1963).

The most appreciative account of Nate Twining as an instructor came from Lt. Gen. Elwood R. "Pete" Quesada. Quesada had been recruited from the University of Maryland by the Air Corps to attend pilot training and primarily to help build up the Training School football team. Cadet Quesada elected to take advantage of this opportunity to learn to fly. One of his teammates on the football squad was instructor Twining. "I remember Twining more as a football player," said Quesada, "than I do as an instructor. Twining was a very decent, pleasant fellow. He was a first lieutenant then, having been in the Army about five years. We got to be good friends on the football team together, and although he was an officer, a rather senior one at that, and I was an enlisted man, he was always extremely friendly to me, which I appreciated and enjoyed. Officers and enlisted men did not mix, but he did make my life very easy.

"What I particularly remember," continued Quesada, "was the fact that I broke my leg playing football, and they wanted me to keep up with the class, so they offered me the chance to take flying instruction during the Christmas holidays when everyone else had gone home or elsewhere for Christmas. They of course had to come up with a pilot instructor who was willing to give up his Christmas. Nate Twining volunteered to be my instructor. So for two weeks during the Christmas break I got special instruction. It was a very decent thing for him to have done and I have never forgotten it.

"I can't recall Nate ever crowing," Quesada said, "about being a little bit senior to the rest of us. Nate was always jolly. I never knew Nate when he wasn't jolly. He never attracted any sense of competition. I always felt that Nate enjoyed his seniors succeeding. I never knew of a case when Nate was ever jealous of anyone. I think that's one of the things that military service teaches us, not to be jealous. Nate would never do anything with an ulterior purpose. I never knew Nate to indulge in a self-serving act as a junior officer or as a senior officer" (personal communication, June 22, 1977).

Twining took his flying very seriously, but he also loved life. He worked hard but he had fun at the same time. One of his colleagues, Col. Harrison H. D. Heiberg, remembered that "there was one instance when our paths crossed that might be of interest to you. It was in the spring of 1926, I believe, while I was in the First Calvalry at Camp Marfa, Texas, and Nate was an instructor at Brooks Field. Among the various odd jobs assigned to me was that of Post Signal Officer. Nate Twining, with Harvey Greenlaw, another classmate, flew in one day in a biplane, landing at the little plot that we kept cleared of the mesquite to serve as an airfield, and looked me up. When they left, I made a radio report of their time of takeoff to continue an extended cross-country flight, and, after reflecting with considerable envy on their ability to flit around the country, put the incident from my mind. Several days later, a radio message was received asking if we had any information on Lieutenants Twining and Greenlaw, who had not been heard from since last reporting to our station. Meanwhile the carefree bachelors of the post had been recovering, as it turns out, from a weekend at a ranch owned by Lee Fischer. Lee Fischer was a wealthy young cattleman with a sumptuous ranch house about forty miles south of Marfa whence his herds ranged over most of the big bend country. After a little questioning, we found that there was quite a house party in progress at the ranch in the honor of an attractive young widow from San Antonio and that two of the very special guests were young Air Force officers, to wit, Lieutenants Twining and Greenlaw. When we finally got a telephone call through, Nate indicated to us that they had damaged their airplane in a rough landing at the ranch and were unable to take off so that would we please notify the base. In due time they were rescued from the ranch" (personal communication, November 12, 1963).

Lieutenant Twining finally received an operational assignment with a pursuit squadron and was stationed at Wheeler Field in Hawaii. One of the officers remembered that, "I was serving as the Company Commander in the old Hawaiian Division at Schofield Barracks, Hawaii, and Nate was Adjutant at Wheeler Field, as the Commanding Officer of a pursuit squadron equipped with little, cloth-covered biplane fighters, aircraft that were really hot stuff at the time. During a major joint exercise with the Navy, we sustained a tropical storm of exceptional violence; it was so severe, in fact, the air operations were presumed to be impossible, and major elements of the enemy Navy air holed up in and near Hilo, some 200 miles away from the island of Hawaii. In these weather conditions, Nate took his squadron, literally at wave-top level, flying only by compass and flying low where there was the only visibility, he proceeded to jump the Hilo Navy contingent in their bunks with such theoretical destruction that the Navy force was presumably damaged and had to be raised from the dead in order to let the war games proceed as planned. I always felt that this was an early exhibition of the same traits that Nate Twining illustrated as an Air Force Commander during World War II, particularly the exploits over the Ploesti oil fields" (personal communication, September 1, 1963).

Gen. Lauris Norstad remembered reporting as a brand new second lieutenant, to his first duty station. "My first Air Force station," said Norstad, "was at Wheeler Field in Hawaii. I lived at Schofield Barracks, and Nate was the senior officer living in the bachelor officer quarters. I was assigned to his quarters area, and I remember so well how nice he was to me. He introduced me to everyone in the quarters, to the people on the post. He was very considerate, very thoughtful, and very nice. I've always liked him, and I've never forgotten that first contact that I had with him" (personal communication, August 22, 1977).

Twining's Air Force career almost came to an end during his tour in Hawaii. His car skidded and crashed, driving the ignition key through his knee, and a spoke from the steering wheel went through his chest. His injuries were so critical that he was given no chance at the Schofield Barracks Hospital. A physician friend, however, managed to pull him through and save his leg. As one commentator said, "Nate Twining doesn't care about fast driving these days." A newspaper reporter later asked him about this particular automobile wreck. Twining pulled up his trouser leg, and pointed with his cigar at a big scar across his knee and said simply, "That was a tough one."

Several years later when Lieutenant Twining was assigned back in the States, Col. David B. Latimer recalled that during the summer of 1935, "Twining was in command of an Air Corps demonstration unit at Fort Benning, Georgia. His unit put on a show of smoke bombs to cover an Infantry attack, and frankly the performance was very poor. I was a tactical officer at the time for the U.S. Military Academy and had accompanied the new cadets on their tours of different Army posts. Lieutenant Twining was then in the East on detached service, but when he learned of the poor performance of the day, having been notified by one of the members of the unit, he returned quickly by air, [and] whipped his unit into such shape that a perfect Air Corps job was performed the following day, with Lieutenant Twining leading the group such a short period of time accomplishing this mission in an outstanding manner" (personal communication, September 19, 1963).

"I saw more of Nate," said classmate Col. Marion P. Echols," after graduation, particularly during the years 1936 to 1940 when Twining was at Duncan Field, Texas, as an Air Force technical supervisor. It was quite obvious to me that he was on his way to the top. He had developed confidence and self-assurance and had become thoroughly informed on the technical aspects of his profession. It had always been my impression that Air Force officers at that time generally felt that their sole duty was to be a pilot and looked down on administrative or technical work. This was particularly true of the Air Force officers who went to Command and General Staff School at Leavenworth, where they almost always finished at the bottom of their class. I was with Nate Twining at Leavenworth, and he was quite different in his approach at Leavenworth, as at Duncan Field. He was a 'take-charge guy' who had become proficient in all phases of his profession. I also remember so well how Nate was blessed with such a charming and unassuming personality" (personal communication, December 3, 1963).

One of Twining's responsibilities at Duncan Field included working with the new flying schools that were being set up for training pilots in preparation for the forthcoming war. Maj. Gen. Daniel E. Hooks said, "I was sent out to one of these schools as a first lieutenant. At that time Nathan F. Twining was a major, and he was an inspector for our area. We used to look forward to his visits, as we knew he would not only tell us where we might be in error but would also show us how to correct our mistakes. He would tell us where other similar schools were running into trouble and how we could avoid such trouble. He was interested in helping us along, not just criticizing. He was expert, open, frank and friendly, and completely honest. We appreciated his help and were always glad to see him" (personal communication, January 21, 1976).

At the completion of his tour at San Antonio Air Depot, Duncan Field, Texas, he was reassigned in August 1940 to the Office of the Chief of the Air Corps in Washington, D.C., as Assistant Chief of the Inspection Division. His initial responsibilities were to make technical inspections of Air Corps equipment and accessories. Within three months, he became Chief of the Technical Inspection Section in the same office. Then in December 1941 he joined the Operations Division. In February 1942, he was selected as Assistant Executive in the Office of Chief of the Air Corps and three months later was appointed Director of War Organization and Movements in the Chief's Office.

He became a brigadier general on July 17, 1942, and the same month was sent to the South Pacific as Chief of Staff to Maj. Gen. M. F. Harmon, Commanding General of U.S. Army Forces in the South Pacific. In January of 1943, he was named Commanding General of the 13th Air Force. On July 25, 1943, he was appointed Commander, Aircraft, Solomon Islands, and placed in tactical control of all Army, Navy, Marine, and Allied Air Forces in the South Pacific, one of the first Joint Air Commands in U.S. history.

Their primary objective was to support the drive up the Solomon Islands. But victory in that theater exacted a very heavy price in men and materiel. Aircraft were either shot down in the jungle or, through maintenance failure, were lost at sea. For those who were flying, as for those tied to the base, the climate was punishing. Mosquitoes carrying malaria and dengue and flies laden with bacteria swarmed into the tents, which in the early months of the war were unscreened, and disease was responsible for as many losses as were the Japanese. In addition, there was the exhaustion, mental and physical, from the boredom of being in the South Pacific islands month after month, a thousand miles from familiar civilization.

At Twining's initial headquarters, the missions were flown from bases without hangars, where the only food was K-rations, and the men were constantly down with malaria. Any sign of improvement would be long in coming.

One of the toughest problems was that of morale. At the outset, it was not sustained at a satisfactory level either among the service units or the ground crews. Each year, malaria affected 788 out of each 1,000 men, and there were insufficient medicines to treat the disease. It was not until August 1943 that the loss of manpower due to malaria infection fell behind the loss of manpower due directly to combat. From the first, Twining strove to have all the services working together as a team. With the relationship that he and General Harmon enjoyed with Admiral Halsey, such a concept became a reality. All the services, plus New Zealanders, worked under one command as a unified operational air force. The command position was rotated periodically among an Air Force, Navy, and Marine officer, as was appropriate in a Navy theater.

Twining's tour was almost short-lived. On January 31, 1943, he was on a combat mission from Henderson Field on Guadalcanal to Espiritu Santo in the Solomons. Along with the regualr B-17 crew of nine were Brigadier General Twining and four others, making a total of fourteen. The aircraft ran into severe weather and after ten arduous hours of flying in heavy rain, they were forced to make an instrument landing in darkness on the ocean. Miraculously, all fourteen in the aircraft escaped with only minor injuries.

Within thirty seconds after hitting the water, the aircraft sank. There was an emergency supply of rations, but unfortunately the crewman responsible for bringing them into the raft was hit by a swinging machine gun as he scrambled to get out of the plane. The blow stunned him, and he dropped the package of food, which sank. The fourteen men were left with one chocolate bar, one bottle of vitamin pills, and a small can of sardines, which one of the crewmen happened to have in the pocket of his flying suit.

There were two rubber rafts. To avoid separation, Twining had them lashed together, and they drifted more than 700 miles before being rescued. They encountered gales of near-hurricane force, broken by two periods of blinding heat. The gales drove the two rafts a great distance from the point where the plane had come down. In an interview with a reporter immediately after the rescue, Twining said, "A storm rose to a terrific height, sending us streaking over the wave tops. We must have drifted 150 miles during this gale. It was like being pulled into a nightmare by a giant devil fish." Twining went on to say, "We were helpless. I just prayed out loud and was joined by the men."

Every crewman was hatless, and three men were without shirts. Luckily, however, Twining had brought his .45 pistol with him. As they floated along, an albatross flew within range of the two life rafts. A sergeant attempted to shoot the bird, but the man's marksmanship was poor and he was unable to hit it. Twining took the pistol and on the first shot killed the albatross, blowing its head off. Back in 1923, in Twining's effectiveness report, he was rated above average in only one thing—pistol marksmanship, and he certainly proved it that day. The bird, divided equally among the men, was tough to chew. One of the crew commented, "The predigested fish contained in the stomach of the albatross was a most delightful dish under the circumstances."

Col. Glen C. Jamison, Twining's Chief of Staff, related that at the time of the ditching, they had only one and one-half canteens of water. "General Twining kept these two canteens," he said, "and would periodically pour out a little water into the cup, dividing it evenly among all of the fourteen members of the crew, and he would encourage all of us to swish the water in our mouth and spit it back into the canteen, doing this over a short period of time, which enabled us to get the most out of the limited water that was available. After the general shot the albatross, I remember that General Twining had a piece of the leg. It was like chewing a tire. But the thing that I remember most about this incident was the manner in which General Twining took charge and did the right thing, and we all knew he was going to do the right thing" (quoted by Gen. Dean C. Strother, personal communication, April 19, 1976).

While they were adrift, there were two occasions on which aircraft flew over their raft, but much to the frustration of the stranded men they were not seen. After six nights and five days, on the morning of Sunday, January 31, a flying fortress piloted by a Lieutenant Bailey spotted the raft. Unfortunately, however, a storm closed in, and contact was lost. After the storm abated, Twining thought they were lucky to have survived its fury and felt that rescue then was too much to hope for. But the next day another flying fortress spotted the rafts and, as Twining said, "It was the greatest sight in my life when the B-17 dipped its wing, showing that it had sighted us." The B-17 summoned two Catalina PBYs, which landed in the water near the castaways. The water was so rough, however, that the aircraft had to wait several hours before they were able to take off. Indeed, one of the Catalinas, on returning to the field, was so badly damaged by the mountainous waves that it had to be beached for extensive repairs. One of the PBY crewmen commented on the roughness of the sea while the PBY was waiting for the waves to settle down so they could take off. General Twining commented to the man, "This is like a Sunday afternoon of sailing compared to the weather these men have been going through during the course of our having been stranded."

It is interesting to note that after this ordeal, one of the first comments Twining made to a reporter was to commend the poilot, Capt. Jasper W. Woodruff of Fayetteville, Arkansas, for his outstanding flying in that weather and particularly for the forced landing on the ocean, at night during a severe storm. He also issued a directive concerning what should be done on behalf of air crews in the event of future ditchings. His purpose in doing so was to assist those who might find themselves in similar circumstances and, hopefully, to prevent such hardships as he and his men experienced.

While Twining was convalescing in the hospital, he wrote a letter to his mother-in-law, giving his personal account of the incident while it was fresh in his mind.

Dear Mother Mack:

In the event you have heard of our recent experience, six days adrift in a rubber life raft, want you to know that after three days in bed am now fit as a fiddle. Suffered only burns and normal exposure.

We were in a B-17 coming from the place where Merrill was located. Storms covered our destination, forcing a landing at sea at 9:45 P.M., January 26. That night and for two days following, terrific storms kept us drifting and made what would have been an easy rescue, a very doubtful one. As time went on, things looked bad, as the weather was poor for searching, but thanks to Hank Everest, who had confidence and a lot of sense directing the search from our base at APO 708, we were sighted on the fifth day and picked up on the sixth, February 1st.

Our B-17 sank 30 seconds after landing, so we had quite a

scramble getting into the rafts. Fourteen persons in all in the airplane were all safe. We were in two rafts and the terribly crowded conditions prevented any rest or relaxation, one of the worst ordeals encountered. Had two canteens of water, but thanks to the rain we caught enough to live on. Had one chocolate bar and one tin sardines that a soldier had in his pocket —not to be sneezed at. Lost our regular rations transferring to the raft. Kept my .45 pistol and shot two birds. Tho not too tasty raw, these helped both morale and stomachs. Fished continuously but could not catch a thing. Sharks hounded us continually; one we named Oscar, who for four days stayed in the same spot eyeing us. We were very kind to these lovely creatures and threw out a shoe which Oscar ate. However, further offerings of shoes were ignored by him.

Behavior of the men was exemplary. But don't know how long it could last in the terribly cramped quarters, no food, and worry about water. When the sun was out it was awful and when the storms hit, one just froze to death. Am sure the rains at night and wind accompanying them were worse than the day at Lihuo when I was there. Saw many water spouts, some awful close—beautiful but frightening. The Goodyear rubber raft is a thing of beauty and dependability.

All men will be returned to duty eventually in good shape, as only minor injuries were received. I expect to be out of this bunk tomorrow and start working on Tojo once again.

Only hope no news was released on this to cause Maude worry. Had the Red Cross contact her as soon as I got in. . . .

Love to Mack and yourself.

[signed]

Nate

Actually, the Air Force had not believed the fliers could possibly have survived in the storm and had abandoned the search for them after two days. But one man would not give up. He was Frank F. Everest, who went on to become a lieutenant general and Deputy Chief of Staff of Operations, ultimately retired as a four-star general in charge of the Tactical Air Command. Calling for volunteers, Everest continued to search, until finally, after six days, one of the planes spotted Twining's raft. It was safe to say Twining and the crew were forever indebted to Frank Everest.

After commanding the Thirteenth Air Force for a year and being promoted to major general, Twining went to Washington in December 1943 for thirty days of rest and rehabilitation. He stopped by the office to see Gen. Henry H. Arnold, who asked Twining, "How do you feel?" Twining responded that he was somewhat tired. Arnold looked at him and said, "You don't look a damn bit tired to me. Report in Italy January first and take over the Fifteenth Air Force." At the time of the transfer, the press release read, "Admiral William F. Halsey, Jr., Commander of South Pacific Forces, in announcing the change, said, 'I desire to pay tribute to the magnificent work of the strike and fighter command under General Twining. Air groups under his leadership had unqualified success in supporting operations at sea and shore.''

Twining was commanding the Fifteenth on April 5, 1944, when his heavy bombers made their first attack on Ploesti (Rumania), which was then the greatest single source of oil to the German armed forces, thus opening one of the most important battles of World War II. Twining said:

> Eight months after the dramatic low-level attack by Liberators from the Middle East, the first bombers from Italy to make the run over Ploesti dropped nearly 450 tons of explosives on the rail yards. Crewmen reported large columns of black smoke rising from the target area—something unusual in railroad results. "Ploesti rail yards were closely intertwined with the great refineries. Following other attacks, photo interpreters, studying pictures of the damage, were convinced that bombing of the oil installations would be feasible. Rail yards were forgotten and oil became the objective.
>
> At the time, the refineries of Ploesti were capable of producing 700,000 tons of crude oil for months, and actual gasoline production was estimated at a figure representing approximately one-third of the total Axis output. By August 19, the day the final punch was delivered, Ploesti's capacity had been reduced to about 77,000 tons per month, a cut of approximately 90 percent.
>
> The battle was waged in nineteen missions flown by heavy bombers, won by bomb-carrying Lightnings and four missions by night bombers of the RAF. The victory was costly: Of 65,413 men who flew over the target during the operations, 2,277 were

lost or missing, and 270 aircraft went down under enemy fire. The loss of men was later reduced by half when more than 1,000 American fliers were returned to their Italy bases from Rumanian prison camps in the first such mass air evacuation in history.

But bare-faced figures tell little of the story. The enemy reacted violently to American swipes, exploiting all the old tricks and bringing in some new. While they still had fuel and pilots, enemy fighter forces were up in strength over the Rumanian lowlands. Newest of the defense measures was encountered in late May, when the refineries were screened by thick, swirling artificial fog thrown up by at least 2,000 smoke pots scattered over the area. The smoke screens were met by Allied airmen with modified bombing and instrument technique and through use of the P-36 spotter sent ahead of the bombing raids to report which targets were more vulnerable as wind drifted the screen.[2]

Twining did not ask the men to take risks that he would not take himself. Brig. Gen. Clinton W. Davies commented that "General Twining, when he commanded the Fifteenth Air Force in Italy, always impressed me with the fact that he went out on missions himself to see what was going on" (personal communication, April 17, 1963).

Twining was also known for his calm, and a somewhat humorous example of this was related by Gen. Leon W. Johnson: "General Twining was reminiscing with me several years ago. He was telling me that Arnold had come to visit him in Italy, when the war was not yet over up in Germany. With the German war going on, Arnold in his own way was just raising hell with everybody he visited. He said, 'Nate, you're doing a lousy job. There's old Joe Cannon up there, and he's not working hard in this thing either, and we're going to lose the war if you all keep on this way. You all have got to put more effort into it, and you've got to make this thing work better than it's going now.' Well, Arnold was really giving him a rough time. While they were talking, in walked an orderly with a piece of paper and handed it to Nate. Nate read it over, and handed it to General Arnold. General Arnold read it, and the comment said that the Germans had just surrendered" (personal communication, July 12, 1978).

With the war over in Europe, Arnold sent Twining back to the Pacific to command the Twentieth Air Force. This was a touchy transfer, because it had been led by Maj. Gen. Curtis E. LeMay.

One classmate remembered, "In 1945, I was a prisoner of war of the Japanese at Hanow, a prison camp in the Akita Prefecture, Northwest

Honshu Island, Japan. Surrender had come when the B-29s began dropping food and medicines, clothing, and some other things that we had not seen for over three years and five months. In a *Time* magazine, there was an article, with photos, of our leaders in this Pacific war. There was Nate Twining with three stars on his collar. I got a thrill and was mighty glad to see it. He had just taken over the B-29 command at Saipan from Maj. Gen. Curtis LeMay. One sensed that being relieved of this command was perhaps a disappointment to General LeMay. In the article, General Twining said, 'Taking over this command from General LeMay is like taking over the Notre Dame football team from Knute Rockne.' It is no wonder that everyone who has ever known Nate Twining admires him for his leadership'' (personal communication, August 27, 1963).

After the war, Twining as Commander of the Twentieth Air Force led a flight of three B-29s that flew from Guam to Washington, D.C., by way of India and Germany. The trip covered 13,305 miles and took 60 hours, 14 minutes with the final leg of the flight, 4,105 miles, from Frankfurt, Germany to Washington, completed in 20 hours, 26 minutes. The three planes carried AAF veterans, all eligible for discharge from the service.

In October 1945, Twining was recalled, and in December he was appointed Commanding General of the Air Materiel Command at Wright Field, Ohio, where he remained until October 1, 1947.

''General Twining,'' related Lieutenant General Craigie, ''was my boss at Wright Field when he was the commander of research and development. Twining had the command, and General Chidlaw was Number Two. I had the engineering division, so I reported directly to Chidlaw; Rosie O'Donnell was my deputy. I recall an interesting incident that occurred during the time General Twining was the commander there. The first meeting of the first convention of the Air Force Association took place in Columbus, Ohio, in about 1948. Nate, Chidlaw, Rosie, and I all went over to Columbus on a Sunday. There was a family in Columbus that was responsible for bringing it about. They were an extremely influential group, owned the bank, the radio station, a shoe factory. That family had a summer place in the woods, about twenty miles outside of Columbus, which they called the Wigwam. The four of us were being put up at the Wigwam, which was their VIP quarters. After dinner the four of us played gin rummy all night long. There was nothing scheduled until eleven o'clock the next morning, when we went downtown and reviewed a parade. Then we returned to the Wigwam. Nate said that we were kind of stupid to have stayed up so late the night before, but since there was nothing for us to do that afternoon and it was going to be pretty busy that night and the next couple of days, he thought we ought to get some shut eye. So we turned in to take a nap. Chidlaw and I had one room, and Twining and O'Donnell were in the next room. The family, that is, Dick Wolfe, had gone into town right after lunch to meet the speaker for that evening, General of the Army Dwight D. Eisenhower, who at that time was Chief of Staff of the Army. The evening banquet was to open the first meeting of the Air Force Association. . . .

"Well, Dick didn't know Twining, Rosie, Ben, and I were getting a little rest. I was awakened out of a sound sleep by hearing this comment, 'Oh yes, General, it looks like Craigie and Chidlaw are getting a little shut eye.' I suddenly realized what was happening, and thinking real fast, I decided well, I just won't wake up. You can't get by with that, but I didn't realize it at the time. . . .

"I met General Eisenhower for the first time at a cocktail party two hours later, when in the most sarcastic voice that I've ever encountered in my life, General Eisenhower said to me, 'General Craigie, I hope I didn't disturb your rest this afternoon.'

"Well, Twining, of course, in his typical fashion, didn't try anything stupid like I did, he came right up out of bed, and with his hand out, said, 'Hi ya, general.' So Twining and O'Donnell came right out in a straightforward manner, but Craigie tried to be smart. I don't remember what Chidlaw did, I guess he didn't get up either. But this incident was just typical of the basic forthright manner in which Twining did everything" (personal communication, February 8, 1977).

Twining's tour at Wright-Patterson was not an easy one. One responsibility he was given when he took command right after World War II was to reduce the number of civil service workers there at Wright-Patterson. Such a reduction of civilians was sure to be controversial and certainly a cause that the congressman in that area would oppose bitterly.

One of the key men in Washington at that time was Gen. Lauris Norstad. Norstad commented that "Tooey Spaatz was extremely fond of Nate. Wright Field was a killer. Because Tooey had such a high regard for Nate, I can remember him saying, 'Nate could and should have great responsibility in this Air Force, and I've decided he ought not to be destroyed by that bunch of civil service people out at Dayton.' So we got Nate out of there, and that's when he was assigned to Alaska" (personal interview, August 22, 1977).

In October 1947, Twining became Commander in Chief of the Alaskan Command at Fort Richardson. The cold war had warmed very rapidly, and there was concern about the possibility of the Soviet Union invading the United States through Alaska. Twining had the job of defending Alaska. He had very little to work with, because there were only two fighter squadrons, no Army or Navy combat forces. Intelligence had indicated a wide variety of options open to an aggressor. "The component forces of the Air, Army, and Navy staffs," reflected Maj. Gen. John M. Breit, "had many plans but there was a great sense of hopelessness among us there, and it seemed to pervade the atmosphere. I remember when General Twining came in as our Commander. He sensed this, and immediately called a meeting. He lit a cigar and addressed us, saying, 'You people look fairly intelligent, so why in the hell are you running scared? First remember the other guys' problems are as bad as ours, maybe worse. Also remember the enemy puts on his pants one leg at a time just like you do.' With that, he turned and left the room. The people in the audience looked about rather ashamed and then spontaneously broke out laughing. Tension was gone, and we got down to work. I remember so well that after General Twining became Chief of Staff, he had this same homely philosophy of leadership that worked so successfully that day" (personal communication, April 26, 1976).

In July 1950, Twining became Deputy Chief of Staff for Personnel, in Washington. In this role, he showed particular interest in the enlisted men, because he realized how tremendous was the cost of training them for the highly technical Air Force. If these men left the service after their first enlistment, it was a waste of money; reenlistment rates had to be stepped up. General Twining felt the answer to this was to make an Air Force career more attractive, with fringe benefits, higher pay, and better housing. He also wanted to instill in servicemen the feeling that their positions were secure and that they were respected by the civilian population. His attitude almost became Air Force dogma. High-ranking officers began to dismiss questions about how big the Air Force should be with the terse comment, "Numbers are nothing but a racket." They preferred to discuss the problem of how to get airmen to look on the service as a career. One general officer even insisted, "I would take a 100-wing force if I knew that every man was well trained and steady on his job."

On June 30, 1953, Twining was named Chief of Staff of the Air Force, to succeed Gen. Hoyt Vandenberg. He was the logical choice for the job, for several reasons. He was extremely popular in the Air Force; one of the Air Force's most distinguished elder statesmen, General Spaatz, favored his selection; and, finally, he had never been identified closely with either the big bomber men or the tactical air boosters. He had proven his administrative abilities, moreover, while serving as Vice Chief and, during Vandenberg's illness, as acting Chief of Staff.

When Twining became Chief of Staff, he believed that the years of fighting to establish air power were over and that the time had come to have the Air Force prove the logic of its proper position by performance. Vandenberg had been unsuccessful in his attempt to get the Air Force a 137-wing program from Secretary of Defense Charles Wilson. When Twining became Chief of Staff, he found that the best the Air Force could hope for was 127 wings, and handed the word down, "No complaints."

Twining exercised restraint in this period of transition. Although convinced that the next war would be primarily an air war, he, as a member of the Joint Chiefs, kept aloof from the interservice rivalries that had beset the armed forces throughout American history. He told his officers, "If you've got a chip on your shoulder, get it off. We're getting along all right. Don't pick fights with other services."[3]

His relations with Adm. Arthur W. Radford, the chairman of the Joint Chiefs of Staff, were particularly good. This was not only because he and Radford were in complete agreement on the advisability of a bold Far Eastern policy, but also because they understood each other's problems. Radford had been a Navy flier, and Twining was from a family that had a strong Navy tradition. That his middle name was Farragut didn't hurt the understanding.

His thinking was always straightforward. "I was a staff officer in the Pentagon when General Twining was Chief of Staff and also when he was Chairman," reflected Gen. Bruce K. Holloway. "General Twining had a very uncluttered mind. He would always do things in a simple way with a simple solution. He didn't bother with thinking about all the possible aspects of bureaucratic and political pressure.

"I remember one day when the General called me down," continued Holloway. "It was when he was Chairman of the Joint Chiefs of Staff. 'One of my problems,' said General Twining, 'is all this excess paper. A lot of it doesn't amount to a hill of beans.' He then pulled open a drawer, actually pulled open three drawers. He pulled out the top one on one side of the desk, and it went all the way to the bottom, and it was full of paper. He said, 'You know what I do? Unless I get something I know I've got to handle right away, I just throw it all in there and let it marinate for a while. You'd be amazed how much of this takes care of itself. Every once in a while somebody comes in and goes through it, and will say to me, "Chief, you'd better take care of this" ' " (personal interview, July 7, 1978).

"I think Twining," said Gen. Bernard A. Schriever, "was more decisive than General White. He had a better sensitivity toward people . . . easier in dealing with people. If he had confidence in you, and respected you, he would then delegate without question. You always had the feeling that 'By God, he's supporting me' " (personal interview, June 29, 1977). General White was simply more standoffish. He was much more intellectual, and less decisive."

Twining supported his people after they were given a job to do. As Brig. Gen. Howard E. Kreidler put it, "When I was commander of the Presidential Wing at National Airport during the Eisenhower Administration, I also had responsibility for the aircraft of the Chief of Staff, then Nathan F. Twining. Each of the pilots on his aircraft was qualified as an aircraft commander. It was required that the first pilot of his crew also make trips in other aircraft as an aircraft commander moving other Cabinet-level personnel. On one of these trips in which we were taking the Secretary of Defense to his destination, the aircraft commander made a serious deviation from procedure in letting down to traffic altitude at destination. The Secretary was unaware of the procedure deviation. I was, and I removed this officer from General Twining's crew, reduced him to first pilot, and put him in a refresher training course. I notified General Twining, but he did not intervene. In due course, the officer was returned to the crew. I was then a young colonel, and I was very impressed that General Twining recognized my awareness that I had responsibility for his safety. It was a sensitive problem, and, frankly, he could have replaced me; but he did not" (personal communication, September 19, 1975).

An observer who had the opportunity to brief Twining as Chief, just as he had Vandenberg, said that Twining would just "sit there politely bored and would never cut you off. But he would tell you when he had had enough. His face sort of went blank and pretty soon he'd lean over to the nearest guy and say in a low voice, 'Man, it was the biggest fish you ever saw.' Or maybe he'd hit the squawk box and inquire, 'Did you get those football tickets?' and the briefer knew that was it" (Lt. Gen. James H. Doolittle, February 7, 1977).

One writer commented, "Twining's easy-going manner stays with him until the end of the day. About 5:30 he sings out, 'Let's close the place up before it burns down.' "[4] and "The word around Air Force Headquarters was that 'the old man is the most relaxed character this side of Mexico.' He is also one of the least talkative."[5]

To some, Twining lacked the guile and polished sophistication of many top military leaders, but as one writer reflected, "He's nobody's dumbbell and most of his opponents have found him a tough, unrelenting adversary in a horse trade. In Joint Chiefs' meetings, where a bevy of Philadelphia lawyers could easily become confused and distraught, Nate lights up a cigar and keeps a clear eye on the real objective. In Air Force eyes, his biggest and greatest victory came when he blocked Army attempts to move into the long-range missile field."[6]

On March 26, 1957, President Eisenhower nominated Twining to succeed Admiral Radford as Chairman of the Joint Chiefs of Staff, effective

August 15, 1957. It was the Air Force's turn to supply the Chairman of the Joint Chiefs of Staff. The first Chairman of the Joint Chiefs of Staff was General of the Army Omar N. Bradley, who was succeeded by Adm. Arthur W. Radford of the Navy. A more telling factor was that Twining had had a great deal of experience in joint Army-Navy-Air command. He had held a joint command in the Far East during World War II, and the Alaskan command was also a joint service responsibility. The decisive factor was Twining's competence in obtaining cooperation among the services.

Twining was surely one of the calmest top military men Washington had ever had. The responsibilities as Chairman did not change him. He was not politically ambitious, not a noted military strategist, nor was he anxious for public acclaim. He had no desire to establish or set any new military doctrine, nor did he really want the job. Twining was looking forward to retirement, and he had seriously considered several attractive offers from private industry. This not only would have helped him build up his near-zero bank account but also would have allowed time for hunting, fishing, and playing golf. He was no special favorite of President Eisenhower or Secretary of Defense Wilson, although both of them admired his integrity, straightforwardness, and his ability to get the other Chiefs to work together. He had a down-to-earth, commonsense approach to solving complex problems and making decisions. If he had not accepted, the Air Force might well have lost the chairmanship to the Army or Navy. Twining did not want to deny the Air Force its turn at this prestigious position.

"I think Twining's selection for Chairman," reflected Norstad, "was not arbitrary. His selection as Chairman, I think, was because there was great controversy between the Chiefs of the services at that time. Max Taylor and Nate were pretty noncontroversial, so they calmed the Chiefs down. I saw this, saw the calmness, and during that time, the Chiefs almost reached the point of working together. They never really worked too effectively. But, after Radford, we needed somebody like Nate because Radford kept the pot boiling. Nate sort of kept the lid on the pot and quieted things down. He had a knack for that, a feel for that. He did quite well as Chairman. There are times when you need someone noncontroversial, and other times you need the individual who is controversial, because he might be the guy that's smashing things out, getting things done. What we needed at that time was someone who could calm things down the way Nate did" (personal interview, August 22, 1977).

Twining became Chairman of the Joint Chiefs of Staff at a time when a number of difficult decisions had to be made that would have considerable bearing on the future. One decision concerned a change in the makeup of our strategic forces. A plan was under study to place all strategic forces under a single unified command. Another concept would put all the weaponry under a single command. The former was an Air Force idea, and placing the weaponry was a Navy one. This was a big decision for the Chiefs. It would drastically change some projects close to the hearts of the separate services, because under a new command certain aircraft and missiles would no longer be the property of the service that had developed them.

Twining, who served his country for almost fifty years, was a very unpretentious man. He was always a great outdoorsman with a passion for fishing, hunting and hiking. "Sometime ago, a friend sent Twining a huge rainbow trout," wrote one reporter. "The general regarded this fish as a thing of beauty, in approximately the same class as a B-52 bomber, which the Air Force ranks slightly above the *Mona Lisa* as a work of art. He kept the fish in his freezer for several months, exhuming it occasionally to show to guests who he thought had the education and taste to appreciate it. Subordinates granted this honor said afterwards that if you never have had a four-star general hold up a dead fish for you to admire, you have no idea how few words there are that seem adequate to the situation."[7]

He did not like service in Washington, but "went to practically every function he was invited to as Chief and Chairman," related Gen. Leon Johnson. "He always tried to get in and out faster than anybody. He hated cocktail parties; he just didn't like that type of activity, but he would take part in them. He would go and make a showing and then get out as quickly as he could. He didn't like these functions, but he did it anyway, and that's why he was a good leader" (personal communication, July 12, 1978).

"General Twining will always be remembered," commented Lt. Gen. Elwood Quesada, "by almost all of his friends for his forthrightness, his decency, and the fact that he was always a pleasant fellow to be around. Some of our officers were a little less than Nate Twining. We were a typical cross section of our population and had some arrogant bastards, too, who were quite a contrast to Nate" (personal interview, June 22, 1977).

When General Doolittle was asked about General Twining's success as a leader, his answer was, "Nate was not an intellectual in any sense of the word. He was, however, a chap with a great deal of wisdom. He had so much common sense. I think Nate's common sense and his acquired knowledge of business is what made him a great leader. And then he was consistently honest. I cannot imagine Nate exaggerating anything the least little bit" (personal interview, February 7, 1977).

In World War II, General Twining commanded more different air forces than any other general and came close to losing his life, distinguishing himself by calm courage in a harrowing air disaster that left him and others adrift in a life raft in the Coral Sea for six days. An airplane in his command dropped the atomic bomb on Japan. He mobilized the Air Force just after war broke out in Korea, and later played a major role in forming the military policy of the United States during the tense moments in Indochina, Formosa, Suez, and Jordan. Twining's almost fifty years of service were packed with action. He continued to grow during his entire career, always taking crises in his stride. As Chief of Staff, he steered the Air Force through the most critical period in its history, the transition from propeller-driven aircraft to jets to intercontinental ballistic missiles.

NOTES, Chapter 4

1. *Howitzer* (West Point Yearbook), 1920, pp. 198–99.
2. *Stars and Stripes,* April 5, 1945.
3. *U.S. News & World Report,* June 29, 1956, p. 63.
4. Clay Blaire, Jr., "The General Everybody Loves." *Saturday Evening Post,* August 17, 1957, *230:* 65.
5. Jack Wilson, "Service Rivalries Aren't Likely to Ruffle the Air Force's Calm Nate Twining,"*Look Magazine,* February 23, 1954, *18:* 120.
6. Ibid.
7. Wilson, p. 120.

CHAPTER 5

GENERAL THOMAS D. WHITE

Thomas Dresser White was born on August 6, 1901, the son of the Episcopal bishop of the diocese of Springfield, Illinois, the Rev. John Chandler White. A point of family pride was that General White's great-grandfather, also a minister, had officiated at the marriage of Abraham Lincoln. Young Tom White attended grammar school in Springfield, and graduated after four years at St. John's Military Academy, Delafield, Wisconsin, in June 1918.

During his years at St. John's, he was into everything: weighing 150 pounds at the peak, he played football for three years; was first string in cross-country, and in his senior year, was a regular on the track team; he sang in the choir; edited the monthly publication *Cadet Day* and the senior yearbook; and was a cadet captain.

A military high school gives a cadet an advantage in many respects, but it also has its drawbacks, as was obvious from White's write-up in the West Point *Howitzer* (the yearbook): "He came to us from a tin school where he had been a tin school captain. What a life he led as a plebe! How often, oh how often, we have heard him recite his honors and his accomplishments as set forth in a clipping from his home Podunk. Life was no long, sweet dream for him in summer camp."[1]

In the plebe system, when a cadet was a product of a military high school and his hometown paper wrote something complimentary that came to the ears of an upperclassman, the cadet was required to memorize it and sometimes even required to recite it backward.

Classmate Lt. Gen. Francis W. Farrell wrote, "He was a handsome cadet, and the authorities at St. John's decided to use his picture on an advertising brochure. This item preceded him to West Point and of course, when Tom was a plebe, the upperclassmen knew of it. However, he took it all in good stead, and I never knew him to sulk or be defeated by this kind of teasing. He was always equitable and cheerful—ready to do what had to be done" (personal communication, October 29, 1963).*

The entrance exam for West Point was not easy. James F. Wahl recalled, "We were two of four who succeeded in passing the entrance exam held at Jefferson Barracks, March 19, 1918, which exam was written by thirty-four persons in all. Tommy White was just 'another scared kid' like I was" (personal communication, October 9, 1963).

But Tom White wasn't too "scared" to jump the gun. With World War I in progress, "adventure stirred deep in him and airplanes started buzzing in his head." Realizing that at sixteen he was too young for Army service, he bolted to Canada and joined the Royal Canadian Air Force. Horrified, his parents yanked him back home and up to West Point, "hoping to incarcerate him there until he matured a bit and stabilized a lot" (Col. H. G. Travis, personal communication, October 9, 1963).

"His family," said his West Point classmate Gen.Lyman L. Lemnitzer, "love to tell how he entered West Point before the 'legal' age of entry and how his father had to pay for the food bill until his son reached his seventeenth birthday."[2] The official statement was "Reported June 14, 1918; permitted to remain at his own expense until legal age for admission," which, of course, was August 6, 1918.

In an interview with the author (April 30, 1963), General White was asked why he decided to go to West Point. He replied, "I think one of the reasons was I was an Episcopal clergyman's son, and there wasn't a lot of money in the family to send me to college anywhere. In fact, I went to St. John's Military Academy because it was an Episcopal school, and they gave reduced rates to Episcopal clergymen's sons. More than anything else," he said, "was the fact that I was very interested in seeing the world. I collected stamps as a kid and that had a great impact on me. I don't think I spent a lot of time thinking about the past. The collecting of stamps made me interested in geography, number one; and secondly, I became interested in various languages that appeared on these stamps and I said to myself: 'Well, how am I going to see the world for free?' The answer was military service.

"I thought," he reflected, "about going to the Naval Academy but I

---

*"Personal communication refers to letter to the author.

anticipated difficulty getting an appointment at the Naval Academy, whereas St. John's was known as an honor school and, therefore, authorized to make a certain number of appointments to West Point each year. Also, if I graduated from St. John's I didn't have to take the entrance examinations. Then I found out I could enter West Point before I graduated from St. John's as long as I passed the entrance examinations and was seventeen years old by the time the academic year began" (personal interview, April 30, 1963).

His widow, Mrs. Constance White, remembered him telling her that "he personally wrote to West Point, his number one choice by that time, and to the Naval Academy for the exams of the previous years so that he could coach himself. West Point didn't send him any, but the Naval Academy did. He got a whole fistful of exams from them" (personal communication, February 11, 1976).

St. John's was very helpful and allowed him to prep every subject required. He spent the entire winter of 1918 preparing for the West Point entrance examination. "The Naval Academy," he said, "had a book that ran back to 1900 with the entrance examination for each year. West Point had no such compilation of old entrance exams. I had trouble with mathematics, but I was pretty sure I wouldn't have too much trouble with the other subjects. I remember working and solving every mathematical problem in the Annapolis examination before I went to take my entrance exams. I used to go over to the classrooms at night and work them all out on the blackboard" (personal interview, April 30, 1963).

Cadet T. D. White began his cadet career on June 14, 1918. Soon after he arrived, he wrote home, "Get out of your head seeing me before next Sept. It is scarcely allowed for plebes to have visitors until after September 1st. Then we have more time to ourselves and are allowed to wander around in the hills a bit. . . . The first leave I can count on won't be until two years from July 22. So that's a long, hard wait but as soon as plebe days are over everything will be better.

"I figure I've *got* to stay here," he continued, "or I'd quit this minute. Perhaps it is doing me good but I long so to go home to the lake, to Gordon's, but every time I hear a railroad whistle it makes me have a strange feeling—like far-off lands—and how I want to travel."

As with any new cadet, he had to learn the system. "After I get started, I can try to 'get by' with a few things. I tried to get by with too many things here and in consequence have quite a number of demerits so far. However, every plebe here has his share of them."

But the same letter reflected that the authorities at West Point meant business. "I might tell you that an order was read," he wrote his mother, "in the mess hall one morning not long ago, and forty-two old men were dismissed for deficiency in the June exams. Six second-classmen and thirty-six third. As you probably know, there is no first class here now, and the second class is 'acting' in the capacity. Among those dropped was the company commander of our company in beast barracks—Cadet Lieutenant Murray. He was a fine fellow but very strict—an athlete rather than a student, I imagine. They are absolutely on the square here, I guess, and anyone goes out regardless."

Because of the acceleration in World War I, the upperclassmen were graduated after an abbreviated course, leaving only White's class, and he became a cadet lieutenant battalion supply officer on October 28, 1918, four months after entering as a plebe, and a month later he became a cadet captain, a distinction that normally requires over three years to achieve.

A classmate explained, "Cadet officers had to be made in a great hurry. Cadet records were screened for those with precadet military experience. Tom's tin school and Canadian record put him high on the list. Those on the list were given a twenty-minute chance to command a company at drill on the parade ground, observed by many tactical officers. Tom's knowledge of the drill and his fine deep command voice pleased the TACS and he was 'in' as cadet captain, the youngest four-striper in Academy history. This was his big break, just seventeen years old, he was off and running" (Col. H. G. Travis, personal communication, October 9, 1963).

When T. D. White became a cadet captain, he was transferred to L Company, "in which the Tactical Department," said one member of L Company, "deemed there was a need for strong leadership. 'Fighting L Company,' as they call themselves, were not so much fighting other companies as they were among themselves. This did not last long after T.D. took over. A relatively happy cadet family developed, as a result of and tribute to T.D.'s firmness and military example" (Col. John L. Goff, USAF Ret., November 18, 1963). This state of affairs continued when "the accelerated graduates" returned to the Point to complete their training.

Tom White's first roommate at the Academy, J. D. Box, made this observation: "A good percentage of our class were already veterans of World War I, quite a few having been battle tested in France. The average age of our class was higher than most. Cadet Captain White was the baby of the class, but in spite of his age and in spite of considerable variance in military experience, he forged ahead to become one of the leading members of the class" (personal communication, November 15, 1963).

"Monday the class election," Cadet White wrote to his mother on May 4, 1919, "for the 1922 *Howitzer* Board was held. I was unlucky enough to be elected editor-in-chief, which while quite an honor carries quite a burden of responsibility and work. The big thing about it is the editor-in-chief appoints all the editorial staff of eleven men with the exception of the business mgr., who is also elected. . . . I think he and I will get along very well and I hope to put out a good book." That same letter to his mother showed White's sensitivity: "Enclosed is a violet I picked while on my first outdoor surveying work."

When White was required to fill out an activity sheet, in answer to the question, "What other activities . . . did you engage in?" his answer was "Editor-in-chief of *Howitzer*." Then, in answer to the question, "Approximately how many hours did you devote to them during the academic year?" he replied, "600 hours!" With so much distraction, it is small wonder that he graduated 148 in the class of 270.

White was extremely impressive in appearance. Classmate after classmate commented on this. Col. Wilbur S. Nye said, "His first impression on most of us was, I think, that he was unusually good-looking, with fine features, an excellent physique, and well set up. He was the perfect picture of a West Pointer, from the very start" (personal communication, October 3, 1963). "After graduation," reflected Fred Trimble, "our ways parted, he in due course went to the Army Air Corps and I to the field Artillery. I next saw him in Washington, during the thirties, and realized that he was the best-dressed officer in uniform I had yet to see, just as he had always been as a cadet" (personal communication, October 11, 1963).

As pointed out earlier, White's class was a war class; within five months after they entered as plebes in June 1918, they were the only class remaining at West Point. As other classes were brought in, White's class had to shoulder the responsibility of being the *only* upperclassmen, just after they completed their own initial summer training. The awesomeness of this was expressed by Nye: "We had to pass on to the new cadets the whole of tradition and discipline of West Point, lest it be lost. In this, T. D. White was one of the outstanding leaders" (personal communication, October 3, 1963).

Classmate Col. R. C. Singer emphasized Cadet White's role in this transition: "My really first clear recollection of Tommy was following the early graduation of all classes except ours on November 1, 1918. Soon after that, all cadet officers and non-commissioned officers were appointed from our class. We suddenly emerged from plebes of only four and one-half months to first classmen [which] under normal circumstances, would have required three years. This sudden, previously unheard of transition placed a great responsibility upon the new first class, particularly upon those selected for cadet officers. We all felt keenly our position as the last connecting link between an unbroken corps of cadets, with its fine traditions of the past, and the future classes. We felt the responsibility that that chain of fine accomplishments of the Corps and our alma mater, with all its traditions, must and would not be broken—that we inherited the responsibility for its preservation and passing on to succeeding classes" (personal communication, October 21, 1963).

One of the things his classmates remembered was that his achievement of high cadet rank did not go "to his head." "He was tall, quite handsome, and striking in appearance," in the memory of W. V. Lunn. "He was a cadet officer, with many stripes on his sleeve, and he wore a star on his collar for academic efficiency. But, with all of this recognition, both military and academic, he was always available to, and active with, the rank and file of the cadets generally. He was considered then by everyone as a natural-born leader" (personal communications, October 1, 1963).

White's roommate commented, "I recall that, with his feet on the table, and reading to me from *The Power of Will* (when he should have been boning his conic sections), he would remark that there were three things he was determined to do: return to the Point as an instructor, go to China as a language officer, and get into the Air Corps. As a matter of fact, we both did two of the three, though not the same two, and I'm quite sure he would have gone back to the Point, except that timing interfered. The demands of his Air Corps career forced him to drop one objective. Perhaps his four stars as Chief of the Air Staff were recompense!" (Col. F. N. Roberts, October 20, 1963).

His desire to enter the Air Service continued after graduation. Col. William E. Ryan remembered that "we both chose the Infantry branch of the service and requested assignment to the Infantry School at Camp Benning, Georgia, in order to learn the broad principles of war combat, its tactics, and use of the most modern and various equipment of warfare. Lieutenant White absorbed all of that, yet expressed to a number of us that a new concept of war had been demonstrated by our Air Corps in World War I. He influenced several of our class to request a transfer to the Air Corps and was quite convinced that air power would be the dominant weapon of the future. I recalled that the Air Service, under the 1920 Reorganization Act, authorized only 1,500 officers and 1,300 men by 1932. Obsolete World War I equipment prevailed, so with this in mind I later transferred to the Corps of Engineers. Little could I foresee that in twenty-four years this arm of the service would develop into 243 combat groups of 80,000 aircraft and 2.5 million men" (personal communication, October 21, 1963).

When Lt. Gen. Edward T. Williams was asked what he remembered most about White as a cadet, he responded, "He has always been a determined fellow. For instance, he believed that he wanted to learn the Chinese language and prepared in his spare time a box full of cards on one side of which was a Chinese character and on the other side was the English equivalent. These he studied religiously and eventually he became a fluent Chinese scholar" (personal communication, October 9, 1963).

After graduation from the Military Academy, the cadets had a ninety-day leave, and Lieutenant White decided, along with some classmates, to go to Europe. "A few of us," said Lt. H. D. Travis, "with money in our pockets, hopped a transport ride to Europe. Tom and I paired off, hired an ex-sergeant who had a big Italian car, and toured the battlefields. We also did Paris, London, Antwerp, Brussels, Bruges, Weisbaden, Switzerland, et cetera, and joined the occupation forces on the Rhine" (personal communication, October 9, 1963).

On July 15, 1920, he was in Paris, visiting the usual sights, and commented in his diary, "On the return we stopped in at Notre Dame Cathedral (paying a fee as usual—something which makes me boil. There are but few churches in Europe where the 'pray,' which should be its watchword, has been shortened into 'pay-pay.')."

On July 27, 1920, he wrote, "In the afternoon after a lunch at the Victory Restaurant, we visited London Bridge, Westminister Bridge, Tower Bridge, St. Paul's Cathedral—very beautiful but still the same old begging boxes—thought they existed only in the Catholic Church."

They traveled to Brussels where Tom alone had the enterprise to call on the American ambassador. Then they rented a car to visit the battlefields. "We saw many, many German coast defense guns and dugouts. . . . The first town of interest," he wrote, "was Zeebrugge, famous forever for the great naval feat accomplished here by the British Navy. At Mihim we saw where twelve tons of British bombs were dumped. A few miles further, we saw acres and acres of graves and two houses and several tents. On a sign we read, 'Here stood the village of Hoage.' "

"It was a great summer; Tom matured considerably, though still under nineteen," said Travis. "I remember so well that in Coblenz, Germany, Tom talked himself out of OD duty on learning the German mark would be devalued to practically zero on the same day. Figuring it would be a shopper's heyday for a few hours before the Germans woke up, he borrowed all the money he could, took off early and made a killing buying oodles of valuable items with good U.S. money. We all wondered how he got so smart so young" (personal communication, October 9, 1963).

After his leave, he reported to his first duty station. "We moved on to Fort Benning," wrote Travis, "for a year of learning how to be an officer. Tom worked hard but was getting restless, and airplanes were in the sky and in his head. It would be a new experience, he said, a gamble maybe, a thrill certainly, but a new branch, a young branch for sure, with room to grow, with room for promotion and a definite goal. The seed was planted in Tommy White's mind, and it grew; but while he was at the Infantry School, he concluded that it had the good earthy foundation, he studied very hard and was one of the outstanding officers" (personal communication, October 9, 1963).

"Two or three of my fellow infantrymen," said General White, "applied to go into flying upon completing the course at Fort Benning. I thought about it, but I had applied for foreign duty—there again you can see that travel bug came in. I had asked for several places and my orders came in to go to Panama. So I thought, well, I will go down there and then I will see what I can do about flying. I hadn't much more [than] arrived there before I wished I had gone into flying" (personal interview, April 30, 1963). He wrote a series of articles for the *Infantry Journal,* and the conditions he described gave insight into why he wished he had gone into flying training. "The climate is terribly hot and humid. Some time is required for the new arrival to become accustomed, perhaps better say reconciled. . . . Due to balmy climate the effort required to take advantage of the various sports and recreations offered generally overcomes the desire . . . even Army people cannot exist on balmy air, or seething surf and waving palms without longing for their own United States. However beautiful and placid the little island may be, however warm and sensuous the breezes blow, the days grow monotonous, the months drag by—three years become appallingly long."[3]

But it was not easy even for him. "I nearly go wild," he wrote to his father on December 28, 1921, "because all I hear, smell, or am able to think about around the house is eat or sleep. Everything seems to center on food. . . . I have sometimes seriously reflected in my mind whether or not I am going insane. Nearly every week some soldier does go crazy here. . . . Yet I haven't the nerve to resign," he continued, "I know I belong in the Army and wouldn't be happy anywhere else—but I sure got the wrong place—and I think the wrong branch down here." Lieutenant White's initial assignment in Panama was as Company Commander and Battalion Adjutant. During the reporting period September 10, 1921, to October 10, 1921, he was rated as simply average, apparently because of his age and perhaps his discontent.

His thoughts were still very much on flying. He wrote to his father on December 4, 1921, "I am wondering what you will write about the Air Service. You agreed so heartily with me about my sizeup of the Army that it quite surprised me. . . . Now, as I wrote, I have wanted to be in the Air Service for years ever since I was at St. John's and the British army had their recruiting agencies in Milwaukee. I wrote home about it then but Mother wouldn't hear of it while West Point was in view and I was 'so young' but nevertheless I think the thing I regret most in my life as I look at it now is that I didn't run away from St. John's and join the Canadian army as Rogers did, and I would have done it if I hadn't passed my W.P. exams. I had the papers and everything for joining the Royal Flying Corps of Canada. . . .

"Now my contention is that in the Air Service I will be 'doing something' all during my preliminary training—learning to fly, which isn't hard at all and the danger in it is very small. To my mind the danger of it doesn't figure at all. . . . It is a young branch and is undoubtedly the arm which is being developed and expanded more rapidly than any other. Hence the opportunities for initiative and ideas are vastly greater than in any other part of the Army."

In addition to duties as a company commander and post adjutant, he had the opportunity to serve as a judge advocate for special court-martial. He served as motor transportation officer and was even assigned duty with the military police.

He continued his study of languages. "Have been doing a good deal of studying lately as well as some writing. You will be surprised to know that I can read all of the first thirty pages of my Chinese lesson book. . . . I can now write the Chinese script—which is supposed to be very hard. I really enjoy such things, and it seems to come easy to me. I can read Spanish, Portuguese, some French and Italian, and a little Chinese, which isn't bad for twenty-one yrs. counting that I have had to do other studies most of my life."

Before leaving Panama, White became Aide-de-Camp for Brig. Gen. J. M. Palmer, who commanded the Nineteenth Infantry Brigade in the Panama Canal Zone. Instead of receiving a rating of "average" as he had from the captains, majors, and lieutenant colonels, Palmer wrote that White was "A young officer of unusual capacity, energy and force. Also possesses an unusually attractive personality."

White commented on this experience in an interview with the author (April 30, 1963): "My last year in Panama I was Aide-de-Camp to General John M. Palmer, who was one of the great scholars of the old Army. He wrote a number of books and was co-author of a work that related to the National Defense Act of 1920, the big reorganization act after World War I. He was the author of *Washington, Lincoln, Wilson: Three War Statesmen,* another on General von Steuben, *America in Arms,* and *Statesmanship or War.* General Palmer had a great influence in my life because he was such a student of history. Another young officer who later achieved great distinction was in Panama from 1919 to 1922, and his General also started him on a reading program . . . Capt. Dwight D. Eisenhower, who was assigned as Executive Officer to Brig. Gen. Fox Conner of the Nineteenth Brigade.

Getting into the Air Service, when you were already assigned to one of the Army branches, was very difficult. Indeed, it appears that in order to transfer to the Air Service it was necessary for White to work out a "deal." "We were very close friends at the Academy," related Col. J. P. Barney, Jr., "and were in numerous scrapes together, and when he transferred to the Air Force he tried to talk me into going with him, but personally, I liked my tanks where I could get out and run. . . . My father was Chief of Purchase in Washington when Tommy wrote to me to see if my father could help him get transferred to the Air Service. At that time the Chief of Infantry was not in favor of allowing any of his West Point graduates to transfer, but the Infantry School at Benning was just getting started and was short of everything so an agreement was reached to the effect that on the day Tommy's transfer was announced, two freight-car loads of office furniture would be shipped to Benning. From that you can estimate his value at the time!" (personal communication, November 4, 1963). He was assigned to Advanced Flying School at Kelly Field, Texas, and again was rated as an average officer. The brief word picture written by his reporting officer, Lt. Col. C. C. Culver, stated, "A fine young officer, energetic in performance of duty, anxious to learn; a very good pursuit pilot."

Some of those going through pilot training did so as officers, as White did; others went through as flying cadets. One of his classmates was Elwood R. Quesada. "When I was a cadet," reflected Lieutenant General Quesada, "and we were at the gunnery range at Houston, Tommy used to go out of his way to be pleasant to me even though he was an officer and I was just a cadet. I always believed it was because he had observed that I read a great deal, and he and I would discuss subjects that he had an interest in. I was a real history buff at that time in my life. We often ate out together. . . . I recall several occasions when I would go with Tommy to a concert; we would also go to art galleries. We didn't like to tell people because we were a little bit fearful that they would think the thing sort of sissy-like" (personal interview, June 22, 1977).

During the course of his pilot training, there was a rash of accidents. White was apparently concerned that his mother had heard of these and was worried. He wrote to her on July 5, 1925, "Do not worry about me because of those accidents last week. As an example of my playing it safe, this is what happened yesterday—after leaving Kelly Field in Ship Number 73, my gasoline pump went out, and I had to run on my emergency tank (fifteen minutes of gas, if full) and turn back. I had pumped up my emergency [tank] some but not enough to fill it. At least it didn't overflow, though I thought I had pumped enough and that the overflow was probably out of order—well I had to land soon—at least within fifteen minutes—Kelly Field was about ten minutes and Fort Sam Houston airdrome about four miles—I didn't take the chance of going to Kelly Field, though I could have made it in about seven minutes—I went to Fort Sam—and got there as my emergency went dry.

"I passed more than 200 hours in the air this month—almost 230 now. In the old days a man was an experienced pilot at 50 hours. Had 55 hours in June alone—second highest in the field—came from getting the extra trip to Fort Sill, which added 10 hours, 18 minutes. One must have 200 hours DH time to qualify as an airmail pilot—just mentioned that as a comparison—haven't any idea of going to the mail! I have almost 100 hours in a DH and and the rest in different types—many more difficult than the DH."

"There are only eight more days of flying until we get our wings. . . . In many ways I feel it is a graduation from the hardest school of all," he wrote his mother on August 30. "I know there is no other institution in the world in which only about 1 in 6 who enter get there. We began with 290 and have 49 left!" He went on to say, "I have some new snapshots. . . . When I graduate, you might put one of them in the paper. I'm proud of getting through this place."

A day later he wrote, "The Army and Navy Register has our orders. . . . I go to Washington, D.C.—Bolling Field! Isn't that beyond one's wildest dream? Imagine me—promoted, getting wings and ordered to Washington almost all at the same time. The only bad feature is that flying is rather curtailed there—but nowhere will there be as much flying as here."

His duty at Bolling Field was to assist in the supervision of the engineering shops for the overhaul and repair of aircraft and engines. "Being Squadron Commander," he wrote, "is like being a company commander in the Infantry—only I have the repair shops like an airplane factory in addition—motor overhaul—new motors and airplanes to be set up—wing making, etc., etc.—my men all work in the shops. It is like being general manager of a factory of 200 employees, with the housing and feeding besides."

He was really excited about his work. "One of the men from the pursuit group at Selfridge brought one of the new P-1 pursuit planes here, and it was given some repairs in my shop so I got to test it. It is a wonderful little ship, and I flew it without any trouble—much to the delight of my squadron, who turned out to see it. Especially since the regular pilot from Selfridge had just wrecked one and nearly wrecked this one getting here when he landed (don't think I'm getting good—I'm just careful and don't take chances)."

"Certainly am awfully busy—no time to attend anything—I am fully enrolled in the School of Foreign Service at Georgetown, which takes all of my spare time—have no days now. As for Xmas presents for me, I think I'd rather have a subscription to the magazine *Foreign Affairs* than almost anything I can think of."

White's assignment to Bolling Field was from October 12, 1925, to April 30, 1927. "When I was at Bolling Field," White recalled, "I went to night school at Georgetown but I don't think I stuck with any of them very much except the language courses. I took both Chinese and Russian, but I put aside any ideas of foreign service because in those days for sure one had to have a private fortune to get to the top of the foreign service. I must have had an ambition to get to the top even in those days, though I never have been particularly conscious of that."

This was a period of indecision for Lieutenant White. Should he remain in the service or enter the Diplomatic Corps? Only twelve days after arriving in Washington, he commented, "I'm waiting for things to settle here before trying to formulate any definite plans of action for the future. One thing is sure. I want to take these diplomatic examinations as soon as I'm prepared for them. I'm quite delighted to find that I'm bored to death with most of the affairs in Washington. . . . Some of the so-called diplomats at the ball the other night gave me such a pain that I've almost lost all interest in trying it. Immediately thereafter I wanted to cling to some of the good old ways of the Army."

In a later letter to his mother, dated Sunday, October 25, 1925, he said, "In talking with the General I was surprised that he suggested that I quit the Army and be a hobo for a few years. He highly recommended it—and he wasn't being sarcastic with me for being unsettled. Said it was quite natural. As I've said before, when it is nice and warm I'm ready to quit and take a chance in the world, but when it gets cold I feel thankful to have a nice job (in a way—plenty of money but too many restrictions)—a place to sleep and eat and above all to hold my head up and *do society with anyone*. That is the thing which probably holds me back from quitting."

On May 28, 1927, Lt. Thomas D. White married Rebekah Lipscomb at Epiphany Church, Washington, D.C. His father, Bishop John Chandler White, performed the marriage ceremony, assisted by Rev. ZeBarney Phillips, who was the rector of Epiphany Church. (At the time of their marriage, White's father was still active as a bishop in the Episcopal Church, living in Springfield, Illinois.) Best man at the wedding was Lt. Walter C. White, who at the time was stationed at Mitchell Field, New York, and among the ushers was Lt. Elwood R. Quesada. After the wedding reception at the Wardman-Park Hotel in Washington, D.C., the couple departed for

China, where he had been assigned for duty in Peking, sailing from San Francisco on June 10, 1927.

He kept a diary of his trip across the Pacific and of his China tour. On board ship, he continued his study of languages. "There are two Capuchin monks aboard going to Guam for sixteen years, rumor has it. They are from Spain . . . I have been practicing Spanish with them. I am surprised to find how quickly I forget—yet I can nearly say everything without thinking so at one time. I guess I know the language very well." He wrote in his diary on June 15, 1927, "I spent most of the time so far reading, also brushing up on Russian, which sounds foolish, I do know. But it is the most interesting language in China. Especially if we go to Peking by way of Fusan and Mukden. I find that I can read a good deal of Russian and my eight months of it at Georgetown have given me the pronunciations correctly, so certainly no harm is done in studying it if I want to—so long as it doesn't interfere with my later study of Chinese. People used to laugh at me, I am sure, when I studied Chinese for recreation at West Point and elsewhere, but I take pleasure in thumbing my nose at all of them now—I haven't seen anyone who wasn't green with envy at the idea of going to China as I am."

He also spent a good deal of time reading. "I am reading," he wrote on June 18, 1927, "*An Outline of Chinese History* which is the latest book on China and is very interesting indeed. I also have enough big books to last me for three or four voyages like this one, including *The Story of Philosophy, Napoleon* by Emil Ludwig, *The Royal Road to Romance,* etc., etc."

White's first effectiveness report, while again rated "above average," had this brief addition by Maj. John Magruder, the Military Attaché in Peking: "This officer has a high degree of intelligence with self-assurance in keeping with his agile and critical mind. Under proper directed influence and not too much conscious restraint, this officer should be of great value to the service." Apparently Magruder was suggesting White, if left alone, would really "move out."

The reporting officer also observed that White maintained his interest in flying. "He shows great initiative and zeal, wholly aside from the financial advantage involved, in keeping up his flying status by frequent visits to the Marine Corps squadron on Hsia He." On August 22, 1927, shortly after arriving in China, White wrote in his diary, "The folks at home think they have me safely away from flying, for four years at least, if not for good." But he was not. He had worked it out with the Marine Corps, which had aircraft in China, to maintain his flying proficiency with them. The Chief of the Marine Corps in Manila had Lieutenant White assigned to one of his squadrons for flying duty, which "required the approval of the Secretary of the Navy." The August 22 diary entry also commented on his first flight in

China that day: "It was a pleasant sensation to be in a ship again and especially to be the first Army pilot to fly in China—except perhaps [for] the world fliers who stopped here. The graveyards and towns were most interesting from the air."

On one occasion, he flew with some Navy pilots. "I am reserving my opinion because this time was all as a regular mission, chasing torpedoes which the submarines were firing for target practice. It was all most interesting from the air. A destroyer usually was used for target practice for the torpedoes, which are real ones, except not loaded. The submarines were very clever at keeping out of sight." He noted quite a contrast: "I'm keeping my eyes and ears open, learning all I can about the Navy. They have many times more things to do with than we in the Army, they seem to have no lack of money or supplies, which we are always short of. The promotion is much more rapid. . . . There are only two officers who have been out of Annapolis longer than I have been out of the Point, yet there are eight who are senior to me."

The next effectiveness report covered from June 30, 1928, to June 30, 1929, gave White a rating as a language officer as "excellent." White's initiative was such that he not only studied Chinese, but also, as the report stated, "Officer independently learned sufficient Russian to translate documents." Actually, he was taking lessons twice a week. A large community of former members of the Russian Army had migrated to China after the Communist takeover. White frequently invited these "White" Russians to dinner to practice his Russian and, of course, was invited in return to dine with them. On one occasion, he wrote home on April 29, 1930, "I went to a Russian dinner last week where we discussed plans for helping an old (Russian) general and his family. . . . He is having a very hard time. I gave him fifty dollars gold last week but he writes that he is having a very difficult time finding work, as the firms in Harbin are afraid to employ White Russians. The Reds put every obstacle in their way."

But the real value of White's preparation for future responsibility was Magruder's comment in 1929, "A good grounding in Chinese language *and in knowledge of Far Eastern affairs.*" White's knowledge of international relations was to be a large factor in his selection as Chief of Staff.

He worked hard at it. "I have had my nose in a book," he wrote on January 27, 1930, "all the time as I am working to catch up the work I lost out while I had the bad foot. Also I want to finish my aero dictionary, which I am working on before Major Magruder is relieved as MA. I have to complete it before I go away." He was also publishing in the professional journals. "Just got the May number of the 'U.S. Air Services' with my article 'Acrobatics on Paper, or How to Write a Chinese Dictionary.' "

"My exam is due next Thursday," White wrote home on April 11, 1930, "hence I am working really too hard. It is boring now, and the lessons prescribed are altogether foolish. I am only waiting until I finish up to let out a holler. I have to let all the really important parts of my work go in order to do the unnecessary things for the exam! Writing the Chinese language is the very last requirement we have—yet it is the subject on which we spend the most time! Not one of us will ever be called upon to write anything—we can dictate what to write to a clerk—then all we have to do is be able to read and know whether or not he had written what he was told."

On June 6, 1930, White was at last given the examination for which he had been preparing for years. It consisted of the translation of a difficult passage from a Chinese newspaper, and the translation, from English to Chinese, of Peck's cards (a selection of Chinese vocabulary words) 401 through 600. Capt. Harker G. Tenney, the Assistant Military Attaché, who did the evaluation, wrote commending White on having "successfully passed his final examination in the Chinese language."

Despite his diligent study of Chinese and Russian, White did not neglect his flying. This was not always easy. One year, instead of going to flying in Manila with the Army Air Corps, he went to Tsingtao and flew with the Navy. "The Navy hurt both my pride and my conscience," he wrote to his mother on July 1, 1930, "which is serious with me. They never let me ride in the front seat of a machine, and only when I insisted was I allowed to land. Everything but the holding of the stick in the air was done by the Navy pilot. Several times I had to go up with enlisted pilots who were just out of the flying school. They wanted to demonstrate what hot acrobatic flyers they were, and I had to endure some stunt flying at the hands of new pilots. It was very poor flying, and I have been flying too long now to let some half-baked youngster try to stunt me."

Lt. Gen. Joseph Smith was a lieutenant stationed in Manila when Lieutenant White came there, and recalled White's nearly fatal accident on September 26, 1930. The next day, the reporter who was present wrote in the *Daily Bulletin:*

> Because of the heavy condition of the landing field, it was necessary for the planes to take off from the concrete runway situated directly in front of the hangars. Lieutenant Backes was first away and got off in good form, while the plane of Lieutenant Thomas D. White was wheeled into position. With the motors roaring and attaining a great speed, White's ship came tearing down the runway in pursuit of Lieutenant Backes who was already circling around the field waiting for the other five

planes. Suddenly the ship, which had by this time almost gained the required momentum to lift her tail from the ground, struck a pile of loose dirt that had been carelessly left on the concrete. The speeding ship virtually leaped at least ten feet into the air, careened to the left and then to the right barely missing several automobiles that had been parked near the hangars. The crowd scattered like magic as a crash was imminent. But by a great display of calmness and head work, Lieutenant White managed to avoid the many obstacles and climbed into the air.

As the plane rose it could be plainly seen that her running gear had been badly damaged. The right wheel was folded under her body making a ground landing almost impossible. Two pursuit ships were quickly wheeled out and took the air in an effort to familiarize the unlucky pilot with the condition of his ship.

Lieutenant White realized that something was wrong as he began circling around the field while the two smaller planes were frantically attempting to make him understand the situation. Everyone expected a crash. The fire department and ambulance were rushed to the scene and the entire personnel of the post stood by ready to go into action as soon as the ship came down.

The two pursuit ships came down apparently having put their message across. Another plane was sent up with orders to have White drop his gasoline to make the incapacitated plane lighter, and lessen the danger of fire if she crashed. The speed boat was ordered to be ready as it was possible that the landing might be made in the Bay. White kept circling the field apparently trying to decide whether to take a chance of dropping into the water or of cracking up on land.

The suspense was breathtaking as there was only one chance in a thousand that either Lieutenant White or his mechanic, Sergeant Langston, could come out of the episode without serious injury.

The pilot at last decided to attempt a landing within the field as he kept circling lower and lower and all onlookers stood ready to rush to the ship as she hit.

Having been warned that his right wheel was gone, Lieutenant White jockeyed around and started down. With the motor cut off he brought the plane within a few yards of the ground and suddenly tilted her to the left and struck the surface on the only good wheel left. Then, just as she hit he swung the ship to the right, and by a miracle the right wing dug into the turf and kept her upright. The impact of the wing digging into the ground caused the machine to turn two complete circles before she finally came to a rest.

Lieutenant White and Sergeant Langston came out without a scratch in what was probably one of the coolest and best planned emergency landings that has ever been recorded. Congratulations came thick and fast as the cool-headed pilot climbed from his precarious perch.

During White's visits to Manila, he stayed with Smith at the Army-Navy Club. They spent many hours talking in the evening. General Smith later remembered that White in the last year "was permitted to roam around and do what he wanted. He traveled around, and he used to tell me he'd take a rickshaw boy and go into the country as much as two weeks at a time, just traveling around, living with the people, talking Chinese, and learning the way of those people. He knew a lot about their art and their culture. He was very interested in that sort of thing. . . . His main objective was to learn how to speak the different dialects of their language" (personal interview, July 6, 1977).

Lt. Gen. Clovis E. Byers, U.S. Army retired, remembered, "While on duty as a language officer in Peking, his courage, imagination, and willingness to undertake the unusual caused him to ask Col. Nelson Margetts, U.S. Military Attaché in China, for permission to visit the battlefront during the early Japanese thrust into Manchuria. The clarity, accuracy, and objectivity of Tom White's reports were such that they were sought throughout the War Department. From this time on, Tom White became a marked man" (personal communication, October 14, 1963).

One of White's classmates was Lyman L. Lemnitzer, who went on to become Army Chief of Staff at the same time White was Air Force Chief of Staff. He remembered, "While Tommy was in Peking, Chiang Kai-shek resumed his civil war against the Communists, and Tommy felt his value as an officer would be enhanced more by observing the fighting than by studying in Peking. He tried to convince Col. Nelson Margetts, a military attaché at the time, of this fact. The Attaché took a dim view of such a risk, but Tommy's determination succeeded in securing authority for a two-week trip of observation. His discerning eyes picked up so much of value that he promptly sent his superiors surprisingly thorough reports and requested an extension of time in the combat zone. Colonel Margetts immediately recognized the great value of Tommy's reporting and happily informed him that 'you are free to remain on the border as long as you're able to find material such as that contained in this comprehensive report!' "[4]

The assignment to China "fulfilled many things for me," reflected White in an interview with the author (April 30, 1963). "I was seeing a very exotic part of the world. I was very interested in the languages, and Chinese was certainly as complicated a one as you would want, but more importantly, from a career point of view, there were only about 800 officers in the whole Air Service at that time. Everybody in the service got to know me by name, if not personally, because I was that crazy son of a gun who was out in China. I met a good many people who were serving in the Philippines. They would come up to China on their way back home and have a vacation and stop over in China. I looked out for them, so I got to know one way or another a great many of the Air Service people. The only point in knowing people or being known is something which inevitably has its part in the way one's life goes."

One unique and lasting contribution during his tour White mentioned in a letter to his mother on January 5, 1930: "The Chinese aeronautical dictionary which I am working on takes most of my time. I hope I will be finished within a month. I don't suppose it is worth publishing, but it should be an original contribution in the way of an official report to Washington." Then, in March, he wrote home, "My dictionary of Chinese-English aviation terms went to the War Dept., in the last pouch with a wonderful letter from Major Magruder. It was my valedictory. But I'd hate to be examined on the terms!"

Not content with the Chinese dictionary, his active mind sought another challenge. "The War Dept. made nice comments about the dictionary," he wrote on May 25, 1930, "but not as nice as the office had expected, I gather. Tenney was quite wrought up over it. One gets little appreciation in the service from anyone but one's own superior officers. The Major made a fine statement about it. Several people in aviation in Shanghai have requested copies and have been very complimentary. I may attempt something of the sort with Russian—though this would be merely transcribing from an English-Russian dictionary to a Russian-English one. I have an official Soviet English-Russian dictionary of military terms which the War Department has not got, and it might establish my ability to speak Russian if I made such a transcription. It would be a tremendous work and would require a Russian stenographer as well as a great deal of personal attention. The dictionary is 268 pages!"

On completion of his tour in China, White was assigned to duty in Washington, D.C. as Assistant to the Chief of the Air Corps, Maj. Gen. Benjamin D. Foulois. During that period, White did considerable work in the Plans Office under Maj. W. R. Weaver, who rated White "superior" in every single category, to wit, in physical activity, physical endurance, military bearing and neatness, dignity of demeanor, attention to duty, tact, initiative, intelligence, force, judgment, common sense, and leadership! This was the first time in White's entire career that he was rated "superior" in all categories. Not unnaturally, Foulois was more reserved in his endorsement: he lowered some categories from "superior" to "excellent," and even lowered some categories from "superior" to "satisfactory." Apparently, an old-timer like Foulois did not believe in granting such high ratings to a mere lieutenant.

There was certainly no lack of variety in the assignments a young officer received in those days. After a tour as Assistant to the Chief of the Plans Division, White became Assistant Engineering Officer at Bolling Field. In addition, he had the responsibility for the prison and was a military police officer.

During his sixteen months, White also served for a time as Mess Officer at Bolling Field; he was rated "excellent" as an airplane pilot, and in the last half-year, July 1, 1933, to January 15, 1934, he was rated as "superior" in almost every category by Lt. Col. B. W. Yount, his commanding officer.

When the United States recognized the Soviet Union, the first U.S. Ambassador appointed to Moscow was William C. Bullitt. President Franklin D. Roosevelt told Ambassador Bullitt he could appoint anyone he wanted to his staff. Bullitt also insisted that he be permitted to have an airplane of his own and that he be able to fly wherever he so desired within the Soviet Union. The Kremlin granted approval, and the newspapers began to refer to him as Moscow's first foreign "flying ambassador." The pilot selected was 1st Lt. Thomas D. White, who was the first, last, and only American to receive a Soviet pilot's license.

"I suppose you could say I tried to prepare myself," commented White, "for the day when we would recognize the Soviet Union. I studied Russian at Georgetown, and that paid off. When I was selected to go to the Soviet Union as Air Attaché, I can't say I did anything to set it up other than the fact that I had studied Russian and some people knew it. It was a complete surprise to me when I was named. I was sent for by General MacArthur when I was a lieutenant at Bolling Field and General MacArthur was the Chief of Staff. I couldn't figure that one out. General MacArthur told me he was sending me to Moscow. I didn't ask anybody for that assignment, but I had made application for more foreign duty" (personal interview, April 30, 1963).

For a man who loved to travel, it was surprising that he was not pleased with this assignment to the Soviet Union. "I felt much as though I were watching," he wrote in his diary on February 15, "my own coffin being lowered into the grave when I watched the gangplank cast off. I'm not as blue as that but I am surprisingly unexcited."

He arrived in Moscow on March 7, 1934, and wrote, "Very tired. Caught a cold and am, as usual in a strange place, rather blue." Two days later he wrote, "Very blue all day. Miss Beck [his wife] and Becky Ann terribly. Long, very blue letter to Beck. Kuniholm and I admit we have not been so low since we were plebes at the Point." And on April 13, 1934, he wrote, "Friday the 13th but seems no worse than any other day. They are all bad!"

He was separated from his wife and little daughter, but that was only one reason for his depression. Part of the difficulty was insufficient funds. The government allowance for food was inadequate. He and the other military personnel could only afford two meals a day on the food allowance. Until the Embassy building was constructed, he lived in a Moscow hotel. He wrote, 'Mr. Bullitt came in during our conference . . . and he simply said, 'let them have three meals for $2.00 a day'—which shows how utterly little he understands the predicament of the rest of us who haven't large fortunes."

In his job as Air Attaché, he attended his first maneuvers of the Red Army within a matter of days after his arrival. On March 14, 1934, he and the other foreign attaches were furnished with bound copies of the Red and Blue Army situations. He wrote that the soldiers wore white for camouflage because of the snow. "Much interested in an aerial sled used for reconnaissance by the Regimental Commander. Had a ride in it. Mounted on three skis with front single ski controlled by cockpit like an auto. Had a pusher type air-cooled engine behind with a set of steel guards in rear of cockpit." He met the Division Commander, whom he described as "very active. 38 years old. Dynamic, rough, positive, rather vulgar."

On March 17, 1934, he visited the Red Army Museum and Club House escorted by a military officer named Smagin who was his liaison with the Soviet government. The club house had a library, pool tables, tea room, and shooting gallery. "I was invited to take a few shots and made 4 fours at 30 yds. Standing. Better than any of the Russians, thank heaven!" His marksmanship training at West Point, and that something extra he had put out at Fort Benning, now paid off.

The opportunity for intelligence gathering was really quite limited for foreigners. Communists put severe restrictions on their travel and on the opportunity to meet the Soviet people and officials. On May 1, 1934, he attended his first parade in Red Square. That night he went to a dinner

given by the Swedish Attaché. He commented that "everyone with pencil
and paper writing down the number of men and units and airplanes, tanks,
etc. I couldn't see the sense in it. I knew for my own information the exact
number of tanks and airplanes. Quite amusing so much bother about a
parade. Shows how little information is to be gotten here!"

But White's opportunity was greater than for any other foreigner
because our Ambassador had an airplane. This gave White the chance to
visit aircraft factories: he saw under construction the aircraft *Maxim Gorki,*
an eight-engined passenger plane; at Factory Number 22, a huge plant, he
saw the production of two- and four-engine bombers, and was given a ride
in one of the latter.

Factory Number 22 in Moscow, he reported, "was producing one four-
engined bomber every day. On the flight line in front of this factory there
were never less than sixty of these bombers waiting for fly-away. I often
suspected, however, that many of them were held up because of defects discovered at the final inspection. Production is on a huge scale in the Soviet
Union but quality is lacking in almost everything."

The tour in the Soviet Union was a broadening experience for the future
Chief of Staff of the Air Force. The essential education was learning about
Communism as it was practiced in the Soviet Union and about the nature of
the people and government officials.

White constantly attended the opera at the Bolshoi and the theaters. On
March 20, 1934, he went to see a play called *Joy Street.* "Quite interesting,"
he wrote, "and I understood about 40 percent of the dialogue. Minister
helped me keep track of plot." And he was learning about indoctrination in
the play. There was "much anticapitalist propaganda involving a strike . . .
even propaganda speeches before the opening act." He went to see a Balzac
play and by now he "could follow most of plot."

He continued his habit of reading and frequented the local bookstores.
He wrote in his diary, "Random note—People in bookstore seem surly and
unfriendly. Maybe have read more anticapitalistic propaganda. I am always
taken for a German. Not complimentary, I understand!" He obtained a
Russian middle-school geography book, which he described as "very
useful."

On March 31, 1934, White invited some of the Russian officers to a
lunch. "All invitations," he wrote, "whether verbal or written must go
through Smagin [his opposite number]. He asked Miss Tolstoy [White's
Russian secretary] not too pleasantly to please make me understand that.
Yet they say we are free to make friends with Russian officers!"

He learned of the authoritarianism of the Communist dictatorship and of the fear the people had of foreigners and for their own security. Even the highest Soviet officials had this fear. White gave a dinner in April 1934 for the Soviet officers, scheduled to be held at the Metropole Hotel but switched to the National Hotel in Moscow. This was done at the insistence of Florinsky, the Chief of Protocol, and upset Lieutenant White, because the new location was considerably more expensive. "We do not know the reason," he wrote, "as there is a private entrance to the Metropole. Probably better guarded at National. It's a great life in a *free* country!" he noted.

Not even a high official was safe. On August 15, 1934, Florinsky disappeared. "The wild stories from books are not so wild after all. At a dinner at the Danish Legation, Florinsky was called to the phone, excused himself, and said he would be back in half an hour. He has not been seen or heard from since! Probably Siberia for him." Florinsky lived in the same apartment building with the members of the staff of the American Embassy. Elbridge Durbrow called him a "built-in spy." Durbrow remembered that after Florinsky disappeared "a great wax seal was placed on his door by the Soviet Secret Police. That was our tip off that he'd been picked up! We never saw him again" (personal interview, December 28, 1977).

With his knowledge of Russian—and vodka—White arranged a dinner party that included the Soviet Minister of War and, as host, made a speech of welcome and toasts in Russian. It must have been nerve-wracking, because he wrote in his diary that night, "Everyone says I kept my feet in almost perfect order and walked to the car and to the hotel from the car."

On March 13, 1934, White attended a dinner given for him and another member of the U.S. Embassy staff, Nimmer. Present were Smagin, Smolin, Florinsky and his assistant Shilo. "I sat between Smagin and Shilo," he wrote. "Shilo gave me some hints as to probable limitations on my flying. Only Ambassador to be allowed to fly. Must get authority for every flight, etc., etc. Will report this to Ambassador as an indication of what underlings are thinking. Afraid to set precedent. Japanese Ambassador has asked for plane and been refused on grounds this plane to Bullitt as personal favor and for personal use."

Nine days later, White and Bullitt called on Voroshilov, Commissar for War. "In my opinion," he said, "he is the strongest man in Russia—controls the greatest army in the world anyway." They discussed flying privileges and "V. agreed to everything—landing wherever we chose, provided we didn't crack up, and housing facilities."

But White was learning fast about the Russians. He left the meeting feeling skeptical about Soviet promises. "I would rather have an agreement to 75 percent of a written document than 100 percent of a verbal request. He [Ambassador Bullitt] feels otherwise."

It was only a few weeks before Bullitt realized how right White was. "Ambassador much discouraged," White wrote on April 9, 1934, "says not a single verbal agreement has been kept. Must confirm everything in writing. I recommended it long ago." He added, "I feel Ambassador should take counsel from the part of his staff with Oriental experience rather than from European side of staff."

The American plane was finally shipped from Hamburg and on May 2, 1934, White went to Leningrad when the aircraft finally arrived there in crates. Again he ran into administrative difficulties and delays. He called on the Chief of the Civil Airport, who said he would have the airplane at the field the next day. White's reaction was, "I doubt it like hell, as nothing has ever been done according to the word given by a Russian."

There were reasons for the delays. In addition to Soviet concern over precedent, they were suspicious that the aircraft might be used for reconnaissance. On one occasion, White found the hangar being searched, looking for photo equipment. The Soviet engineers came out from the factory near the hangar where the aircraft was to be housed. White was overheard to say, "I wouldn't like to be the first passenger in the *Maxim Gorki*." They thought, he said, that "I had noted some serious structural deficit which they said their enemies wouldn't tell them about but hoped I would. I forgot I represent the greatest airplane manufacturing country in the world."

It was suggested to White that he fly back to Moscow under escort of Soviet planes, but he refused. He was furious, and his response in his diary was blunt: "The dirty lying sons of bitches." He instructed them not to move the plane.

Finally, one of the U.S. State Department officers got into the dispute. "Loy Henderson from the U.S. Foreign Office told the Soviets to quit beating around the bush and talk straight," White commented in his diary. "They finally did. The plane was to be considered as a civil machine and must conform to all civil air laws. Also it was to be considered Mr. Bullitt's personal machine, and the invitation will not be renewed to any other succeeding ambassador."

On May 14, 1934, the aircraft was finally assembled. Great credit was due to the American mechanics, because the engine started on the first try. White flew almost daily, and on May 23, 1934, he received his Soviet transport pilot's license, marked "No. 01," the first ever given to a foreigner. His American mechanics received their mechanic's licenses, and they were numbered "NO.s 01, 02, 03."

Once the aircraft was operational, it did not take long before White was challenged. On June 25, 1934, an article appeared in the *New York Times* with the headline, "Bullitt Crashes in Embassy Plane." The article continued, "Ambassador Bullitt and his pilot, Lt. Thomas D. White, had landed upside down at Leningrad, but neither was injured and the plane only slightly damaged." Bullitt called the American Embassy and "attributed their escape to Lieutenant White's adroit piloting."

Bullitt was on his way to meet his young daughter who was coming to Leningrad from the United States. He and White had taken off from Moscow Airport shortly before 1:00 P.M. in a Douglas observation plane in which they had recently toured the southern part of the Soviet Union.

In the June 25 issue of the *New York Times,* Bullitt described the crash in his own words: "We had left Moscow just before noon. Midway we met bad weather. Coming within sight of the airdrome, my experienced pilot, Lieutenant White, stopped the engine for the landing, but then seeing that the field was marshy, he tried to start the motor again. The motor refused to work.

"Lieutenant White kept his presence of mind and tried to maneuver to the left, but he could not prevent the plane from landing upside down. We found ourselves in a queer position, but fortunately we were strongly strapped in. Two minutes later we were free. I didn't experience one moment of emotion, and here we are both unscratched."

Bullitt had a sense of humor. As they got out of the airplane, he muttered, "Tommy, never let the Russians know there was anything unusual in the landing." They got out of the airplane nonchalantly, lighted cigarettes, strolled across the field, and greeted the astonished reception committee without saying a word about their spectacular arrival. White later commented, "I'm not sure that they still don't think that was the way to land an O-38F."⁵

After the narrow escape, Bullitt sent a reassuring cablegram to President Roosevelt, which was printed in the June 25th *New York Times:* "Plane landed upside down, but we emerged right side up. Trust no one has reported to you that we are dead. We are both unscratched."

Years later, when White was selected as Chief of Staff, the *New York Times* commented on this incident: "The tall man who smiles easily was the only American military pilot to ever dunk an American Ambassador in a Soviet swamp and then go on to become Chief of Staff."

With Bullitt, White flew over much of the Soviet Union. They were even scheduled to fly from Moscow to Vladivostok. "Ambassador apparently calling off flying to Vladivostok. Ship all set to go, but I am glad not to go. Felt it was an opportunity that I couldn't fail to take in the interests of the War Dept."

The Soviet Union had set aside for the use of foreign diplomats a vast preserve for hunting and fishing in the north, but it was so difficult to reach that few ever went. But after five months of duty in the Soviet Union, White determined "to go fishing and forget my troubles," as he wrote in his diary. "I want to go yet know damn well that the grief and troubles involved will far more than outweigh any pleasure. . . . I haven't had one single moment of unadulterated fun since I left the U.S.A.!"

He finally received permission to go to the fishing camp, and he wrote on July 18, 1934, "Perfectly marvelous here. We had a hell of a time getting here but it is even better than I had dreamed possible." This fishing trip afforded him a further insight into what life was like for the people there: "He got permission," reflected his widow, Constance White (his second wife). "God knows how—I doubt if one could do it now if stationed in the Soviet Union—to go on a ten-day fishing trip way up in the north. He had to go by train. Whenever he went on this kind of trip, there was always a little man assigned to stay with him (a member of the NKVD). Tommy had to take the train to get there, and that little man always went along.

"To reach the fishing camp, they had to cross a lake from the train station. The boatman who was to be his guide and take him to the camp was late, and the little man had to leave to get the boatman. While Tommy was waiting, the railway station master and his wife and family were very kind to him. They had a bunch of kids, and they took Tommy into their home to have some tea. He remembered lumps of brown sugar they put in the tea as a sweetener. They had a thoroughly good time, and then this little guy showed up with the boatman, so they pushed off to the fishing camp.

"When the ten days were over, they came back and he looked forward to seeing the station master and his wife and kids. But Tommy had made a mistake in visiting their home—he gave one of the children a dollar bill—he should never have done that. When the station master's wife saw him coming, she ran up screaming at Tommy, 'Go away, go away—don't come near my house. My husband's gone. They came and took him away.' That wretched little man had reported that station master for talking with Tommy and having him in his home, and because of this they had put the station master in concentration camp. This was very upsetting to my Tommy, and he was glad to leave the Soviet Union. That kind of stuff really got him down" (personal communication, February 11, 1976).

But intelligence gathering was unquestionably part of the trip. Gen. Lyman L. Lemnitzer observed that Lieutenant White's "excellent air intelligence reports from Moscow were commended, and he earned the reputation as a close observer of the Soviet's growing air power."[6]

In spite of the frustrations, pressures, lies, suspicious atmosphere, and hard work, he did not lose his sense of humor. His fellow Embassy officials were concerned over electronic bugging. When they first moved into their new Embassy building on June 21, 1934, White noted in his diary, "The elevators don't work, neither does the doorbell, the water doesn't run out of the washbasin, no hot water; but I will be satisfied if only the floor and ceiling doesn't collapse." Then, on July 2, 1934, he wrote, "You can't make me believe there is any mysterious spying going on. A dictaphone (judging by poor plumbing, etc.) simply would not work here!"

After some months, White's first wife and daughter joined him in Moscow. It was not a happy marriage, and eventually one of White's friends in the American Embassy, Elbridge Durbrow, helped him obtain a divorce. "There was a quick divorce procedure in the Soviet Union, which was also available to foreigners. The Soviets had one desk for getting married and another for divorce—you could just go up to the desk and say, 'I don't want to live with my spouse any more' and get a divorce. Tommy knew about this, and one day he came to me and said, 'Becky and I have tried to make our marriage go, but it just doesn't seem to work. We want to divorce quickly and quietly.' They dreamed up a reason for Becky and their daughter to return home—to get her teeth straightened or that her mother was ill. We all went down to the train to send her off. They were a well-known couple to the Diplomatic Corps so there was a large crowd at the railway station. No one knew that I'd gotten them a divorce that morning. The Whites didn't want to make a big thing about it" (personal interview, December 28, 1977).

Major Faymonville, Senior Air Attaché, was impressed with his junior. He evaluated White "superior" in handling officers and men and in administrative and executive ability. White was rated as a foreign language expert in Russian, Chinese, and French, all learned on his own. He was also rated "superior" in all other categories: physical endurance, military bearing, tact, initiative, intelligence, and so on. Again, such a high evaluation was too much for the endorsing officer, Brig. Gen. H. W. Knight, in Washington, who wrote, "I know neither the reporting officer nor the officer reported upon. However, I cannot conceive of an officer who is qualified to a preeminent degree in each and every qualification listed. It would seem that the reporting officer has allowed his enthusiasm for the officer reported upon to unduly influence him in the preparation of his report."

What was even more significant was White's diplomatic ability. He was highly thought of by the career State Department officers, whereas Major Faymonville did not get along with them. "While serving in Siberia [1918–1920]," reflected Ambassador Loy Henderson, "Faymonville, like his Commander, General Graves, developed a distrust of the Department of State and that attitude . . . manifested itself almost immediately from the time of his arrival in the Soviet Union. He was, so to speak, a lone wolf . . .

it was rare he let anyone, even Ambassador Bullitt, see what he was sending in (in the way of intelligence reports)" (personal interview, January 25, 1978).

Following his assignment to Moscow, White was transferred to the Office of the Military Attaché in Rome. He now had the opportunity to learn Italian and to improve his French, as his duties took him to Greece, Britain, and throughout Europe. His titles were Assistant Military Attaché, Assistant Military Attaché for Air, and Finance Officer. During this first year on the continent, his rating officer, Col. J. B. Pillow, a colonel in the Cavalry, gave White, soon to be promoted to captain, an overall rating of "excellent." He was known as an outstanding linguist.

White's old friend from the State Department, Elbridge Durbrow, was now assigned to Naples. "Tommy called me on the phone and said, 'Derby, I'm up in Rome. Can you do me a favor? Becky and I have decided to get remarried by a ship captain on the high sea. Could you find out if it is legal?' I determined it was, and found a ship captain to marry them. So I got them together again" (personal communication, December 28, 1977). But unfortunately, they still could not get along and were shortly divorced for a second and final time.

In the fall of 1937, Captain White was called home to attend the Air Corps Tactical School at Maxwell Field. His selection marked him for future leadership but the assignment upset his private plans. "He was coming over to England," reflected Constance Millicent Rowe, with whom he had fallen in love and who was to become his second wife, "for us to be married. Then he was appointed to the Air Force Tactical School and he wrote to me and said it was difficult for him to leave. He had a ten-day spring holiday, and instead of his coming over to Great Britain to marry me and come right back again, he asked me if I would come over to the United States. I saw nothing wrong with it. My parents did not approve. They wanted him to come there, but I could not care less. To me, his school was more important to him than coming to England. So we were married in New York" (personal interview, February 11, 1976).

"Everyone seems to like Connie," White wrote to his mother on April 3, 1938, "and I think she is really happy and enjoys Maxwell and the people here. Our first night here was awfully funny. . . . Just after dinner we were having our coffee in the living room when the doorbell rang. I went to the door and there stood a huge man with black moustache, cowboy hat and a sheriff's badge on his lapel. He demanded to know whether or not we had a marriage license. I recognized Major Bill almost at once and then behind him trooped a whole gang of hoodlums in every conceivable costume, each with a bottle of liquor which they placed on the dining room table. . . . It was simply grand from my point of view—nothing could have broken the ice so beautifully and they were all charmed with Connie, who took it so sweetly and naturally."

He showed serious apprehension in his work at the Air Tactical School, as is reflected in this comment he made in 1938: "A man forms his opinions from what he sees and hears. It was my good fortune to have seen much of Europe in the three years just prior to reporting to Maxwell Field. I have come to the Air Corps Tactical School with the firm conviction that all we learn here may be of vital and practical importance to our country and ourselves within the near future." Mrs. White said that while they were stationed at Maxwell, "Every evening after dinner, he would go upstairs to the library and really study" (personal interview, February 11, 1976). And it paid off, for he graduated at the top of the class. He was rated "superior" by Col. H. A. Dargue, one of the same officers who had supported Billy Mitchell, and who now gave White a glowing evaluation.

On completing the academic program at Maxwell, he was assigned to Command and General Staff School at Fort Leavenworth from September 3, 1938, until June 20, 1939. Mrs. White described their life there as "the same routine, after dinner he studied. They used to do a lot of work with map study. I used to help him put together the maps they used for their map study problems. He would put them on the floor and ask me to put the maps together for him, so I'd get down on the floor and piece them together" (personal interview, February 11, 1976). Then, in July 1939, a fateful year, White, now a major, had his first exposure to Maj. Gen. Henry H. Arnold, being assigned to the Office of the Chief of the Air Corps, working under H. H. C. Richards who was Chief of the Information Division.

"My job," he wrote home, "as Liaison Officer simply means that I am contact between G-2 (Intelligence, etc.), General Staff, and the Air Corps. Examples: Approve and arrange all foreigners' visits to Air Corps stations and factories where the Air Corps has contracts. All foreign flying of our airplanes, all reports to attachés. . . . The intelligence part of it is . . . consolidating, recording, and disseminating the data from *all* our attachés and other sources." Major White was rated as "excellent" by Colonel Richards, but the endorsing officer added to this evaluation, "I do not concur in the above report. I consider this officer as 'superior' based on my observation of the work of this officer during the period covered"—signed, Maj. Gen. H. H. Arnold, Chief of the Air Corps. For the next six months, White remained in Washington as the Chief of the Intelligence Section.

In the summer of 1940, before his promotion to lieutenant colonel, White learned, with mixed feelings, that he was to be sent to Rio de Janeiro,

Brazil. "I asked to go to troops instead of abroad but the general [Arnold] wouldn't agree, so while I didn't say so in so many words the inference was plain that I would much rather be in Brazil the next few years than sitting on my tail in his office or sweat shop! . . .

"This all happened because the Chief of Staff decided he wanted an aviator in Brazil as Military Attaché and because there is a hitch about ladies going to Europe at present. There will be a vacancy in Rio this spring —having been released by Gen. A. to go to Italy, it was not hard to get him to agree to my going to Brazil instead. I did none of the 'getting'—Colonel McCabe, G-2, did all that. Both he and General A. asked me if I wanted to go. I didn't hesitate too much. I don't know who will go to Italy. Anyway it is better to be the boss and alone than to be an assistant."[7]

Before he could leave for Brazil, he had another aircraft accident. He wrote to his sister, "My crackup has delayed things some, and it now means selecting another ship. . . . I can't seem to crack up," he continued, "without getting on the front page. This time because a photographer happened to be on the spot and got a really remarkable picture in the one where the water is still boiling up around the nose. I was in the nose at that time trying to get out. It wasn't pleasant to feel trapped, though as soon as I was oriented there was no difficulty about climbing out into the hull, where we stayed until the ship keeled over—just as the Sea Scouts and the Navy arrived. We have no good explanation for the wreck except that the ship isn't strong enough to take a fast landing on the water.

"I have a small cut on my nose at the bridge," he said in closing, "which will probably leave me a slight Heidelbergian scar and a rip on the left side of my head just above my ear. It has practically healed now, and the three stitches are out. I have a shaved spot now which will take a while to grow. So all is well which ends well, and I guess I can count myself lucky not to have had worse in fifteen years of flying." Shortly after his recovery, he and Constance flew to Rio, where they remained for a year and where Tom acquired competence in another language, Portuguese. His efficiency report said he "now speaks it fluently."

In March 1942, Colonel White became Acting Chief of Staff for the Third Air Force in Tampa, Florida, and did so well that he was soon moved up to Chief of Staff of the Third Air Force and received his first star. It was his first real opportunity to exercise leadership over a large group of officers and men. An episode related by Brig. Gen. John J. Borbridge throws light on the high standards White demanded of officers serving under him. "It was necessary," writes Borbridge, "that I examine each day the guard report, and I noted an entry on one day that said, "M.P.s were called out at midnight last night to the Big Orange (which is a beer spot in Tampa frequented by enlisted men and officers off duty) because of a disturbance, with the statement that a colonel threatened to shoot a sergeant in an argument over a girl who is a civilian employee at Third Air Force Base Headquarters.' I went to the colonel involved, whom I knew very well, and asked him what happened the night before. He said, 'Nothing, we went down to Big Orange and had a couple of beers.' I then asked who he was with. He mentioned one of the majors. I then went to the major, asked the same questions and received the same answers. I could not leave the remarks for all to read in the guard reports, so I went to the Chief of Staff, General White, and told him of the entry in the guard report. He instructed me, 'Tear that page out and put a statement saying you removed it by my order and it will be in a confidential file in the Adjutant General's office,' which I did. General White called in the colonel to explain the situation and after listening to him gave him a choice of standing court-martial or retiring at his permanent rank, which was then captain. The next day, the colonel was out of the service."

As a brigadier general, White was to receive a new type of evaluation. The rating officer was required to answer the question "Of all general officers of his grade personally known to you, what number would you give him on this list and how many comprise your list?" Maj. Gen. St. Clair Streett, Commander of the Third Air Force, wrote, "I consider General White the finest brigadier general of my acquaintance. He is superlatively effective and loyal. He is fast, certain, and tireless. He thinks clearly and objectively. He is fearless and direct. His gentlemanly characteristics are only equaled by his soldierly attributes. He is respected and admired by all with whom he comes in contact."

But despite the praise, White was troubled about his assignments. "I got some I certainly didn't want. I had some terrible blows. I was sent for when I was down in Tampa to come to Washington. General Barney Giles told me I was to be Commander of the Twentieth Air Force. To me this was the greatest assignment in the Air Force. Before I was able to leave, General Arnold sent for me. I went down to his office. General Clayton Bissell was sitting there at his desk. This is where some of my sins of being interested in foreign places and languages caught up with me. General Bissell was A-2 (Intelligence), and he had gone in to tell General Arnold that the Chief of Staff of the Army, General Marshall, had told him he was going to be the next G-2 for the whole Army. General Arnold asked General Bissell who should replace him as A-2, and he said 'Tommy White.' So when I walked into General Arnold's office, after General Bissell had just left, General Arnold said to me, 'Tommy, I don't give a damn what anybody has told you, you are now the A-2.' And that was the end of being commander of the Twentieth Air Force. That was a real bad break'' (personal interview, April 30, 1963).

He was disappointed, of course, but it certainly gave him visibility with General Arnold. Arnold, who could be plenty tough, wrote of White's performance in the spring of 1944: "An outstanding Air Staff officer whose clear thinking, logic, energy, and extraordinary personal qualities have lifted Intelligence in the Air Staff to the highest level ever enjoyed.''

Finally Brigadier General White received what he had longed for since the beginning of the war. On September 30, 1944, he became Deputy Commander of the Thirteenth Air Force in the Pacific. In this, his first combat command, he was to serve under Maj. Gen. George Kenney and with Brig. Gen. Ennis P. Whitehead, who had been fighting in the Pacific for over three years. As a veteran commander, he scrutinized White's effectiveness from the first in these words: "General White is a brilliant officer. He has a magnetic personality. He is superior either on command or staff duty. Of all the brigadier generals known to me, I place him No. 3 on my list of 81.''

Such a high rating is significant coming from such an unsparing commander. Whitehead's capacity for work in the energy-draining climate of the Pacific received frequent comment by Kenney: "Whitehead . . . so busy he didn't know or care what he ate; Whitehead was worn down to a shadow, losing weight, and unable to sleep.'' Several months later, he wrote, "A great leader and aviator, that man Whitehead, and a driving operating genius, who planned every operation down to the last detail to ensure success. He was no yes-man to anyone but no one ever had a more loyal right-hand man than I had in Ennis Whitehead. He was durable, too. In spite of the way he punished himself, I instinctively knew he would last through the war.[8] . . . Just above average in height, he had the figure of an athlete, the quick step of an action man, and a pair of the coldest blue eyes that ever bored through you. I certainly would have had a tough time if the Japs had had a Whitehead.''

At the war's end, White, now a major general, from January 15, 1948, to September 24, 1948, served as Commanding General of the Fifth Air Force, and for a fortnight was temporarily in command of all the Far East Air Forces. Of this period, Whitehead wrote of White, "He is a superior officer in every way with a fine forceful personality and extraordinary leadership ability. . . . He improved the overall combat effectiveness of the Fifth Air Force and thereby made a great contribution to the security of American forces and interests in the Far East. He has no superior as an Air Force officer of his grade. While he is fully competent for any staff assignment in the USAF, he is also superbly fitted for high command. . . . Due to his unusual ability as a commander, I recommend that as far as is possible he be used for command duty."

Although he would have preferred remaining in the Far East, White was then recalled to the Pentagon, where he served for an unprecedented thirteen years. "When I came home from the Pacific theater in 1948," he reflected, "I was made Chief of what we called Legislation and Liaison, and I was never unhappier with an assignment in my life. I had always had a rather low opinion of politics and politicians. I just hated the idea, and I remember having quite a discussion with Secretary Stuart Symington. He said, 'You are going to learn more in this job than you ever did in your life.' I just pocketed that advice, unbelieving, but that experience probably came in as handy as anything I had had" (personal interview, April 30, 1963).

The position of Director of Legislation and Liaison was a challenge. The two directors prior to White were fired, for reasons explained by Maj. Gen. Robert Eaton. The difficulty arose from the fact that there was someone in Secretary of the Air Force Stuart Symington's office in whom Symington had more faith, on such matters, than he did in any Air Force officer. This individual was James D. MacIntyre. "If you wanted to find out something," related Eaton, "you could get in touch with MacIntyre and he'd tell you. He had the complete confidence of the Secretary. Well, from the moment General White came in things changed. When he learned of the situation, he went in and had a knock-down-drag-out with Symington on who was going to advise the Secretary and represent the Air Force in L&L matters. He told Symington, 'Either I'm going to be the head of your legislation shop or else MacIntyre is going to be head.' It could have gone either way. Pete Quesada had a similar argument later and lost, but Tommy won. I knew from that moment on that Tommy White would be Chief of Staff because he was a very smooth fellow, a very smart fellow" (personal interview, August 14, 1979).

It proved to be an important assignment for both White and the Air Force. The time was critical: from 1948 to 1950, the Air Force was building strength to cope with the threat of Soviet aggression in the cold war. The programs needed congressional approval and appropriations, and the results depended to a great extent on White's persuasiveness. His performance was so outstanding that Symington twice wrote letters of commendation to the Chief of Staff. In the second, dated April 24, 1950, Symington wrote, "During this period General White has been assigned as Director of the Legislation and Liaison Division of this office. In this assignment he has been responsible for the Air Force legislative program, for the processing of congressional inquiries, investigations and correspondence, and for maintaining liaison with the Congress and of other Governmental agencies in connection with these matters.

"General White is one of the most capable officers of any rank whom I have known. His character and personal traits are without question of the highest order. His affable personality, his quick comprehension of the broad phases of any high staff or joint staff problem, and his tireless energy, make him particularly well-suited for the highest level of assignments.

"General White has been a great asset to my staff, and has rendered a great service to himself and the Air Force in this position."

On April 25, 1950, now a lieutenant general, White was assigned as Director of Plans, Office of the Deputy Chief of Staff, Operations. In this role, he was responsible for preparing war plans in collaboration with the other services, supervised the preparation of position papers on Joint Chiefs of Staff matters for the Chief of Staff, and assisted the Chief of Staff during Joint Chiefs' meetings and deliberations. This was a particularly important post at any time, but especially so during the Korean war, which began in June of 1950. White remained in this position until July 1951, when he became Deputy Chief of Staff for Operations.

In June 1953, White was selected as Vice Chief of Staff of the Air Force. His greatest contribution in this role was his vision. "General White recognized," commented his Assistant Vice Chief, Jacob Smart, "the absolute essentiality of our developing space technology and devices that would have military application. He recognized that the space age was coming. It wasn't here, but it was coming. We had a program among others that was called MISS (Man in Space Soonest). We were pressing hard for that. This view was not widely held, particularly it was not held by "Engine" Charlie Wilson, Secretary of Defense, and former president of General Motors. I recall being sent up to Secretary Wilson's office to receive his dictum which I was to deliver to the Chief that we 'should stop all this foolishness about men on the moon and concentrate our activities on problems here on earth.' Specifically, Charlie Wilson directed that the Air Force, which was leading the thing, cease and desist—and it was my job to draft the directive saying so. . . . *Sputnik* saved us when it came in October 1957, and the Department of Defense was strangely silent" (personal interview, August 14, 1979).

White's advocacy, the space mission, "in that particular period was with the ballistic missile," remembered Smart. "General Ben Schriever was in charge of this project, and General White was one of his strongest supporters. White made Schriever's work possible. First, we carried the ball for

Schriever with the Secretary of the Air Force and the Secretary of Defense to acquire the resources and the authority to move ahead. Secondly, he defended Schriever from people who were over eager to help him; that is, who gave him more help than he could use. General Schriever was being called to Washington at least every week, and General White moved heaven and earth to give Ben an airplane he could sleep in. The people in Washington didn't realize what a chore it was to fly across the United States in those days from Vandenberg Air Force Base, a six- to nine-hour flight one way and much longer going the other way. Well, Ben would work all day, fly all night and go to work to meet the people in the Pentagon at working hours the next morning" (personal interview, August 14, 1979).

In July 1957, White was selected as Chief of Staff of the Air Force. James Douglas was Secretary during White's initial tenure as Air Force Chief. When asked why he thought White was selected as Vice Chief under Twining, Douglas commented, "Roger Kyes, Deputy Secretary of Defense, was immensely impressed, and I think he exerted his influence by saying there was only one candidate that he was interested in becoming Vice Chief—Tommy White, and Kyes was very credible on any matter with Secretary of Defense Charlie Wilson. I think Kyes was right at the start preparing the way for Tommy White's becoming Vice Chief. After Tommy was Vice Chief, nobody had any question that he would succeed Nate Twining" (personal interview, July 13, 1978).

One of White's first decisions as Chief of Staff was to tie together a disconnected command. Brig. Gen. Robert C. Richardson, III, one of his planning officers said, "White was interested in getting the Air Force position established. He had a study made of the speeches delivered by major Air Force generals on Armed Forces Day and his comment was, 'They're making speeches all over the place, against me, for me, with the Navy. Nobody has told these fellows what the party line is; they're all at odds with each other. I can't fight the Navy and Army for counterforce, for SAC, for B-36s, and all the rest, when I've got major commanders out making public speeches against our position.' General White's solution was to circulate a series of papers. They were never to be more than two pages long, and each stated the Chief's position in a paragraph or two, then proceeded to give the arguments in support of it. They were mailed to all senior commanders, who were instructed to keep them in loose-leaf notebooks and to keep the notebooks in their desks. The letters were signed by General White, and this was the source for their speech writers to refer to on any of the issues. For example, one paper gave the reasons why the Air Force was for counter force, and the letter made sure the generals didn't argue for 'massive retaliation.' If any general needed documentation, it was all in General White's letters, containing the best arguments the Air Staff could put together" (personal interview, December 28, 1977).

Lt. Gen. Royal B. Allison explains White's success as Air Force Chief of Staff in these words: "The Air Force needed a leader like General White, particularly at that point in its history. When the Korean War was over then, there was needed at the helm a man who understood how to work successfully in Washington within the executive branch and within Congress. General White was eminently well qualified to do that. In addition, the Air Force was sort of trying to find its way. . . . White's grasp of overall strategy and his ability to sort of look out beyond today's world and see what might be important in the future is what really set him apart. He believed in the space program, and he did more than most men of his time to assure that the Air Force had a special kind of mission" (personal interview, July 6, 1977).

He had made his position clear when he was Vice Chief of Staff of the Air Force. On October 21, 1954, the *New York Times* quoted White's speech to the seventy-sixth National Guard Association Conference. White had said that formidable modern weapons probably would make any war "as short on time as it will be terrible in destruction." He added, "The outcome of such a war will be decided with the forces ready to go." His leadership was directed toward keeping the Air Force ready.

White was well aware of the Soviet threat to U.S. security. There was certainly no relaxation of preparedness on his part. In an Armed Forces Day speech before the Military Order of the World Wars on May 20, 1955, he warned it would be "foolhardy" to assume that the United States automatically would keep its technical arms lead over Russia. "It has become habit to believe that we are bound to win any technological race. . . . This is dangerous complacency.[9] . . . We must be realistic. The airpower that we have today is not the answer for all time."[10]

On November 29, 1957, White announced at the National Press Club the decision to speed the United States readiness for combat use of long-range ballistic missiles, placing the missile program with the Strategic Air Command. The intermediate and intercontinental ballistic missiles were in the Air Research and Development Command. He emphasized that existing air power was not sufficient. The next step was for the Air Force to control space—the twenty miles of atmosphere encompassing the earth as well as the regions beyond. This was the essence of his thinking: "We are working into the future, and in the future I see integrated forces of manned and unmanned [aircraft] systems, for missiles are but one step in the evolution from aircraft to true spacecrafts." This comment was reported in the November 30 issue of the *New York Times*. On October 2, 1958, the same paper reported his statement that the Air Force was considering equipping the Air National Guard with surface-to-air Bomarc missiles because, "the Air Force maintains continuous and critical self-analysis of both the active and its reserve forces."

Although a strong advocate of unmanned missiles—the Atlas, Titan, Minuteman, and all the others—White never ceased to emphasize the importance of the manned bomber. He reasoned first that the manned bomber was flexible, that it could be put into the air and moved close to the target and await orders to attack or return. Secondly, the bomber crew has the ability to select targets, return and hit again, make reconnaissance flights and evaluate the effects of the strikes. "Missiles," he said, "can do neither."

During the controversy over manned versus unmanned aircraft, in testimony before a Senate preparedness subcommittee by then Senator Lyndon B. Johnson in March 1959, White said, "I feel there has been a great downgrading of our manned bomber force. The missile is a romantic and exotic piece of equipment that has caught the public imagination, but I, for one, am not prepared to stake the existence of the nation on missiles.[11] "After all," he said at another time, "man is the only computer with a judgment circuit."[12] This was part of White's brilliance. He could see beyond the glamor of what seemed to be the weapon of the future—the missile—to its lack of flexibility. The Air Force of the future would need both. A lesser man would have "hung on to manned planes," and a man more limited than White would have been content with missiles.

As early as December 14, 1957, on the anniversary of the Wright brothers' flight at Kitty Hawk, North Carolina, White said in a speech to the embryonic Air Force Academy that the idea that manned aircraft would soon be a thing of the past was wrong, that the missiles of today "are but one step in the evolution from aircraft to piloted spacecraft.

"When the B-52 finds its way to the museum, it will not be because man has been eliminated from flight. Rather," he said, "it will be because new equipment has been perfected to propel him higher, drive him faster, keep him in motion longer and enable him to do more tasks better."

"It is quite obvious," he said, speaking before the National Press Club on December 6, 1957, "that we cannot control air up to twenty miles above the earth's surface and relinquish control of space above that altitude and still survive. . . . We airmen who have fought to assure that the United States has the capability to control the air are determined that the United

States must win the capability to control space." He pledged he would lead the Air Force in the race for control of space.

On occasion, General White would let off steam when things did not go right. Maj. Gen. Robert M. Ginsburgh, who had been on his staff for two years, remembered, "He would let loose with a couple of swear words. It was not an extended chewing out of anyone on the staff, but he would say such things as 'Can't anybody do things right? This is so simple.' But it would be very short and very much to the point, and then it would be over and you'd go out and feel like, 'Hell, I let the old man down, and I shouldn't because I know what kind of strain he's under.' But I never saw him press down any senior officer. He never, in my presence, was critical of anyone senior to me, whereas General LeMay, if you were in a staff meeting, got rather brutal sometimes on the senior staff to the extent that I, as a junior officer, felt a little embarrassed" (personal interview, August 4, 1977).

"I can remember one time, in particular," said Brig. Gen. John Baer, "when we were shooting these early test missiles, the Atlases and the Titans and so forth, and General White was interested in it. He always wanted the report the day before the firings on his desk when he came in in the morning. We used to have a dickens of a time getting them in or getting all the information he wanted. I was never quite sure why we had so much trouble in getting them but we did. Sometimes he would get furious. He told us, 'You know, that's the most important project you have.' We still couldn't get him the information he wanted, and I think he was justified in getting mad at us but it was hard to get the work out of the appropriate staff. I remember one time a major general was in who had not performed as General White wanted regarding this, and General White really worked him over. But I think characteristically, he worked with a mode of encouraging and being positive and happy with people. . . he would bite only occasionally. I've been with other people whose characteristic mode was that they bit everybody all the time. It was just the way they did their business and as long as they got results, I guess, that's all right. General White did not. He sought to have a positive stroke in the way of getting his work done (personal interview, August 17, 1977).

Gen. George S. Brown, White's executive officer for two years, and later, Chief of Staff of the Air Force, commented, "I've seen General White pretty darned rough with people on occasions. I've seen him stack real abuse on some colonels. On the other hand, I had the feeling that he would be the first to regret it when he cooled off. But the reaction really was that you should have been flattered he was steaming on their direction because he was letting it out and it was a safety valve for him, although I'm sure they didn't look at it that way" (personal interview, September 14, 1977).

Brown realized that White had a very strong affection for Secretary of the Air Force James Douglas. Yet, "on the other hand, General White used to get terribly upset with Mr. Douglas because he was so slow and deliberate about reaching a decision. His meetings on program reviews and those kinds of things, budget meetings, were painfully slow and monotonous, and General White finally got to the point where he would send me. He wouldn't go on most occasions. General White's mind was just like a steel trap. It worked very fast" (personal interview, September 14, 1977).

Shortly after Brown became White's executive officer, the annual Air Force Association convention took place. "They were to have a lunch for the Chief of Staff, and General White was to make a speech," said Brown (personal communication, September 14, 1977). "So he called in his aide, Tim Ahearn, and myself, and he turned to me and said, 'You get together with Bob Dixon and the two of you guys write me a speech. Then give it to Tim Ahearn. Tim will put it into language that I'll find easy.' So we collaborated on this speech, which turned out to be pretty good. Well, General White was worried enough about it that he personally carried it to the Deputy Secretary, Don Quarles, to get it cleared, and Quarles read it and suggested a few minor changes. Then Tommy White delivered it. Next morning he called me into the office. 'Colonel,' he said, 'do you know what it's like to pick up the telephone and find the President of the United States on the other end giving you hell?' I said, 'No, sir.' And he said, 'Well, it was about that speech you wrote.' Apparently the speech had taken the Army on a couple of things, and General Eisenhower picked it up in the press. I guess Eisenhower felt he'd better nip this in the bud. He had a brand new Chief of Staff of the Air Force, and if this guy started out and kept up this tactic, he was going to get out of hand or get into trouble so the President lowered the boom on him right away." What White had said was "The other services" have not had "an overall adjustment to the present era equivalent to the Air Force adjustment." (He was referring to the policy of massive deterrence in nuclear warfare with air power as its dominant element.) "The other services have had some rigorous self-examination to do, and face still more in the future, just as we do.

"The key writer of this speech was Col. Robert J. Dixon. The issue was 'what did we say,' and 'was what we said accurate, was it or wasn't it politic, how impolitic was it, was it constructive or destructive?' So, I dug out the text, went through it again and thought to myself, knowing the President had called, I wouldn't change a word. I sent that message back in, and that's the last I heard of it. We must have touched a nerve . . . that doesn't mean that the nerve didn't need to be touched. General White never got upset with me about it" (personal interview, November 10, 1977).

White had a "think group," as did Arnold during World War II. In 1959, as Chief of Staff, he formed a small group called the Long-Range Objectives Group, comprising three officers, one sergeant, and a secretary. Those three officers were then Maj. Abbott Greenleaf, Col. Bob Richardson, and Col. John Frisbe. It was not to answer to the Air Staff, which at that time was under Gen. John K. Gerhart, Deputy Chief of Staff for Plans and Policy; they reported only to White. One of the major tasks of this group was to give thought on how to improve the management of the Department of Defense. The three men would periodically have conversations or briefings with White from fifteen or twenty minutes to several hours. Lt. Gen. Greenleaf remembered an interesting impression of White at that time: "General White was a very, very reflective person, and he wanted the original results of our study unmodified by the staff. In fact, it was a source of some intrastaff irritations that General White insisted that we report directly to him. We would brief General White and then subsequently brief General LeMay, who was Vice Chief at the time, and the rest of the senior officials on the Air Staff. I knew of no other group that General White handled the same way as he had handled this particular long-range objectives group. . . . He remarked to me on many occasions that he considered it his principal duty to be that of a member of the Joint Chiefs of Staff, and not that of supervising the efforts of the Air Staff on behalf of the Secretary of the Air Force. He considered his responsibility to be that of an advisor first to the Secretary of Defense and then to the President on national security matters. I sensed that General White believed that there was a basic dichotomy between how the department was structured and how the department should work and that he considered some of the functions, which military department secretaries and the Chiefs of the Services exercise as members of military departments, were in conflict with the responsibilities of the Service Chiefs which they had as members of the Joint Chiefs and advisors to the President and the Secretary of Defense. In addition to studying the organization and management of the Defense Department, there were other projects that they worked on, such as strategic force policy, the role of ICBMs, the role of deterrent strategy, and other issues that were key at that time. He had us prepare policy or decision papers on this for him, and these were very closely controlled. It was my understanding that I was no longer on the Air Staff while doing these projects, but was working directly for General White" (personal communication, June 8, 1977).

White made a point of getting around to see members of the Air Staff. It was his policy when he came to the Pentagon on Saturday mornings to "wander down the halls and see who was working and stop in and chat with them. We never knew precisely where he was," said Ginsburgh. "I recall a friend of mine, a lieutenant colonel somewhere down in Plans, calling me up one day and saying, 'Guess what happened to me last Saturday afternoon? I was working like mad on one of these JCS papers, and all of a sudden this big tall guy in civilian clothes comes down and says hi and sits down. I did a double take. It was General White.' " Ginsburgh commented that these little trips were very helpful because General White "would find out things that we wouldn't have found out if he had just been sitting in the office, both in terms of substance and policy and in terms of the capabilities and characters of the individuals on the Air Staff" (personal interview, August 4, 1977).

When asked why he felt White was so successful, Ginsburgh responded, "He had intellect. He had really a wide range of interests. He was quite a linguist, as you know. In that connection he used to keep several pads on his desk and he would write notes to himself and to his office staff—whom he felt very close to—and who were expected to read everything on the desk or behind his desk to keep up with what he was thinking. On one pad, however, he made notes using the Cyrillic alphabet. Cyrillic was Russian, but he used English words with the Cyrillic alphabet. Well, I had taken Russian when I was in graduate school at Harvard. Not that I knew much, but I knew enough to be able to transliterate and see that they were English words and get a little insight into other things he had on his mind" (personal interview, August 4, 1977).

One of White's executive officers, Col. Robert G. Moll, who was traveling with him on an official visit to a number of South American countries, remembers White speaking as the guest of honor at a banquet at Venezuela Officers' Club in Caracas. Two microphones had been set up—one for him and another for the translator. At the appointed time, White was introduced and, as some public officials do, began his speech in the language of the country. But the General continued to speak in Spanish for some twenty minutes, and the appreciation of his audience was something to behold. "By his mastery of their language, he accomplished more than many others could have no matter how convincingly they may have spoken" (personal communication, August 3, 1977).

Consideration for others was also a characteristic of White's. Brig. Gen. John J. Borbridge remembered, "While I was serving as Headquarters Commander of the Third Air Force, my daughter, a teenager, was taken seriously ill with a ruptured appendix, gangrene having set in. General

White heard of the plight that my daughter was in and called me into his office. He said, 'Barb, I hear your daughter needs blood transfusions, and I don't want you going outside this Headquarters for additional blood. I'll personally have mine checked, and if it is the right type she is welcome to it.' From such a busy man who had so many problems on his hands, you can imagine the feeling that I had for General White to have taken the time to show this thoughtfulness for my daughter.''

His Director of Plans commented that White was admired by his juniors. "He always picked things up so quickly," said Brig. Gen. John Baer. "The other thing was that he would always go down and make a good case for the job you had done with your plans so that you knew that when he went to the Joint Chiefs of Staff, you were confident that he would get some good resolution of your problems. We felt as young officers that we liked to work with a winner, not that General White always won, but you had the feeling that he'd give it a good shot and if he came back and you had lost what you wanted, he'd have a logical explanation, saying, 'I decided that I wanted to compromise on it or give it up,' or whatever he did. Sometimes other people would come back and wouldn't know why they gave up or have any idea of what happened. I think the key to General White was his energy and his interest.

"The other thing is that General White treated you well. Sometimes, and interestingly enough, if General White came back and we had done well with what we had prepared, we were as happy as a winning football team. I think that is one reason why people liked him. He was such a gentleman and such a winner. He was so considerate. Just in talking with you, like he'd say, 'Johnny, well, that's a good brief, thanks a lot, you're a lot of help to me.' But sometimes he'd bite a little bit if he didn't like the way you put it together. He might say to me, 'This is just not an adequate briefing,' or he'd say, 'You haven't done enough homework on this' and he said, 'I want somebody to get some work done on this so that we will have a logical position' '' (personal interview, August 17, 1977).

He did not limit his consideration to officers. His concern for the enlisted man was given final emphasis when he invited three NCOs to attend his retirement ceremony on June 30, 1961. These NCOs had been associated with General White earlier in his career, and honoring them in this way was White's method of saluting all career servicemen.

"General White," said Ginsburgh, "thought that one of his primary responsibilities as Chief of Staff was to ensure the future leadership of the Air Force. I believe he worked very hard in this line of succession. Examples were LeMay, McConnell, Burchinal, and Brown. Now at that time, of course, LeMay was a four-star general; McConnell was a three-star about to become a four-star; Burchinal, I guess, was a relatively new major general; and General Brown was a new brigadier general. I think General White had his eye on Allison as a possible follow-on. Allison, at the time, was just a colonel, but General White had some other colonels in mind. What I'm saying is that General White, through that kind of foresight, had an impact on the Air Force for a long, long time" (personal interview, August 4, 1977).

It might seem strange that anyone would believe Gen. Curtis E. LeMay would need to be developed. "General White had a certain feeling of admiration towards great combat leaders and a certain humility towards them," said Lt. Gen. Royal B. Allison. "He believed that General LeMay was a man of great strength in the Air Force. We were moving into an era where the Strategic Air Command was going to be the heart of our deterrent position. To overlook LeMay in this, leave him out in the field, or in a sense put him out to pasture would be doing a great disservice to our Air Force in the military structure. He had earned the right to be in a position of authority, and while he lacked certain characteristics that General White would like to see in a man to be Chief of Staff, he believed that General LeMay's overall ability and the image that he had created in the minds of the military, the young military people, the young Air Force people, particularly, of a tremendous combat leader was something that was needed. General LeMay met all the requirements that one might lay down for being Chief of Staff, and on balance, it was the right thing to do. It's a little hard to think of anyone grooming General LeMay, but that's what I know General White had in mind" (personal interview, July 6, 1977).

"It was clear," said Allison, "that from his reputation and what one heard about what he was doing that he had a real flair for dealing with the broad issues facing the Air Force, and with the Air Force relationship to the other services and to the Defense establishment generally. This, of course, was a role that did not require and does not today require that a man have great skill in combat leadership. General White was really more of a soldier-statesman. He was more of a soldier-statesman than any of his contemporaries by inclination and by nature. He just fit that role to a degree the others did not, without in any way taking anything from the others. He was quite different from Gen. Nathan F. Twining. General Twining was the kind of old soldier who liked to put his feet up on the desk, and one can almost visualize him chewing tobacco. You know, a down-to-earth sort of old salt-type of fellow. General White's military career filled the more diplomatic types of assignments. These were the type of assignments that polished any rough edges and developed more of the soldier-diplomat-statesman" (personal interview, July 6, 1977).

It is characteristic that White became quite an accomplished ichthyologist. He applied the same determination to the study of ichthyology that he did to everything else he'd done. While stationed in Brazil as Air Attaché, he and his second wife became very interested in rare tropical fish. He fished for them and Mrs. White made watercolors of these fish. They made a very outstanding contribution to ichthyology, and White and his wife discovered certain previously unknown species. Scientists later named some species after the Whites. One species was given the name *Cynolebias constanciae*, and another was named *Cynolebias whitei*. So appreciative was the scientific community for the work done by the Whites in ichthyology that the Brazilian government awarded Mrs. White the Cavalier Medal of the Southern Cross. In the history of that medal, which was established in 1822, she was the only wife of a serviceman to receive that award.

One of his drivers when White was Chief of Staff, Chief Master Sgt. Thomas E. Schoolcraft, said, "I was impressed with General White's ready knowledge to discuss anything that might come up. We were driving across Newfoundland's countryside when he asked me to stop; we walked into a nearby field where he picked up a small beautiful wild flower; he called it by its name (Latin, I assume) and told me it was a member of the orchid family" (personal communication, January 20, 1978).

When White succeeded Twining as Air Force Chief of Staff, he was called a "global strategist." "Soldier-statesman" would be another appropriate title. His Air Force career was unique in its breadth, with a tour in Panama, four years in China, a year in Moscow, then Italy, and Greece, and finally Brazil—all before World War II began. He commented that at the Air Tactical School in 1937 one of his classmates kidded him, saying that "I had served so long in embassies that I wore a bowler hat, spats, gloves, and carried calling cards for the instructor to our first conference." But the assignments abroad developed subtle talents and balanced his military duties in the Pacific theater in World War II and in Japan in the postwar era.

One of his most meaningful tours was in the Soviet Union. He received an education on the evils of communism that was superb preparation for an Air Force Chief of Staff who had a key role in our country's national security and that of our allies' security against the dangerous threat of communist bloc nations under Soviet leadership. He learned firsthand of the ruthless Soviet leadership. He saw Soviet leaders disappear, never to be heard from again. In a speech he made to the Air Corps Tactical School in 1938, he remarked that "every single officer of the Red Armed Forces whom I knew has since been executed."

Ambassador Loy W. Henderson said of Lieutenant White's tour, "I think that Tommy learned a great deal about adversity in Moscow, about difficulties and how to overcome them, how to have patience when you are in a very exasperating position. He learned how to deal with difficult international problems, and his relations with other members of the diplomatic mission at that time were very valuable to him" (personal interview, January 25, 1978).

The group of men selected for duty in Moscow had exceptional ability. George F. Kennan, who had served under White at St. John's Academy and who was Third Secretary in 1934, went on to become the U.S. Ambassador to the Soviet Union, said of White, "He served in Moscow (in 1934) with the same enthusiasm and distinction that marked his military career generally, but did not remain very long, and soon went on to better and bigger things" (personal communication, January 16, 1978). So did others in that early Moscow group. The Second Secretary, Loy W. Henderson, went on to become U.S. Ambassador to Iraq, India, and Iran. Charles E. "Chip" Bolan, the Third Secretary, became U.S. Ambassador to the Soviet Union and India. Elbridge Durbrow, Vice Consul, went on to become U.S. Ambassador to South Vietnam.

White won for the Air Force a reputation for resourcefulness, replacing that of merely being "mighty fly boys." This type of leadership was needed, as White quietly stated and restated before the Secretary of Defense, the Joint Chiefs of Staff, and others his belief that the Air Force needed preponderance over the Army and Navy. He provided the necessary balance of leadership forged in battle and tempered with a farsighted responsibility for the future, which was greatly respected in Washington.

White had some disappointing assignments, but he faced up to the challenge, worked hard, and always seemed to come out ahead. Ultimately and deservedly he arrived at the very peak of his profession as Air Force Chief of Staff. Perhaps the simplest tribute was expressed by his World War II enlisted orderly, Francis L. Murphy, who commented, "In my opinion, there have been a lot of people around with stars on their shoulders, but few deserved them more or wore them with greater dignity than Tommy White" (personal communication, January 6, 1978).

NOTES, Chapter 5

1.   *Howitzer* (West Point Yearbook), 1920, p. 169.
2.   Gen. Lyman L. Lemnitzer, *Assembly,* Fall 1971.
3.   Lt. Thomas D. White, 4th Infantry, "Service in Puerto Rico," *Infantry Journal,* 1923, *23:* 17, 20.

4. Lemnitzer, p. 113.
5. *Time,* May 18, 1953, p. 25.
6. Lemnitzer, op. cit.
7. Letter from Lt. Col. Thomas D. White, December 27, 1939.
8. George C. Kenney, *General Kenney Reports* (New York: Duell, Sloan and Pearce, 1949), pp. 11–12.
9. Gen. Thomas D. White, Armed Forces Day Speech, May 20, 1955.
10. Speech to National Press Club, December 1957.
11. *Air Force Times,* March 21, 1959, *19:* 16.
12. *Air Force Times,* May 6, 1961, p. 21, col. 8.

PART TWO

THE AIR FORCE CHARACTER

INTRODUCTION

Character can run the gamut from bad to good. There are people with strong character, good character, weak character, bad character, and no character. And you can say of a man, "He's quite a character," meaning he is odd or strange.

"The noun *character* carries with it not only good connotations, but also bad ones. It is used to describe an individual's moral strengths and unique or distinctive traits, all of which combine to give him a reputation and to those who know him, a degree of predictability under various and sundry circumstances. The point, however, is that character is not necessarily a good thing to have—it can be equally bad. (Brig. Gen. Herman Rumsey, personal communication, February 10, 1976).

Although character connotes many meanings and shades of reference to different people, most of us assume that when we refer to a person's character we are thinking in terms of those traits or qualities that most pertain or are descriptive of that person as an individual. It is, of course, a common term used in the rendering of miltiary efficiency reports or ratings qualified by the accompanying explanatory or descriptive words or phrases such as 'good,' 'excellent,' 'of high morale,' and the like. It can also, of course, be used with appropriate accompanying definition [to describe] undesirable traits or qualities, but I would say that on balance it is normally used affirmatively in conjunction with words or phrases descriptive of desirable qualities. Thus, for example, when a rating officer describes a subordinate as having a 'strong character' we refer to the best rather than the worst. However, it is to us an all-inclusive term, and whether the word *character* is used or not, we assume . . . [that] when we say a person has integrity, high moral standards, honesty, fairness in dealing with others, respect and loyalty to subordinates and superiors alike, a keen sense of responsibility, dedication, and so on, we are in fact detailing the individual's 'character.' ''

Certainly men have become brigadier generals or perhaps even higher in the Air Force who were not men of strong character by the high standards just described. There have been ruthless, ambitious, and selfish men who get their first star, maybe even a second star. But once these qualities become clear, they usually go no further in rank, fortunately. When a man has strong qualities of leadership, but is of low moral character, there is always the danger that his subordinates will be influenced by his bad characteristics, to the detriment of the leader and of the group. But if the leader is a man with both strong qualities of leadership and high moral character, he will endure and he will achieve better results.

The presence of character in a leader is quickly recognized and its absence swiftly felt. Character, good or bad, breeds emulation. A bad character is like a bad apple spoiling the other apples in the barrel. It is the sterling character that produces the winning team. A leader cannot normally rise any higher than his subordinates—he cannot do the job alone.

Character is the essence of leadership in American democracy. However, not everyone gives character the same emphasis or importance. One general officer who gave very serious thought to this was Maj. Gen. Dale O. Smith, USAF, Retired.

"I took the same approach as you have," General Smith wrote to the author (January 17, 1976). "You might call it the U.S. Army approach because it is so common to American military biographies, of relating leadership to the military virtues: duty, honor, country, character, selflessness, honesty, etc. The list of virtues is almost endless. But then I ran into so many historical exceptions that I began to doubt this approach. The great Khans were merciless, and ruled by fear. Tamerlane was another. Alexander was homosexual. Caesar was a wily politician. Napoleon deserted his Army in Egypt. Certainly, *character* as we define it was not one of their virtues."

In personal interviews and meaningful correspondence, I asked over a thousand officers of the rank of brigadier general and higher, "What role does character play in successful leadership?" In brief, the most frequent responses emphasize just how important character is: "Character is the essence of leadership."[1] "Good character is a must for leadership, it's the keystone."[2] "Character, and I am speaking of strong and good character, has everything to do with leadership."[3] "Character and leadership go hand-in-hand."[4] "Character is of considerable importance in leadership."[5] "In my belief, it is one of the most important."[6] "Strength of character plays a most decisive role in leadership."[7] "Strength of character is a prime requisite of a successful military commander."[8] "Character is the most essential attribute of a successful military leader."[9] "It is essential to leadership in a democracy such as ours."[10] "Character is the cornerstone of leadership."[11] "Strong character is one of the more fundamental requirements of leadership."[12] "Character and leadership are like the popular song, 'Horse and Carriage.' Both go to make marriage. You can't have one without the other."[13] "You can have character without leadership, but not leadership without character."[14] "All important."[15] "Without character one cannot be a leader."[16] "Everything."[17] "It is basic."[18] "A very considerable one—perhaps the most important."[19] "Everything. Without good character, it is impossible to be a good leader."[20] "Character is the number one attribute of leadership."[21] "Without character, there cannot be any leadership."[22] "Character is all important."[23] "A major one."[24] "No character, no leadership."[25] "Good character is the keystone of leadership."[26] "A major role."[27] "A man without character cannot lead, at least in our society."[28] "The most important—without it there is no true leadership."[29] "It is almost the whole works."[30] "A leader without character is a poor leader or no leader."[31] "Character is the backbone of leadership."[32] "Character is leadership."[33] "Without character, there can be no leadership."[34] "With few exceptions, in all history, it is all important."[35] "I don't believe that anyone can be a good leader without having inside him the qualities of good character. In short, good character is the basic element in all good leadership."[36] "All important in leadership."[37] "The No. 1 attribute."[38] "A dominant role, if not *the* dominant role."[39] "Character is the base on which leadership is built. Without it, there would be no such thing as a leader."[40] "It is an indispensable ingredient."[41] "Must have character to be a leader."[42] "I do not believe anyone can achieve leadership unless his character inspires admiration and complete confidence."[43]

But what is character? How do you define it? The answer is that character as a leadership quality should not be defined—it should be described.

NOTES, Chapter 5

1. Maj. Gen. Fred C. Tandy.
2. Maj. Gen. Pearl H. Robey.
3. Brig. Gen. Edwin W. Chamberlain.
4. Brig. Gen. Edgar A. Sirmyer.
5. Brig. Gen. Joseph L. Whitney.
6. Maj. Gen. Frederic E. Glantzberg.
7. Maj. Gen. William D. Old.
8. Maj. Gen. Edward H. White.
9. Maj. Gen. Harold A. Bartron.
10. Maj. Gen. Gilbert Hayden.
11. Maj. Gen. Samuel R. Brentnall.
12. Maj. Gen. Herbert L. Grills.
13. Brig. Gen. Charles H. Caldwell.
14. Brig. Gen. Sheldon S. Brownton.
15. Brig. Gen. Clyde L. Brothers.
16. Maj. Gen. Albert Boyd.
17. Maj. Gen. George R. Acheson.
18. Maj. Gen. Francis L. Ankenbrandt.
19. Maj. Gen. Harold H. Bassett.
20. Brig. Gen. George H. Beverley.
21. Maj. Gen. Charles F. Born.
22. Maj. Gen. Charles C. Chauncey.
23. Maj. Gen. Jared V. Crabb.
24. Maj. Gen. Frederick J. Day.
25. Maj. Gen. John P. Doyle.
26. Maj. Gen. Walter H. Frank.
27. Brig. Gen. Walter R. Graehman.
28. Maj. Gen. Richard A. Grussendorf.
29. Brig. Gen. Wilfred H. Hardy.
30. Maj. Gen. Frank O'D Hunter.
31. Maj. Gen. Joseph H. Hicks.
32. Maj. Gen. Junius W. Jones.
33. Maj. Gen. William L. Kennedy.
34. Maj. Gen. Morris J. Lee.
35. Brig. Gen. William L. Plummer.
36. Maj. Gen. Lester T. Miller.
37. Brig. Gen. Russell J. Minty.
38. Maj. Gen. James F. Phillips.
39. Maj. Gen. John M. Schweizer, Jr.
40. Maj. Gen. Delmar T. Spivey.
41. Maj. Gen. Gordon P. Seville.
42. Brig. Gen. Ernest K. Warburton.
43. Brig. Gen. Benjamin G. Weir.

CHAPTER 6
DUTY

When Woodrow Wilson was inaugurated as President of the United States, he petitioned in his inaugural address, "I pray God I may be given the wisdom and prudence to do my duty." Duty is the essence of military service and life. The true compulsion on an officer must be a sense of duty if he expects to succeed as a leader.

Brig. Gen. Prentiss D. Wynne, Jr., recited a story that truly gets to the heart of what character is all about—a sense of duty (personal communication, February 21, 1976).

"I knew very few top field commanders, but I did know one quite well," said General Wynne, "and that was the late Gen. Emmett ["Rosie"] O'Donnell, who provided me with what I consider to be a perfect example of character as a leadership quality. The time was 1950 or 1951, I can't remember exactly, but the place was Riverdale, California, the town nearest to March Air Force Base. 'Rosie' was a major general commanding the Fifteenth Air Force, Strategic Air Command, and I was a lieutenant colonel at Headquarters for the Fifteenth Air Force. Rosie was a flier's flier and loved the boys who could produce with an airplane. My job at Headquarters for the Fifteenth Air Force was A-2, Intelligence, and frankly Rosie O'Donnell thought that Intelligence in the Air Force was an absolutely useless appendage, and I tend to agree with him that in peacetime it might be. Anyway, Rosie liked to play golf, particularly when things were slow in the office. So, as 'useless,' I was the one he called when the idea hit him to leave the office for a quick eighteen holes of golf, and I'd better be out front in less than five minutes, ready to play or else!

"At the time in question, major league baseball was having one hell of a time agreeing on a successor to Commissioner K. S. Landis. The owners had been trying for months to find someone that twelve of the sixteen owners could agree upon, since it was necessary to have twelve agree for approval.

"So, one morning, while working at my desk the squawk box buzzed, and it was Rosie saying that Spike Briggs, owner of the Detroit Tigers at that particular time, had just arrived in town—let's go play golf. And we did, at the Riverside Golf and Country Club, where we all belonged.

"About half-way through the round, Spike Briggs told Rosie that he thought Rosie was the perfect solution for the problem of finding a new baseball commissioner, and he had canvassed the other owners, and they agreed. The job was to pay $50,000 per year plus an unlimited expense account, which was real money in those days! Germane here is the fact that Rosie, at that time, depended solely on his paycheck for financial survival; I know this to be true because our respective wives were, and still are, best friends.

"Back to the golf game. Rosie replied he had to think about it. A few holes later, he stopped abruptly and said, 'Spike, I can't accept. I was a poor boy from Brooklyn that the U.S. government picked up and educated at West Point and I haven't repaid that debt! I'd love the job, and I know many of the players, managers, and owners well, but I just can't quit the service now.' Nothing further was said. Spike Briggs spent the night at March Air Force Base and the next day returned to Detroit. Sometime later, a new commissioner was appointed. End of story!

"Unfortunately, to me," General Wynne continued, "there were not a couple of thousand troops around to witness this incident, because to me, that experience was truly important. Call it selflessness, devotion to duty, sense of fair play, or what you will, it exemplified why the people who worked with Rosie O'Donnell would break their backs to do what he said needed to be done."

General Spaatz's outlook was similar to General O'Donnell's. When I asked Spaatz why he decided to make a career of the service, he responded, "In the first place, when you're educated at government expense, you are conscience or duty bound to at least give some service to the government and then decide after having given a reasonable amount of service whether or not a military career is something you want to follow. But, after coming into the service, I found it a very fine life. I enjoyed all of my years of service."

Inevitably, the performance of duty requires one to do unpopular things. "In 1943, I was serving in the U.S. Army Air Corps," wrote Brig. Gen. Archie Higdon, "and during that period of time there was a very large basic training center that was not functioning in a satisfactory manner. Inspection ratings were extremely low, and my superior, a lieutenant colonel, and three of his staff, including myself, were sent from a much smaller basic training center to the unsatisfactory center. Our inspection ratings had always been very high. The center commander, a major general, was ordered to place the four of us in charge of all training in his basic training unit. He followed orders even though some of the people there had equal or higher rank than we had.

"We were treated on a personal basis as if we were enemy officers. However, we firmly believed that the national mission came first. By extremely tough, long days, seven days a week, we corrected the flagrant shortcomings in training procedures and raised officer and noncom performance from below-adequate level to quality performance, and the center output in quantity and quality moved up very rapidly, as shown by the inspection reports.

"Some of the lazy officers asked for and received transfers overseas, where they were soon promoted. None of us were promoted, even though recommended several times. Even so, we never let down, and that center continued to produce the quality and quantity of graduates needed to the end of the war" (personal communication, February 4, 1976.)

These officers performed their duty as they saw it and not only suffered the ire of the others but sacrificed their personal promotions as well. It was not unusual because this is part of the price of duty.

Another example was given by Brig. Gen. Lewis W. Stocking. "I can relate one anecdote,' wrote Stocking, "involving the leadership demonstrated by a subordinate of mine, which to me illustrates character. I had an occasion to relieve a fighter squadron commander because he would not exact the meticulous standards required when nuclear weapons were introduced to a unit. The man relieved was a likeable person, an excellent pilot, and popular with all his people. His replacement was charged with finding and correcting all discrepancies in the least time possible and with establishing—demanding—new procedures immediately. Obviously, his was a difficult position, for a young officer, brought into the organization from outside. He was not 'a hatchet man,' but a normally sensitive person and, fortunately, a leader. A couple of weeks later, I visited the squadron, acknowledged his task as a lonesome and difficult one. He replied, 'Well, sir, I knew that what I had to do would be unpopular with a lot of people. I could not let myself dwell on what the mediocre think. I had to keep telling myself that the good guys in this squadron recognize and approve of what I'm doing, and that's what counts' " (personal communication, January 23, 1976).

Another aspect of duty is to always give a job one's best. General Arnold wrote to his son-in-law on January 20, 1940, "Now, as to duty in Washington. As you know, I have always cursed every day I served in Washington, and I haven't stopped since my first assignment there in 1911. But somehow or other fate decreed that I would come to Washington and I would repeat and repeat and repeat all of the previous cursings out. Furthermore, I can't say that I ever enjoyed one day of service that I had in Washington, but it apparently is necessary as part of one's career. Furthermore, during my entire service I've never yet asked for a single assignment of any kind. I have let nature take its course. I have not fought the problem. No matter where they sent me, I went and I did the best I could under the circumstances."

"In my career," wrote Lt. Gen. Allen P. Clark, similarly, "I decided to do my best always, but never to push for a certain job—simply to try to turn each job into a successful and meaningful experience in service to the Air Force.

"A lot of my service was in personnel, and I did not choose it nor did I particularly like it, but I was promoted in it several times. Even though I did not like the assignment that I had, I pursued the policy that I had learned in POW camp that I was to follow for the rest of my Air Force career, and that was as I say to do the best job I could in every assignment that I had."

He added that one of the most difficult aspects of duty in military service is the problem of serving under someone one does not like. He related, "As a POW I was forced to serve under a man, through the misfortunes of war, whom I heartily disliked and whose methods I disapproved of strongly. I served under this man because there was no escape from it. When the war was over, I was proud that I had learned to serve under someone I disliked, and, frankly, after that experience I concluded that I could now work with anyone, regardless of how bad they were.

"I guess what I am saying is that I learned that human relationships and working relationships are terribly important and that it is usually possible to serve another loyally and effectively even when you don't personally care for him or his methods" (personal communication, February 16, 1976).

Another aspect of character is to be made of the kind of stuff that does not expect a pat on the back every time a job is done well. That is just not the way the world operates. Certainly, in most cases a subordinate will be disappointed if his superior does not give praise where it is due, but perhaps the greatest praise for a job well done is to be handed another assignment and told to do it as well. One who expects praise for every job well done will probably turn out to be a malcontent. In the military, one is expected to do a good job and should be expected to move on to the next assignment without stopping for applause. If the work truly merits praise, one will probably get it, but certainly one should be able to proceed without it. You see your duty and you do it.

If one adopted the outlook of Lt. Gen. Gordon Blake, the need for recognition would not be a problem. When asked the question, "Why did you achieve the rank of three-star general?" he responded, "My personal philosophy about work probably has a major influence on any success I've had. It starts with my mother, who insisted that I do things right. But it was many years later before I crystallized it into a personal work philosophy. Actually, this happened while I was Vice Commander, PACAF, in the late 1950s, through reading about a Japanese way of life which embodied pride in work as one's primary reward. Later a Japanese acquaintance told me this was known as *yamoto damashii.* I have found this a great drive toward excellent performance as well as an insulator from the more conventional rewards, such as acclaim, raises, promotion, etc. These become nice to get but not essential" (personal communication, June 19, 1976).

Part of duty is simply just that: working hard at each and every job. A good leader can inspire his subordinates not only with the necessity for hard work but also with that something extra; can inspire the individual to emulate his leader; and, at the highest level of leadership, can inspire him to the point where he would be literally ready to die for his leader. In answering the question of how one gets that something extra out of an individual, Maj. Gen. R. L. Delashaw commented that "Foremost among Air Force leaders I have known was Lt. Gen. Ira C. Eaker. He was my Commander as a colonel when he commanded the Twentieth Pursuit Group at Hamilton Field, California. I was a new second lieutenant at this time, and Colonel Eaker personified to me the professional leader. I knew that he could and did do anything he demanded of other officers and men of the group. I also remember so well that he was at work when I got to work, and he was still there when I left for home in the evening."

Working hard at your job is what Brig. Gen. Allen C. Edmunds meant when he said, "The two absolutely important characteristics, in the quality of character in leadership, in my opinion, are commitment and concern. Commitment to the mission, task, or whatever, and concern for those whom you must command in the fulfillment of that mission or task" (personal communication, March 15, 1976).

Brig. Gen. Ross A. Garlich worded the same idea another way when he remarked, "Stated concisely, character is the innate quality in an honest individual which *causes* him to give automatically and without equivocation the best he has in him toward the fulfillment of the responsibilities he has accepted" (personal communication, March 4, 1976).

Another example of giving the job that something extra involves General Arnold. He was visiting various parts of an air base he was inspecting, but was doing it after normal duty hours. He remembered quite well going into a hangar and finding a man in overalls working on an aircraft engine. Intrigued, he found that the individual was not an enlisted mechanic, as he had initially thought, but instead was a young lieutenant, James Doolittle. I asked General Doolittle if he were indeed the lieutenant General Arnold had found working. "I was," he said. "I've always been very interested in mechanical things and I was interested not only in flying airplanes, I was interested in maintaining airplanes and later in the design and manufacture of airplanes. When I was a lieutenant flying, if I wasn't in flying clothes, I was very apt to be in overalls working on the engine or working on the airplane. I wanted to fly as well or better than anyone else, and I believed that in maintaining them and as an engineering officer that I would learn more about engines, and as much about the airplanes and the mechanics who are working under me. I requested the opportunity to go to the Engineering Maintenance School, and while there you could usually find me with a screwdriver or a pair of pliers or a wrench in my hand on the line." But then General Doolittle was reminded of the fact that General Arnold found him working "after hours." He responded very simply, "I was never one to leave a job before it was finished. If I had to work a little longer to get it done that day, then that's what I did" (personal communication, February 7, 1977).

I was intrigued by the fact that, when talking with general officers of the 1929 through 1933 West Point classes, the name of one officer was referred to often as a person who significantly affected and molded their development in a lasting way. As related by Maj. Gen. John M. Breit, "When I entered the U.S. Military Academy in July 1929, a new Commandant of Cadets had just been assigned. His name was Lt. Col. Robert C. Richardson, Jr., class of 1904, with twenty-five years of service. As events evolved, his tour at West Point coincided exactly with my four-year tenure as a cadet. His character made an immediate impression on my class and me. The impression at first was 'a hard man,' but this was revised over the four years to 'the best damn officer in the U.S. Army.' We, the class of 1933, voted to ask Colonel Richardson if he would consent to be an honorary member of our class. He accepted graciously, and he was as proud of being a member of our class as he was of his own.

"Colonel Richardson had definite ideas about his job as Commandant of Cadets. His personal appearance was an example to all cadets—perfection in dress, bearing, cleanliness, and behavior. He maintained a 'rogue's gallery' of photographs of all 1,200 cadets in the Corps, together with their names. He studied his photos every day, and in a short time he associated the names and faces of all 1,200 men. He made surprise inspections during study hours, with a view of understanding cadet behavior and habit changes since his cadet days of twenty-five years ago. He punished with demerits for flagrant violations, but he always explained why. He inspected cadets and ranks at various formations, calling each man by name as he passed. He appeared at all cadet activities, from intramural sports to dances, and expressed appreciation for all things that were well done.

"He made it his personal duty to teach our class the traditions, courtesies, and customs of the service. He obviously cherished this assignment by his display of complete sincerity and devotion to his subjects. Over many hours of instruction, the class learned what made the Army tick, in minute detail. We learned how long to stay at a formal social call and how to die in the service of one's country. Needless to say, we considered the social duties to be trivia, but each presentation was illustrated by a true-life example, either personal or from first-hand knowledge. Thus the trivia was programmed into the memory bank along with everything else.

"In the broad context, Colonel Richardson's course was a description of character as a leadership quality; the dedication of one's self to the mission of the service. Two attributes that Colonel Richardson dwelled on at length were, first, never question a change of station assignment. It is ungentlemanly and negates orderly planning for the Army mission. If the War Department in its infinite judgment plans to send you to Zamboanga, then you go to Zamboanga and do your best. You'll probably have an experience that you will talk about for the rest of your life. This was illustrated by Pershing proceeding to Zamboanga as ordered, winning the confidence of the Moors, and thereby ending the Moor revolt. Pershing's ascendancy to bigger and better things had started. Second, never grumble if you are assigned more responsibility than your contemporaries. This merely means that your contemporaries have been tested and found lacking when you have been tested and passed. This was illustrated by a personal experience at a post where his brother lieutenants repaired to the officer's club each noon for beer call while he performed the many tedious duties as Post Fire Marshal, Post Police and Prison Officer, Post Athletic Officer, etc.

"The two Richardsonisms just cited always stuck in my mind, and I abided by them. I suppose that they have partly molded my own character. I will try to illustrate both points by personal examples. First, never question change of assignment. The end of World War II found me as a regimental combat team commander in Italy. My division was the Thirty-fourth, commanded by Maj. Gen. Charles Bolte. By mid-1946, I was in Army Ground Force Headquarters, G-3, and General Bolte was Deputy Commander, Army Ground Forces. He called me in one day and said I was wasting my time doing a captain's job and a colonel needed broader horizons. Therefore, he was sending me to the newly created Air War College at Maxwell Air Force Base as a student. My reply was "Yes, sir," and I proceeded to Maxwell and enjoyed a splendid course under Maj. Gen. O. A. Anderson. At the end of the school year, Headquarters Army Ground Forces ordered me to Alaska as G-3 Alaskan Department. I thought this strange because the Unification Act of 1946 was to be implemented soon, which would abolish the Alaskan Department. However, I proceeded as ordered, and on arrival in Alaska found that there was no Alaskan Department but a Joint Alaskan Command with Army, Navy, and Air Force components commanding. All joint J-3 jobs were full, as well as all Army G-3 jobs. I was advised by the senior Army officer of the joint staff to seek employment with the Alaskan Air Command. I did and was assigned as Deputy for Plans. It occurred to me that if I was to work for the Air Force for two years in Alaska after such a fine year of training at Maxwell I might as well transfer to the Air Force. So I did. And later developments proved that proceeding to Alaska as ordered was a 'turning point in my career.'

"Second, never grumble over added assigned responsibilities. When I graduated from the National War College in 1951, I was assigned as the Air Force member of a joint planning team on the Joint Chiefs of Staff organization. The Director of Plans was an Army major general, Slayden Bradley, and the Chairman of the Joint Chiefs was General of the Army Omar Bradley. The planning team to which I was assigned consisted of an Army colonel, a Navy captain, and me, an Air Force colonel. Our job was Middle East contingency plans. As time passed, I began to notice that I was getting more and more work as Primary Action Officer, which meant drafting the initial papers, obtaining Army and Navy consent from my team members, staffing the paper in the services, and briefing the Chairman when the paper appeared on the JCS agenda. Soon I was spending nights and weekends working while my teammates enjoyed business as usual. I was fairly provoked but said nothing. One day Gen. Slayden Bradley advised me that the Air Force wanted to transfer me to a new job as Deputy Air Provost Marshal. He said that General of the Army Omar Bradley strongly advised my acceptance of the job at once. I thought, 'My God, I really fouled up somewhere,' but I only said, "Yes, sir," and reported accordingly. Several months later I was promoted to brigadier general. Years later, after retirement, I was in casual cocktail conversation with a friend of mine who informed me that I had been taking the 'heat' very well in the Joint Chiefs and that that was reflected in my selection folder by letters from the JCS superiors. This last statement is hearsay only. I've never seen my own file, in all my active service.

"In closing, if you want to describe character for our young officers tell them to give unstintingly of themselves in furtherance of the Air Force mission. All station assignments and job assignments provide a high degree of self-satisfaction. Guess it all adds up to selflessness" (personal communication, April 26, 1976).

Another aspect of the duty concept is evident in the remarkable patience of our military leaders. General of the Army George C. Marshall was asked by a newspaper reporter in 1951, after Marshall had been successfully Chief of Staff of the Army during World War II, Secretary of State, and Secretary of Defense, what the most exciting moment was of his life. His response was "Being promoted to first lieutenant!" Why? He had spent five years as a second lieutenant.

Patience was certainly a characteristic of Generals Arnold, Spaatz, Vandenberg, Twining, and White, men who remained in the service during the periods of slow promotion between World Wars I and II. During the early years of our aviation history when the first man was killed in an airplane crash (in 1908, Lt. Thomas Selfridge of the Field Artillery), Arnold was thinking of promotion. "It was a plan that has occupied every second lieutenant since the beginning of armies. I was trying to get to be a first lieutenant. In those days in the regular Army, your chances for remaining a second lieutenant for six or seven years were very good. . . ." Arnold became a second lieutenant on June 14, 1907, and was not promoted to first lieutenant until April 10, 1913, thus spending almost six years as a second lieutenant.

Arnold became a captain three years later, a major a year after that, then jumping to the rank of full colonel (temporary) on August 5, 1917, skipping over the rank of lieutenant colonel. Arnold explained the reason for this jump in his own words, which are likewise revealing as an insight into his character. As quoted in Chapter 1, he wrote in his memoirs, "Promotion came rapidly in wartime—especially in an Air Force in which only a few relatively junior officers knew how to fly. . . . My wife and I looked at these eagles on my shoulders, and though we were certainly pleased to see them there, they seemed unreal, even embarrrassing. Youngsters in those days, just didn't get to be colonels."[1]

General Spaatz was commissioned a second lieutenant (of Infantry) on June 12, 1914. His early promotion situation was better than Arnold's because Spaatz was able to get in on what little action there was going on prior to the United States becoming involved in World War I. In June 1916,

Spaatz was assigned to Columbus, New Mexico, serving with the First Aero Squadron under General John J. Pershing in the Punitive Expedition into Mexico and as a result of this action was promoted to first lieutenant on July 1, 1916. In May 1917, he joined the Third Aero Squadron in San Antonio, Texas, and in the same month was promoted to captain.

On November 15, 1917, he again got into the action, being assigned to France with the Thirty-First Aero Squadron, serving in the American Aviation School at Issoudon continuously until August 30, 1918. During this period, he received a temporary promotion to major. After the war, he reverted to the rank of captain, but was again promoted to major on July 1, 1920. He then spent another fifteen years as a major, not receiving his lieutenant colonel's leaf until 1935.

General Vandenberg spent a total of twelve years as a lieutenant, receiving his promotion to captain on August 1, 1935, after having been commissioned a second lieutenant on June 12, 1923. It was then another five years after making captain before he became a temporary major.

Thomas D. White started off brilliantly: he graduated from the Military Academy on July 2, 1920; was commissioned a second lieutenant of Infantry; and on the same day was promoted to first lieutenant! While this was quite a contrast to the slow promotions between the wars, any ego trip would have been short-lived, for on December 22, 1922, he was returned to the grade of second lieutenant. He was not promoted to first lieutenant again until August 24, 1925. Then it was ten years before he became a captain, receiving that promotion on August 1, 1935, after serving over fifteen years as a lieutenant.

But perhaps the most significant example was that of Nathan F. Twining. He entered the Military Academy in June 1917, and because of World War I his class was accelerated. He graduated and was commissioned in November 1918 as a second lieutenant of Infantry. He became a first lieutenant on January 1, 1920, but was not promoted to the rank of captain until April 20, 1935, thus spending seventeen years as a lieutenant.

In summary, one can see that promotions were extremely slow for our first Chiefs of Staff of the Air Force. Arnold was a second lieutenant for six years, and, although things were better for Spaatz because of World War I, he still spent sixteen years as a major. Vandenberg served twelve years as a lieutenant, White fifteen years, and Twining an unbelievable seventeen years as a lieutenant. Their patience and sense of duty were most remarkable, for during the years of slow promotion they chose to remain in the service rather than enter more lucrative opportunities in the civilian world. One wonders why they remained.

Arnold, in fact, had considered leaving the Air Corps to join the embryonic Pan American airlines. Indeed, he was offered the presidency of the airline. But when he was exiled to Fort Riley, because of his continuous efforts to support Billy Mitchell, he concluded, "That was the end of my plan to resign and become president of our newly founded Pan American Airways. I couldn't very well quit the service under fire."[2]

General Spaatz was also offered the opportunity to get in on the early development of Pan American. At the time Arnold was offered the presidency, Spaatz was asked to be vice president. He was asked during an interview why he decided to ignore these temptations. "Well, it's awfully hard," he responded, "to give any reason except that you liked the service. There certainly wasn't any incentive; that is, the same incentives to stay in the service between World War I and World War II as there are now (1962), because there was no apparent threat of any war or any likelihood of any war in those days. However, there was the challenge of developing the Air Force. Most of us who came into the old aviation section, the Signal Corps, believed there was going to be a growth of military aviation, and we had confidence in its being a dominant force for defense and decided to stay with it. There is a different situation now, where you have a big military requirement for years to come—as far ahead as anyone can see."

General Twining, reflected on promotions, "you go through different phases in life. We were lieutenants some fifteen years; we were not always worrying about promotions in those days. I have a kid in the Air Force [this was in 1962], and he gets worried once in a while about promotions, and I say, 'Listen, bird, I was a lieutenant seventeen years—you haven't got a squawk coming.' We were lieutenants so long, and we just felt we would be lucky if we ever got to be major, that was a big hump then, that was where we were going to retire (as majors) at the rate we were going. If it hadn't been for the war, most of us probably would have retired as majors or lieutenant colonels. You see, our commanding officers were those ranks. The highest commander I ever saw was lieutenant colonel until the war came. Horace Hickam came down to our field to become Commander. He was a lieutenant colonel, and I said when I first saw him, 'Oh my gosh, he's way up there. Most of the commanders in those days were majors."

Thomas D. White did consider leaving the service in his younger years. When asked, "After you entered the service, what was there about it that made you decide to stay?" he replied, "Well, that is a tough question because I was more conscious of a real strong desire to get out in my early days. I either didn't have the nerve, or I simply figured that I was in a pretty good billet, but was not too satisfied in the Infantry as a junior officer [he was detailed to Brooks Field, Texas, on September 14, 1924, and officially transferred to the Air Corps on March 3, 1927]. I was definitely not very happy for a long time."

Not even the flying changed his position right away. "Did you have any doubts," he was asked, "when you started flying?" He responded, "Yes, actually, I did. I remember very well after I had finished flying school, for some extraordinary reason, I didn't know why, I was ordered from Kelly Field to Bolling, and I could never figure out why until I ran into the personnel officer. I said, 'Tell me why I was sent to Bolling Field. I just can't understand it.' He said, 'Oh, because I thought you wanted to be near your folks.' I said to him, as far as I know my family had never even been to Washington, D.C.!' I thought then about getting out. I used to go to New York. I had very definite correspondence and interviews with some of the officials in the Chase National Bank. One day I was going back to Bolling and I flew over Manhattan. I looked down—it must have been about 12:30 on a Saturday, and I saw all those thousands of people down there who looked like thousands of ants. I also remembered seeing the junior executives with their golf clubs in the lobby of the bank dashing out to go to some club out on Long Island which they couldn't afford to belong to, working like dogs to try to keep up. There I was up in the sky in a fabulously expensive 08-4 which probably cost $50,000, and I was free as a bird. It was then and there I said the hell with it. I will stay where I am in the service, where I was doing things that interested me."

The military is always confronted with the demands of duty—duty rosters on the bulletin board, duty details, the duty to keep your equipment in good condition. The concept of duty is constantly before you in every phase of military life.

But duty is more than a detail roster on the squadron bulletin board. Duty with these men carried the requirement to do their job to the best of their ability, whether they liked it or not. Duty was doing what one ought to do, when one ought to do it, as one ought to do it. It was a matter of doing their work well for the sake of all. This is summed up well in the Bible: "Whatever thy hand findeth to do, do it with thy might" (Ecclesiastes 9:10).

There are jobs within the military that are certainly not glamorous. But duty means doing the day-to-day routine jobs well. No matter how much one may love one's work, there are some aspects of the job that are not easy or pleasant.

Duty is a life not centered on oneself. These men saw their duty to God, to their country, and to their fellow man, and they did it. This duty required sacrifice—the loss of personal comforts, money, their health, and sometimes their lives. They lost themselves in a cause bigger than self. A sense of duty called for this kind of sacrifice.

But there are rewards for this sense of duty—for the sacrifice. Their lives were filled with a sense of worth, an immeasurable sense of satisfaction. They were given the opportunity in military service to make the best possible use of their lives.

These men had an aim and purpose in life. Was it because they were ambitious? Ambition is the desire to do or to become. It may be limitless. It comes from within. There are many ambitions for many different things. There can be ambition for power, popularity, money, and prestige. Ambition can be either good or bad. It moves men to overcome obstacles, but it needs direction and control. When there is direction, it is good. One of the greatest motivations for achievement in history has been ambition. But the motives that induce people to follow a particular ambition are not always the highest, not always noble. Ambition to be powerful, or to make the most money, or to achieve the greatest fame were not the goals of these men. Their aim was to follow the creed of service to God and country, and to their fellow man. Their achievements came from hard work for a noble purpose—service.

They were selfless men. Selflessness entails sacrifice, surrendering something for a greater cause. The selfish person thinks first of himself, whereas the unselfish thinks first of the welfare of others. These men gave themselves—their time, their health, their wealth, their energy—all to achieve worthwhile goals. To them, sacrifice was a way of life.

Their sacrifice was personal, measured in long hours at work away from their families, neglecting leisure pursuits, and sometimes even forgetting their health. They also did not worry about amassing wealth. Service was sufficient. And, of course, when duty called they were ready to give their lives.

A military career is not the best-paying job, nor is it the most comfortable or easy. Indeed, it is a very dangerous profession. What motivates this desire to serve and to sacrifice? Love of one's home and family, of one's community and country. This causes many men to give up much. But the greatest and highest motive for the daily sacrifice of those who serve is their love of God and country.

NOTES, Chapter 6

1. Gen. Henry H. Arnold, *Global Mission* (New York: Harper, 1949), p. 48.
2. Ibid., p. 122.

CHAPTER 7
HONOR

William Shakespeare said, *To thine own self be true, and it must follow as the night the day, thou canst then not be false to any man.* And Ralph Waldo Emerson wrote, "Honor is venerable to us because it is so ephemeral. It is always ancient virtue. We worship it today, because it is not of today. We love it and pay it homage, because it is not a trap for our love and homage, but is self-independent, self-derived, and therefore of an old, immaculate pedigree."

While honor may not be "of today" to some, it is, has been, and must always be a part of the American military establishment. General Arnold said firmly to the officers of the then Army Air Corps in 1941–42 that

> It is an unwritten law, but as binding as the unwritten common law in the English system of jurisprudence—that any army officer's official word, spoken or written, can be depended upon to be the absolute truth. High on the list of military crimes goes the false official statement. This does not mean that an officer cannot or does not tell his young son that there is a Santa Claus, or his wife that he was, believe it or not, waiting for a streetcar. It does mean that when he makes an official statement it is true without evasion or equivocation. The military profession takes great pride in its reputation in this regard and its senior professionals will never forgive any deviation.[1]

231

This was particularly important when testifying before Congress. "I remember," said Lt. Gen. Elwood R. Quesada, "that during the testimony after World War II, we were getting ready to go down and testify on the Hill. General Spaatz, who had become Chief of Staff, called us in before going down to testify and said to us, 'I don't want any of you to ever lie' " (personal communication, June 22, 1977).*

In *The War Lords,* Alfred Goldberg wrote that "Spaatz had the common touch, identifying naturally with his fighting men and visiting combat crews frequently. He had great concern that his men put their trust in him and their other leaders, insisting that they be told the truth about operations and their effects. Because he felt that misleading information and wrong impressions could be harmful to the morale of the fighting men, Spaatz personally took great pains to correct and set right such lapses."[2]

General McKee (who was nonrated, yet was Spaatz' Deputy Vice Chief of Staff) said of Spaatz, "He was a man of great integrity. He had the respect of everyone above him and everyone below him. You could see his integrity in every action that he took. There were not any cliques around General Spaatz. He was fair with everyone, and he didn't give a damn whether you were rated or nonrated" (personal communication, July 6, 1977).

Gen. Theodore R. Milton had a similar outlook toward Nathan F. Twining. "I'm a great admirer of Twining," he said. "Twining was a man of enormous honesty. It sticks out all over him. You can't imagine Twining doing anything that wasn't the right thing to do in his judgment. No devious business, no trickery. I don't think you could ever point to anything that he did that was brilliant, but everybody trusted him. And this I think on the part of anyone who was ever around Nate Twining resulted in their having an enormous respect for him, and this is quite a good leadership trait. If everybody respects you and thinks you're wonderful, why, you can get anything you want out of the people" (personal communication, April 9, 1976).

Theodore R. Milton was forever indebted to one officer for demonstrating character. "I think General LeMay had enormous traits of character," he said. "He always did what he thought he ought to do, right or wrong. I remember something he did for me during 1943. I led some missions in the Eighth Air Force and when we were making bomb drops on Bremen they put up some smoke screens that fooled us, and we didn't do a very good job of bombing. We lost a lot of airplanes, and as a result of the poor performance and the loss of aircraft the brass came up from London for the critique of this mission and quite frankly they were looking for a

---

*"Personal communication" refers to letter to the author.

scapegoat. The mission was not a disaster, it just wasn't a very good job, and it was one of the first real tries we had in going into Germany itself. So, anyway, one or two people got up and had a story which no one challenged, but I personally made a mistake in part of my performance in leading this mission, and, being new, I got up and stated what mistake I thought I had made. I started where I thought I went wrong and went on to describe the errors I had made and how I shouldn't have done it, and before I knew it the critiquing officers were all over me. Present in the group was then Col. Curtis E. LeMay. And most all of the people around were senior to him, but as he saw these senior officers going after me he got up and said, 'Wait a minute, now.' He then turned to me and said that 'If that's the worst mistake you ever make, Milton, you'll be all right.' What he had done was to let the senior people know that perhaps they had lost their perspective in their effort to look for a scapegoat. Colonel LeMay's comment silenced these people and that ended the inquisition and, indeed, the whole briefing." Milton then went on to say that what impressed him was that "There was nothing in it for Colonel LeMay. I wasn't even in his group. Colonel LeMay sat there, and listened to what they were doing, and decided that these people were going about it in the wrong way, that I had simply made an honest mistake. . . . We picked up the wrong initial point coming in, and . . . the smoke screen . . . fooled us. . . . I think this was typical of the way Colonel LeMay behaved in his whole career. He was fallible, he made some mistakes now and then, but he always stuck to what he felt was right. I don't think he ever tried to tailor his attitude or behavior to whatever might have been the current fashion. He was his own man" (personal communication, April 9, 1976).

Since the time when Gen. Curtis E. LeMay became SAC Commander in Chief, Strategic Air Command had a system in which numerous requirements had to be performed by each unit as they maintained their readiness. Some commanders anxious to stand high in the ratings resorted to filling in requirements that were not actually performed. This was, of course, dishonest. A real insight into this issue was offered by Brig. Gen. Richard N. Ellis, who stated, "I spent some fourteen years of my military career in Strategic Air Command either as a wing or division commander. It was probably the most demanding and finest command in the Air Force during those years, and it may still be. Strategic Air Command was blessed with strong commanders at the top and in my opinion pretty much up and down the line throughout its Air Forces, divisions, and wings. It was a strongly competitive command, and one of the means of measuring performance throughout an organization's area of operations, logistics, and administration was a management control system. It was designed . . . to provide command emphasis and intention in important operational and combat related areas, but also . . . to support administrative and even recreational or morale areas. Attention was drawn to the key areas by weighting these areas heavier than functions of lesser importance to the mission accomplishment. There were commanders, however, within SAC who used the management control system as an end within itself—who tolerated, by their acceptance and probably active encouragement, the 'penciling' of accomplishment . . . sensed by subordinates. . . . Although these units appeared to be performing well in the monthly analysis, they had lost their integrity. The commander had no integrity, and the lack of it permeated down through the system. Some of these individuals progressed well, promotion-wise, due to strong-appearing performance, but eventually the 'paper strength' of the unit would be revealed by deficient performance during an operational readiness inspection, poor crew performance on evaluation flights and the like, and the unit would be swept clean by the old man; that is, General LeMay, for example, who would absolutely not tolerate this type of lack of integrity. A commander whose unit hadn't been scoring too well in the management control system and whose unit had failed in a readiness inspection, and whose record was proved clean by the inspector usually got help and a second chance; but God help the commander in whose unit false reporting and other hanky-panky was found to exist. He usually just suddenly disappeared out of the system. While admittedly the type of weak commanders I have described were very, very few in number, I use this example to demonstrate the absolute necessity for integrity and the insistence upon high standards of conduct and honesty by the man at the top. The great majority of us subordinate commanders knew this and appreciated it and admired General LeMay very much. However, there are always a few misguided individuals, I suppose, who don't get the word and who presume to climb to the top on false pretenses. It just won't work, and the tragic part is the lowering of morale throughout a unit that falls heir to a commander who lacks integrity—again, the most important ingredient of leadership and in turn character'' (personal communication, January 20, 1976).

Hayden Pearson, in a story in *A Treasury of Vermont Life,* put into perspective the most noble and cherished of all the qualities of leadership —honor—when he said,

Years ago as a young lad I was helping an old man build a section of wall on a sidehill slope of a farmyard. For almost two centuries, Old Ben's familiy had been famous dry-wall builders. Old Ben was the last of the line. We had dug the trench wide and deep, three feet or more, so that the big foundation stones would be below the frostline. Slowly the wall rose. The old man was very particular about each rock and chinking piece. To an impatient lad the old craftsman was unconscionably slow. The idea of chinking rocks below the soil surface was particularly irksome. "Who's going to know if these are chinked or not?" was a boy's question. The old man's astonishment was genuine as he peered over his spectacles. "Why," he said, "I will—and so will you."

This is what honor is all about. Honor has as its foundation our own self-respect and esteem—our actual integrity and worth. Put very simply, a real test of honor is what we would do if no one was looking and if we knew we would never be caught. If one would be honorable under these conditions, he is truly a man of honor. He is noble—a man of strength who stands above all men and dictates to the consciences of others. It is this quality of honor that urges men to chivalry and to sacrifice. It is an inward strength which sustains a man when he is doubted by others—where it is enough if one knows inwardly he has been honest.

"When Gen. Thomas D. White became Chief of Staff," reflected Edith Cafferey, White's secretary during his tour as Chief, "he wanted to sign everything personally that required his signature. The condolence letters, for example, were prepared by his staff. The number of letters became so voluminous, he simply couldn't keep up signing all the letters personally, so we, the staff, on our own decided to use the signature machine to take some of the load off. Somehow a response to one of these condolence letters . . . was placed on his desk, without a note on it explaining what we had done. He called me in immediately after he read it, and, very distraught, his head in his hands, he said to me, 'Edith, I feel like such a hypocrite getting a thank-you note for a letter I did not sign" (personal commuication, February 1, 1978).

White's public relations officer during his tour as Chief of Staff, Maj. Gen. Arno H. Luehman, remembered an occasion when General White was Chief of Staff: "We were being briefed by an intelligence officer, in fact the Chief of Air Force Intelligence with regard to a pamphlet the Air Force was going to put out outlining Russian capabilities. The first thing that flashed on the screen, the first slide the intelligence officer showed us, was a picture of the cover of the pamphlet. It had Russian letters, supposedly spelling out missiles, but it was spelled out with Russian characters in the Latin phrase. In other words, not really Russian—not in Russian script. General White immediately said, 'Hold it a minute. I'm not going to be a part of your discussion if you're going to put out something that's supposed to look like Russian, nor will I permit that pamphlet to be published. It's neither accurate nor honest'' (personal communication, 1977).

"I suppose one could take the dictionary's definition of character," said Senator Barry Goldwater, a two-star general in the Air Force Reserve, "and come out all right but, as long as you asked me, here's the way I look at it. A man's character is wrapped chiefly around his honesty, which means his ability to be honest with every person and everything he touches. I have never known a leader in any field in my life whom I held in high regard who had any hint or taint of dishonesty. What particularly impressed me was that these people in high positions did not make any great to-do about their honesty, and if you'll notice, one of the first things a man will say about a commanding officer who is a capable and outstanding leader is that he's an honest man and I know I can depend upon him" (personal communication, September 22, 1975). If you have honor, you don't have to go around talking about the fact that you have—your people will know.

Maj. Gen. Frederic H. Miller makes the point that integrity and honor are givens. "Looking at the personality traits, integrity would have to be high on the list. But ask yourself this question—should it be possible for an officer to survive long in a military service without integrity? It seems to me that those without integrity should be fired early in the process if the officer evaluation system is worth anything at all. Hence, I think it is a fair conclusion, that all or nearly all of the potential leaders come with a built-in integrity since they survived the system. In other words, it is such a basic attribute for all officers that it shouldn't be special for the 'great' leaders. One of the problems, however, is that OER [Officer Effectiveness Reports] systems tend to rate job performance rather than personality characteristics. This comes from the mistaken belief that OERs should be used by the officer rated to improve his performance. That's wrong—it needs to be a separate counseling system. Officer Effectiveness Reports will continue to be relatively useless as long as the rated officer has access to them.

"The 'duty, honor, country' creed of the Military Academy is in this category to some degree. It also represents a personality characteristic that should be found in all officers, but it is not necessarily. What I'm saying is that these characteristic traits, of a personal nature, ought to be expected of the potential leaders if the selection and evaluation process of the military service is worth anything" (personal communication, January 23, 1976).

Not everyone agrees that honor and duty are so important. To some, job performance is about all that counts. As suggested by Brig. Gen. Chester J. Butcher, "Perhaps I can offer a few constructive comments on what might get the attention of the young people in today's Air Force. Words like *selflessness, integrity,* etc., sound too much like an OER check sheet and too 'Boy Scoutish' for this generation. You don't give them vague definitions, concepts or theories—give them performance. The first and foremost characteristic of leadership is that the boss has got to know his job. Translated simply, 'Is he technically qualified?'; 'Does he work the right problems?'; (and I can't overemphasize this point) 'Does he know how to go about problem solution?' From the answer to these questions, all else falls into perspective. I adhere to the premise that from basic intellectual honesty and technique stem all the characteristics you and others have listed as desirable. The one element missing is the human interaction—a very necessary aspect, but much easier to find or develop" (personal communication, January 23, 1976).

Former Air Force Surgeon General, Lt. Gen. K. E. Pletcher, would disagree. "If I were to assess an individual for character in its best connotations, I would look for honesty. . . . I'm willing to accept something less than the highest intelligence if I can be assured of honesty and loyalty" (personal communication, March 11, 1976).

A less sophisticated but certainly blunt way of saying the same thing was when Maj. Gen. Archie M. Burke remarked, "On a personal basis I guess the best I can do, in describing to you what character is in leadership, is to repeat what one of my superiors is supposed to have said of me, 'He isn't the brightest guy to ever come down the pike, but he's the most honest SOB alive I have ever known.' That's good enough for me" (personal communication, December 15, 1975).

Often honesty is simply a matter of one's word being one's bond: "I had a personal experience with Hap Arnold which illustrates his fairness in keeping his word," reflected Brig. Gen. Russell E. Randall, "Hap was a major, commanding the Sixteenth Observer Squadron at Fort Riley, on a so-called punishment tour for his support of Billy Mitchell. I was serving at my first post after graduating from Kelly Field, and it was in the fall of 1926.

"To replace the old DHs at Riley, we received some new Curtiss observation planes. We were only a handful of pilots, and Arnold announced a new policy. Each pilot was to be assigned his own aircraft and crew chief; he was to have his name printed on the side, and when he wanted to go on the frequent weekend cross-country flight he could also have complete control of his own airplane when it was in commission.

"This was a boon to most pilots, because previous normal cross-country approval was based on seniority, and the ranking pilots got first choice on trips and airplanes.

"The following weekend my ship, *Pegasus,* was in spotless condition, and I requested a flight to Omaha taking a classmate with me. At the assignment briefing by Hap Friday at noon, he announced that, since Captain Boland wanted to go to Kansas City and since his airplane was out of commission, he could take mine and I could go to Omaha as a passenger with Lieutenant Fisher! This was not only contrary to his previous promise, but I too had promised to carry my roommate to Omaha. So I opened my big mouth and said, 'But sir! Didn't you say we could take our own airplanes if they were in commission? And I have promised to take an officer with me.'

"Hap glowered at me and said: 'If you want to go to Omaha—go with Fisher; Boland, you can take Randall's airplane and go to Kansas City!' He then slammed the door and went home, and I thought, 'How could he break his word?'

"In two hours Hap was back, and he took me out behind the hangar and said, 'Randall, do you know you were insubordinate this morning?'

"'I replied, 'Yes, sir.' '' "He then said, 'Well, all West Pointers are insubordinate; so you take your airplane and your classmate and fly to Omaha this weekend and thank you for reminding me. That's all!''

"And he kept his word and I continued to think the world of him."

One of the best expressions of what honor is all about was provided by Lt. Gen. Robert E. Pursley, who said, "I believe our military leaders need to evidence an exceptionally strong characteristic of adherence to high principles. That involves more than a snappy salute and a 'can do' spirit. There is ample room for such traits. But in a society obviously beset with unethical infections at every military interface—i.e., with other government officials, with business, and with foreign elements—there is an additional premium on ethical behavior, high morality, and unimpeachable principles. A military leader has the responsibility, in my judgment, to establish such standards and to live by them. If and when superiors or other governmental elements flout such standards, the military man with sound leadership qualities should make his views known and see the adverse element changes or he should resign or retire. Only by such strong adherence to principles can the military do its job—defending values as well as people, defending principles as well as property" (personal communication, March 5, 1976).

NOTES, Chapter 7

1. Lt. Gen. Henry H. Arnold and Brig. Gen. Ira C. Eaker, *Army Flyer* (New York: Harper, 1942), p. 71.
2. Alfred Goldberg, in Field Marshal Sir Michael Carver, ed., *The War Lords* (Boston: Little, Brown, 1976), p. 580.

CHAPTER 8

SERVICE BEFORE SELF

On December 31, 1942, Secretary of War Henry L. Stimson attended a surprise party for Army Chief of Staff George C. Marshall, in the office of one of the Deputy Chiefs of Staff, then Gen. Joseph T. McNarney, Air Corps. Present were Generals H. H. Arnold, Brehon B. Somervell, Lesley J. McNair, and a few others. At this occasion, Stimson made some remarks about Marshall, which he later recorded in his diary: "I had been accustomed throughout my life to classify all public servants into one or the other of two general classes: one, the men who were thinking what they could do for their job; the other, the men who were thinking what the job could do for them, and that General Marshall I thought was in front of all those of the first class. Then I expatiated on his single-mindedness and his selflessness and his deep feeling for his friends. I said that I thought that in this case the proverb was very applicable: 'He that ruleth his spirit is better than he that taketh a city.' "[1]

On June 12, 1944, a week after the D-Day invasion of Europe, General of the Army George C. Marshall, along with General of the Army H. H. Arnold and Adm. Ernest King, made an inspection trip to Europe. With General of the Army Dwight D. Eisenhower as their escort, the officers went over and up and down the beaches in jeeps. They stopped at noon at a field lunch mess; and as they sat on ammunition boxes eating their lunches, General Marshall very suddenly turned to the Supreme Commander and said, "Eisenhower, you've chosen all these commanders or accepted the ones I've suggested. What is the principal quality you look for in selecting a commander?'' Eisenhower responded, that ''Without thinking, I said selflessness'' (General of the Army Dwight D. Eisenhower, personal communication, May 3, 1963).

One of the highest tributes to a leader is that he be so effective in his leadership that his men give their all—indeed, they will literally be willing to give their lives—in carrying out orders. How does a leader accomplish this? Unquestionably the most important quality engendering this loyalty is the quality of selflessness. It implies the ability of an individual to put service above self, to put the welfare of others and the unit ahead of his own. This means making sure food and shelter and rest are available to the troops before the leader takes care of himself. It means placing the goals of the unit ahead of his personal ambition. It means seeking to relate the success to the unit rather than looking on the success as an individual accomplishment of the leader. An example given by Lt. Gen. James V. Edmundson (USAF, Ret.) is that of Gen. Curtis E. LeMay during the time he was a group commander in the Far East in World War II. LeMay made the decision to lower the bombing altitude on missions over the Japanese empire from 25,000–35,000 feet to 5,000–10,000 feet. This simple decision, General Edmundson related, helped bring the war in the Pacific to a successful conclusion far sooner than would have otherwise been possible and without the need to execute a ground invasion, which would have been costly in lives, materiel, and time. ''Those of us who commanded the groups under General LeMay,'' related Edmundson, ''knew that his decision was reached in absolute honesty. There were no ulterior motives. We accepted the difficulty of this decision and the courage it took for him to make it in the face of so much 'expert' advice which held that bombing at lower altitudes would produce prohibitive losses. Finally, we were delighted that his professional judgment on which his decision was based proved so correct. He accurately predicted that Japanese defenses would have difficulty in adjusting to the new tactics and that the increased accuracy and bomb load permitted by the reduced altitude would result in each mission being flown over the empire being vastly more effective than the ratio of lives lost to bomb tonnage becoming more favorable.''

An example of an Army officer who put service before self and greatly influenced him was related by Maj. Gen. James W. Spry. ''One whom I consider to have great character was an Army general, Thomas T. Handy. I had the pleasure of being his Chief of Staff for about a year in the Headquarters of EUCOM in Frankfurt, Germany, after World War II. General Handy had charm, courtesy, common sense, sincerity, honesty, and courage in abundance. I personally saw him verbally castigate a visiting deputy secretary of defense because the office of the deputy was constantly sending us vague and conflicting instructions in spite of our many complaints. General Handy was the perfect host with no pretense of fawning to visiting dignitaries, and he did not have any reluctance to be candid and honest to speak his mind as he did to the deputy secretary of defense.

"A very meaningful example of the character of General Thomas T. Handy was illustrated by the fact that he served throughout most of World War II in Washington, D.C., as Deputy to General of the Army George C. Marshall, even though his great ambition was to be a field commander in one of the war theaters. I knew that General Handy had requested a command from General Marshall, but had been told he was needed in his present position. In all my many conversations with General Handy, while I served under him, I never once heard him utter a word of complaint that his ambition had been denied. His devotion to General Marshall was complete, and he spoke of Marshall almost with reverence. In short, here was a most capable officer, with a DSC from World War I, who subjugated himself to serve where his boss had told him he was needed. No glory for him; no hero headlines; but he willingly performed where he had been told that he could best help his country and his superior. This is a display of character" (personal communication, March 6, 1976).

In addition to service before self, although not as vital, is a kind of humility displayed by officers when they become commanders of a unit. General Spaatz expressed it like this: "I think that a very important thing is that when you are in command of anything—a squadron, group or whatever it may be—the unit doesn't belong to you, you belong to the unit. Some of the officers in the military had the idea when they were in command of a unit that it was a personal thing, that the organization belonged to them, which of course was the wrong attitude" (personal communication).

Spaatz was one of the most unassuming, unpretentious, and humble leaders of World War II. Sir Michael Carver commented that "Eisenhower named Spaatz and Omar Bradley as the outstanding generals to serve under him during the war. In 1948 he wrote to Spaatz, 'No man can justly claim a greater share than you in the attainment of victory in Europe.' Arnold considered Spaatz the outstanding airman of the war, and Bradley referred to him as a 'deceptively quiet and brilliant man.' Portal and Tedder held him in the highest esteem as a commander, and Sholto Douglas, who had come to know him well, wrote that 'of all the relatively unknown military leaders of World War II, Spaatz was probably the greatest.' That he was relatively unknown suited Spaatz, for he had no concern about status and image. His achievements as a commander and a major architect of the Allied air war in World War II deserve a full measure of historical recognition. May he be accorded his due."[2]

After Nathan F. Twining achieved great high command, "Superior rank and heavy responsibility changed him little," said classmate Maj. Gen. Herbert M. Jones, "if at all, and as you know, this is not always the case. He is very loyal to his class and classmates and rarely misses a class affair that he is able to attend" (personal communication, April 19, 1963).

When General Twining was inducted into the Aviation Hall of Fame, former Air Force Secretary Jim Douglas gave him a glowing introduction. Twining's brief acceptance speech revealed his basic humbleness. He simply said, "Ladies and Gentlemen, first I would like to thank my dear friend Jim Douglas for his wonderful introduction of me. To be inducted into the Aviation Hall of Fame means more to me than I can ever tell you. Thank you for this great honor." End of speech. This talk was one of several given during the course of the presentation. The reaction of the crowd to Twining's words was greater than to any of the other talks, and General Twining received a standing ovation.

But humility did not and does not mean they were not confident men. "I would say one of the important things in character is self-confidence," remarked Lt. Gen. Jimmy Doolittle, "and I very carefully distinguish between self-confidence and conceit. I think a man has to have confidence in himself, in his ability, in order to instill confidence in him in others, and he's got to be very careful that his word is self-confidence and not self-adulation" (personal communication, February 7, 1977).

When Doolittle discussed leadership and his success with me, one of the major hurdles I had to overcome was the basic humility that General Doolittle displayed about himself and his career. For example, I asked him what role humility played in the success of a man. General Doolittle responded that "All I have to do to remain humble is to think of the stupid things that I've done in my life" (personal communication, February 7, 1977).

The truly successful leader is one who has a lifelong interest in his men, particularly in their well-being. Brig. Gen. John D. Peters, USAF retired, said to me, "I guess if I were to characterize leadership . . . I would have to say that the most important aspect is *concern for people*. That in itself, I think, indicates a certain selflessness. It also indicates that the selflessness is motivated, not by ulterior motives, but rather because of the concern that one has for the people upon whom he depends" (personal communication, January 7, 1977).

Brig. Gen. Clarence J. Galligan reflected that "I believe that

I can provide one very simple example of character, if you will agree that 'selflessness' and 'concern for others' are reasonably synonymous. Sometime in 1944 I was a colonel commander of a troop carrier group working with the OSS—the British resupplying and evacuating partisans in Yugoslavia, Greece, Italy, etc. Part of the so-called Balkan air force. My Commander was Brig. Gen. Tim Manning (Slot Wing). He visited my station, and I met him as he landed. It was quite cold. I was dressed in a woolen shirt but without a flight jacket—then considered part of the uniform. At his inquiry, I told him I had worn out my jacket. He departed for Fifteenth Air Force Headquarters. Late that evening he returned —having flown perhaps two extra hours to give me a flight jacket that he had picked up at Bari, Italy. His concern earned my deepest respect and loyalty—or otherwise reinforced both" (personal communication, October 26, 1976).

An excellent example of this concern for people was given by Brig. Gen. P. C. Sandretto. He told me a story about Brig. Gen. Alfred Warrington Marriner, known as "Si" throughout the Air Service.

"The incident I remember about General Marriner occurred in 1929 at which time Si was asked to set up a communications school at Chanute Field in Illinois. When the time came for submitting effectiveness reports, Si sent some high ratings for the members of his command, whereupon his commanding officer censured him. What happened was a long and bitter argument over the ratings. The commanding officer ended by saying, 'The ratings you have sent to me are too high. If you will not lower them so that they are the same order as those of the remainder of my command, you give me no alternative but to lower your personal rating because these ratings indicate you have failed to do an adequate job in rating the members of your command.'

" 'Very well,' Si replied, 'make my rating what you wish, but I tell you that if the quality or performance of my staff is not as good as I have indicated, these men would not be in my command. I will not change these effectiveness reports.'

"Was General Marriner correct in what he had done? Some ten years later, the country was engaged in World War II. Of the members of that particular command that General Marriner had, 60 percent remained and were in the service when World War II started. Of that group that remained, of whom General Marriner wrote such high effectiveness reports, 80 percent obtained the rank of general officers. Two of the members obtained the rank of lieutenant general" (personal communication, March 17, 1976).

A further essential aspect of leadership involves community relations, because the welfare of a military installation and its effectiveness in accomplishing the mission depends on the civilian communities at home and overseas.

"In my own case," wrote Maj. Gen. Ben I. Funk, "I believe that my understanding of human dignity and the importance of the individual can best be illustrated by events which took place during my military career between 1951 through 1954. During this period of time, I was assigned to the U.S. Air Force in Europe and placed in command of the Air Depot in Erding, Germany (near Munich). The mission of the Air Depot was to provide material support, supply and maintenance, to the Air Force organizations in the European theater of operations. At the time I took command, the personnel complement of the Erding Air Depot was approximately 4,000 Air Force military and civilians, plus 4,000 German nationals. As you may recall, this was during the U.S. occupation of Germany, and there was very little fraternization between the Americans and the Germans.

"The policy at the time I took command was to have as little association as possible both socially and professionally with the Germans. I believed this policy to be wrong because I felt the same sense of responsibility for the German personnel as for the Americans. The efficiency of the Air Depot was also of concern to me, because I knew that the productivity of neither the German nor the American workers was as good as it should have been, simply because they were not working as a team. As a result, I established a German-American Club, with representatives from all depot organizations. Both the German and the American representatives elected presidents of their respective groups each year who then served as joint presidents of the German-American Club. The burgomeister (mayor) of the town of Erding and I were advisers to the German-American Club and met with them on a monthly basis to assist in resolving any social or professional problems that arose between the members during the period. As a result, relations between the town of Erding and the U.S. Erding Depot greatly improved as well as did relations between the German and American workers at the Air Depot. It is significant to note that efficiency and productivity increased to the point that Erding Air Depot won the outstanding depot award for the entire U.S. Air Force throughout the world.

"In the area of humanitarian welfare, another matter occurred during this period of time—that is, during the fall of 1953—which may possibly illustrate character as a leadership quality. It had been the custom, since occupation of the Erding Air Depot by the U.S. Air Force after World War II, for the American personnel to contribute to Christmas support for about 5 orphanages in the local Erding-Munich area, with a total of about 600 orphans. At a staff meeting in October 1953, the subject of Christmas support to orphans was discussed, and I asked the question, 'How many orphanages and orphans are there in all of Bavaria?' The answer from my German-American staff adviser was, 'Approximately 114 orphanages with about 15,000 orphans.' I suggested that the Erding German-American Club consider the possibility of sponsoring a fund-raising campaign with a goal of $25,000 to provide Christmas gifts for all these orphans this particular year of 1953.

"The decision was enthusiastically unanimous, and by mid-December the German-American Club had raised $37,500 and had procured about 75,000 presents consisting of candy, toys, toothbrushes, soap, pens, pencils, tablets, etc., for all ages of orphans. The presents were individually wrapped by name, with five for each orphan, and were distributed by Santa Clauses flying Army helicopters to the remote locations, Air Force trucks to the less remote ones, and the German railroad transporting about 1,500 orphans from more local areas to Erding Air Depot where 1,500 airmen gave up their Christmas dinners at local mess halls in support of the orphans. . . . The local Air Force theater provided German versions of Mickey Mouse movies for entertainment.

"As I recall, *Newsweek* at the time reported the whole affair as the world's biggest Christmas party. I don't believe I ever saw a happier group of individuals than those orphans being called forward by name by Santa Claus to receive their presents or those Germans and Americans who witnessed the event" (personal communication, January 12, 1976).

The value of community relations was pointed out by Brig. Gen. George M. Higginson, who emphasized that one aspect of character in a leader is the ability to understand the needs of others, the ability to deal with other people in ways that provide satisfaction. If a leader is able to do this, he will have the loyalty and support of his subordinates. "This is not to suggest selfish motives, but merely that the only things of value in this world are other humans and that there is little point in any interaction that is not mutually beneficial and satisfying. Thus, a knowledge of psychology and an ability to deal with others fairly and openly will generate confidence."

Why is a man ready to give his all for a leader? Certainly consideration of others is part of the answer.

"On December 17, 1961, my father passed away," reflected A1C Forrest W. Werts, "and I was asked to return home to bury him. General O'Donnell found out and saw to it that I was returned to the CONUS with the least amount of delay and confusion. During the twenty days that I was gone, my wife, then pregnant, and daughter were looked after. At Christmas time the General saw to it that my daughter received toys under the tree. This act of kindness alone helped to calm the sadness and anxiety during that period. I also received a sympathy card from General O'Donnell.

"I, as well as the rest of the staff came in close contact with the General. When he asked a question of any man, you were expected to come out with a straight answer without flowery statements. When a person was reprimanded, it was done so severely but with fairness.

"General O'Donnell's ability to command his men, yet have a concern for each man's welfare and morale makes him a great man as well as a great general. He is one man that I would consider it an honor to follow anywhere even through hell."

Sometimes simple recognition of someone is important. "I will never forget that as a young officer I was stationed in England during World War II, and while I was there General Arnold had come over for an inspection trip. He had landed at the airfield, and I was simply there among the crowd, but Arnold recognized me, which I thought was remarkable. He called over to me and asked me to come over to him, and we then proceeded to take a walk. During the conversation he asked me how I was and how things were going. It made a great impression upon me." Milton at the time was only a young lieutenant, but Milton's father had been a career officer within the military, and his father had known Arnold, since they were stationed at various duty stations together. Indeed, it was Arnold who gave young Milton his first interest in flying by giving him his first airplane flight when he was only twelve years old. Milton went on to become a four-star general in the Air Force.

Even a sincere and genuine interest in the opinion of others is appreciated. "An experience in my military career that occurred in 1940 still remains very much a part of my memory," said Brig. Gen. John A. Desportes. "At ROTC training at Fort McClellan, Alabama, my instructor was a regular Army major. He obviously had a personal interest in me, as evidenced by frequent private conversations. He told me one day that he did not believe in giving orders. Instead, he believed in 'asking' subordinates to perform certain tasks or missions. His opinion was that over 95 percent complied willingly and cheerfully to this approach. Of course, the small number that did not could be handled in a more 'direct' manner. It was not at all strange to me that this major's company was rated as the best in the entire camp" (personal communication, February 12, 1976).

Former Lt. Gen. K. E. Pletcher said, "I have known people with a high level of intelligence, but whose loyalty was suspect because of burning ambition to get ahead by whatever means. I am a believer in the cliché that good luck is the coincidence of preparation and opportunity" (personal communication, March 11, 1976).

"My career was somewhat out of pattern in that I spent the war in a POW camp in Germany," remarked Lt. Gen. Albert P. Clark. "I was given a 'sympathy promotion' to colonel upon return in 1945. I was about the last one on the list to get such a promotion, and had I not earned it I probably would not have gone beyond colonel in my career. As a young officer, I was intensely ambitious. My misfortunes in the war had a profound effect on me, and I had plenty of time to decide that a driving ambition was not a virtue but a vice and caused men to do things that were immoral and damaging to others and to the service" (personal communication, February 16, 1976).

This aspect of character was summed up by Lt. Gen. J. H. Moore: "I can recall an anecdote to illustrate the importance of character in leadership. An Air Force officer was promoted to general officer rank. One of his subordinates remarked he got his promotion 'without stepping on anyone' " (personal communication, April 10, 1976).

"I believe 'selflessness' and a 'high sense of duty' come to my mind most often as qualities that describe character in military leadership," stated Brig. Gen. Archie S. Mayes. "This is occasioned by my memory of several outstanding Air Force leaders that I have worked for directly, such as Generals Walter Sweeney, Jr., William W. Momyer, John D. Ryan, Bruce Holloway, and John C. Meyer. All these individuals differed greatly in personality, but in the eyes of the people working for them their sense of duty, selflessness, and interest in subordinates was beyond question. Each looked for and demanded the same characteristics from their key staff and subordinate commanders. The individual who possessed these characteristics along with the trait of being candidly honest in direct dealings with these men faired well under them. In spite of a reputation for toughness in some cases, I never found it necessary to beat around the bush in my dealings with these men if I had the facts and I was candidly honest with them in every respect. In summary, they were not only strong in the characteristics of character I have mentioned—that is, selflessness and a high sense of duty—but they could also quickly detect these qualities in those who were under them" (personal communication, January 20, 1976).

Today, there is some concern that the quality of selflessness is being replaced by self-seeking or unjust ambition in the services. "Over recent years it is my belief that we see many in leadership positions who are not leaders," said Brig. Gen. Thomas B. Kennedy. "This situation derives from the emphasis on promotion through recognition, which tends to make those who have flaws in their character claw their way over the more ethical. Frequently, the true leader attributes to others the same sense of values he possesses; thus he fails to recognize the subtle lack of essential leadership characteristics and allows the clawer to rise to a position of great responsibility. This may not be disastrous until the chips are down, and then it may be too late'' (personal communication, January 19, 1976).

One reason for a young officer to be aware of the importance of character is the fact that if those at the top have character, they will be looking for this same quality in those working for them. If they see these qualities in individuals, they will seek them out in the hope that they can develop these men as their successors. It is clear that one of the responsibilities of a top leader is the importance of developing qualified leaders to succeed them in years to come. If this continues—the perpetuation of men of character at the top—then the concern of General Kennedy will be unfounded. If not, the Air Force and our country are in trouble.

Perhaps the epitome of selflessness is a leader's willingness to sacrifice his own advancement to do the right thing. ''Heading the list of qualities that characterize the outstanding professional military officer,'' said Brig. Gen. Robert A. Duffy, USAF (Ret.), ''is selfless integrity. This quality enables the officer to unhesitatingly subordinate personal considerations to the attainment of objectives which have a high priority for his unit, service, and country. Most younger officers can visualize and accept the need for this selfless subordination in the context of open conflict. Suppression of personal ambitions in this context is almost a given.

''Less simple,'' he went on to say, ''are situations in which the officer, to best serve a large national issue, must persevere in convictions which in the short term may appear at odds with the stated interest of his own service and thus may appear to threaten his career aspirations. These may be less dramatic than in combat, but the challenge to courage and integrity is just as demanding, and the probability of encountering this situation is infinitely higher.

''The military leader can encounter this challenge in numerous assignments when he serves the Joint Services Commands, the Joint Chiefs of Staff organization, defense agencies, and . . . the civilian management of the Defense Department and the services. I can recall specific instances in my own career when Air Force officers made difficult decisions adverse to the Air Force's immediate program funding aspirations but, in their perception, vital to the national interest. One example is Polaris, which became a very effective strategic system largely because of a high-caliber team of dedicated Navy professionals, but also with the help of Air Force officers.

''The invention which led to a submarine-based Polaris was the solid rocket motor, which replaced the highly volatile, dangerously flammable liquid fuel rocket in the original proposal. I had no involvement in the solid rocket motor development, but I was involved directly in what was then known as the Western Development Division in assuring Colonel (later Lieutenant General) Terhune and Gen. Bernard Schriever that we could and should lend equipment and a part of our development team to the Navy for the Polaris development.

"Later, as a staff officer in the Office of the Director of Defense Research and Engineering, I conducted performance analyses on the Polaris missile which validated the capabilities claimed for the proposed Poseidon system, which aided the Navy significantly in acquiring approval to proceed with full-scale development. In each of these activities, where interservice rivalry ran high, I encountered no instance of conduct by a professional officer of either the Air Force or the Navy which was motivated by short-term special interests for their respective service taking precedence over those of the nation as a whole" (personal communication, February 23, 1976).

Another example of this type of character in a military leader was portrayed by General Schriever in his overall conduct on the Intercontinental Ballistic Missile Program. He is an outstanding example of an officer who had the courage and character to support a widely unpopular cause with all the integrity and intensity he could muster. "Specifically," said Brigadier General Duffy, "I think of the gigantic task that General Schriever and Gen. Sam Phillips assumed in seeking to convince the Air Force and the nation's leader that a highly automated weapon system, Minuteman, was the best response to a clear and present threat to our security. To make that case convincingly required an unswerving dedication to a development philosophy which constantly ran counter to the established system. For example, in such fundamental matters as parts and spares provisioning each echelon of the logistics functions traditionally injected into this system needs which inflated total program costs. General Schriever defeated this practice by an edict which eliminated intermediate maintenance echelons and thus avoided the accumulation of excessive supplies. To go on as another example, he enlisted the support of both the Logistics and Strategic Air Commands to remove excess manning at all levels. The resultant force has a remarkable readiness record, and the costs of providing the ICBM capability are only about one-third the cost of the comparable aircraft force, disregarding the airplane's obvious time to target disadvantage, for the same function. Many vested interests had to be swayed in the efficacy of this solution. If the integrity or courage of either Schriever or Phillips had even slightly wavered, I believe the conviction necessary to implement this plan would have been missing, and we would have had a lesser deterrent at a much greater cost as a consequence.

"The examples pale when compared with the action scenarios from combat leaders, but I believe they have importance when you think of the number of our officers who must daily maintain our standards even though they do not get exposed to hot war situations (personal communication, February 23, 1976).

Noncombat courage and unselfish integrity mean a willingness to sacrifice your personal advancement for the good of your service and of your country. Part of achievement is to be able to enjoy the accomplishment with a clear conscience.

"It is my feeling that, while a lack of character at times may be evident from the outside, the existence of character in specific instances can be seen and evaluated only from within. I believe this to be so since the exercise of character imposes self-sacrifice. Who, really, other than the principal himself, would know the extent of the sacrifice?" (Brig. Gen. John M. Hutchinson, personal communication, January 31, 1976).

Character is not really something a leader has to think about. Just as Goldwater has said that people in high positions did not "make any great to-do about their honesty," Gen. George K. Sykes has said that character requires "no maintenance attention."

Gen. George K. Sykes went on to say, "this complex definitional problem is pretty much wrapped up in the word . . . *selflessness* when it comes to defining the quality of character. Somewhat strangely related, in the sense of ostensible contradiction, is the reference made to General of the Army George C. Marshall as being complete within himself. In brief, a man can only be truly selfless (i.e., *externally* focused with respect to his assigned, or assumed, role in the military hierarchy) if he is *indeed* 'complete' *within* himself and the *total*—psycho-moral-social—*balance.* All the noble and important externally oriented qualities of honor, duty, service, etc. can only stem from a foundation of internal integrity that is so firmly structured it needs no maintenance attention. With this vital personal base, the military leader can easily and naturally formulate decisions and take actions that are for the good of the country, his service, his unit, or his men. And his perception of what is good is not adulterated by personal considerations, no matter how strong, that inevitably will surface as conflicts.

"I do not say military leaders must be nonhuman. I say that successful sustained leadership of men in combat, or being trained for combat, calls for an uncommon degree of subjugation of self to the greater cause on enough occasions to make it literally a mandatory quality for top military leaders. We have all worked for top military leaders we did not like for some reason or another, but I've never known one at the very top who was not able to subordinate personal consideration when the objective demanded it" (personal communication, February 10, 1976).

NOTES, Chapter 8

1.   Secretary of War Henry L. Stimson, *Diary,* December 31, 1942.
2.   Sholto Douglas, in Field Marshal Sir Michael Carver, ed., *The War Lords*
     (Boston: Little, Brown, 1976), pp. 580–81.

CHAPTER 9
COURAGE

No one would consider an officer to be a leader and a man of character if he lacked the quality of courage.

The Bible says, "Whom shall I send and who will go for us? . . . Here am I: Send me" (Isaiah 6:8). This exemplifies the courage a real leader must show. Later I will discuss decision making in leadership. But "The time always comes in battle," wrote S. L. A. Marshall, "when the decisions of statesmen and generals can no longer affect the issue and when it is not within the power of our national wealth to change the balance decisively. Victory is never achieved prior to that point; it can be won only after the battle has been delivered into the hands of men who move in imminent danger of death . . . courage is the real driving force in human affairs . . . every worthwhile action comes of some man daring what others fear to attempt."[1]

Courage is an indispensable aspect of character. It is to an airman what life itself is to a man. As a young Air Force officer, Lt. Gen. J. H. Moore, USAF Ret., observed an event that made a lasting impact on him for the rest of his military career. "I can recall," he reflected, "an anecdote to illustrate the importance of character in leadership. I commanded a Pursuit Squadron on Bataan during World War II. After three months of constant battering by the enemy, the loss of most of our aircraft, little food, and finally having to fight on the ground as infantry troops, we all felt pretty discouraged and felt that the situation was pretty hopeless. I visited

Corregidor one day and ate lunch in the officer's mess outside an entrance to Malinta Tunnel. It was late, I was the only one eating, and shells from Japanese guns on Luzon began landing within close hearing distance, and I thought I would be prudent to go back inside the tunnel. At that moment General MacArthur strode out to the dining area and calmly sat down at the table reserved especially for him. He exuded such calm confidence that I not only forgot the Japanese shells but began to feel that things just couldn't be as bad back on Bataan as they seemed. It was so overpowering that I took that feeling back to Bataan that day. It was extraordinary" (personal communication, January 19, 1976).*

This was an example of one of the more obvious and certainly indispensable requirements of leadership, courage in combat. Brig. Gen. Thomas B. Kennedy, in discussing leadership, made the comment that his impressions of leadership character were in many ways derived from when he was a junior officer. He cited an incident that occurred during World War II when he was a junior officer under a wing commander named Marden M. Munn. "Each night," he reflected, "when the operational orders would come in for the next day's mission, Wing Commander Munn would casually drop by the operations office, where I was, and inquire as to the target. Invariably, if it was a difficult target, he would say, 'I think I need to get some flying in. I think I'll fly lead tomorrow.' He was an outstanding pilot, and we all knew that when he flew it would be an excellently led mission. By this simple process, he developed the respect and leadership essential to performance by many people of difficult and hazardous tasks" (personal communication, January 19, 1976).

Kennedy went on to reflect on a similar incident of leadership by example. During the course of the Vietnam conflict, when he was commanding the airlift operation—which included the defoliation aircraft— they had an ever-increasing amount of battle damage and wounded crew members. "I was having difficulty," he said, "in convincing the staff above that we should receive increased fighter cover. The then Air Force Commander in Southeast Asia, Lt. Gen. Joe Moore [the same Moore who gave the MacArthur anecdote] resolved this problem by flying with us. Observing the intense ground fire, he immediately directed the essential changes in operating procedures. "While these are minor examples of the kind of appraisal that you are undertaking, these characteristics of personal courage combined with intelligent competence and dedication to getting the mission accomplished with realistic consideration of the human aspect of

*"Personal communication" refers to letter to the author.

the situation convinced me that General Moore was a true leader" (personal communication, January 19, 1976).

Similarly, Maj. Gen. Frank Nye reflected, "An example of character that comes to my mind based upon my experiences involves Lt. Gen. James V. Edmundson, now retired and living in Sarasota, Florida. I was his operations officer for about four years while he was in the position of heavy bomber group or wing commander. His integrity, reputation, judgment, and other facets of character were cemented together by his personal example. He always led the tough missions; never the milk runs. He never asked anyone to do anything that he wouldn't or couldn't do himself. He was never satisfied with any position except Number One. He was the greatest leader whom I have personally worked for. His demonstrated character resulted in outstanding leadership" (personal communication, February 2, 1976).

A more complete illustration of the role of courage in leadership was provided by Maj. Gen. William P. Fisher: "To me, character in a military sense in a leader is the quality of evaluating, deciding, carrying through, and accepting full responsibility for these actions and accomplishing his mission or assignment. To be successful militarily, character must be accompanied by judgment and common sense, which to my mind are of equal importance. Our great military leaders have always appeared to be strong in these areas.

"Gen. Curtis E. LeMay, as a wing commander, exemplified these qualities when, early in World War II in the bomber offensive against Germany, he realized that daylight bombing accuracy was very poor and results were not commensurate with losses. It was obvious to him that the major reason for this was the weaving path flown to avoid the accurate anti-aircraft firing encountered. All bomber personnel also knew that accuracy could be achieved by flying at a level, steady path during the time period required to enable the Norton site to establish the target course and dropping angle. In other words, one to three minutes of straight and level flight prior to the bomb release point. It was also the accepted consensus that this would allow pinpoint accuracy to be achieved by the antiaircraft batteries and bomber losses would be disastrous.

"General LeMay, after much consideration and analysis of missions, decided that this did not necessarily follow and that any small increase in losses would be more than compensated for by the complete destruction of targets. He, therefore, personally led his wing on a heavily defended target and achieved the required accuracy and results with *little* increase in bomber losses. This established the method of daylight precision bombing which enabled the Eighth Air Force to continue effectively in spite of heavy anti-aircraft defenses" (personal communication, January 20, 1976).

Courage is not absence of fear or never being afraid. There probably is no such thing as a man without fear. Those who appear unafraid have simply overcome their fear. Maj. Gen. Thomas N. Wilson reflected on courage: "Twice from positions of leadership—once as the pilot of a bomber crew and once as a fighter group commander—I've been called upon the following day to fly identical airplanes to ones that, by all odds and probability in the history of the type of aircraft, should have killed me the day before. I say 'I was called upon.' It was my own decision to take my crew up the following night in another of the original 'widow makers,' the Martin B-26, at the same hour before midnight, off the same runway and pass over in the darkness the watery grave of the aircraft in which we had crashed the night before and miraculously escaped death. The flight had to be taken to prove something to each of us.

"It was somewhat the same thing sixteen years later when, the day following a crash, I strapped into an identical supersonic fighter and lit the afterburners for takeoff. No one had ever previously survived a forced landing of a supersonic aircraft on an unprepared surface. I did the day before when my aircraft exploded and caught fire at extreme altitude and at supersonic speed—and the ejection system failed—there was nought to do but ride it down. It was an unnerving experience.

"But the takeoff and flight the following day was nothing short of abject, nerve-shattering terror. Still, it had to be done if I was to continue to command and lead that fighter group." I'm sure these acts of courage were not lost upon his organization as an element of leadership (personal communication, November 17, 1976).

A final anecdote on this point was supplied by Maj. Gen. Franklin A. Nichols. "In the early part of 1943 in New Guinea, I was operations officer of the Seventh Fighter Squadron flying P-40s. The commander of the Fifth Fighter Command was Brigadier General Wurtsmith. . . . I was asked to get eight pilots who had had night flying experience for a special night mission. We had only seven pilots who were qualified, including myself. On being briefed concerning this mission, we were to dive bomb a Japanese convoy thought to be in Burma Bay, New Guinea, and a B-17 would drop flares for us to bomb the ships. General Wurtsmith attempted unsuccessfully to have this mission canceled because it was too dangerous, and there was more risk involved than results that might be gained. . . . As a result of this order, he volunteered to be my Number Eight man in the second flight, saying that if he had to send his pilots on such a hazardous mission he would go himself. What made the mission particularly hazardous was the fact that all of us pilots had already flown two combat missions that day and had been on the flight lines since 6 A.M. that morning. There were very poor lighting facilities at our airfield and absolutely no guides between our airfield and the target 200 miles away. Weather at night was, because of the Stanley Range of mountains, always critical and unknown on this type of mission. In addition, this type of mission had never been tried before, coordinating between fighters and bombers, and we were relying upon the bombers to provide us the light. That night while we were waiting for the word to go, as if we did not have enough problems, we were bombed by the Japanese bombers twice, which disrupted communications and runway availability. It was around 3 A.M. when we got the word to cancel since the bomber reconnaissance aircraft could not find the Japanese convoy.

"This story has never been told before, largely because General Wurtsmith was killed after the war. But this to me is an example of the quality of character in a leader, and was portrayed by a senior officer in acting beyond the call of duty when he had everything to lose and nothing to gain in risking his life except the respect of his fellow officers and pilots within his command" (personal communication, February 6, 1976).

General Doolittle's comment regarding courage was philosophical. "I have never had," he said, "and do not have now any fear of death. I do hope that when the Grim Reaper comes he takes me promptly and painlessly. I do not want to suffer. Death is a terrible thing, and nobody wants to see anyone else die. But I have no fear of death myself; possibly this makes it a little easier for me to accept it in others than for someone who greatly fears death" (personal communication, February 7, 1977).

These are examples of combat courage. But, as suggested by Maj. Gen. David T. Liebman, "It is my belief that greatness of character can be established outside of the field of battle. In fact, the statement has been made by you [the author] that a wartime staff position can often be many times more demanding than a position where one is literally under enemy fire" (personal communication, January 13, 1976).

Part of what courage requires is a willingness to speak up on the issues. As described by Maj. Gen. R. L. Delashaw, "One caution that I feel is very important is that rank gives validity to opinions, and often it moves to silence contrary opinions. A good leader needs the opinions and thoughts of those who work for him and must achieve a relationship where there is a free exchange of ideas until such time a decision is made. Very few leaders were successful when deprived of the opinion of their subordinates" (personal communication, April 7, 1976).

Even more to the point is the importance of having the courage of one's convictions—of not being "yes men."

"My definition of character," stated Brig. Gen. E. L. Ramme, USAF Ret., "is largely encompassed in integrity, but it is also composed of respect for others. I believe this can best be reverse-illustrated by traits which demonstrate a lack of character; i.e., 'yes-men' certainly lack character; those who accept gifts from contractors or others, who may or may not contemplate a future favor, demonstrate a lack of character.

"As to respect for others, one good example is to praise subordinates publicly but to criticize only in private. Integrity can be identified in many ways, but one of my favorites is evidenced by a commander who does not want 'yes men' around. He is one who says, 'If you disagree with me, I want you to say so, but if after I consider your proposals my decision should be different from yours, then you are to support it as enthusiastically as if you had thought of it" (personal communication, January 26, 1976).

"The principal qualities I sought in selecting my immediate and most trusted assistants, aside from their professionalism, were integrity, dedication and maturity of judgment," said Maj. Gen. J. F. Rodenhauser. "I wanted and needed men who would not hesitate to inform me immediately of any mistake or irritable situation they felt their actions or decisions might bring about so that remedial action could be taken before sources outside the organization 'surprised' me with a cause cèlébre. Inasmuch as I was asking these outstanding leaders to bare their breasts professionally in a highly competitive selection system, such a relationship demanded a very high sense of duty and great mutual trust between them and myself" (personal communication, February 10, 1976).

Maj. Gen. Gilbert L. Pritchard commented, "In my judgment, character is personified by other identifiable traits. Those include courage, not only on the battlefield but also courage to stand up and be counted when the issues are clear; courage to develop and practice intellectual honesty and integrity; and, finally, courage to cope with an issue as it arises rather than put if off and procrastinate" (personal communication, January 21, 1976).

This courage to speak up was also emphasized by Maj. Gen. Haywood S. Hansell, who said, "You ask me to describe what character is as a leadership quality. I think that one of the basic fundamentals of character is the quality of integrity. I mean by that a willingness to question cherished beliefs without disparagement and without equivocation—honest criticism and loyal acceptance of responsible decision.

"To give you an example, an officer who I held in very high esteem was one who went on to become a lieutenant general in the U.S. Air Force, by the name of Roger Ramme. Ramme was my Deputy Commander when I commanded the Twenty-First Bomber Command in the Marianas. Roger often disagreed with me, sometimes violently, but always for cogent reasons and always in private. Sometimes I accepted his views and modified my position. Sometimes I overrode his objections or discounted his views. But always the results were the same: Roger accepted my final judgment as his own and turned his great energies to execution of my decision. I am certain that he never hinted at our disagreements. He had a courageous mind, good common sense, and true loyalty. I valued him not just because I could rely upon his honest and unbiased judgment, whether or not it agreed with mine, but also because I could rely upon his loyalty and integrity. I would have been glad to serve him if our positions had been reversed" (personal communication, January 15, 1976).

A final perspective, offered by Brig. Gen. Herbert G. Bench, shows that some officers have the courage to put their career on the line. Character may even be synonymous with courage, because if a man has courage he will not acquiesce to selfish motives in order to attain objectives or to reach selfish and personal goals. "I will say unequivocally," wrote Bench, "that the greatest deterrent to developing dedicated young leaders is the present system of encouraging our young officers to be 'yes men' and to 'not rock the boat' " (personal communication, February 19, 1976).

General Bench then went on to give an example. He said, "I will give you a prime example with which I'm intimately familiar. My last year in active duty was as Number Two man with the Army-Air Force Exchange Service [AAFES]. As Deputy to a disgruntled Army brigadier general, I was told by him to 'stay out of the way' and study the past history of the Army-Air Force Exchange Services and that he would run the show. He would not permit me to participate in any decisions or make recommendations or even express my views when called upon. I was determined to represent the 'blue suiters' and went to my Air Force boss. I stressed the need for the Air Force to make a complete investigation of the activity in Dallas of the AAFES. All the responses were very similar and along this vein, 'Herb, the Army is the major stockholder in that corporation'; 'Herb, you are probably right, but we must get along with the Army'; etc. The hard cold facts were that there were many bad and selfish decisions being made. In my opinion, the Chief was operating the exchange in isolation and without a free line of expression or communication from the primary user (the soldier and airman). My allegation was proven to be correct, to the embarrassment and chagrin of all the men in uniform.

"Though I had recently made permanent brigadier general and could have probably spent eight more years in active duty, I refused to accept the passive, futile role when my own bosses would not support me. My letter of retirement stated that the two lieutenant generals mentioned who were my bosses would only take a line of least resistance, and therefore my only choice was to perform in a gutless, ineffective capacity or retire. The day after I submitted my letter of retirement and was reassigned out of AAFES, I wrote a letter to the *Washington Trade Journal* explaining the sorry situation to AAFES Headquarters. For that, General Ryan sent me a letter of admonishment, to which I responded and told him he would never have done it if he had any idea what was going on" (personal communication, February 19, 1976).

The message Bench was trying to get across was that in his opinion an officer not in combat should have both courage and unselfish integrity, which means among other things a willingness to sacrifice personal advancement if it is for the good of the service. Bench put his comments in perspective when he said, "I do not mean to advocate having a bunch of rabble rousers, but we need honest men of courage who do not hide behind rules and regulations. We need officers who will risk their own professions to see that others are treated fairly. A man who has the strength of his convictions will be respected, admired, and followed" (personal communication, February 19, 1976).

What a strange phenomenon it is that some men will die for their country but will not sacrifice a slot on the promotion ladder to defend a principle or an idea. Yet there have been those who did sacrifice their careers. In the postwar years, Air Force Maj. Gen. Orville A. Anderson was outspoken in his evaluation of the basic moral issue in our confrontation with communism. Anderson phrased it this way: "Which is the greater immorality—preventive war as a means to keep the USSR from becoming a nuclear power, or to allow a totalitarian dictatorial system to develop a means whereby the free world could be intimidated, blackmailed, and possibly destroyed?"

General Twining was very concerned about this issue; he wrote,

> General Anderson was convinced that the greater immorality lay in our decision to permit the development of a militant system of power capable of destroying the free world. He regarded the "immorality" of a preventive strike against the USSR as the lesser of two moral evils. His views were, of course, unpopular, because they contradicted the administration's desire to maintain a status quo, and they were never given a fair hearing by the State Department or, for that matter, by the military establishment.
>
> General Anderson did not advocate a sudden nuclear attack on the Soviet Union. What he did advocate was a power maneu-

ver in which an ultimatum would be delivered to the Soviets to free the enslaved satellite countries of Europe and to stop subversion and aggression on the land mass of Asia. In terms of his logic, if such an ultimatum had been delivered to the Soviets, who were then in no position to offer effective resistance, Russia would have been forced to free both Eastern Europe and Southeast Asia. If such an ultimatum had been delivered and not accepted by the USSR, the United States could undoubtedly have eliminated Russia's power base for generations to come.

This view was not consistent with that of the political administration so General Anderson was in the words of General Twining, "prematurely retired" in 1950 under the Truman Administration.

NOTES, Chapter 9

1. S. L. A. Marshall, *Men Against Fire* (New York, Morrow, 1947), pp. 208–209.

CHAPTER 10
DECISION MAKING

In a discussion between General of the Army Dwight D. Eisenhower and myself, General Eisenhower commented, "I have pondered the question of leadership quite a bit, and I think I can come back to take as my starting point the statement that Napoleon is reputed to have made: 'Genius in leadership is the ability to do an average thing when everyone around you is going crazy and at least hysterical.' When you come right down to it, leadership is, of course, being exerted all the time in the capacity of boosting morale, confidence and all that, but leadership is most noticeable when tough decisions have finally to be made. This is the time when often you get conflicting advice and often urgent advice of every kind. Now this is the kind of leadership that's often concealed from the public. . . . But making decisions is of the essence in leadership—that is, handling large problems whether or not you are at war or at peace. When you make these decisions, it is not done with any reaching for the dramatic. It is almost everyday and commonplace. You reach a conclusion based upon the facts as you see them, the evaluations of the several factors as you see them, the relationship of one fact to another, and, above all, your convictions as to the capacity of different individuals to fit into these different places. You come to a decision after you've taken all these things into consideration. Then you decide and say, 'That's what we'll do' " (personal communication, May 2, 1963).

The wartime leader is a lonely man. At no time does he feel his loneliness more deeply than when he has to make a critical high-level decision dealing with life and death, success or failure, victory or defeat. It is an overwhelming responsibility that few people desire and one for which considerably fewer people are qualified. But making decisions is part of leadership, and in wartime the general who does not have the strength to make decisions and the judgment to be right a large percentage of the time does not remain long in a position of high leadership. Generals are human and are subject to the strains and stresses of the mind just as other men are, particularly because the general's responsibility is greater than that of the lesser man. His mistakes can be counted in death and destruction, and this is a responsibility that no sane man takes lightly.

Secretary of War Henry L. Stimson wrote in his diary on May 10, 1943, "Very bad news came to me from Marshall and Lovett in regard to General Arnold who had a severe heart attack last night. He is at Walter Reed Hospital and our hope is that it may be a nervous attack due to his overwork, but it is a bad blow to the strength of our smoothly working military machine. Arnold has come into his own since the day three years ago when I had to fight for his official life and he is a tower of strength in all of the conferences, for he has a quick mind and he doesn't hesitate to make his views clearly felt. He is not as cautious and diplomatic as Marshall who is a good counterpoint to him, but on the other hand he (Arnold) does not hesitate to espouse the unpopular side of a discussion and make it very clear even in the face of his Chief."[1]

From the first meeting with President Roosevelt, General Arnold spoke his mind and was immediately informed that army and navy officers who were uncooperative were sent to Guam. Exile was not new to General Arnold. He didn't change. He continued to espouse the cause of air power and its role in the defense of our country. That aspect of his character—the determination to fight for what he believed—was to pay off later. Nine months after being advised of where 'uncooperative officers' were sent, General Arnold was invited to a small dinner at the White House, where he was received cordially and individually by the President.

"Good evening, Hap," the President said. "How about mixing you an Old Fashioned?"

General Arnold responded, "Thanks, Mr. President. I haven't had one for about twenty years, but I assure you I will enjoy this one tremendously."

Then they proceeded to discuss aircraft production, the building of an air force, and other matters. Later, at the end of the small, informal session, General Arnold commented, "I realized I was out of the 'dog house.' "[2]

An excellent perspective is offered on the role of character in decision making by a story told me by Gen. Wade Haislip. In 1949, General Haislip was called by Gen. J. Lawton Collins, who had just been informed he had been designated as the next Chief of Staff of the Army. Collins called him on the phone and said, "Wade, I've been informed I am to be the next Chief of Staff of the Army, and I'd like you to be my deputy. Will you take the job?" Haislip responded, "Why do you want me? You and I have not agreed on anything in thirty years." Collins replied, "That's exactly why I want you." Collins did not want a "yes man." No outstanding leader does.

Air Force Gen. Joseph T. McNarney remembered his first encounter with Gen. George C. Marshall: "I was serving on the General Staff in Washington in the War Plans Division just before we got into the war, and at that time I was a lieutenant colonel. I was made Chief of Plans Division under the Joint Plans Division, which was then making joint war plans with the Navy. One day, General Marshall sent down for some information on the plans we were working on but my boss was not there, so I went up. This was the first time I had ever seen General Marshall and the first time he had ever seen me. We got into a little argument. I went back to my office to get some more information to prove my point, along with a map I needed; I put the map on the floor to show him my point, and we had another little argument about it. I was a brash young man, I guess, but I didn't back off. General Marshall kept asking me questions, and I finally got a little bit irked. I said, 'My God, man, you can't do that!' He then dismissed me. I walked out of his office, and his secretary, who was an officer from the class of 1914, tapped me on the shoulder and said, 'Don't worry about that. That's what the old man does every time. He was just feeling you out.' " Marshall must have been favorably impressed. McNarney rose from the rank of lieutenant colonel to four-star general during World War II under Marshall.

McNarney went on to say of General Marshall, "He disliked the 'yes man.' He wouldn't have anything to do with the 'yes man.' If anybody agreed with him the first time, he would look upon him with some suspicion. Of course, it didn't necessarily always mean that because maybe agreeing with him on that was the proper thing to do. But to come in and agree with him right away, he didn't like that. He was not a 'yes man,' and he didn't like that in people under him. He wanted frank expression of your views" (personal interview, August 22, 1962).

General of the Army Omar N. Bradley had a similar experience with General Marshall. After he had worked for a few weeks for Marshall, shortly after he had become Chief of Staff just before World War II, Lieutenant Colonel Bradley and his assistants were called into Marshall's office. "Gentlemen," he said, "I'm disappointed in you. You haven't yet disagreed with a single decision I've made." Bradley said he replied,

"General, that's only because there has been no cause for disagreement. When we differ with you on a decision, sir, we'll tell you so" (personal communication, February 15, 1963).

When I asked what the relationship of a commander with his people should be during the decision-making process, General Spaatz responded, "I certainly wanted to have the respect of the people around me, but I didn't want them to have any fear. I always encouraged all members of my staff and the commanders to feel free to discuss anything with me they wanted to. And I always liked to have at least one man on the staff who disagreed with the others. To have a real good 'no man.' He had to be a pretty smart, talkative individual."

When asked the purpose of the "no man," Spaatz answered, "To challenge before the decision is made. But all this has to take place before the decision is made. That is the difference between what I call a successful commander and an unsuccessful commander. If there's no challenge before the decision, and after the decision is made, the challenge comes up, then there's indecisiveness, which in military operations can end in disaster."

This type of character was greatly sought after by the top leaders in World War II. Gen. William F. McKee, as a lieutenant colonel, was part of a group of officers who briefed Generals Eisenhower and Spaatz on matters relating to air defense in the North African campaign. One of the briefing officers was Col. Fred Anderson. Spaatz was very impressed with Anderson and immediately wired General Arnold requesting that he be reassigned from Washington to North Africa for a key assignment in Eighth Air Force. Arnold responded that Spaatz could have Anderson only if he would recommend him for promotion to brigadier general; he did, and Anderson remained with Spaatz.

When McKee was asked how Anderson made such an immediate impact, he responded, "Because Fred Anderson spoke up and didn't mince any words. He said what he thought and not what he might have thought General Spaatz would want to hear. This was a key thing in Spaatz' leadership. In fact, I followed that in my career—I told my Chief what I thought—but you better know what the hell you're talking about" (personal communication, July 6, 1977).

Gen. Albert C. Wedemeyer, in a discussion with me on decision making, stated that "In the field of ideas, every person participating in the discussion should have the full and unintimidated opportunity to express himself. In my experience in war planning when I was Chief of the Plans and Strategy Group, General Staff, in Washington, back in 1940–41, I tried with my staff to mix up the group as far as age and experience were concerned. I tried to have older officers with a great deal of experience

—practical experience—and then to balance the group with the younger officers. My objective was to exploit the enthusiasm and creativeness of the young officers and to mix that up with the mature judgment of the older men. I encouraged the younger officers to speak up and not to hesitate to give me the full benefit of their knowledge and experience. They were never intimidated one iota with the senior men or with me as their Chief. One's rank had nothing whatever to do with the operation of that little planning group" (personal interview, July 23, 1962).

General Twining, in a similar vein, commented, "Another thing about leadership is that you should say what you think. Nobody can be so great that they don't have to listen to others. Some people think they are, and that's where they get into trouble. Sure, they can be geniuses on the piano or the violin or a specialty like that, but that's not leadership, that's personal accomplishment. In leadership, you have got to have the ability to sit back and listen to your staff or an individual who briefs you, men who can speak with authority. You have got to have the courage to sit down and listen, have them say what they think is right, no matter how sore you might get at them. You also need to have a commander who will come in and tell you off when he thinks you are wrong. I have had that happen to me many times, and it's been helpful to me. It sure takes the ego out of you too" (personal interview, March 3, 1977).

General Schriever put it another way: "I want someone I can trust, who I know is going to be loyal to me, but not necessarily agreeing with me. He can come up and tell me I'm full of crap, but I want him to be loyal to me. You can sense loyalty in a person. I started early in my career taking people who were controversial. Because they were controversial, other people didn't want them, but I'd want them because they were smart, and they would tell me not what I wanted to hear but what they really thought" (personal communication, June 15 and 29, 1977).

Elaborating on his comment that indecisiveness was weakness of character, Spaatz remarked, "Marshall didn't like to listen too long to anyone discussing anything, what you might call beating around the bush. He liked the direct approach. When he asked questions, he liked direct answers. It was very important when you went to see General Marshall that you know the subject you were going to discuss with him. General Arnold was the same way. He was very impatient when anyone came in to see him and didn't know what he was talking about."

Another quality of leadership was pointed out by General Laurence S. Kuter: "I have not wanted people who would find out just what I told them to. I wanted people who would study the problem, particularly their phase of a problem, and find a way to solve the problem. I wanted people who were perfectly willing to tell me I was completely wrong in an idea, or a concept, or an approach, *provided they tell me how, where, and why it was wrong.*"

Kuter said that "General K. Saville was a splendid example of a vigorous or a violent 'no man' of Tooey Spaatz's staff. Saville was never known for his tact, and would say to Spaatz, "Chief, what you say makes no goddamn sense whatsoever for the following reasons: 1, 2, 3, 4, 5—and General Saville was usually right.' "

A leader must create the best atmosphere in a command for decision making. Gen. Edwin W. Rawlings described his decision making: "All my effort," he said, "when I was running Air Materiel Command was to seek out and assign the good people I could get for the particular key jobs I had. If you work at it hard enough, naturally you get the best ones for the best slots. Then it becomes easier to get a good one to replace him when he has to leave, because one of the qualities of a good leader is that he is always training someone to follow him, so it begins to snowball. There are all sorts of ways of doing it. I did it with a monthly review of our operation with my commanders and key staff. We would look at all of our problems, and each top man was given the opportunity to express his philosophy, his attitude, and to keep everybody abreast of the facts and problems he had to deal with at that particular period of time. Generally, people are a lot better than we think they are, so the responsibility of the top man, I think, is to create an atmosphere where they can use their full horsepower. Part of that is knowing the problems the top man is dealing with, what factors surround these problems, what is the top man's personal philosophy. By that, I don't mean 'yes men.' One of the grave hazards of command is that too many people will tell you what they think you want to hear. So you have to work very hard at creating an atmosphere [in which] they are willing to disagree with you. This is not easy. If you take decisive action, they are apt to think you will hold it against them if they disagree. My philosophy was one of wanting everybody to say what he thinks, because none of us is smart enough to think about everything. Somebody will have an idea or a thought that might change our course if we knew it. Now, once you make the decision, that's something else. You expect everybody to carry out the decision, and if they don't you are in trouble. But if you have created this atmospshere to draw out a lot more people's ideas, they are more likely to be happy, for it they aren't happy, they aren't going to work as well."

While a leader does not want a "yes man" around, this does not mean challenge for the sake of challenging or speaking out just to be heard. Rather, it consists of making constructive and worthwhile comments during the decision making process. For example, General Arnold's deputy before

World War II was a lieutenant general who, after a short period of time, was reassigned. Gen. Ira C. Eaker explained that Arnold was somewhat disappointed in the way he had handled the job; moreover, he tended to be slightly contentious. "Arnold would tell him to do something," said Eaker, "and he would argue about it. So Arnold replaced him very shortly and sent him overseas, down to Australia. I always assumed that he wanted somebody to work with him under pressure who would carry out his orders and who was a little more progressive and dynamic" (personal interview, October 4, 1977).

Gen. Leon W. Johnson gave a contrary example. "I worked with Spaatz," he reflected, "when we moved down into Bushey Park before Eisenhower came in in Great Britain in World War II. He came in and took a building right adjacent to the one Spaatz had that we'd already set up and had there. Spaatz was a very straightforward commander. He was a no-nonsense person.

"He got us all together when we got there and said, 'we're over here to fight a war. Now, we don't want to bother these units with reports coming in here. You go out and see the units and don't have reports coming here. The commanders don't have time to send their reports to headquarters! Within ten days, he was in my office and said, 'How much training did the Ninety-Seventh Group do last week?' Rather stupidly, I said, 'General, we don't know. We don't bother our groups to send in reports on how much training they're doing.' So he stormed out of the room. I should have gotten the reports some way or other" (personal communication, July 12, 1978).

Several weeks later, Johnson made the same mistake with Spaatz, seeing a side of Spaatz that few people had ever seen and that he surely hoped he never would again. "Eaker and Spaatz were in one night," he remembered, "and they said, 'That's a good report on personnel that has come in. Let's send this one in; that's exactly like it for our operations.' So they turned to me and said, 'Get this one out like this.'

"The next morning when I went to Spaatz's office, he said to me, 'Did you get out that report?'

"I said, 'No, sir, I haven't.'

"He said, 'I want to get out that report.'

"I said, 'Well, General, it doesn't fit the situation, in my opinion.'

"He said, 'That's the report I want, get it out!'

"I said again, 'General, that report, in my opinion, doesn't fit operations.'

"He said, 'Well, I want you to get it out.'

"I said, 'Well, I can get it out, but . . .'

"And he interrupted and said, 'God damn it, get out of here and get it out.' It was his report, so I finally did write the report the way he wanted. It seemed to me that every time he said something was white, I'd say it was black, or vice versa. I don't blame it on Spaatz in the least because I think if there's a fault, it was my fault in not accepting . . . a decision" (personal communication, July 12, 1978).

I asked Lt. Gen. James Doolittle if it was correct that Gen. Dwight D. Eisenhower did not want him as his air commander in the North African campaign early in World War II. Doolittle responded that that was correct, saying that at a staff conference General Eisenhower had given a briefing on his view of the plans for a forthcoming invasion and then asked for the views of the group present. "Patton told him what he would do, and then Eisenhower said to me," remarked Doolittle, "the first thing we will do is to capture the airfields. I should have said, 'Yes, General Eisenhower, that's the first thing we have to do after the group troops are ashore, secure the airfields.' It was so obvious. I then did as stupid a thing as could be done. I continued to talk and said, 'General, the airfields will be of no value to us until we have the supplies, the oil, the gas, the bombs, the ammunition, the supporting men, the food and the facilities to take care of them.' This was all true. But it wasn't what I should have said. What I was doing was pointing out to my superior that he didn't know what he was talking about. I should have merely said, instead of what I did say, 'General Eisenhower, you are quite right. The first thing that we must have are the airfields and after that, with all possible expedition, get in the supplies to accomplish this.' I watched Eisenhower's face as I spoke; I could have chewed my tongue off because I knew what I had done. But it was too late. It took me a year to overcome that. I am not suggesting that you should be a 'yes man.' What I am suggesting is what you should not do is to imply that your superior is a little stupid for not having mentioned these things all at the same time. I do not believe in being a 'yes man.' I do believe in using tact in getting ideas over" (personal communication, February 7, 1977).

General Arnold commented that flying and air power had a new, modern, ever-changing, and progressive technology. "It, perhaps more than any other [service], is impatient with the conservative," he said, about decision making in air power. "The best telltale mark," he continued, "of the over-conservative is the doing of nothing for fear of doing something wrong." On one occasion, he remembered, an order was given to go out on a mission, but the base operations officer demanded that the unit not leave until they had received clearance. The officer pointed out that that was in the regulations. Actually, that might have been an appropriate procedure in peacetime, but not in wartime. Waiting for this written clearance, delaying the flight for five minutes, did not seem to bother the operations officer:

"in the regulations; it had to be done." To Arnold this was an example of a "dull, unimaginative officer living by the bread of conservatism, ever fearful of the slightest deviation from routine, holding it better to do nothing than to do something contrary to established precedent."[3]

General Arnold was a dynamic decision maker. An officer who was with him for many years, Maj. Gen. Howard C. Davidson, reflected, "I had a good chance to observe General Arnold, for I worked with him as Nineteenth Bombardment Group Commander at March Field and later as executive officer to Chief of the Air Corps when Arnold was assistant chief. Arnold was quick to make a decision; some of them were wrong, but most of them were right, because Arnold was constantly seeking for information on people and subjects concerning the Air Corps. Even at social gatherings such as cocktail parties and dinners he was picking everyone's brain. If a bush pilot came to Washington from Alaska, Arnold would invite him around and entertain him while he found out all he could about Alaska."

Arnold's thirst for information was insatiable. He was instrumental in getting an officer who was with the Army liaison office in Berlin before World War II to give talks to the Air Staff. He used every possible opportunity to have American manufacturers go to Europe to study aircraft production there. He even arranged to be briefed by Lindbergh before the latter's trip to Europe; and on his return Lindbergh briefed Arnold on the capability of the German air force. Arnold then took Lindbergh around to members of the General Staff, to the Secretary of War, and everywhere else he could get him, so that he could tell the story of what he had seen in Germany. This obviously assisted the Air Force with its mission, because Lindbergh's insight helped to corroborate the concern that Arnold had about the build up of the German air force.

General Davidson also commented that in the process of leading and making decisions, "Arnold was very impatient and short-tempered. His impatience helped him to get things done quickly, and fortunately he could not remember four hours later what had made him angry. He was too impatient to read long-winded reports, and as an executive officer I would have the staff summarize in about one page what they had expressed in many pages."

General Arnold's approach to decision making was contagious. Another officer very close to him before and during World War II was Maj. Gen. Lester T. Miller, who told me, "General Arnold was an officer of broad vision, [especially regarding] his concept of the Air Force and his influence on a global plane as pertained to World War II. He used everything at his command, including the members of our country's legislature, to get the force he needed to carry out the Air Force mission. In 1939 I was a member of his staff in Washington, and one day he came to a staff meeting and said, 'What would you buy to strengthen the Air Force if you were given $100 million today to spend as you saw fit?' All of our eyes popped out like we were being strangled, and then he told us that the president had asked him the same question. We were not to answer the question now, but to think it over for twenty-four hours and bring in our written answers. This we did, and, of course, there were almost as many answers as there were officers. Some would buy trainers and flying fields, others fighter aircraft, others to strengthen the bombers, but from all these answers General Arnold presented a well-rounded program to the president which was approved instantly, and the money was given us with full steam ahead.''

Miller said that in making decisions, Arnold sought the advice of other people; after obtaining their input, he proceeded to make his decisions.

But Arnold made it clear that a commander should not attempt to make all of the decisions. It would be overwhelming. How far a man goes within the military depends on his ability to delegate and to get the most out of his subordinates. One must delegate the more petty decisions. General Arnold once commented on the role of the staff officer as being one in which the staff officer must "Keep the commander informed of the state of his command at all times, and yet he must avoid passing up to the commander petty decisions and a mess of infinitesimal detail."[4]

Concerning decision making, General Spaatz was asked what went on in his mind during World War II when he sent men out on a mission in which he knew that the losses would be high. His response: "It's awfully hard to say what goes on in your mind, because, in the first place, you can't dwell on it. An air leader is somewhat different from the ground commander in peacetime. In the years between the wars, you would have in the flying business a man or two killed every so often. But you could not just close up shop even in peacetime just because someone was killed. You had to keep on your operation. That sort of thing steels your mind for war.''

When Spaatz was asked to comment on how one develops the ability as a decision maker, he responded, "I think decision making is based upon two things. One, is the knowledge of your own forces, their capability and your ability to size up the enemy forces. That is, if the operations that you're carrying on would let you do that, but there are times when you have to commit your forces even though you know the enemy forces can possibly be stronger. That is true with some of the air battles that we fought over in Europe in World War II. Formations of bombers took some pretty tough beatings at the hands of the German fighters, but if you're making decisions where you lose a lot of men in one battle you must size up against these losses whether or not what you are doing has anything to do toward finally winning the war. You have all these factors to keep in mind all the time.''

"I remember having a conversation with Eisenhower," Spaatz reflected, "in January or February, along in there, when I was still operating, I was Strategic Air Force Commander, in operational control, when we had some pretty heavy losses. We had a raid, an operation against —I'm sure it wasn't Berlin—but we lost thirty or forty planes, and he asked me whether we could take the losses.

"I said, 'What's that got to do with it?'

"General Eisenhower . . . said, 'Are we getting control of the German air force?'

"I said, 'If we have to take the losses to control them, then we have to take it, that's all.' You can't have a war and worry about that. What you have to worry about is whether you're winning or not. If you have a hopeless loss, then that's stupid. But if you're winning, then it's not. Maybe someone smarter could have done it with fewer losses, but the situation that existed at the end of 1944—the German air force was still pretty strong, and there was no hope of making an invasion of Europe if we were going to be met by a strong German air force. Unless that air force could be subdued or forced back, either one or the other. I think we did part of both—they were partially subdued and partially forced back—and the net result was there were only about two or three German airplanes that appeared at the Normandy invasion. If they had had two or three hundred airplanes there, that thing would have become a shambles.''

General Doolittle contributed a specific example of the soundness of Spaatz's decision making. He said, "General Spaatz took over from me in North Africa. General Eisenhower was happy for a while, and then he brought General Spaatz down to run the show. The first thing that General Spaatz did when he got down there was to improve our communications and to establish more effective intelligence. By intelligence, I mean in the sense of learning as much as possible about the enemy's capabilities and intentions. In the early days, we did not wholly command our troops, at least the air troops, because we were dependent upon the British for communications and intelligence. Spaatz, when he came down, immediately corrected that by putting in his own communications system so that he was free of the British, and he immediately started developing his own intelligence system so that we would have those two all-important functions in our own hands. That, to me, was a very wise thing to do, and I'd been too stupid to get at it. If you have the communications, and if you have the intelligence, then your decision making was made with a great deal more input, and the decisions were sounder'' (personal communication, February 7, 1977).

General Spaatz demonstrated his wisdom again during the controversy over whether or not, in the immediate post–World War II era, the Air National Guard should be integrated with the Air Reserve. There were many who were strong advocates of this integration. Spaatz was called to testify. His briefing officers and staff advisers were unanimous that they should be integrated. Spaatz carefully listened to all of these comments and made no response. He went to testify to Congress and, to the surprise of all, took a position against integration. His Assistant Vice Chief of Staff, Maj. Gen. William F. McKee, commented on why he took this position: "General Spaatz was a wise man. He knew that the integration of the Air Reserve and the Air National Guard was just not politically feasible. He decided he was not going to waste his time and effort going up against a stone wall. It was as simple as that" (personal communication, July 6, 1977).

Asked why he thought Spaatz was a good decision maker, General Eaker said, "General Spaatz was the only officer I ever knew who never made a mistake. General Eisenhower made this comment about Spaatz many times in my presence" (personal communication, October 4, 1977).

General Quesada remarked that the chief requirement of being a decision maker is to be a wise decision maker; asked how one becomes a wise decision maker, he responded, "Have the courage to make the decision, [have] some judgment, and keep your emotions out of it. I'll go back to my father, who was a very successful banker. He mastered four languages, English with an accent, but spoke Italian, Portuguese, Spanish, and French perfectly. I remember one time I was with him and a group of other bankers. My father, because they were of different nationalities, switched from language to language. Someone said to him during the conversation, 'How can anybody be intelligent enough to speak four languages as you have here?' My father—being humble, as I am not—said, 'You're not intelligent when you speak four languages, you're only intelligent if you speak them wisely.' I never forgot that, never" (personal communication, June 22, 1977).

General Vandenberg was another firm decision maker. "After World War II, General Vandenberg invited me," said one of his West Point classmates, Col. D. H. Galloway, USA (Ret.), "to join Central Intelligence when he was appointed Director of that Agency. He made me Assistant Director in charge of one of the divisions. In this post, I was closely associated with him and privileged to sit in and observe at conferences at the highest level of government. I was astounded at Van's ability to more than hold his own with some of the foremost members of our and other governments. He would listen, digest and weigh what was being said and advocated and then with charm, tact, and intelligence make brief remarks that would either uphold or demolish some contention. It was then that I noticed he had acquired another characteristic. He never went off half-cocked, but when he felt he was right he never backed off" (personal communication, December 23, 1963).

This kind of strength was observed by another commentator who said, "Van can become vocal when he wants to make a point, (but) he will listen at length before making a decision. Once it is made, that's that. A member of the staff said, 'The general can become convinced of a point and all the arguing in the world will not change his mind.' "⁵

Gen. Dean C. Strother, who was very close to Nathan F. Twining during World War II, having been with him in Europe as well as in the Pacific, said of Twining's leadership, "You sensed that he was right, you sensed that he knew what he was talking about and when he was talking about a particular subject, you felt that he was sound in the advice that he gave, so you simply listened to it and did what he suggested. He didn't force his advice upon you, but he had a calm way of discussing matters, and getting the message over to you. You knew he was sound, and he had that wonderful quality of common sense" (personal communication, April 1976).

"I was Assistant Vice Chief," related General McKee, "When Nate was Vice Chief of Staff of the Air Force. I'll tell you the story about the B-47 program. If it hadn't been for Twining, we'd have probably never had the B-52. The Inspector General made an investigation of the B-47 program and wrote up a report that was quite thick which came on General Twining's desk. This report in effect said that the Chief of Staff of the Air Force and the Secretary of the Air Force were stupid in going ahead with the B-47 program. It would kill a lot of people, cost a lot of money, and wasn't going to be any damn good. That was the conclusion of the report. It was the hottest thing I'd ever seen. The newspapers would have loved to have had it. They would have had a story for practically every page in the report. It was a story that would have carried on for years. Things where they could draw conclusions about the stupidity of the military, wasting the taxpayers money. So Twining read the report, and shook his head and said to me, 'Bozo, what in the hell am I going to do with this?' I said, 'Well, every night before you go home, put it in the safe there by the righthand side of your desk and lock your safe. If you want to read it some more, you can get it out the next morning, but be sure every night that you put it in that safe and lock it up and don't let anybody else see it. That's what we did. And that report never went anywhere. If Twining had taken the recommendations of the report, we wouldn't have had any B-47, and that would have meant we wouldn't have had any B-52. At least not for many years. Twining didn't give the report any credence because with his knowledge of aircraft, and he had a great gift for that, he knew that in the airplane business you could not just stand still. You had to go forward. That's where Arnold was so great, and we never would have had the Air Force that we did if it hadn't been for a man with the vision of Arnold. Twining had a lot of that same vision, and he was willing to stick his neck out. There he was sitting on a red-hot piece of paper. If this thing had gotten out, he probably would have been blown out of his chair and his position. But he had enough guts to go ahead and say, 'to hell with it' '' (personal communication, July 6, 1977). Time obviously proved that Twining's evaluation of the worthiness of the B-47 was justified. It was the backbone of our strategic air force, an excellent workhorse, and also a very, very safe aircraft.

Gen. Thomas D. White said, ''The first thing that comes to my mind in decision making, which may not be the most important thing, is don't become bogged down in detail. . . . So many of the people who can't make decisions are very often the people who can't see the forest for the trees. They get bogged down in detail.''

To avoid getting bogged down in detail, a leader must delegate and then be ready to accept the consequences if the subordinate to whom he delegates makes a mistake, and must be able to back him up.

General Lauris Norstad's comment on decision making was that you ''have to have confidence in your judgment. You learn over a period of time how often you're right and in what areas you are right. Almost all my military life I was matched with the best people in their fields, in the military field. I got to be pretty good, and I knew that my judgment in the area of my chosen profession was good. When the chips were down, and there was opposition to my judgment, it was the good opposition—some of the best. History will bear me out that my decisions, made in the face of this competent opposition, were the best'' (personal communication, August 22, 1977).

An important aspect, of course, within the Air Force is that decisions both in time of peace and war may cost human lives. It takes courage to be a decision maker, and there are many who prefer staff positions simply because they prefer to provide the staff work with which the decisions are made, but they are not willing to accept the responsibility for these decisions. It also is inevitable that sometimes wrong decisions will be made. General Arnold's philosophy on this was that, ''What I can't change, I don't worry about. The old Chinese have a proverb, remember, which runs something like this, 'What will not matter a thousand years from now does not matter now.' Certainly one has to have a philosophy such as this in making decisions where human lives are involved.''[6]

NOTES, Chapter 10

1. Stimson, Henry L. World War II Diary, 1943.
2. Arnold, *Global Mission,* p. 194
3. Lt. Gen. Henry H. Arnold and Brig. Gen. Ira C. Eaker, *Army Flyer* (New York: Harper, 1942), p. 13.
4. Ibid., p. 183.
5. John A. Giles, "General 'Van' " *Flying,* July 1948, 43:271.
6. Arnold and Eaker, p. 132.

EPILOGUE
THE PATTERN IN COMMAND

What does command entail? To be a successful commander requires a willingness to devote twenty-four hours a day, seven days a week, to one's command. This will often mean that one's wife and family will have to take second place to the mission. In addition, the commander and his family must be willing to live in a goldfish bowl, because their actions are closely observed by both subordinates and superiors. The commander must be willing to learn, teach, stress, and live with the basic and often elementary fundamentals necessary to develop his unit and still believe his talents for "bigger things" are not being wasted. He must like to be with young people and to live with their energy and the problems they create. The commander of large units must be able to delegate, and when he does delegate he must be willing to accept the responsibility for the failure of his subordinates. Command is complex: the commander must be able simultaneously to handle training, maintenance, tests, administration, inspections, communications, messes, supply, athletics, discipline, job proficiency, awards, and public relations. He must be able to do all these things at the same time.

The top man must be able to take orders, because no leader is ever really in a position of not having to answer to someone or to some group. The commander must be willing to compete with other units in peacetime, without losing the spirit of cooperation or losing sight of the fact that all the individual units together make up the whole team. Often he is expected to accomplish the impossible with inadequate means. If things go wrong, the successful commander accepts the responsibility, even though the failure might rest with his staff, subordinates, or higher headquarters. He must be able to do the best he can with whatever he has—which may on occasion be very little. He must be able to produce the hard work and leadership to create a superior unit with average manpower. It is the commander's job to inspire the men to put out their maximum and thereby build a superior unit.

The responsibility for the failure of a unit or mission rests with the commander. He must realize that failure generally results in his relief from command. Command requires a man who can physically and emotionally cope with the responsibility and strain without losing his effectiveness and his patience. Often, the only compensation is personal satisfaction; there is generally very little reward or glory, particularly in peacetime. And the reward may go to a superior, rather than to the man most responsible for the performance of the unit or the accomplishment of the mission.

I concluded from this comparative study that there is a common pattern of leadership qualities. A writer for the *Saturday Evening Post* commented, when Vandenberg became Chief of Staff, "In his new job Vandenberg succeeds two definite personalities—Generals 'Hap' Arnold and 'Tooey' Spaatz. Arnold is a mercurial, table-pounding human dynamo who had a precise and bold blueprint for airpower and who drove men into accomplishment by sheer force of his personality. Spaatz, the Number One strategic air commander of the war, who had inherited the difficult job of putting together the pieces after headlong demobilization had wrecked the Air Force, is a grizzled introvert who has a hard-bitten, exact conception of what this country needs to keep air supremacy. . . . Vandenberg is sharply different from both Arnold and Spaatz. He is smooth, polished, persuasive, a born diplomat—invaluable qualities in these days when so much depends on having Congress and the public on your side. . . . 'With Van,' a deputy says, 'There's no stomping, screaming or beating on desks, but when he gives an order, it damn well better be carried out.' "[1]

Others have described Arnold thus: "stern and hard task master who pounded on the desk and hammered on the table"; "We were afraid of him"; "impatient"; "impulsive"; "impetuous"; "forceful"; "aggressive"; "positive"; "even-tempered—that is, always angry"; "persistent"; "ready to accept and demand seemingly impossible tasks"; "inspirational"; "a goer"; and "enthusiastic."

In contrast, Spaatz has been labeled "intuitive," "lazy," "stable," "taciturn," "quiet," "thoughtful," "casual," "short of speech," "inarticulate," "indifferent," "not a spit and polish type," and one who "lacks discipline."

Vandenberg has been called "quick," "tough," "personable,"

"diplomatic," "far-sighted," "lazy," "aggressive," "indifferent," "smart," possessing "self-control," and "unflappable." More specifically, "I never saw Van roar or rave around about everything as Arnold [did]"; he avoided exaggeration (which Arnold did not) because "The case for air power is good enough without compromising it or stretching it"; and "Vandenberg's animation and eloquence in private conversation make it clear that his behavior in public is simply an expression of shyness" (no one could call Arnold shy).

Nathan Twining was referred to as the "general everybody loves," "a gentle person," "solid," "honest," "trustworthy," "straightforward," and "a very down-to-earth person who would slap you on the back while making comments during storytelling such as 'smart as a warehouse rat,' 'I felt like a monkey at a family reunion,' and 'Man, it was the biggest fish you ever saw.'" He was considered not as polished as General White, as being "easy to approach," "silent," "least talkative," "the most relaxed character this side of Mexico," one who was "not an intellectual in any sense of the word," and who did not become a "great leader because of his intellect."

Finally, the description of General White who has had it said of him, "He was a soft-spoken man who impressed me as being sensitive to the needs of others;" that "White was not one of those flamboyant young brigadiers. He was just a prodigiously hard worker who managed his time effectively and efficiently." One writer wrote of his appearance that "General White looks as much like a New York banker or diplomat as he does a general." When it was announced he was to succeed Twining, one of the commentators wrote, "The nomination of General Thomas D. White to be Air Force Chief of Staff, succeeding General Nate Twining, who is moving up to be Chairman of the Joint Chiefs of Staff, makes a sharp switch from hero to intellectual."

With all these differences, where is the pattern? Actually, the preceding descriptions by themselves are superficial. It is when one studies the careers of these great men in depth, as we have done here, that the successful leadership pattern unfolds. Profiles of these men reveal the qualities that they had in common and that made them great. Their character was of the highest—they shared the integrity, the humility, the selflessness, the concern for others, the respect, and the self confidence that are present in most top American leaders. This book shows that these five generals also had in common a thorough knowledge of their profession. Although Arnold, Spaatz, and Vandenberg obtained no cadet rank at the Military Academy, their cadet years reveal that they possessed leadership among their peers plus an independence, ruggedness, and spirit of adventure necessary to enter flying in the early hazardous years. White excelled quickly as a cadet, and Twining was on the way but graduated before the end of his second year. The latter two were acknowledged as leaders among their peers and the active military officers above them. Arnold commented, after having been somewhat rebellious as a cadet, that he was going to take his career in earnest, as did the other four. A decision to devote one's life to a military career, and the motivation to be an outstanding leader, are obviously necessary before an officer can make the most of his other qualities.

An officer must be a leader in everything he does and says and as such must reflect his true character as a man. The extent to which the individual man can accomplish his high goal is a measure of his true worth to himself and to society.

It is not my thesis that a man of character is perfect. Not even a strong man is without weaknesses, nor is a weak man without strengths. But a man of high character can be depended on at virtually all times in all situations and in all aspects of life. To speak of leadership is to be able to say of a man, "I can depend on him, not always to be right necessarily, but to do his best and do what he considers to be right. I can depend on him to be honorable in his dealings with his men. I can depend on his fairness, on his moderation and temperance. I respect him. I admire him. I trust him."

Our leaders must have and instill in their followers a spirit of earnest patriotism and unconditional loyalty to our country. John Curran has said that "The condition upon which God has given liberty is eternal vigilance." This is a part of the Air Force mission—to keep the eternal vigilance.

We must instill in our military men and women the will to fight for our freedom, to go beyond the instinct of only having a willingness to fight for self-preservation. We want our military people to have an aggressive spirit for right.

One reason for needing leaders with character who care about each man under them is that, unlike societies where the individual is of little consequence, our men in the Air Force were born and raised in an atmosphere of freedom where each individual is important. They will not respond with enthusiasm to a leader who belittles the significance of the individual.

Part of the strength of our country has been that each individual has the right to make choices. Our leadership must provide that choice, and each person must work at protecting our freedom. The strength of an individual's character is the basis of our moral defense, which in turn is our nation's first line of defense.

Plato once wrote that only the dead have seen the end of war. Whether or not these wars are fought with sticks and stones, bows and arrows, bombers or missiles, the essence of it all is that men are always well behind these weapons. The men who make up the Air Force of our nation, a free nation, are individual instruments that will help keep us a free country. These men must be led by men of character.

We are grateful for the example of the leaders we have here described.

NOTES, Epilogue

1. Sidney Shallett, "Man in a Hot Spot," *Saturday Evening Post,* May 29, 1948, p. 23.

Index